Homest

Learn To Grow Own Food, Provide Own Energy And Fresh Water, Heal Yourself While Living No-Debts Life

2

The trademarks that are used are without any consent, and the publication of the trademark is without permission or backing by the trademark owner. All trademarks and brands within this book are for clarifying purposes only and are the owned by the owners themselves, not affiliated with this document.

Table of content

Introduction

Homesteading is a self-sufficient lifestyle to reconnect with nature. This lifestyle is really beneficial for you to get rid of numerous problems. You can reconnect to nature and invest for your health. It will lead you to spend a healthy life and reduce tensions.

Homesteading is not easy because it requires you to grow your own food and raise animals for food and byproducts. It will keep you healthy and active because your grown food will be free from chemicals and other harmful ingredients. You can sell surplus items in the market for money. If you want to enjoy a homestead lifestyle, you should maintain good physical health because an ill and fatigued person is unable to manage this lifestyle.

This book is designed for your assistance so that you can enjoy a good lifestyle without any problem.

PART ONE
Home Garden

Gardening has always been part of society. In ancient times people simply tilled their own piece of land to provide a meager supply of crops. This would have to be enough for them and their families to survive on until the next crops were ready. It is from this period that humans first started to understand the power of a wide range of plants to heal; although these plants were generally cultivated and not grown themselves. Studies have shown that the very first type of gardening was forest gardening; which is conducted on the banks of rivers within the jungle. It is believed barriers were created round plots of land as early as 10,000 BC!

Alongside growing vital supplies, the wealthiest individuals would have planted gardens simply for the aesthetic pleasure. There is some evidence of this in the 16th century BC! However, it was not until the 19th century that this became something which was popular an affordable to everyone. The creation of a peaceful and beautiful space from the existing materials is very much a western traditional. The great gardens of the Eastern countries often seem to be at odds with their environment. Whilst this can make for a striking image it is much more difficult to keep this type of garden maintained.

When you look at creating your backyard garden and ensuring the soil is fertile; it is essential to consider the native plants you will be putting in the ground. These are the ones which are most likely to flourish and will require very little attention. Anything which does not naturally grow in the environment you have to offer will need extra care and attention to ensure it thrives.

Perhaps most importantly of all is the fact that gardening should be fun. There are enough other things to take your stress and attention; taking care of your backyard should not be one of them. With a little work your backyard can become a fertile garden and give you hours of pleasure!

photo made by: Salvadonica Borgo del Chianti

The Importance of Planning

Although ¼ acre is a reasonable size garden it may be challenging to fit everything in. This will depend upon your design for your garden. In fact, at this stage you must see your backyard as a blank canvas. Even if there are already plants in the garden it is possible to move them or even eliminate them in order to create the right space for your needs. Planning the garden will allow you to visualize what your backyard will ultimately look like and make the most of every bit of available space. The following planning tips should help:

1. Growing Food

The first question you will need to ask your self is are you hoping to grow food? If this is a yes then you will need to consider which crops are most beneficial to you. There are many different ones which can be grown but you should focus on those which you enjoy eating. You will also need to decide if you intend to grow more than you need and sell any on. Considering the size of your back yard this is not necessarily a good idea.

If edible produce is high on your agenda then you will need to consider which part of your yard is going to be dedicated to them. You can opt to turn the entire back yard into a vegetable garden which will provide you with a good quantity of vegetables. It is worth noting that some products can be grown earlier in the year and others later; providing there are enough nutrients in the soil you can turn the soil after removing your first crop and plant a second.

It is also worth considering raising the beds as this will reduce the strain on your back and can protect some plants.

2. Tools – Storage and Requirements

You should also consider your tools. You may already have a shed or garage. However, if you do not then the first thing you will need to consider is whether you need a small shed or a lockable tool shed. A fairly small shed can provide a space for tools and to pot new plants. However, it will take up some of your available space.

You should also consider the impact of a shed and its use to store tools. Whilst you may have a space in your home or garage which could be used; this does not mean it is the best solution. Walking back and forth to your house will take time away from gardening; especially if you need to remove muddy wellies each time! Whilst you want to enjoy the gardening it is probably not something you want to occupy every moment of your time!

3. Seating Area

Even if you are intending on simply creating a fertile backyard for growing all these different vegetables, you will find that a small seating area will be appreciated. This will provide you with somewhere to stop and review your work as well as a spot for you, your family and even your friends to enjoy the backyard; especially on a hot day. It is worth thinking about how much you currently entertain company. If this is an important part of your life then it is likely that you will need an area for you all to relax. You will want this to have a view of the garden but may not want people looking at soil beds with very young vegetables in. You will, therefore, need to consider adding some screening in to ensure you present the right view.

A seating area is usually next to the house; this is for convenience although it does not have to be. You may find it necessary to dig part of the garden in order to level the ground; this soil may be good to add to raised beds.

4. Pest Control

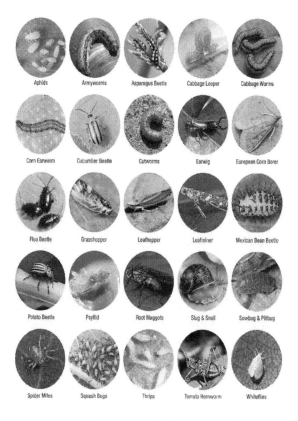

Aphids	Armyworms	Asparagus Beetle	Cabbage Looper	Cabbage Worms
Corn Earworm	Cucumber Beetle	Cutworms	Earwig	European Corn Borer
Flea Beetle	Grasshopper	Leafhopper	Leafminer	Mexican Bean Beetle
Potato Beetle	Psyllid	Root Maggots	Slug & Snail	Sowbug & Pillbug
Spider Mites	Squash Bugs	Thrips	Tomato Hornworm	Whiteflies

You cannot spray your crops with pest control substances as this may be harmful to you when you eat the produce. However, there are a number of natural ways to help prevent pests eating the fruits of your labor. One of the best ways of limiting access by pests is to mix your plants; this will actually prevent many pests from being attracted to the plant as they tend to be attracted to only one sort. By mixing them it will appear there is not enough of one specific type to be worth attacking. This should be tackled at the planning stage as you will want to work out an approximate number of crops you would like to produce.

It is also worth watering your plants early in the day; this will ensure the soil stays dry during the day and makes it less attractive to many bugs.

5. Borders and Fencing

Raised beds eliminate the need for borders in many ways. Obviously you will need a border round your backyard; if you do not already have one. However, you need to consider which the best borders are. Walls are excellent at keeping wildlife out of your yard. However, the wall can create a significant amount of shade across a section of your garden; reducing the ability of the plants to grow. Natural borders such as hedges can be effective although small animals maybe able to get through. These are excellent for the aesthetic appeal but generally block light and require maintenance. The third option is a fence which is solid at the bottom to block the path of most animals but mesh higher up to let the light through.

14

As these items may need to be added before you start planting it is important to consider them at the planning stage. They can also be used to add definition to your backyard.

6. *Flowering Plants*

Even if your sole aim is to grow vegetables you may wish to consider adding a few flowering plants into the mix. Many vegetables do produce flowers and these can look fantastic as they grow. However, they will be for a short time only. BY adding a few perennials and long flowering shrubs you will not be adding any significant work to your backyard but will add an extra touch of color which can be very satisfying.

7. *Play Area*

If you have family it is important to remember that the garden will not just be for you. Depending upon the age of your children they may wish to get involved. You may find that it is best to create a small patch where they can experiment with planting without damaging your plants. Alternatively they may be experienced enough to assist you. You will need to have tools ready for them and teach them the importance of keeping these tools clean.

The other factor of having children is that they will want somewhere to play. If you are working hard to produce vegetables you will not want them running across your plants and beds. The best idea in this scenario is to build a play area for them; and factor it into your plans. Surprisingly this does not need to be a large space. A den can be built which incorporates a swing, slide and even some climbing bits and yet have a very small floor area.

8. Height

One of the key skills when successfully planning your ¼ acre backyard garden is to envision it on a 3D scale. Your garden is not flat! There are many plants which can grow up a wall or trellis; you can even plant some in stacks. Simply plant the ones which prefer shade under the ones that like full sunshine.

You can also opt to create a small greenhouse which will allow you to get plants started when the weather is not quite warm enough. Even a small greenhouse will have several shelves; allowing you to grow more plants in a small space than simply flat planting.

Other options to expand your available space include window boxes and planters on the edge of the paths and seating areas. They can add to the effect of your backyard whilst increasing the available space to plant.

Fertile Soil and Planting

Of course you can plant hundreds of plants and still get very poor results; even after planning where the sunlight will fall in your garden and which plants like the most sun. This is because the secret to a well developed and attractive / successful garden is in having fertile soil. Just like any form of life a plant requires nutrients and water to survive. If your garden has not been used for a long time then you may already have a good level of nutrients in the soil. However, if this is not the case then you will need to follow these steps to improve the quality of your soil:

1. Manure

Any type of manure can be a valuable addition to your soil. Depending upon your location you may be able to visit a local farm or horse center and take away some of their excess manure. This will smell! If this is not a possibility you may find some in the local adverts or you may have to purchase some at your local garden center.

It is essential to put manure on your crops at least three months before harvesting. This is to avoid any issues with bacteria. However, the best time to do this is actually in the winter! Once you have dug your vegetables up and turned the soil over, cover it with

18

manure and then cover the manure with plastic. This will allow the manure to breakdown into the soil without any weeds growing.

You may find that you have a hankering for keeping a few chickens; even in a ¼ acre backyard you will have room for this; four or six chickens need remarkably little room to be comfortable. You would then be able to use the chicken manure on your plants! You can even allow the chickens to roam on empty beds with compost on them; the chickens will root around for food and help the compost blend into the soil.

2. Compost

This is an excellent alternative or addition to manure. You should plan to have a compost pile in your backyard or even site a couple of compost bins. You can then add any waste which will degrade; whether dead plants or food waste from your kitchen. It will take several months before the compost at the bottom of the pile is ready to use. This can then be applied to your soil to return valuable nutrients. This can be done on an ongoing basis as the natural process of decay removes any harmful bacteria.

3. Look for Deep Plants

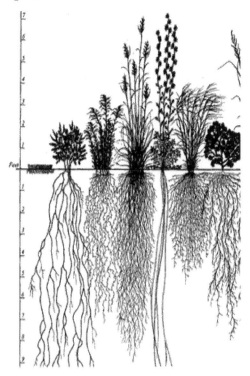

Some plants have extremely deep roots. Comfrey is a good example as its roots have been known to go as far as ten feet into the soil. Even the humble stinging nettle has deep roots. By allowing these plants to grown in a small area you will be tapping into the nutrients and minerals which are far beneath the surface and beyond the reach of most plants. Once the plant is established simply remove it and add it to the compost heap to allow the deep rooted nutrients to be made available to the other plants!

Both Comfrey and nettles are considered weeds but, with a little control, they can occupy corners or edges of your plot which are otherwise not useable.

4. Mulch

This is one of the most obvious and common ways of adding natural nutrition to the soil. Mulch is generally added to the top of your soil and provides a layer of protection against temperature changes. It also prevents many bugs from; attacking the plants; they can eat the mulch instead. A by-product of this is the breakdown of the mulch and the addition of nutrients to the soil. Mulch can even offer a good level of protection against weeds. It is advisable to add new mulch every year; usually at the beginning of the season.

5. *The Value of Paths*

Paths do more than separate your different plants or add structure to your garden. They also allow you to move freely around your plants without needing to step on the soil. Walking across a planting bed is likely to damage crops and will compact the soil. This can damage the roots and even limit the amount of nutrients and water which can get to the plant.

Creating paths also allows you to plant in your beds right to the edge. Surprisingly optimizing the number of plants in any given area is good for the soil; it helps to protect the soil from excessive temperatures. This can help to ensure the moisture is maintained.

If you need to create paths across a bed it is best to use mulch as this can be broken up by walking on it and then transferred to the plants which need it the most.

6. *Tillage*

Many gardeners will remove the dead plants at the end of the season and then turn the soil over. However, this can actually be damaging to the soil structure. A better way of preparing the soil for the next season is simply to cover the plants in mulch, compost or manure; as mentioned before. This will kill off the last bits of the old plants and add the nutrients directly to the soil.

There are a few plants which this technique may not work with, such as rye. However, you still do not need to till the soil; simply cut the plant just above the crown and late the upper part of the plant decompose in with the mulch. This should be done after the flowers have arrived.

7. *Planting*

There is more to having a fertile garden than simply having the right soil! You need to know the right place and time to plant the various plants that you are hoping to grow. This can be a difficult process; however, the following tips should prove beneficial:

Most plants like to be planted in the spring; this is the time which they would naturally start to grow. It is generally recommended to plant them outside as seeds, just after the last frost of the year has happened. Frost will kill many plants or simply damage their ability to grow properly. Of course, when the last frost is will depend upon exactly where you are located. It is possible to plant your seeds inside between two and four weeks before the last frost hits. The warmth of your home or a dedicated potting shed will ensure they have a head start. However, it is worth noting that this is a time consuming option. Planting inside means you will need to plant every one twice. It will also be essential to water them regularly and make sure they have enough nutrients in a small pot of soil. Allowing your plants to establish themselves in the relative safety of your inside space will assist them in settling in when they are re-planted into the garden.

It is also worth looking at the seed packet to verify their instructions. The general guideline above works in most cases but there are always exceptions.

The Seeds

This is an important consideration; the tips above will ensure there are enough nutrients in the soil for anything to survive. However, you must then know how to plant your seeds! The majority of vegetables and flowering plants like to be placed just below the surface of the soil. But, there are a few which need to go on top of the soil. Of course, your newly planted seeds will be at risk from birds and you may need to consider adding netting to protect them whilst they settle in. If you do not protect them you will need to assume you will lose a fair quantity of them. To ensure you have enough left you will have to overplant them.

Transferring your Plants

If you have opted to get your plants started inside you will need to transplant every one of them! It is important to make sure every seedling is not watered too much; they should never have wet leaves overnight as this attracts disease.

In general once your seedling has developed its first set of green leaves you will be able to move it. This should be done in the morning so that they can be lightly watered for the day. It is also important to mist them with water regularly for the first week after their move; this will help to give them enough moisture and allow them to settle into their new home.

There are specific tips for individual plants and you will find it useful to consult an online guide after you have chosen which plants to grow.

Additional tips to Ensure Your Backyard Garden is Optimized and Fertile

By now it should be obvious that the key to successful gardening is in planning your plot and in making sure the right nutrients are in the soil. Alongside this there are a few other considerations which can help to ensure your backyard garden is a success.

Know your Soil Type

Adding nutrients naturally to the soil will help you plants to thrive. However, there are a number of different soil types. Your plants may require different types and it is important to know which is the best one for the type of plant you wish to add to your backyard garden. There are usually guidelines on the back of the seed packets to ensure you choose the right one. The main soil types are as follows:

1. Sandy

Sandy soil is made up of large particles and it struggles to hold any water in it. When you scoop a handful of this soil up you will find it is dry to the touch. Unfortunately most plants will not like this type of soil as the nutrients will simple be washed away before the plant can access them.

Sandy soil can be confirmed by scooping up a handful and rolling it in your hand. You should then moisten it slightly; if the soil crumbles in your hand it is sandy and not good for many plants.

2. Silty

This type of soil consists of much smaller particles and it is more capable of retaining onto the moisture. Simply add a little water to a handful of soil and roll it into a ball; if it rolls and leaves dirt on your hand then it is silty. This type of soil will retain the moisture for longer. However, it is cold to the touch and drains badly meaning that many plants will struggle to survive in this type of soil. It also worth noting, that it is very easy to squash this type of soil. This will reduce the amount of air able to get to the roots and thus damage the plant.

Despite being better at holding onto the water it is not as good as you would expect at retaining nutrients. In fact; its ability to retain water can make it too wet for many plants.

3. Clay

This is the best soil for retaining water without over watering the plants. It has tiny particles. If you wet it and then make a handful into a ball you will find it is sticky to the touch However, if clay soil is dry it will be smooth and moldable. The tiny particles which make up clay soil are perfectly formulated to balance water, air and nutrients; making sure all three items are there for when your plants need them.

Unfortunately clay can be very heavy when wet; making it much more physical work to get your plants into the ground. In the summer it will become hard and you will struggle to dig into it! You must get your plants in at the right time to benefit from this delightful substance!

4. Saline

This type of soil is generally limited to exceptionally dry areas. It derives its name from the fact that there is an excess amount of salt which has built up in the soil. The salt will prevent most plants from being able to access water; leaving the plant to die of dehydration. This type of soil is also very difficult to germinate as seeds have no means of surviving once in the soil.

Saline soil is commonly see as barren land as it is very difficult to successfully farm; even if you manage to get an irrigation system in place. You can usually tell this type of soil just by the fact there is a dusting of white across the surface of the ground. In addition, should you manage to get any plants in the soil to start growing they will have white tips on their leaves and grow very badly. It is generally considered to be not worth the effort f growing in this type of soil.

It is unlikely that your backyard will have this soil type; however, if it does then you may need to look at digging large sections of it out and replacing with better quality soil. Alternatively raised beds can provide the opportunity to introduce new soil but it will need regular watering.

5. Peat

Your soil will be peat if it is a very dark brown or even black color. This type of soil has a large amount of organic material combined with high levels of water. In fact, this type of soil will have started to form nearly ten thousand years ago! It is the result of huge ice glaciers melting extremely quickly and destroying plants. These plants decayed very slowly under the water to create what is now referred to as peat.

Peat cannot be rolled into a ball, no matter how hard you try. It will feel like a sponge when you pick it up and if you squeeze it you will actually be able to produce water! In this state it is simply too wet to grow plants. However, if you put it where it will drain the peat will become an excellent base for plants to grow in. It will lock in water for the plants during dry spells and protect the plants from excess water in the wet months! However, if you allow it to get to dry in a hot summer there is a risk of fire.

6. *Loam*

This type of soil is actually a mixture of silt, clay and sand. It will often have humus added to increase the nutrient level. It is possible to create this type of soil in your garden by adding the mixing ingredients. However, it is also worth noting that different backyards will naturally favor different types of soil and, without constant attention, your loam soil may return to its original base.

Loam will generally be dark and will crumble in your hands. This is because it consists of very small particles which encourage water retention whilst allowing air to access the roots.

You may find it helpful to scoop a piece of your soil into a jam jar and, after putting the lid on, shake it thoroughly. You can then leave the jar on the side and within twenty four hours it will have settled into distinct areas. Sandy soil will be at the bottom with silt on top of it and clay at the very top. Once you have established how much of each you have you will be able to tell what kind of soil you have and how best to adjust it to get the right balance.

Of course, it is also important to consider what type of soil your plants will prefer as some will grow better in dryer soil. At the planning stage you will even be able to assess the soil type in your garden and adjust different areas to best suit your intended planting regime.

To achieve a successful backyard garden you will need to plan your garden and decide which plants are the most important to you to grow. When considering whether to grow carrots, parsnips or even cauliflowers you must think about the end use. If you are not growing enough to sell and are not actually very keen on carrots then they will not be the right plant for you!

Creating a fertile backyard is possible and even ¼ acre can provide a good range of produce which will help you and your family live a more sustainable and environmentally friendly lifestyle. However, it will be hard work; particularly in the start up phase. Creating raised bed, paths, separating areas and adding nutrients to the soil is also physically demanding. You must have a passion to do this and complete the project or your backyard will only ever be half a fertile garden.

Of course, once you have picked your first crop and tasted the delights of home grown food you will almost certainly be hooked. There is very little which can compete with the flavor of your hand grown vegetables; especially as the satisfaction of having grown them adds a special element.

A backyard garden is also an excellent opportunity to spend time with your children as you either teach them about gardening or learn together. Not only will you be building your relationships you will be providing them with an important skill for the future.

When you plan and start to create the backyard garden you have been dreaming of it is worth remembering the most important elements:

- The better the quality of the soil the better your plants will grow. Test your soil and adjust it to establish the best possible combination. This will be easier if you are creating raised beds as you will need additional soil anyway.

- Vegetables generally like to have plenty of water. You will need to remember to water them regularly if there is no rain. Water butts can be a useful way of collecting rain water to assist with this. You should also make sure there is water sources situated round your backyard so that you always have water to hand.

- Sunshine – Some plants like the shade but most vegetables prefer to have six or even eight hours of full sunshine; this will ensure they are strong, have a better resistance to bugs and disease and grow larger.

It is also worth considering your planting style. Neat rows can look good and be easy to maintain with mechanical equipment. However, it will not produce as high a yield which is important when your space is limited. The alternative is to pack your vegetables in close together and even add a few ornamental flowers in to create a feature. This can look much better if you are concerned about the view from your kitchen window.

On a final note, there are many different types of each vegetable! Simply choosing to plant tomatoes is not enough. You will also need to select your tomato type. This should be based on the type which is best suited to your garden and you are most likely to enjoy eating. Adopting this method will ensure your backyard garden is not only fertile and productive but useful!

Tea Herb Gardening

You've always dreamed of growing your own herbs. You are fascinated with the natural world, and want to start growing your own plants to care for a variety of everyday ailments you face in your life.

But when you take a look at the world, you are instantly overwhelmed. There are so many different plants you can grow and different uses for those plants, so how do you know which to pick?

How do you know which ones are going to work for your growing season and preferred growing style? How do you know which ones are going to work for your ailments?

When it comes to botany, it doesn't have to be a stab in the dark. With the right knowledge, you can grow beneficial plants that will give you the results that you want in a matter of weeks.

Learn how to use these herbs in tea, and you have your hands on a continuous source of all natural remedies you can call on at any time. With the plants outlined in this book, you have everything you need to grow the herbs you will actually use, and grow them in a way that will help them live.

There's no end to the wonderful things you can do with these herbs, so if you are tired of using pills for everything, and are ready to dive into the wonderful world of botany, you have come to the right place.

There is a green thumb in all of us, it just takes a little extra digging for some.

So are you ready?

Let's get started.

Teas for Taste

Although there are many healthy benefits to drinking your own herbs, there's times when you simply drink it for the taste. These herbs are all delicious, so if you only drink them for the taste, you are in for a plethora of health benefits besides.

Read what they do and how you can use them, and you are going to have your pick of the crop when it comes to teas!

Herb:

Mint

Use:

Taste, upset stomach, headaches, anxiety

How to Grow:

Mint grows well both indoors and out, and will thrive in a pot. Make sure it gets plenty of direct sunlight, water when the soil has become dry to the touch.

Tea Time:

Purchase a box of loose leaf black tea to keep on hand. This will add body to whichever herb you choose, and will help with the undertone flavor of your tea.

Select a few of the leaves you wish to use, and set them out on a paper towel overnight. Once dried, crush in your hands then add to a tea ball or bag. Add a small scoop of the black tea as well, then secure the top.

Steep in hot water for 5 minutes, and enjoy!

You can also enjoy these herbs as is, without the black tea as an addition, but the flavor can be a little harsh that way, or it may feel that something is missing. At the same time, if you want to add a dab of sweetness to your tea, opt for something natural such as honey or stevia.

Herb:

Cinnamon

Uses:

Eases nausea and indigestion, relieves anxiety, gives warmth to the body

How to Grow:

Cinnamon is a tropical tree that can be grown indoors in a large pot. It needs plenty of moisture and direct sunlight, so make sure you place it near a large window and mist it often.

Tea Time:

Purchase a box of loose leaf black tea to keep on hand. This will add body to whichever herb you choose, and will help with the undertone flavor of your tea.

Select a few sections of the bark you wish to use, and set them out on a paper towel overnight. Once dried, crush in your hands then add to a tea ball or bag. Add a small scoop of the black tea as well, then secure the top.

Steep in hot water for 5 minutes, and enjoy!

You can also enjoy these herbs as is, without the black tea as an addition, but the flavor can be a little harsh that way, or it may feel that something is missing. At the same time, if you want to add a dab of sweetness to your tea, opt for something natural such as honey or stevia.

Herb:

Lemongrass

Uses:

Antibacterial, anti-parasitic, antifungal, healing

How to Grow:

Use a large pot to grow this herb in a windowsill. Simply moisten the soil when it gets dry and ensure it gets a lot of direct sunlight.

Tea Time:

Purchase a box of loose leaf black tea to keep on hand. This will add body to whichever herb you choose, and will help with the undertone flavor of your tea.

Select a few of the leaves you wish to use, and set them out on a paper towel overnight. Once dried, crush in your hands then add to a tea ball or bag. Add a small scoop of the black tea as well, then secure the top.

Steep in hot water for 5 minutes, and enjoy!

You can also enjoy these herbs as is, without the black tea as an addition, but the flavor can be a little harsh that way, or it may feel that something is missing. At the same time, if you want to add a dab of sweetness to your tea, opt for something natural such as honey or stevia.

Herb:

Echinacea

Uses:

A preventative herb, drink this herb to maintain optimal health.

How to Grow:

This is a very dry plant with a large taproot. Plant out of direct sunlight in late spring. This plant is a perennial.

Tea Time:

Purchase a box of loose leaf black tea to keep on hand. This will add body to whichever herb you choose, and will help with the undertone flavor of your tea.

Select a few of the leaves you wish to use, and set them out on a paper towel overnight. Once dried, crush in your hands then add to a tea ball or bag. Add a small scoop of the black tea as well, then secure the top.

Steep in hot water for 5 minutes, and enjoy!

You can also enjoy these herbs as is, without the black tea as an addition, but the flavor can be a little harsh that way, or it may feel that something is missing. At the same time, if you want to add a dab of sweetness to your tea, opt for something natural such as honey or stevia.

Tinctures for Trouble

Whether you have a stomachache or some other ailment, you are going to be glad you have these herbs in your garden. They are all incredibly easy to grow and use, and taste great.

Use them for a variety of reasons, and enjoy excellent health benefits no matter which herb you have chosen!

Herb:

Ginger

Use:

Settles an upset stomach, wards off the flu and colds, aids with nausea

How to Grow:

Ginger is easy to grow indoors in a large pot. It requires rich soil and filtered sunlight, so make sure to place it in a bright room in indirect sunlight. Water when the soil is dry to the touch.

Tea Time:

Purchase a box of loose leaf black tea to keep on hand. This will add body to whichever herb you choose, and will help with the undertone flavor of your tea.

Select a root you wish to use, then take a knife and slice thinly. Lay the pieces out on a paper towel to dry overnight, then add to a tea ball or bag. Add a small scoop of the black tea as well, then secure the top.

Steep in hot water for 5 minutes, and enjoy!

You can also enjoy these herbs as is, without the black tea as an addition, but the flavor can be a little harsh that way, or it may feel that something is missing. At the same time, if you want to add a dab of sweetness to your tea, opt for something natural such as honey or stevia.

Herb:

Chamomile

Uses:

Relieves anxiety, helps with sleep, soothes a sore throat and upset stomach.

How to Grow:

Start the seeds in a pot indoors in late winter. Once spring arrives and you are no longer worried about frost, transfer the plant outdoors. The plant requires very little water even in the hottest months, so water occasionally.

Tea Time:

Purchase a box of loose leaf black tea to keep on hand. This will add body to whichever herb you choose, and will help with the undertone flavor of your tea.

Select a few of the leaves you wish to use, and set them out on a paper towel overnight. Once dried, crush in your hands then add to a tea ball or bag. Add a small scoop of the black tea as well, then secure the top.

Steep in hot water for 5 minutes, and enjoy!

You can also enjoy these herbs as is, without the black tea as an addition, but the flavor can be a little harsh that way, or it may feel that something is missing. At the same time, if you want to add a dab of sweetness to your tea, opt for something natural such as honey or stevia.

Herb:

Rosehips

Uses:

This herb is an excellent source of vitamin C and can greatly boost your immune system, giving you excellent preventative care as well as help when you are sick.

How to Grow:

Rosehips grow at the base of a rose plant. Simply grow your roses as you normally do, and take full advantage of the rosehips growing at the base.

Tea Time:

Purchase a box of loose leaf black tea to keep on hand. This will add body to whichever herb you choose, and will help with the undertone flavor of your tea.

Select a few of the pods you wish to use, and set them out on a paper towel overnight. Once dried, crush in your hands or with a nutcracker if your hands aren't strong enough, then add to a tea ball or bag. Add a small scoop of the black tea as well, then secure the top.

Steep in hot water for 5 minutes, and enjoy!

You can also enjoy these herbs as is, without the black tea as an addition, but the flavor can be a little harsh that way, or it may feel that something is missing. At the same time, if you want to add a dab of sweetness to your tea, opt for something natural such as honey or stevia.

Herb:

Blackberry Leaf

Uses:

Will aid in relieving diarrhea, reduces discomfort from sore throats, excellent source of vitamin C, boosts the immune system.

How to Grow:

Quite literally the leaves from a blackberry plant, you can grow this outdoors quite easily. Make sure you know the growing season for blackberries in your area, and you can also harvest these leaves from wild plant sources.

Tea Time:

Purchase a box of loose leaf black tea to keep on hand. This will add body to whichever herb you choose, and will help with the undertone flavor of your tea.

Select a few of the leaves you wish to use, and set them out on a paper towel overnight. Once dried, crush in your hands then add to a tea ball or bag. Add a small scoop of the black tea as well, then secure the top.

Steep in hot water for 5 minutes, and enjoy!

You can also enjoy these herbs as is, without the black tea as an addition, but the flavor can be a little harsh that way, or it may feel that something is missing. At the same time, if you want to add a dab of sweetness to your tea, opt for something natural such as honey or stevia.

Soothing Teas

Sore throats and headaches are no fun. Digestive issues and aches and pains are also no fun. With these herbs, you are going to find the relief you need without worry.

These herbs are all easy to grow, easy to use in teas, and easy to enjoy! Grow a variety or grow a lot of your favorite. Either way, you are going to have everything you need to satisfy that ache or pain while enjoying your tea at the same time.

Now, you can have your tea and drink it, too, and enjoy a world of health benefits as you do.

Herb:

Lemon Balm

Uses:

Soothes anxiety, helps with sleeping problems, aids in digestion, fights off viruses and can aid in healing a cold.

How to Grow:

Lemon balm is an easy herb to grow, especially if you live in warmer climates. Make sure your plant has partial shade during the hottest part of the day, and water often.

Tea Time:

Purchase a box of loose leaf black tea to keep on hand. This will add body to whichever herb you choose, and will help with the undertone flavor of your tea.

Select a few of the leaves you wish to use, and set them out on a paper towel overnight. Once dried, crush in your hands then add to a tea ball or bag. Add a small scoop of the black tea as well, then secure the top.

Steep in hot water for 5 minutes, and enjoy!

You can also enjoy these herbs as is, without the black tea as an addition, but the flavor can be a little harsh that way, or it may feel that something is missing. At the same time, if you want to add a dab of sweetness to your tea, opt for something natural such as honey or stevia.

Herb:

Alfalfa

Uses:

Excellent for your heart and aids in relieving cystitis. Possibly fights against cancer. Good for circulation.

How to Grow:

Can be grown indoors or out in a large pot. Simply make sure there is plenty of direct sunlight and that you water daily. Don't keep the soil wet, but keep it moist.

Tea Time:

Purchase a box of loose leaf black tea to keep on hand. This will add body to whichever herb you choose, and will help with the undertone flavor of your tea.

Select a few of the leaves you wish to use, and set them out on a paper towel overnight. Once dried, crush in your hands then add to a tea ball or bag. Add a small scoop of the black tea as well, then secure the top.

Steep in hot water for 5 minutes, and enjoy!

You can also enjoy these herbs as is, without the black tea as an addition, but the flavor can be a little harsh that way, or it may feel that something is missing. At the same time, if you want to add a dab of sweetness to your tea, opt for something natural such as honey or stevia.

Herb:

Burdock

Uses:

Excellent for blood circulation, provides relief with arthritis, rheumatism, and various skin irritations.

How to Grow:

Plant in a large pot with plenty of drainage. This herb requires plenty of sunlight and rich soil. Though it grows easily in the wild, it's a little more difficult to grow domestically.

Tea Time:

Purchase a box of loose leaf black tea to keep on hand. This will add body to whichever herb you choose, and will help with the undertone flavor of your tea.

Select a few of the leaves you wish to use, and set them out on a paper towel overnight. Once dried, crush in your hands then add to a tea ball or bag. Add a small scoop of the black tea as well, then secure the top.

Steep in hot water for 5 minutes, and enjoy!

You can also enjoy these herbs as is, without the black tea as an addition, but the flavor can be a little harsh that way, or it may feel that something is missing. At the same time, if you want to add a dab of sweetness to your tea, opt for something natural such as honey or stevia.

Herb:

Catnip

Uses:

Excellent for relieving colic or stomach pain. Aids in digestion, perfect for relieving bloating.

How to Grow:

Catnip grows readily both indoors and out. Plant in any pot you like, just make sure it's contained – it will quickly take over your garden if you aren't careful.

Tea Time:

Purchase a box of loose leaf black tea to keep on hand. This will add body to whichever herb you choose, and will help with the undertone flavor of your tea.

Select a few of the leaves you wish to use, and set them out on a paper towel overnight. Once dried, crush in your hands then add to a tea ball or bag. Add a small scoop of the black tea as well, then secure the top.

Steep in hot water for 5 minutes, and enjoy!

You can also enjoy these herbs as is, without the black tea as an addition, but the flavor can be a little harsh that way, or it may feel that something is missing. At the same time, if you want to add a dab of sweetness to your tea, opt for something natural such as honey or stevia.

In Sickness and In Health

There are times when you drink tea because you are sick, then there are times when you drink tea to keep from getting sick. With these herbs, you have the best of both worlds.

These teas are all excellent to help heal any ailment you are feeling, but they are also great to drink for preventative reasons. There's no end to the wonderful benefits you are going to get from these herbs, so grow a wide variety of them all over your home and garden, and never be without the remedy you need.

Herb:

Dandelion

Uses:

This herb is an excellent source of vitamin A. It will aid in relieving anemia and prevent an iron deficiency.

How to Grow:

This flower will grow readily indoors and out. Plant in the pot of your choice and make sure it gets plenty of direct sunlight throughout the day. Dandelions also enjoy plenty of water, so water daily.

Tea Time:

Purchase a box of loose leaf black tea to keep on hand. This will add body to whichever herb you choose, and will help with the undertone flavor of your tea.

Select a few of the leaves (or even the flowers) you wish to use, and set them out on a paper towel overnight. Once dried, crush in your hands then add to a tea ball or bag. Add a small scoop of the black tea as well, then secure the top.

Steep in hot water for 5 minutes, and enjoy!

You can also enjoy these herbs as is, without the black tea as an addition, but the flavor can be a little harsh that way, or it may feel that something is missing. At the same time, if you want to add a dab of sweetness to your tea, opt for something natural such as honey or stevia.

Herb:

Green Tea

Uses:

Green tea is loaded with antioxidants and disease fighting properties. It is believed to aid in preventing and fighting cancer, and can even aid in weight loss.

How to Grow:

If possible, transplant already established green tea plants. Plant them in a pot with filtered sunlight, and make sure you water them often. If your only option is to grow them from seeds, stay consistent and optimistic, as it can take a few years to grow plants large enough to provide tea.

Tea Time:

Purchase a box of loose leaf black tea to keep on hand. This will add body to whichever herb you choose, and will help with the undertone flavor of your tea.

Select a few of the leaves you wish to use, and set them out on a paper towel overnight. Once dried, crush in your hands then add to a tea ball or bag. Add a small scoop of the black tea as well, then secure the top.

Steep in hot water for 5 minutes, and enjoy!

You can also enjoy these herbs as is, without the black tea as an addition, but the flavor can be a little harsh that way, or it may feel that something is missing. At the same time, if you want to add a dab of sweetness to your tea, opt for something natural such as honey or stevia.

Herb:

Hops

Uses:

Excellent in relieving insomnia and full of calming effects, this herb will relax you. Also aids in digestion and relieving stomach pain.

How to Grow:

Grow this herb outdoors against a trellis. The vines are going to climb vertically out of the mounds you plant the initial hops inside.

Water occasionally, and make sure they are out of direct sunlight.

Tea Time:

Purchase a box of loose leaf black tea to keep on hand. This will add body to whichever herb you choose, and will help with the undertone flavor of your tea.

Select a few of the pods you wish to use, and set them out on a paper towel overnight. Once dried, crush in your hands or with a nutcracker, then add to a tea ball or bag. Add a small scoop of the black tea as well, then secure the top.

Steep in hot water for 5 minutes, and enjoy!

You can also enjoy these herbs as is, without the black tea as an addition, but the flavor can be a little harsh that way, or it may feel that something is missing. At the same time, if you want to add a dab of sweetness to your tea, opt for something natural such as honey or stevia.

Herb:

Sage

Uses:

Thought to be good for oral health, including the gums. Eases stomach cramps and aids in digestion, considered one of the best herbs for all around wellness.

How to Grow:

Sage grows well both indoors and out, and can be grown in pots or directly in your garden.

Water often, maintaining a moist soil but not overly wet.

Tea Time:

Purchase a box of loose leaf black tea to keep on hand. This will add body to whichever herb you choose, and will help with the undertone flavor of your tea.

Select a few of the leaves you wish to use, and set them out on a paper towel overnight. Once dried, crush in your hands then add to a tea ball or bag. Add a small scoop of the black tea as well, then secure the top.

Steep in hot water for 5 minutes, and enjoy!

You can also enjoy these herbs as is, without the black tea as an addition, but the flavor can be a little harsh that way, or it may feel that something is missing. At the same time, if you want to add a dab of sweetness to your tea, opt for something natural such as honey or stevia.

Herb:

Eyebright

Uses:

Relieves itchy and dry eyes. Soothes eyestrain and eye irritation. Soothes eye inflammation.

How to Grow:

Can be grown in large pots both indoors and out. Sprinkle the seeds evenly across the surface and cover with soil, then water occasionally, keeping the soil moist but not wet.

Tea Time:

Purchase a box of loose leaf black tea to keep on hand. This will add body to whichever herb you choose, and will help with the undertone flavor of your tea.

Select a few of the leaves you wish to use, and set them out on a paper towel overnight. Once dried, crush in your hands then add to a tea ball or bag. Add a small scoop of the black tea as well, then secure the top.

Steep in hot water for 5 minutes, and enjoy!

You can also enjoy these herbs as is, without the black tea as an addition, but the flavor can be a little harsh that way, or it may feel that something is missing. At the same time, if you want to add a dab of sweetness to your tea, opt for something natural such as honey or stevia.

All Year Round Teas

There are times when you don't want to be limited by the seasons, and want to be able to enjoy teas from your own herbs all year round. With these herbs, you have the option to grow them either indoor or out, so no matter where you live or what the weather is like, you are going to have a variety of fresh herbs to fall back on.

Enjoy these herbs in teas, or enjoy them soaked as their own tea or tincture, and reap all the incredible health benefits from each and every one.

Herb:

Eucalyptus

Uses:

Use this to relieve any respiratory ailments you may be having. It's excellent for relieving mucus and phlegm issues. Will clear chest congestion quickly.

How to Grow:

Select a variety that has been designed to grow indoors, and use specialized indoor potting soil for the plant as opposed to regular potting soil. Plant in a large pot and make sure it gets plenty of sunlight throughout the day. Water sparingly.

Tea Time:

Purchase a box of loose leaf black tea to keep on hand. This will add body to whichever herb you choose, and will help with the undertone flavor of your tea.

Select a few of the leaves you wish to use, and set them out on a paper towel overnight. Once dried, crush in your hands then add to a tea ball or bag. Add a small scoop of the black tea as well, then secure the top.

Steep in hot water for 5 minutes, and enjoy!

You can also enjoy these herbs as is, without the black tea as an addition, but the flavor can be a little harsh that way, or it may feel that something is missing. At the same time, if you want to add a dab of sweetness to your tea, opt for something natural such as honey or stevia.

Herb:

Garlic

Uses:

Helps prevent heart disease, excellent at fighting off a variety of infections, known to help fight and prevent cancer. Excellent for blood circulation.

How to Grow:

Plant in a pot either in your windowsill or out in your garden. This plant requires some sunlight throughout the day, but it doesn't need constant sunlight. Water occasionally, keeping the soil damp but not wet.

Tea Time:

Purchase a box of loose leaf black tea to keep on hand. This will add body to whichever herb you choose, and will help with the undertone flavor of your tea.

Select a bulb you wish to use, and set it out on a paper towel overnight. Once dried, take your knife and thinly slice off the end the clove, then add to a tea ball or bag. Add a small scoop of the black tea as well, then secure the top.

Steep in hot water for 5 minutes, and enjoy!

You can also enjoy these herbs as is, without the black tea as an addition, but the flavor can be a little harsh that way, or it may feel that something is missing. At the same time, if you want to add a dab of sweetness to your tea, opt for something natural such as honey or stevia.

Herb:

Lavender

Uses:

Lavender has an incredibly calming effect and will aid in insomnia. Helps calm anxiety and panic attacks. Excellent stress reliever.

How to Grow:

Grow in a large pot with a lot of drainage. Keep the plants in a well-lit area, but make sure they aren't going to be in direct sunlight constantly.

Water when the soil is dry, but water a lot when you do.

Tea Time:

Purchase a box of loose leaf black tea to keep on hand. This will add body to whichever herb you choose, and will help with the undertone flavor of your tea.

Select a few of the leaves you wish to use, and set them out on a paper towel overnight. Once dried, crush in your hands then add to a tea ball or bag. Add a small scoop of the black tea as well, then secure the top.

Steep in hot water for 5 minutes, and enjoy!

You can also enjoy these herbs as is, without the black tea as an addition, but the flavor can be a little harsh that way, or it may feel that something is missing. At the same time, if you want to add a dab of sweetness to your tea, opt for something natural such as honey or stevia.

Herb:

Marshmallow

Uses:

Relieves congestion, soothes coughs and provides relief for sore throats, will clear out chest congestion and phlegm, believed to hasten healing from a cold.

How to Grow:

Start germination in the fridge in a small bit of soil. Once the seeds have sprouted, transfer to a pot and cover with soil.

Grow in filtered sunlight and water often.

Tea Time:

Purchase a box of loose leaf black tea to keep on hand. This will add body to whichever herb you choose, and will help with the undertone flavor of your tea.

Select a few of the leaves you wish to use, and set them out on a paper towel overnight. Once dried, crush in your hands then add to a tea ball or bag. Add a small scoop of the black tea as well, then secure the top.

Steep in hot water for 5 minutes, and enjoy!

You can also enjoy these herbs as is, without the black tea as an addition, but the flavor can be a little harsh that way, or it may feel that something is missing. At the same time, if you want to add a dab of sweetness to your tea, opt for something natural such as honey or stevia.

Herb:

Oregano

Uses:

Disinfectant, antibacterial, antimicrobial, believed to aid in curing the common cold and the flu.

How to Grow:

Oregano can be grown easily in a pot on your windowsill or in your garden. Plant a lot of seeds together and cover with soil, water often but not with too much water at a time.

Tea Time:

Purchase a box of loose leaf black tea to keep on hand. This will add body to whichever herb you choose, and will help with the undertone flavor of your tea.

Select a few of the leaves you wish to use, and set them out on a paper towel overnight. Once dried, crush in your hands then add to a tea ball or bag. Add a small scoop of the black tea as well, then secure the top.

Steep in hot water for 5 minutes, and enjoy!

You can also enjoy these herbs as is, without the black tea as an addition, but the flavor can be a little harsh that way, or it may feel that something is missing. At the same time, if you want to add a dab of sweetness to your tea, opt for something natural such as honey or stevia.

Vertical Gardening

No matter wherever you live, it is really a fact that having a vertical garden in your home will truly give you a lot of benefits. The plants in a vertical garden are basically mounted on a wall so that you may get the green walls full of plants of vegetables and flowers in front of you. It is true that when you are opting for growing a vertical garden, a limited space will be available to you but if you use that space in an apocopate way then your vertical garden can prove to be perfectly aligned for you.

You can grow so many types of vegetables and flower plants according to your desire but you should be very selective in determining the type of plant which you grow during different seasons of the year. Like, there are several plants which cannot be grown in direct sunlight during summers so you should make them grow during winters. Setting up the complete framework for the vertical garden is also the most crucial part which requires a lot of care and some specific skills to work on.

Various types of material can be used to set up the frame but the best one is to use the one that is made up of PVC. Different layers incorporate different materials which can enhance the durability of the frame without any doubt. So, working with the vertical gardening can prove to be so much beneficial for you for sure. All you need is proper planning along with few other tips which will definitely help you a lot in setting up your vertical garden where you can grow various vegetables, berries, herbs and flowering plants as well.

Getting started with vertical gardening

For making your vertical garden, you should be very well aware of the fact that a proper wall is required for making a perfect vertical garden. So, when you are getting started with it, firstly you should choose the right wall on which you are going to work for making your garden. You can choose any wall of your home where there is an access to direct sunlight. Basically, the extent to which you may choose to have the right wall depends upon its length along with the amount of sunlight it received during the whole day. If you are going to plant those plants which require some specific conditions to grow, then you should choose that wall where all the necessary conditions and requirements of their growth will be fulfilled.

Making of frame

If you do not know much about making the frame then do not worry at all. Basically, the vertical garden has got the basic structure which is entirely made up of three layers of fabric, sheet of plastic and the upper frame. Just before hanging the frame, you are required to build the whole setup first, so that installing the frame can become easier for you.

Building the frame is another task which is going to be done by you. But, when you are choosing the material for making a frame, you should not go for a metallic one, as it will prove to be additionally expensive without any doubt. Wood should also not be your choice for building the frame as for it, you will require a continuous treatment off and on so that it can be protected from moisture around.

Attaching the plastic sheet

The next thing which you should look for is the process of attaching the sheet of plastic with the already installed frame. The plastic sheet will be directly attached to the frame and will act as a backing for the layer of fabric along with helping to prevent the water from falling off the frame. The material which can be used here is the PVC, but in case you are opting for a wooden wall, a way of ventilation is required to be present at the back end.

Attaching the fabric

Now, after going through the steps which have been mentioned above, you are required to make attachment of fabric to the already installed frame. This is exactly that place where the growth of your plants will take place. Along with that, it will help in holding the water for the plants. For this purpose, you can simply make utilization of padding of carpet but this is not the only option. You can opt for any other fabric material as well which can help in retaining the water without letting it rotten.

Here, at least, two layers of fabric are required. Then make them attached to the already installed frame by taking help of screws and staples made up of stainless-steel. This will be done in exactly the way as you opted for making the canvas stretched across the pre-installed frame. Go for attaching it in a way that it cannot become detached and also, the way in which it will look pretty.

The irrigation system

An irrigation system is definitely required if you want your plants to grow on a surface that is vertical. This will help in providing moisture to the plants you have grown. For this purpose, the use of poly tubing along with the fittings can be the best option. If you do not know from where to get it then do not worry as it will be easily available from any of the irrigation suppliers near you.

Irrigation drippers and standard sized valve can be another option to be used for irrigating your plants. For this, a propagation timer should be used along with the dripper so that you can set up the irrigation time from minutes to even seconds.

In order to avoid rusting, you should make the frame attached to the wall by making use of a stainless steel tool. If you desire to have your frame removed, then using hooks can prove to be fine and otherwise, you can also look for using brackets which are screwed into the wall along with the frame.

Selecting the right plants

After setting up the frame along with plastic sheets and other equipment completely, now you are completely ready to choose the right plants to add in your vertical garden. Along with many other things, you are required to look for the access of sun, humidity level, wind, cold and the shade at the place where you are going to grow your plants. You are required to be very selective in having the right plants as the growth of plants really depends upon the factors which have been mentioned above.

Potassium and phosphorus are two very important and effective fertilizers which are used for making the soil of any place more cultivated. So before you are going for plantation, in addition to wood ash you must also add a bit of potassium and phosphorus so that the soil of the top most layer becomes more and more cultivated.

For winters, you can opt for the plants like ferns, iberis, and hostas etc. For summers, the best plants which you can choose to grow may include weigela and blueberries etc. In addition to this, you should also follow this tip that those plants which are native can grow better in the vertical garden as compared to the other ones.

Inserting the plants

The outer layer of fabric is the place where you are going to insert your desired plants. First, make a cut in the horizontal direction in the material with the help of a razor. Then, try to get the maximum amount of soil from the roots of the plants and then insert that into the cut you have made earlier. By making use of a staple gun, at least, five staples made up of stainless steel are required to be inserted there so that you can attach the backing of plastic with the cloth around the root ball in a semicircle form.

Now you have to make a small hole in the top layer which you made, after making the hole, just put the seed into it and cover it up. Now you are done with working on your very first vertical garden. All you should do is now keep watering the garden regularly so that the seeds you have planted must get enough nutrition and care that eventually they may become a healthy plant one day and give you out the highest output in the form of vegetables and flowers.

And that's done. Now after inserting the plants, all you are required to do is to choose the right design using which you are going to set up the whole vertical garden. For getting some ideas, here are some of the pictures which will greatly help you for sure.

Vertical gardening for saving your money and to add more beauty to your home

Saving your hard earned cash never seems to be so much easy as you have to put a lot of effort to work on it but with the easiest techniques of modern vertical gardening, the hard earned cash of yours can be saved wisely and without facing any sort of problem. It involves the techniques of reducing your expenses so that you can live a self-sufficient and sustainable life.

If you are not scared of working some extra hours doing hard work and if you are absolutely comfortable in waking up before the rooster then your aim of working on vertical gardening and desire of saving your money can be greatly achieved. All you have to do is to completely commit to the aim you have in your mind and leave everything else.

Today is the world of pacing fast which can lead you towards none other than a path down to debt. Due to so many expenses in your life, it can be possible that you may face so many kinds of worse situations as well but you have to keep calm because panic will lead you nowhere but to distress only. If you want to live a sustainable life and want to bring improvements in the way of life you are leading then, the modern ways of vertical gardening can definitely help you out in doing so. Through vertical gardening, you will least likely to depend on others and will become the helper of your own.

It may be possible that a time may come in your life or maybe you are currently suffering from the situation of shortage of money and thus, you are unable to feed your family as you should be or maybe you are unable to buy gasoline for the vehicle you possess, then what will you do? You will think of doing something that will not only help in saving your present money but will also make you able to earn more and more by using a place in your own home without depending on anyone else.

If such ideas reside in your mind then the next step which you must take is to make yourself able to learn actively the techniques of vertical gardening so that, you may live a sustainable life without having any problem of shortage of any cash or facility which you want in your life.

Initial goals for vertical gardening

After finally deciding that you are going to opt for a making your own garden for improving your standard of living somehow and also to look for some sustainable ways of earning a livelihood, it's time to set up your initial goals which you are going to achieve shortly regarding vertical gardening. The first goal should be the preservation of your vertical garden if any, or the preservation of stock of fruits and vegetables which you have in your home in order to make sure that you will always have something to eat at home during the time when you are going to grow a new backyard farm in your home.

So, after preserving the stock of fruits and vegetables to have during the vertical gardening period, you are good to go for using your backyard as a farm for growing fresh and vegetables in your home. This will make you able not only to save the cost but also you will be less dependent upon the things which you get from outside.

When you are putting efforts to live a self-sufficient life, there are some initial costs which are required to be faced by you and without which, you cannot start a journey towards maintainable life. If you have got worried, then do not worry at all. All the initial costs which you are going to bear will pay for themselves in near future for sure and the time in which these costs will be fulfilled is totally dependent upon you that how you manage your time while working on the process.

Vertical gardening does not mean that you are required to build your own vertical garden or to have your food items at home by which you can become able to reduce the level of expenses you have. There are several other methods as well by which the process of vertical gardening can be made possible by working in the following self-sufficient activities:

- If you and your neighbor are having their own vertical gardens in which different fruits and vegetables are being grown, you both can cooperate with each other by bartering different fruit and vegetables for mutual benefits.

- When you have planned to set up your own farm in the spare space present in your backyard, you are required to purchase some items initially, the most important of which is seeds. Once you purchase them and sow them into the soil, the next and only cost which you are required to bear is to water them. You can also save some seeds for using them in your vertical garden for next year as well.

- Using the used material creatively will lead you towards ultimate success like if you have any unrepairable refrigerator in your home, you can use that for storing the extra seeds to be used next season. Many glass jars which are no more in your use can also be used for the same purpose, or you can also use them for preserving any other food items and feed for your chicken as well. You can easily use milk cartons to start seedlings in it.

Tips to easily grow vegetables and flowers in your vertical garden

The basic key to vertical gardening is to become able to live a sustainable life. It will also help you out in adding beauty to the walls of your home. If you are looking for the ways by which you can start your working to become more sustainable, you are required to follow some steps which I am going to mention below. These steps will make you able to accurately work upon the vertical gardening activities with much ease.

Appreciate your life. Yes! Appreciating your life is the main rule of making your life sustainable. You are not allowed to listen to anything said by naysayers. Do not bother about any comment on your lifestyle with raised eyebrows and try to find your own strength during tough and difficult situations as well.

Take steps to grow your own food at home. You can grow own vegetables by taking help from the vertical garden. No matter whether you live in city or village, replace the spare space and the vertical garden in your home into a vertical garden or farm, grow vegetables and fruits on your own and make your own fish farm followed by learning the way of hunting the fish.

If your house is having a fireplace, then convert that place into wood and store wood at that place. This wood can be used by you for getting heat during winters and thus you can become able to save extra energy which you were about to use instead of wood.

Stop relying upon the habit of always buying new stuff which you want in your daily routine. You can reuse and recycle various objects and thus can save your cost a lot. You can buy second-hand clothes, furniture, and hand tools and by doing so you can save a huge amount of money which can be used in some other beneficial and productive way for sure. The saved money can also be used for paying off the debt which has burdened you since long or you can better make your own decision that how the saved money can be used in an effective way.

Stop buying most of the paper products which you buy every week in the form of tissues, paper towels and napkins etc. You can save money by replacing these paper items with old cloths or rags which are no more in your use.

Reviewing your current budget is very necessary as it will help you out cutting down the extra costs which are not necessary for you. If you are under a burden of debt then cutting down the costs in your budget will help you out in sorting out the extra cost which you bear. Cut down all the costs which are burdening your budget as well.

In order to get a tremendous quantity of all natural and healthy sweetener for you and your family, you can raise your own honey bees at home and the honey which you will get after pulling the hives twice a year will give you an endless amount of honey which is far more economical than the honey which you get from market. The flowers which you grow in your vertical garden are then can be used by honey bees to extract juice to make honey.

When you are planning for making a vertical garden in your backyard, you can use the heirloom seeds as they have got the benefit that you are not required to purchase them again and again and you can save these seeds for a longer time by saving the extra costs.

Wherever you live, it is quite easier for you to live a sustainable and self-sufficient life without facing any extra problems. But to be successful in it, you are required to work step by step and do not work on more than one steps at a time. By knowing the basics of vertical gardening, you will most likely to take care of all the needs of not only you but your family as well right from your own backyard farm.

With all these tips, you would become able to get rid of any problem which you may face during the whole process which can be related to anything and any step which you take while working on vertical gardening. Your experience also matters a lot so try to use your experience a well when you are going to comprehend and apply all of these tips I am just going to tell you. Growing your own vertical garden.

Small layers should be edged

If the garden bed which you are using for vertical gardening is narrow or small, you are in really a great need of containing edges at the place. As the place you choose is flat and there may be a chance that due to rainfall or heavy wind, the garden layer will be blown or taken away so its corners should be edged so that rain would not be able to take the soil of the top most layer away.

If your garden layer is large enough you do not have to edge that because the seeds there have been planted by you at such a faraway distance that will not allow the rain or wind to carry the stuff with it. So, you should be considering this tip while working on the garden that in case your garden is small, you should make edges so that you may not face any problem later on.

Material should be crunched

The organic material which you add to the layer in your vertical garden must be in crunched form. This is because, if for instance you are adding dry leaves of some plants as organic material and you are not adding them in crunched form it is possible that as soon as you water the layer, all the leaves, and organic material just gets washed away from that area and all the nutritional material gets lost. So, you should be taking care of this thing and keep this very useful tip in your mind that whenever you are going to add organic material in the layer, make sure that you are adding it in crunched form.

This will get mixed with the soil already present and helps in making the soiled sponge so intact that it would not get washed away while you sprinkle water over it or due to rainfall.

Organic materials should vary in quantity

When you are preparing the mixture of organic materials of various kinds for making a pile be added up in the organic layer, you add various kinds of materials so that it can help in increasing the effectiveness of the whole material. But the tip is, you should use varying quantity of all the materials you are using together. A varying amount of organic materials helps in retaining the original contents of the soil thus help in making your vertical garden more effective and productive.

Make deeper layers

It has been observed that if the garden layer in which you are making layers for the vertical garden is deep, it will help your plant to get more nutrition from the soil and this tip is specifically for those plants which are having a longer tap root than others. The tip is, you should make the garden layer deep so that the tap root of the plants grow in the vertical direction and will get more and more space to grow. In case the layer is shallow and not so deep, the roots of plants will grow in the horizontal direction and it will not grow as it should, thus leading to the poor growth of plant due to poor nutritional input. So, you should be having a deep garden layer to get the best results out of it.

Vertical garden for decoration

It is known to many of year people that watching something green can help in releasing of stress. So, does the gardening is, if you are having a garden at your home then you can help yourself in getting out of any stressed situation you have by sending some of your time in the garden as it will really help you out in the release of all kinds of stress you have.

Decorating a garden and keeping it in the latest way is an art which should be learned by everyone so if you are having a garden at your home then you should make it more beautiful by adding more and more ornaments and other tools to it which will definitely enhance its beauty. Do not worry about the ways by which you will become able to make your garden more decorative as it would just require some easy steps to be done and that's it.

It is absolutely perfect to grow herbs and other plants in your garden which provides a soothing effect to your eyes. Apart from it following are some of the benefits which you will definitely get in order to get your dream garden within your home.

Although the greenery itself is self-sufficient for making the garden good looking and beautiful to eyes but certain ornaments if added to it can give you a really great look of your garden. Several kinds of ornaments can be used in order to make the garden attractive and to enhance its look. A vertical garden can prove to be so much eye catching and it will help you in getting peace of mind, in addition to the decorating properties which it has.

The ornaments which are made up of stones or cement such as statues or other things like that can help the garden owner in using the garden space for some useful purposes in order to make the garden beautiful. If you also want to enhance the look of your garden then several kinds of ornaments including the statues, fountains or waterfalls etc. should be an essential part of your garden.

93

Brings extra beauty to your garden

Use of several ornaments as an essential part of your vertical garden will definitely help you out in bringing extra beauty to your garden. No matter what kind of ornament you use, either it is a fountain or a cement statue, wind chimes or garden rocks, everything will work for enhancing and adding real and elegant beauty to your garden and you are not required to put any sort of extra effort on it as well.

Gives a relaxing atmosphere

In addition to enhancing the beauty and look of your garden, decorating your garden with several types of ornaments will help you in having a really relaxing atmosphere which cannot be possible anywhere else. Of course, it is a known fact that greenery always proves to be a tonic for those minds who are having stress and frustration to help them getting rid of it.

The ornaments in your vertical garden will add much better beauty to it and will help a lot in giving a more relaxing environment to everyone who wants to have some peaceful time. Like, if you are sitting a waterfall in your garden, you will be having a soothing effect on the mind as it would seem to be natural when you would be taking advantage of a waterfall in your home.

Makes the outdoor looks great

If you are having a garden in your home, it would make the outdoor look of your home really well presented but if you have added various kinds of ornaments into it then definitely it would help you out in making the outdoor looks even better than before.

Of course, it is a matter of fact that overall ornaments will help you out in enhancing the beauty of your vertical garden and giving you a lasting and soothing effect for your mind but it is also a proven fact that as your garden is an important part of the outdoor portion of your home, it will specifically enhance the looks from outdoor and will definitely help you out in making your garden looking great.

Makes your mood better

If you come to home after having a hectic routine or if you are in bad mood, you are definitely in need of some therapy which will change your mood from bad to best at once. The garden at your home and its decorative ornaments will definitely help you out in making your mood better by letting you breathe deeply in the open air with greenery and good atmosphere all around so that you may relax and concentrate on your future task.

These were some of the benefits which are definitely associated with the decoration of your vertical garden with various kinds of ornaments and if you think that you can get out of stress and can be happy while you are in your garden, and then you are absolutely right.

Some more tips to consider

With the passage of time as you have made your garden, you will notice that the volume of the layers you just have made will surely get decreased due to the fact that rain, wind and many other factors are incorporated to make the layers thin with the passage of time. Now as you are thinking of what to do with them, I must say the organic layer should be filled up using the crunched leaves so that when it gets mixed with other material, it should take the time to make the layer thin. Otherwise, if some other material is used, it will make the layers thin eventually thus you will have to refill it just after a short span of time.

Add sand to the layers time to time

The layers you have made for the vertical garden are perfect and you can cultivate any herb or vegetable plant on it but you should be considering this fact that something should be added to make their working even better. What is that? The answer is sand. Yes, the ordinary sand which you see in your daily routine. Twice or thrice in a year, you must sprinkle dried sand on the layers of your garden you just have made.

You do not need to mix it with the material residing in layers. Just you have to sprinkle it and that's all. Various worms that live in the soil and making it fertile do not possess teeth and they use sand to grind the material to release out nutrients. So adding sand will definitely add a much better proportion of nutrients to each layer.

Perennial Vegetables

Perennial plants make an amazingly beautiful addition to your home garden. They bear beautiful flowers and grow leaves with great tastes and fresh aromas. They are easy to maintain and stay productive for many years.

It is true that perennial vegetables do not require that much maintenance, but they do have some specific requirements during the year. It is vital to provide them with the best soil, water, and weather conditions to get the ultimate results in the form of organic home grown vegetables, beautiful visual treats and unusual smells in your flower beds with low maintenance requirements.

They have an average life of more than two years. They die and re-grow from the same root crops. Therefore, leaving some of the underlying plants in the soil during harvesting season is pertinent so that they can grow back in the next spring all by themselves.

Garden Landscaping for Perennial Vegetables

Select the types of perennials that you want to have in your garden beds according to the climate conditions of your area. You can use this temperature chart to determine what zone you live and which type of perennial plants will suit the weather conditions of your region.

Zone	Temperature
1	Below -50 F
2	-50 to -40 F
3	-40 to -30 F
4	-30 to -20 F
5	-20 to -10 F
6	-10 to 0 F
7	0 to 10 F
8	10 to 20 F
9	20 to 30 F
10	30 to 40 F

Perennial plants are hard by nature and can survive a few days in containers. But it is important to transplant them from their containers or pots to your perennial garden beds as fast as possible. Discard weeds or moss before transplanting the plant in your garden bed. Get them established in the backyard before the temperature gets freezing outside. Those plants which have survived diseases and are struggling to live now must be avoided. Also, avoid buying overgrown and leggy looking plants. In sunny spells, bring a shade over them so the soil can stay moist. It is inevitably vital to keep your perennials moist. Water them regularly.

When to Plant:

• **Mid to Late Spring**: This period is the ideal time for your perennials because they can get the chance to establish before the heat of summer.

• **Summer Planting**: It is very useful. It is not recommendable to divide and transplant your perennials in summer. Just don't let your perennials get dry. Watering them is essential.

• **Fall Planting:** It allows early blooming in spring seasons. It is also the best season to divide your perennial plants.

Perennial Plant # 01: Cardoons:

Cardoon looks similar to artichoke or thistle. It is an attractive silvery plant. Remember to blanch its stems before eating. To do it, wrap the plant into bundles and surround it with straw. Then pile up the earth around it.

It grows from seed easily, prefer a sunny spot, and tend to increase to a massive plant. In winter months, it provides an unusual vegetable dish.

Perennial Plant # 02: Sorrel:

It is a lemony herb. It works perfectly in sauces for fish. Its leaves turn bitter after flowering.

It grows as a perennial in warmer areas. It must be cropped soon after two months of sowing. It is an early spring vegetable and mostly used as a salad leaf. It grows back after being harvested.

Perennial Plant # 03: Salsify:

It is a great perennial vegetable that you can easily grow in your garden. Only start by sowing seeds of the spring season. Just keep weeds down. Ongoing care is very easy. Its roots will get ready to lift from mid-autumn. Water only if the weather is dry.

Leaving them in the soil throughout winter season is good. If you have winters where the ground gets solid cold, then lift some roots beforehand and store them in boxes of damp sand. It will allow you to access them as required.

Perennial Plant # 04: Scorzonera

Another fabulous addition to your landscape for perennial vegetables is Scorzonera. It has many excellent health and medicinal benefits.

It is sowed, maintained and harvested just like Salsify. Seeds are planted in winter, need less water and roots get ready by mid-autumn. Similarly, it is good to leave its roots in the soil throughout the winter season.

Perennial Plant # 05: Sylvetta Arugula

It is a perennial heirloom. It contains a sharper, fiercer bite than another regular arugula.

It is famous a wild rocket or wild arugula. Also, you can also make a peppery pesto sauce out of it. Its green pointed leaves are used in salads and egg dishes.

Perennial Plant # 06: Miner's Lettuce

It is a tasty salad green. It tastes rather like spinach when sautéed or boiled. It is high in vitamin C.

It is grown in areas which are partially shady. It is ideal for multi-tiered forest gardens. It is hardy and favors a nice mulchy soil during winter especially in colder climates.

Perennial Plant # 07: Dandelion

It has signature friendly yellow flower heads which are incredibly tasty. It grows on lawns and abandoned spaces.

They can be eaten as a salad green or made the tea of which strengthens your liver and kidneys. Its greens are excellent when added to pasta dishes.

Perennial Plant # 08: Watercress

It is a tasty perennial green. It has a unique, meaty and spicy taste that works well in sandwiches and soups. It is rich in iron to vitamins A and C.

Consider growing watercress if you have a hydroponic system at home or an area that's rich and damp on your property. Just keep weeds down. Ongoing care is very easy.

Perennial Plant # 09: Sea Kale

They taste like Asparagus a bit. Its leaf stalks are blanched until semi-soft. Its young leaves are eaten like collards or spinach.

It is commonly found along tide lines of England and Europe. It is easy to make it a part of your home garden. Just keep weeds down. Ongoing care is very easy.

Perennial Plant # 10: Groundnut:

These are American groundnut which is also called the Indian potato. These vines can grow up to six feet long. It is a perennial vine and produces edible beans and tubers. They can also be grown up for dense plantings like a trellis.

In spite being an excellent addition to your garden, unfortunately, it doesn't get that much attention. Most of the perennial vegetables are harvested in the fall and during harvesting, some should be left in the ground for next year's growth.

Perennial Plant # 11: Walking Onions:

This delicious perennial vegetable is self-propagating. The bulb of onion blooms on the head of this beautiful plant.

They require moist garden bed with well-drained soil. You can replant the bulbs. They enjoy full sun. However, they tolerate winter season too.

Perennial plants are easy to maintain and can bear vegetables for many years however their growing conditions vary according to their types. They carry amazing flavors and tastes. You can use them as greens or fry and boil them according to your taste buds. You can also use them in preparing soups and making salads. There's no limit on their uses.

Winterizing Perennial Vegetables

Perennial plants make an amazingly beautiful addition to your home garden. They bear beautiful flowers and grow leaves with great tastes and fresh aromas. They are easy to maintain and stay productive for many years. You can divide them and grow your perennial garden as much as you have space and capability.

It is vital to provide them with the best soil, water, and weather conditions to get the ultimate results in the form of organic home grown vegetables, beautiful visual treats and unusual smells in your flower beds with low maintenance requirements. Also, remember to add natural compost in your perennials. It will help them grow healthier with natural ingredients.

It is true that perennial vegetables do not require that much maintenance, but they do have some specific requirements during the year.

Maintaining your Perennials:

It is very easy to maintain your perennials. They do not require much care and maintenance. Some important guidelines include;

- Prune your perennials regularly.

- Water during drought.

- Water early mornings. It will prevent evaporation.

106

- Control all kind of pests and diseases well on time.

- Divide perennials every two to three years.

- Divide them from the center.

- Regularly remove dead flowers. It will encourage blooming.

Perennial plants make an amazingly beautiful addition to your home garden. They are easy to maintain and stay productive for many years. They bear beautiful flowers and grow leaves with great tastes and fresh aromas. You can divide them and grow your perennial garden as much as you have space and capability.

Temperature Requirements of Perennial Vegetables:

Perennial herbs like garlic, chives, edible canna and yacon grow in the hot and humid zone of East Texas to coastal Carolinas. This zone is not tropical but features hot, humid temperatures of both summer and winter.

One highly populated area of perennial vegetables is the cool maritime that runs from San Francisco to Alaska panhandle. Asparagus yellow, sea beat, Turkish rocket, daylily, and asphodel grow here in dry to mesic moistures. Their bulbs, broccolis, roots, leafstalks, flower buds and tubers are edible.

A lot of perennial vegetables like walking onion, welsh onions, ramps, udo, camass, chicory and mallow in cold temperatures of eastern and central U.S., Europe and Asia. They include giant herbs like watercress, Chinese and American lotus too. They can live in dry to mesic moistures.

Other perennial vegetables like nodding wild onions, showy and common milkweed, yampah, rhubarb and Arrowhead grow in extreme cold weathers such as Canada, northern U.S. and some portions of Asia and Europe. Some giant herbs like Maximilian sunflower, sun-chock and watercress whereas micro herbs like watermill, duckweed also grow in the same region in dry to mesic moisture. Their green shoots, flower buds, green leaves, seeds, tubers, leaf stalks and starches are edible.

Winterizing Perennial Vegetables:

Many of your perennial vegetables such as artichokes, Jerusalem artichokes, horseradish, asparagus, and rhubarb may survive winter better with a little care and maintenance.

Winterizing Artichoke:

For winterizing artichoke, check if small pups are coming out. If they are, then remove the mother artichoke entirely ad protect the baby plants.

Clip back the large thistle type or globe artichoke rosette. Take leaves, compost or mulch and cover the plant with six inches or more with it. Put a plastic cover box and place it on the station during the harshest time of the winter season. When weather moderates, remove the box.

Winterizing Horseradish:

It survives winter season comfortably. You only need to cover it with light mulch during the coldest part of the season.

Harvest it after several good touches of frost in the seasons of falls to make it best potent to the harshness of the winter seasons.

Winterizing Asparagus:

Mulch the beds of asparagus plants with hay, weed-free straws, chopped leaves or similar materials for up to four to six inches. Remove mulch from half of the bed in the following spring.

Removing the mulch with allow the perennial vegetable to come back more quickly. Where the mulch remains, the plants will get out later. Thus it will naturally extend the asparagus season of your garden.

Winterizing Rhubarb:

Divide the plant of rhubarb in October every two to three years if it is crowded and well-established. Remove half of the roots, crown, plant and all. Fill fertilizers mixed with organic compounds, rotted manure or compost in the hole.

Plant the removed rhubarb to another spot in your garden. It will ensure a good crop for next season.

Excellent Perennial Vegetables for Garden

Perennial plants are fun to grow. They have an average life of more than two years. They are easy to plant and require very less maintenance. They die and re-grow from the same root crops. Therefore, leaving some of the underlying plants in the soil during harvesting season is pertinent so that they can grow back in the next spring all by themselves. Divide your perennial vegetable plants every two to three years. Just divide the plant from the middle, reach the root, divide it and then transplant one part to another garden bed.

110

In this chapter, we will be discussing some great perennial vegetables and valuable tips to sow, maintain, harvest and re-grow them;

Perennial Plant # 12: Radicchio:

It is a sharp flavored perennial vegetable. It grows a tightly clumped head which is edible. It requires full sun and well-drained soil. Keep the soil highly fertilized too. Many people consider it to be biennial but under favorable conditions such as weather and soil, it can turn into a perennial.

Radicchio has dark red leaves with white veins. It is similar to cabbage or lettuce. For starting up sow its seeds or plants in early spring and they will be ready to be harvested in late fall. Remember that it re-grows from these roots automatically in next spring therefore it is pertinent to leave some of the root crops in the soil during harvesting season. Its leaves have a bitter flavor but are largely used in salads. You can add salt and pepper to reduce the intensity of its bitter flavor.

Perennial Plant # 13: Rhubarb:

111

Rhubarb is a hardy perennial vegetable. Many people consider it a perennial fruit as well. It stays productive for many years. Therefore, it is important to plant it at a place in your perennial garden where it won't get disturbed easily.

If you want to add this beauty to your perennial garden, plant it in the sun and moist. Also, keep the soil well drained. Spread a 2-inch layer of compost into the ground before sowing it. Do this when the air temperature is 80 degrees Fahrenheit or above. In the early spring of the first year of its growth, apply a balanced fertilizer. It will be ready for harvesting in its second year. After six to eight years, its stalks will start getting thinner, at that time divide the plant and transplant half of it to another flower bed in your perennial garden.

Perennial Plant # 14: Jerusalem Artichokes:

This beautiful perennial vegetable is from the family of sunflowers. They can be eaten raw or cooked. They grow edible tubers like potatoes. They can be a better choice for people with diabetes because their carbohydrates break down into fructose instead of glucose.

It is important to handle your perennial tubers with care as their skin is fragile. It is good to leave 15 to 24 inches space between the plants when sowing. They grow tall and bear yellow flowers like sunflowers. As you do with other perennial vegetables such as asparagus and globe artichoke, leave some root crops of Jerusalem artichoke in the soil during harvesting season and then they grow back from them in coming spring by themselves.

Perennial Plant # 15: Asparagus:

Asparagus is a hardy perennial vegetable. It can last for decades under favorable conditions in your perennial garden.

Before sowing or transplanting asparagus, mix the soil in your garden bed with a 2-inch layer of thick natural compost. Place two plants of this beautiful perennial vegetable 12 inch apart from each other. New plants will take around six weeks. It is harvested in the spring. Like globe artichoke, asparagus also needs the sun and moist. They require well-drained soil too. In the second year of its growth, it will be ready for harvesting. Leave some of the root crops in the ground so they can re-grow in the next spring.

Perennial Plant # 16: Globe Artichoke:

Globe Artichoke is a vast and attractive perennial vegetable. Growing this perennial plant in the sun and moist is important. They produce beautiful purple flowers. Some of these flower buds are not cut off during the harvesting season. Their flower buds are edible.

Keep the soil well drained. The plant needs consistent moisture into the ground to grow well. You can start your new globe artichoke perennial by (I) seeds or (II) a divided root. Keep two plants 24-36 inches apart. It is advisable to lay a 2-inch layer of compost into the soil before sowing or transplanting this beautiful fuzzy purple perennial vegetable. Grow them in rows.

Perennial Plant # 17: Good King Henry:

Good King Henry is a small perennial vegetable. It is from the family of spinach. Its seeds are an edible grain. Its flower buds are eaten like broccoli and shoots like Asparagus. It is a great plant.

114

They need consistent moisture in the soil to grow well. Keep the soil well drained. They are easy to plant and require very less maintenance. It is important to plant it at a place in your perennial garden where it won't get disturbed easily.

Perennial vegetables are a beautiful addition to your garden not only visually but also it grows healthy vegetables for longer periods of time. You can eat their edible parts in some ways like soups, salads, etc. Also, these plants require low maintenance. Some of the perennial plants can stay productive for more than a decade such as Rhubarb. You must add perennial vegetables such as globe artichoke, asparagus, Jerusalem artichoke and radicchio in your garden beds this spring and enjoy their beauty and produce for years.

Perennial Herbs to Grown in Garden

You can start your perennial herbs garden in your backyard. They also produce amazingly beautiful aroma in summer. They become accessible and handy this way. Above all, you can even grow them in containers, but it is advisable to grow them in garden beds as they live long and produce for many years. Herbs are perennial, biannual and annual too. Some people also dry these perennial herbs for offseason, and other may freeze them as well. They are very famous for perennial gardens because they stay there for years and add beauty to the visual landscape. Also, they provide an excellent, continuous harvest for your kitchen.

In this chapter, we will be discussing some of the most famous and beautiful perennial herbs and useful tips to grow and maintain them;

Perennial Plant # 18: Sage:

This perennial herb has a bitterly strong flavor. It grows in many colorful types. It is commonly used in stews, herb bread, stuffing and sausages. It has a beautiful floral spike. It has soft green leaves. It can plant anywhere in your garden beds, and it can be grown in most climates.

It can be planted anywhere in your garden beds, and it can be grown in most climates. You can also dry up its leaves like many other perennial herbs. It dies in fall and then grows back in early springs.

Perennial Plant # 19: Rosemary:

It is a lovely perennial herb. It grows blue flowers. Its leaves contain a pungent aroma. It has needle-like spines. Bees are very attracted towards this herb. It is a flavorful addition to any dish such as roast chickens, cooked meats, and vegetable stews.

It is also used in bathtub waters. Soaking in this water can relax your muscles after a tired day. It also becomes a fantastic addition to bread and biscuits. It can easily be grown in containers. You can dry its leaves up for use in off seasons as it does not grow in cold climates.

Perennial Plant # 20: Winter Savory:

This bushy and hardy perennial herb contains a peppery flavor. It requires relatively drier soil. With aging, its leaves tend to become sparser. Therefore, it is important to take cuttings and start new plants every three to four years.

It is added to teas, herb vinegar, herb butters as well as many other dishes. It has many medicinal qualities as well.

Perennial Plant # 21: Chives:

This perennial herb is a part of the onion family. It best compliments the salads, vegetables, eggs, dips, and sauces. It has green hollow spears. These spears contain a mild onion flavor. It is very simple to use as well. Just take out its fresh leaves and add the edible flowers in your dish to get that light, flavorful onion taste in your food instantly.

Chive is a lush plant. Therefore, it is important to divide it every three years. It is very easy to plant this perennial herb. It dies in fall and grows back in spring. You can start it from seed and soon it will be cultivated into a large plant with clumps of bulb and tops.

Perennial Plant # 22: Thyme:

Another amazingly beneficial and useful perennial herb is thyme. It grows beautiful tiny flowers. It is very flavorful. It produces small green leaves and contains a fresh aroma. You can keep the dried leaves in a closed, airtight container.

You can grow thyme almost everywhere. It can grow for decades. It is also very easy to propagate it from its cuttings. You can also cut down the stems and hang to dry them up to use later. It requires very less maintenance and care.

Perennial Plant # 23: Green Oregano:

Its leaves have a great sage-like flavor. It is a perennial herb that does not do well in the winter season, but you can shelter it with straws. It requires continuous pruning. Its stems can grow roots where they touch the soil. It usually comes back in form in springs. It stays green in some zones as well.

You can only dry bundles of green oregano and use it in off seasons. It is utilized in all kinds of foods including drinks and ice creams. However, it goes amazingly well with all kind of tomato dishes.

Perennial Plant # 24: Mint:

Mint is a very useful green perennial herb. It produces beautiful purple flowers on a single spike. Its leaves have an intense flavor. It also exudes a sharp amazingly fresh smell. It best compliments peas, sauces, vegetables, teas, and chocolates.

It is invasive. Therefore, it is important to contain it. You can grow it in some containers or pots. If you want to grow it in soil, then plant it in a bottomless container and place that container in the ground to contain it.

Perennial herbs make a beautiful addition to your garden. Most of these herbs require the same kind of maintenance. They are usually tough plants and can grow in most of the climates. Therefore, it is very easy for you to grow them even in your backyard. You can enjoy the visual landscape and healthy benefits both from your little perennial garden. Remember to make a note of the flavors that you prefer over others and then plant your perennial herbs accordingly. It will help you obtain your favorite flavors in teas, stews, sausages, chocolates, peas, etc.

Edible Perennial Plants

Perennial fruits are considered to best edible perennial plants especially if you want to grow them in small gardens. They don't take as much space as other fruits trees do. They grow fast and produce for more years than annual or biannual fruit plants. They must be grown in full sun. Some perennial fruits grow fast while others may test your patience. But either way, they add beauty to your visual landscape and also rejuvenate you with their pleasant fragrances and fresh tastes.

Growing perennial edibles have their benefits; for example:

• They make effortless gardens.

• They are organic.

• They need less tillage than other vegetables.

• They help retain carbon in the soil of your garden too.

- The soil structure of your garden is also not disturbed during their cultivation.

- They also extend your harvesting seasons, especially in early spring.

- They are also low maintenance plants and much less work.

It is advisable to start with one or two plants and then to propagate from them to save money. If you want to start your little garden of perennial fruits, then here are some of them along with the much-needed tips to grow and maintain them throughout the year;

Perennial Plant # 25: Blueberries

Perennial blueberries bear fruits in the third or fourth year of their growth. And they do not produce many fruits after five or six years of their growth. They do not grow well in neutral and alkaline soil beds. They require acidic soil. Always plant them in full sun. Keep the soil bed organic, well-drained and moist.

Propagating this plant is trickier and can test your patience. There are three varieties of blueberries i.e. (I) Highbush berries, (II) Rabbiteye berries and (III) Southern highbush berries. Highbush is self-fruitful whereas rabbit eye is not, therefore, plant at least two rabbiteye plants together for pollination. Similarly, southern highbush berries also do well when two or more crops are planted together. Dwarf ones can be planted in containers or pots and thus can be accommodated in tight spaces. These are probably the most delicate small perennial fruit to grow in your home garden. If you still want to develop them then, it is important to keep the soil rich with an acidic fertilizer and moist without being soggy.

Perennial Plant # 26: Brambles:

Perennial blackberries and raspberries come in some colorful varieties. Brambles include blackberries and raspberries. Perennial blackberries bear fruits in the second year of their growth just like the perennial raspberries. They come in both thorny and non-thorny versions of plants.

Keep the soil well drained. However, they can tolerate poor soil but require full sun and light shade sometimes. These plants can easily turn your perennial garden into a jungle by growing suckers and long canes therefore it is important to prune the tops timely.

Perennial Plant # 27: Kiwi:

Kiwis are beautiful perennial fruits. They come in hard varieties too so you can choose according to your climate and weather conditions. They grow best in a neutral or slightly acidic soil. Keep the soil well drained too.

Hardy perennial Kiwi plants bear the small size of fruits. It is important to keep the ratio of male and female plants in kiwi bed accurate. You can plant one male plant with two to four female plants for pollination. Add a light amount of fertilizers in early springs. For propagation, do cuttings in midsummer. It is vital not to fertilize the plants over. Pruning is essential, but you must remember to prune male plants after flowering and female plants after harvesting only.

Perennial Plant # 28: Grapes:

Perennial grapes are woody vines. They require a deep and red loam. Keep the loam well drained. They can grow up to 50 years. Always plant them in full sun. They bear fruits in the first growth year.

Pruning perennial grape plants are important. Provide them with a fence or trellis to grow on. Also, provide them with a lot of air. It will prevent fungal infections. It is important to tie these plants, so the fruit does not hang on the ground. It can rot there quickly. They come in some varieties. Therefore, you have the freedom of choosing them according to your climate and other needs.

Perennial Plant # 29: Strawberries:

It is one of the easiest perennial fruits to grow in your home garden. Plant them in the fully sunny area. It is important to plant your perennial strawberries in garden beds where you have not plant nightshade crops in last two to three years. Nightshade crops include tomatoes, potatoes, etc. It will help in preventing the spread of Verticillium Wilt.

Perennial Strawberries require sandy loam which must be slightly acidic as well. Most perennial strawberry plants begin producing fruits in their second growth year. It is good to spread a thick layer of compost on the soil of your perennial garden bed every spring. It is important to cut the top growth after harvesting season. Don't cut the crown. They can last up to five years depending upon proper maintenance and rich fertilizing.

Perennial Plant # 30: Raspberries:

They are delicious and tart perennial edible plants. They are a few different species of raspberries. Growing them from seeds will take a couple of years to produce fruits.

Other famous perennial fruits include currants, serviceberries, honeyberries, jostaberries, mulberries, lingonberries, elderberries and gooseberries. Perennial fruits look beautiful during their growth years and taste yummy when to get harvested and placed on your dinner table. They require low maintenance, but it is vital to select the type of perennial fruit according to the climate and other conditions of your living zone. Once chosen wisely, it is the time to enjoy watch them growing up and becoming part of your food.

Pepper Growing

Hot peppers are extremely healthy vegetables, which are not difficult to grow. There efficaciousness lies within the fact that they are a rich source of Vitamins and other nutrients. Therefore, it is essential to provide a guide about how to grow hot peppers. In order to provide a brief elaboration regarding the fact, this book is written with all of the important pieces of information.

To begin, the book incorporates the types and various classifications of the hot pepper. Furthermore, the method to grow Jalapeno, Cayenne and Anaheim are included. In addition to this, the methods to cultivate cherry peppers as well as Serrano pepper are also discussed in here. Moreover, the book also incorporates the tips to keep pests and insects away from your plants. Finally, the understanding of overall planting conditions to grow hot peppers is also elaborated.

Therefore, this book serves as an astounding guide about growing hot peppers at home. This book is written in such a manner that it will facilitate all kinds of readers. Not only the professional gardeners, but also, the beginners will understand the tips and procedure for growing hot peppers. Thus, this book teaches the methods to grow five major kinds of hot pepper.

Types and Varieties of Hot Peppers

Despite their spicy taste and hot nature, hot peppers are still used by a number of people. These peppers come in a huge variety. Their properties like taste, color and shape varies differently. Some of them are present in tropical regions, while others are usually cultivated in comparatively dry parts of the world. Furthermore, there taste is high and their color is tempting. This chapter intends to provide a detailed analysis of the different kinds of hot peppers. Some of these peppers are as follows:

1. Cherry pepper:

Cherry peppers possess following properties:

i.   These peppers are also known as pimento peppers.

ii.   Cherry peppers are similar to a heart shape.

iii.   They are around 4 inches wide and 4 inches long.

iv.   These peppers are not very spicy. On a Scoville heat index, they enjoy 500 rating.

v.   Mostly found as red stuffing inside the olives.

2. Anaheim pepper:

Anaheim peppers possess the following properties:

i.   Another pepper which is not highly spicy is the Anaheim pepper.

ii.   This pepper is generally reddish maroon in color. They are long and thin kind of peppers.

iii.   Anaheim peppers generally possess 1000 to 5000 scoring on the Scoville heat index.

iv.   Therefore, the pepper with the highest score is extremely spicy.

3. Jalapeno pepper:

Jalapeno peppers possess the following properties:

i. The jalapeño pepper is one of the most important and widely used forms of peppers used in the United States.

ii. Numerous individuals like it since it is hot yet not overpowering.

iii. These peppers are generally red or green with a length of 2- 3.

iv. Their Scoville heat record is around 5,000. Moreover, they can go anywhere in the range of 2,000 to 8,000.

v. At the point when utilized sparingly, they include only the perfect measure of hot flavor to most Mexican dishes.

vi. Numerous individuals additionally profound broil jalapeños loaded down with cheddar for a wonderful starter.

4. Serrano pepper:

131

Serrano peppers possess following properties:

i.   The Serrano pepper looks like a jalapeno pepper. However, this pepper is much spicier.

ii.   On the Scoville heat record, the Serrano pepper can be somewhere around 10,000 and 25,000. This pepper is generally little in size and green in shading.

iii.   As per a general saying, if the pepper is smaller in size, they will be spicier.

5. *Cayenne pepper:*

Cayenne peppers possess the following properties:

i.   This is another kind of hot pepper. Because of its spicy taste, it is used by a lot of people in food items.

ii.   The cayenne pepper is red in color.

iii.   It is large and utilized in powdered structure.

iv.   Furthermore, this pepper has been utilized as a part of common prescriptions for a long time because of reported recuperating traits.

6. Tabasco pepper:

Tabasco peppers possess the following properties:

i.   The Tabasco pepper is utilized to make Tabasco sauce.

ii.   In the event that you have ever tasted how hot Tabasco sauce is, you will not be astounded to discover that the Tabasco pepper has a Scoville heat list of somewhere around 30,000 and 60,000.

iii.   The real pepper is under 2 crawls in length and can be green, red, yellow or orange in shading.

7. *Thai pepper:*

Thai peppers possess the following properties:

i.   The Thai pepper is grown in Thailand along with some of the other neighboring countries.

ii. It is one of the spiciest peppers of its family. Its score on a Scoville index differs from 50,000 to 100,000. Interestingly, these peppers enhance thee taste in such a manner that the person eating the food will keep on drooling over the food.

iii. The Thai pepper is one of the littlest peppers, measuring in at not exactly an inch.

iv. It is utilized as a part of the numerous fiery Thai dishes at eateries in the U.S.

8. *Ghost pepper:*

Ghost peppers possess following properties:

i.   Ghost pepper, also known as Naga Jolokia, is literally the spiciest pepper.

ii.   It possesses such high Scoville index of 1,000,000 that it is included in the Guinness Book of World Records.

iii.   If you ever got a chance to taste this spicy pepper, then be careful while consuming it. It can burn your mouth with its spicy nature for about half an hour.

9. *Habanero chili pepper:*

Habanero chili pepper is another kind of the hot pepper family. Some of the properties of this hot pepper are as follows:

i. Habanero chili pepper is another spicy kind of pepper with ubiquitous utilization worldwide.

ii. These peppers, which can change its color from green to pink to yellow, are not longer than 3.

iii. Interestingly, the size of these peppers does not matter. They can cause severe burns even if they possess small size. The Scoville heat index for these kinds of peppers can change from 150,000 to 350,000.

How to Grow Cayenne, Jalapeno and Anaheim at home?

One interesting thing about these kinds of peppers is that they can be grown in homes without a huge problem. In order to grow these types of hot peppers, some of the steps must be followed. This chapter intends to provide the procedures to grow Cayenne, Jalapeno and Anaheim pepper at home.

How to grow Cayenne pepper at home:

Cayenne peppers are also familiarized as Capsicum annuum. These peppers are usually grown in the pots to maintain a cool yet suitable temperature and environment. Therefore, they are usually not grown outside. Hence, these pepper plants can be moved outside after the warm climate is passed. At that time they gloom bright with red colors of the peppers. Peppers require a long developing season and warm to hot temperatures for fruiting. Furthermore, they demand depleted soil and normal watering system. They do not require extensive care either. Following is the procedure to grow Cayenne peppers at home:

1. Buy a soil mixture or create one of your own soil mixtures by adding only one part of sand, one part of garden soil and a single part of moss.

2. Now, you must fill a compartment from the inside with half inch filled with the self-created soil mixture, and water completely. Permit the pot to deplete for one day.

3. Sow a few seeds quarter inches deep. Put the dirt aside. Expel your pepper plant from its compartment, and relax any roots that wind around the root ball. Place

the plant in the focal point of the pot. Put enough soil under the pepper plant so it is planted at the same profundity as its past developing level. Utilize the rest of the dirt to cover.

4. Place the seeds in a sunny window. Developing seeds grow best at around eighty degrees Fahrenheit. Squeeze out all with the exception of the most grounded seedling. Develop pruned pepper plants in normal family unit temperatures of seventy degrees Fahrenheit at a spot near daylight.

5. Move these peppers outside when daytime temperatures are reliably fifty five degrees or higher.

6. Water pepper plants to avert drying out, yet do not keep the soil immersed with water. Utilize a pot with waste gaps, and place a saucer with edges under the pot or set the pot in a plant stand to permit free seepage. Flood until water runs unreservedly out the base of the pot. Water when the top inch of soil is dry to the touch. Satisfactory and unfaltering watering system is vital for most extreme natural product generation and organic product size.

7. Treat pepper plants, taking after producer's proposals, or utilize half-quality all the more frequently for a consistent supply of supplements. A compost mix with higher phosphorous than nitrogen helps peppers deliver more natural product. Overwintering pruned peppers can be treated with a higher nitrogen equation to empower rich development, decreasing nitrogen again in the spring.

How to grow jalapeno at home:

The procedure to grow jalapeno pepper at home is as follows:

1. Sow seeds around two months from the time you need to transplant them into your greenhouse. Put two seeds in little pots loaded with the blend of soil. Plant seeds about quarter crawl profound. Water altogether.

2. Put the pots in a sunny window. Keep up the temperature at 80 degrees Fahrenheit, since jalapenos require a dirt temperature of 80 degrees Fahrenheit to sprout well.

3. Check the dirt temperature with a thermometer. Keep the plant watered; however not saturated. Pivot the pot a fourth of a turn every four days if the light source is a window. On the off chance that both seeds sprout, evacuate the weakest one.

4. Take care of your plant by providing the suitable conditions for it. Moreover, regularly provide water as well as the required sunlight to ensure a proper growth of your plant. Transplant it after all risk of ice is past.

How to grow Anaheim pepper at home:

If you intend to grow Anaheim pepper at home, then you must follow the steps given below:

1. Develop Anaheim pepper in a sunny zone of the greenery enclosure that has all around depleted soil. Besides, the pH of the soil must exist in 5 and 7. You can do various tests in order to measure the pH of the soil you are working on. In order to regulate the pH, you can add various chemicals in the soil accordingly. As indicated by the test outcomes, revise the dirt with limestone to raise the pH, or fuse sulfur to lower it. Moreover, addition of fertilizers can also help in the maintenance of the dampness of your soil. Transplant the seedlings when the dirt temperature surpasses fifty degrees Fahrenheit.

2. Mulch the dirt with dark plastic before transplanting the seedlings in the event that you live in a cooler region or on the off chance that you need to begin your plants early. Notwithstanding warming the dirt, the plastic additionally advances soil-dampness maintenance and keeps weeds under control. Grow the plants after creating small holes.

140

3. Care must be taken and one must sow the Anaheim seed with appropriate space. All of the seeds must be spaced 2 feet apart in lines. Moreover, these lines must be separated from each other by a distance of 3 feet. In addition, the area in between the beds must be 14 inches for proper growth with the provision of wide area.

4. Water Anaheim Chili properly in the entire developing season. Moreover, keep the dirt consistently damp. If the soil is dry then it can hinder the growth of your plant. Above all, try not to spray the soil which is not to be used afterwards.

5. Presently, include some manure in the planting bed. Disseminate 2 tablespoons of manure in a trench which is dug around all of the plants. The trench must be 4 inches farther from the stem of the plant and abstain from getting manure on the plant. Addition of the manure at nearer places can burn the plant. Then again, burrow a 1-inch-profound long trench on either side of a column and the soil mixture in them. Afterwards, fulfill the trench, water them and clean them properly.

6. Wash your hands with a cleanser and water before taking care of Anaheim pepper. Moreover, one must not smoke near the plants. Tobacco can trigger plants to build up the Tobacco Mosaic Virus, which stains the foods grown from the ground the leaves to yellow and build up a mosaic example. Hence, if you want to have healthy yields, use gloves as well.

How to grow Cherry Pepper and Serrano Pepper at home?

Cherry peppers as well as Serrano peppers are two other major types of hot pepper. It is extremely simple to grow them at the house. Moreover, the cherry peppers as well as the Serrano peppers possess high nutritional values. These peppers are not only used to control cholesterol level, but also, they are used to eradicate the chances of arthritis.

How to grow cherry pepper at home:

The method to grow cherry pepper at home is given below:

1. One must develop pepper plants in proper sunlight. Once the temperature reaches fifty degrees Fahrenheit in the evening, the right time for plantation has come.

2. Pour fertilizer into the dirt before planting. Dig holes and add manures. This will improve the nature of the plant. Moreover, they will also help in the growth. Add the soil to fulfill these holes. Water them appropriately.

3. Include natural fertilizers to improve the growth of your plant. These plants will need mulch as well. Once you have included the mulch, you are good to go.

4. Water the cherry peppers instantly after they are planted. The amount of water must be such that it wets the soil but the water content does not exceed the desired level. However, if such a situation occurs that the plants become dry, then add the sufficient but not extra amount of water.

5. Once the plant is loaded with one or two small fruits, then you can gather them. In order to gather these, use scissors to cut the peppers. Try not to pluck them with your hands as they are spicy and can cause burn in the area.

How to grow Serrano pepper at home:

The method to use Serrano pepper at home, one must follow the steps given below:

1. To begin, sow the seeds of in a pot with a homemade soil mixture. Seed develops best when soil temperature is 70F or higher. However, if the temperature is below fifty, then various problems can take place in the process of germination.

2. Moreover, one must not place these plants in the light deficient areas. If these plants do not get proper sunlight, they fail to grow.

3. Do not place your plants outside in ice cold weather. If the plants are hampered because of the snow, then it becomes extremely difficult to save them and grow other plants.

4. Move the plants outside once the soil is warm and pleasant. If the soil is not appropriate, then do not take the plants outside.

5. Use dark plastic or column spreads to speed soil warming and early development. Use various homemade manures to warm up the soil. This will help in the growth of the plant.

6. If you do not desire to use dark plastic, then you must mulch the plants after they are settled. This will maintain the dampness of your soil. Moreover, they will also help in controlling the weeds.

7. Peppers are sensitive when the temperature reaches extreme conditions. They face problems in both extremely hot as well as in the extreme cold weathers. Therefore, you must choose mild temperature with enough sunlight.

8. A large amount of nitrogen manure may advance the rich vegetative development. Moreover, these peppers have depicted positive response to phosphorus manure as well. However, with the addition of a chemical, the organic component of your fruit will be decreased.

9. Furthermore, try to maintain even levels of calcium and other nutrients in the soil as well.

Tips to Grow Your Plants from Pests and Insects

Growing vegetables in your own garden provides you great opportunities and variety of food. However, if proper care is not taken, then these vegetable can be attacked by numerous pests and insects. In this way, bug control is very essential to avoid such issues. On the negative side, pesticides contain large amounts of perilous poisons that may leave its residues on the foods grown from the ground. Astoundingly, natural pesticides which are home-made are safer and efficacious. In addition, they can be produced using each one of those things which are not expansive.

Utilization of the following homemade recipes can be used to grow plants and keep pests away:

1. Garlic Sprays:

The strong fragrance of garlic keeps numerous insects away from the vegetables. For this common pesticide, blend 10 to 12 garlic cloves with 1 quart of water and mix them together. Now allow the mixture to settle for 24 hours. Afterwards, strain it through cheesecloth covering the opening of a glass container and incorporate 1 cup of cooking oil. This concentrated mixture works efficiently for a number of days. In order to increase the efficiency, put one tablespoon of cayenne pepper in a jar and place it in the mixture you have created. Now let it stay for an extra 24 hours before straining the liquid. Strain the liquid and you are now good to use the spray.

2. Red Chili Pepper:

This pepper is widely known for its ability to add taste in pizza and to incorporate flavors in the food items. In a similar manner, red pepper powder can be used to make a locally developed pesticide that is efficient enough to keep pests and insects away. In order to make the mixture, blend 1 tablespoon of red pepper powder, 6 drops of washing powder and 1 gallon of water and mix all of them

146

together. Sprinkle the pepper spray on the vegetables as per the requirement. In order to get better outcomes, reapply the spray. This will keep the pests away.

3. Vinegar:

It works especially well for weeds in the garden. The essential issue with vinegar is that it can hurt numerous varieties of plants. In this way, it is recommended to use a pad to brush the vinegar particularly onto the leaves of the weeds one is endeavoring to execute. This keeps the vinegar from getting onto distinctive plants and ensures that the entire leaf surface is secured with the vinegar.

4. Cleanser and Alcohol Sprays:

To start, blend a teaspoon of fluid cleanser in some rubbing liquor in one quart of water. Once you have thoroughly mixed them, you can apply them on the plants. However, before the application, test the mixture on two or three leaves to guarantee no harm is done to the plants. Sprinkle the solution on the top and base of leaves to protect them. Moreover, you can also apply this mixture using a pad or a brush. Once you have applied the mixture, and then wait for some time. After a few minutes, wash the leaves swiftly with cold water.

5. Baby Shampoo Sprays:

A baby shampoo is very effective yet harmless cleanser. Moreover, it does not contain any chemicals. On the contrary, if there are some chemicals present in the shampoo, then their content ratio is extremely low. Therefore, it can be used to keep away numerous insects. This spray can protect indoor as well as the outdoor plants, including aphids, scales and insect vermin.

6. Lime Sulfur:

Lime sulfur is an old but still used cure for pests. It is used by both professional and simple gardeners. This blend is used to kill most sorts of pests. In addition, it is also used to eradicate eggs of insects and other insects. Lime sulfur also has fungicidal impact and can be used on normal and ornamentals trees. On the brighter side, care must be taken since lime sulfur associated with plants near the house will recolor the paint. Apply as per the requirement.

7. Tobacco Water:

Strangely, tobacco and cigarette butts are helpful for eradicating worms. They can be used to kill various species of aphids and termites, In order to create tobacco water, blend tobacco along with water to create a blend that creates a brownish mixture. After the mixture is settled, put it on the soil. However, keep this mixture away from the children as it can be extremely dangerous if drunk.

8. Oil Sprays:

Firstly, take 1 tablespoon of washing agent and include 1 cup of cooking oil from a fresh oil bottle. This concentrated liquid must be mixed with water before use with an extent of 4 teaspoons of oil mix to 1 half quart of water until the mixture is completely ready. At that moment, place the oil mixture in a glass container in a calm, dry and cool area. Apply little parts of this spray on the affected areas. This will keep the mites and midges away from your pepper.

Some of the advantages of using these natural pesticides are as follow:

148

i. Economical:

Making your own pesticides is extremely beneficial since it costs less and provides encouraging results. By far most of the responses for these pesticides are overwhelming. They are extremely economical and beneficial.

ii. Secure:

These mixtures include those ingredients which are secure. Therefore, they are used by many farmers as well as ordinary gardeners.

iii. Non-Toxin:

Most of the homemade pesticides do not use substances that contain harmful ingredients. They possess nontoxic ingredients and efficacious results. Therefore, they are extremely beneficial.

Therefore, the use of homemade pesticides to improve the growth of your plants is extremely beneficial. They will provide you an opportunity to enhance the quality of your work by simply using those substances, which are easily available at your home. Moreover, these pesticides do not possess any harmful ingredient that might cause problems to the growth of your plants. The ingredients utilized are easily available in the grocery stores and used in various houses as common items. Therefore, one must use these homemade pesticides to get maximum advantage.

Understand Planting Conditions to Grow Hot Pepper

Plant the peppers on such areas which receive adequate sunlight. To begin, choose a soil that contains high minerals and is not attacked by any of the pests or insects. Moreover, the soil must not be saline. Afterwards, dig holes to plant the seeds; however, maintain appropriate spacing between the holes. As a result, the plants will get enough space for their growth. Moreover, manures and fertilizers must be added in order to improve the condition of the soil. In addition, maintain a thorough record of the plantation date. In this way, you will succeed in eradicating the growth issues. Moreover, you will be able to maintain and follow a complete timeline of the plant growth. Some of the important things and tips which must be understood before growing the peppers are included in this chapter. Following are the conditions used to grow hot pepper:

Cultivate using plant or seeds:

Usually the gardeners with efficient skills and abilities try to cultivate these hot peppers. However, a large portion of us must begin planting our own particular plants 8-10 weeks before transplanting, which ought to be done 2-3 weeks after the normal last ice.

Most pepper seeds sprout grow at a temperature of 70 degrees F.; however, germination can be hampered if the temperature is not appropriate. Hot peppers can be extremely tricky at time. Moreover, they might demand warm soil for their growth. To speed up the procedure, put the seeds between sodden sheets of paper towel, place them in zippered plastic packs, and put the sack in a warm place. When the pepper seeds sprout, deliberately plant them in individual holders, for example, pea pots. At the point when the main leaves emerge, move the plants to a sunny southern window until you can transplant them into the garden. Try not to set out your pepper transplants until night temperatures reach around 55 degrees F.

How to cultivate:

Cultivation of hot pepper can be challenging at times; however, it is not difficult if handled properly. In order to get better results, two tips must be followed while cultivating the hot peppers:

1. Water with some restraint:

Peppers are parched plants. They require a moderate supply of water from the minute they grow until the end of the season. In any case, peppers won't endure a soaked soil that waterlogs their roots. The dirt must deplete well, yet hold enough dampness to keep the plants underway. To keep up a legitimate equalization, before transplanting, work some natural matter in the dirt to upgrade dampness maintenance. Use mulch to keep unreasonable vanishing from the dirt amid the dry summer months.

2. Do not over-treat:

This tends to make the pepper plants create rich foliage to the detriment of natural product generation. Put a normal ratio of fertilizer on plants. You can likewise side-dress the plants with a light sprinkling when blooming begins, just to give them a help if necessary.

Tips to improve growth:

To enhance general pepper generation, consider utilizing the accompanying systems.

1. Plastic Mulch:

To get an ambitious start with your peppers, cover the readied bed with dim hued polyethylene mulch a week prior to transplanting. This will warm the dirt underneath and give a superior developing condition to youthful pepper plants. The mulch will likewise help the dirt hold dampness all through the season as the plants develop.

2. Sidekick Plantation:

Another technique to improve the growth is to plant other vegetables. Some of the sidekick plants are tomatoes, parsley, basil, and carrots. Try not to plant peppers close to fennel.

Tips to harvest:

The harvest time is very important in case of a hot pepper growth. As the pepper differs in its taste at different levels, it is essential to harvest them at the point when they have achieved maximum flavor. Despite these peppers can be used without any harm at all stages, yet it is recommended to use the, after they are fully ripped. In order to harvest the hot peppers properly, some tips must be followed. The tips that might prove beneficial while harvesting the peppers:

1. Similar to summer squashes and cucumbers, peppers can be generally gathered at any stage. The usually used pepper, for instance, is collected green. Despite the fact that most fruits will turn red, orange, or yellow. Peppers can be collected at any phase of development; however they develop their complete taste when they are completely ripened. Therefore, to get better results, one must wait longer

2. Successive reaping builds yields. If you pluck un-ripped fruits then the plants might suffer in the future as well.

3. Permitting natural products to completely age upgrades flavor as well as the yield. Additionally, you will need to hold up until late in the season before collecting table-prepared peppers.

4. In order to eradicate the chances of less fruit production, one must plant two or three plants at a time. Permit one plant of every plant to completely age to develop, and harvest the other all through the season. Likewise, when you are picking peppers, abstain from pulling on the organic product, which may sever a branch or even evacuate the whole plant. Utilize a sharp blade or garden shears to cut the intense stem.

Square Foot Gardening

Cover photo made by: <u>Alachua County</u>

Spring is right around the corner, and your mind is turning to greener things. Though you may still be looking at a winter wonderland outside, it's not going to be long before the snow is nothing more than a memory, and you will have months of warm sunshine to look forward to.

This summer you want to do something different. Sure, you'll still spend as much time as possible down by the pool and hanging out with friends, and you know you're going to kick your workout regimen into high gear, but that's not all you want to do.

154

This summer, you want to grow something. You remember your mother's or your grandmother's garden, you remember helping them water and pull weeds, and most of all – you remember the vegetables. When you have your own garden, you give yourself the freedom to enjoy a variety of fresh vegetables and herbs without spending a lot of money at the store.

Or, perhaps you are more about the aesthetics than the veggies, and you want to grow a garden full of flowers and other gorgeous plants. You enjoy the beauty each flower boasts of, and you love the bees and butterflies it attracts.

But then you look around your yard, and you see that you have very limited space. You remember the row after row of plants in other gardens, and you wonder if you can pull of something even remotely like that with the space you have available.

The answer is: yes – you can.

With the right tools and skills, you can grow a garden virtually anywhere, with the tiniest amount of space you can imagine. Square foot gardening has grown in popularity the past few years, and with little wonder. This form of gardening allows you to make the most of the space you have, giving you the ability to garden regardless of where you live.

In this book, I am going to show you how this is possible, and provide you with the skills you need to grow your own garden, no matter how much space you have.

This summer, you really can grow the garden of your dreams. All it takes is a little skill and creativity, and your garden can be as beautiful as the garden you remember.

Let's get started.

So You Want To Grow A Garden?

There are many reasons people choose to garden – sometimes that reason being they enjoy the process. While gardening in and of itself is a rather easy hobby, if you don't know how to handle the space you have available, you may end up more frustrated than anything.

Square foot gardening is a gardening technique that can be used in 2 ways. The first method is planting a garden literally using only the bare minimum amount of space. This can be anywhere from a literal foot to 4 or 5 feet squared. The interior of the garden is then carefully divided to provide space for a variety of different plants.

The second method of square foot gardening is to maintain the internal division of the garden, but to spread the garden all throughout your yard or living space. Gardening this way allows you to plant a greater variety of plants that have different growing requirements.

Regardless of your situation and how you plan to garden, you are going to follow the same method constructing and planting your plot. So, grab a pen and several pieces of paper, and we'll get started.

First things first.

The very first thing you must decide is what kind of plants you wish to grow. The reason this is important is because plants do have different requirements, and you must follow the guidelines in order to help your plants flourish. On your paper, write down a list of the plants you would like to grow, then get online and learn what those plants need.

If you are only working with a small space, you will need to grow plants that have similar needs to each other. This will eliminate the game of balancing which plants are grown where, and allow you to enjoy a fuller crop when the time comes.

At the same time, if you are going to spread your garden throughout several parts of your yard, determine which plants ought to be grown in which sections.

For example:

Plants which need partial shade throughout the day are better near fences, whereas plants that require full sunlight do well when planted close to the side of the house that gets the most sun in the afternoon.

Any plant you want that requires a lot of sun needs the afternoon sunshine – look around your house and determine which side of the building this is before placing the garden.

If you live in an area that doesn't get a lot of sunshine, you can do this backwards.

Pay attention to the sunlight in your yard, and take note of where you get the most sunlight during the day. Then, get online once more and search for plants that would do well in your conditions.

You'll then be given a list of plants you can choose from for your garden, and plant with confidence they will grow!

Gardening, though easy, does require knowledge and some skills. Put in the time and effort to learn what you need to do in the beginning, and your garden will flourish.

Location, Location, Location

You have your list of plants you hope to get into the ground this spring, but that's not all you need to do. I mentioned the importance of location in the last chapter, but in this chapter, I am going to show you how to set up your yard for your garden.

In these diagrams, you will see two things. The first thing you will notice is that they are divided all throughout the yard, planted in different locations that are optimal for the plants they grow.

The second thing you will notice is that each of the diagrams is further divided into the garden themselves. Not only can you see where each of the gardens are going to be in the yards, but you can also see which plants are going to be grown within the garden.

This is an exciting part of gardening, and it gives you complete freedom to be creative. You can make multiple copies of your grid and try a variety of different patterns. The benefit to outlining your own yard before you begin is that you don't have to commit to anything until you are in love with the layout.

Skipping this step may not seem like a big deal, but once you start placing seeds in the ground, you can't go back and change your mind, even if you realize you would like the plants better elsewhere.

Grab your pen and paper, and draw a rough diagram of your own space.

Use a ruler to mark different lengths, and use these lengths to represent larger spaces in your actual yard.

For example, consider every inch on the ruler to represent 1 foot in your yard.

Use your ruler to create a grid, following the same layout as the space you have.

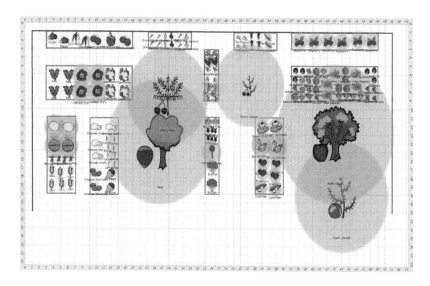

If there are any defining features in your yard space, include these in the grid. In the first grid, you can see that different trees have been included in the space, and in the second grid, you can see that trees, planted pots, and even the garbage can were included in the outline.

If you have anything in your own yard such as a bird bath, statues, play areas for your kids, pet areas, or anything else that will have an effect on your garden, place this in the diagram. This will give you an active visual as you plan the placement of your garden in your yard.

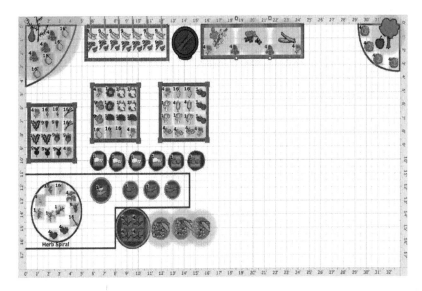

Many beginning gardeners are tempted to skip this step and simply dive into the building of their garden, but location is important for more reasons than one, so take the time to do this.

As I said, location is going to matter when it comes to the plants you grow, but that's not the only reason it will matter.

Children and pets are often too wrapped up in what they are doing to notice a garden, so an ill placed garden could potentially become a digging site, or get trampled during a game of football or soccer. Gardens that are sharing their space with children or pets should be placed off to the side, where they won't be bothered.

You must take into account there are people who do take things that don't belong to them, and a garden that is grown too close to the fence or an open part of the yard may be subject to unwanted visitors and attention.

On the other hand, gardens that are planted too close to roadways and drives will be subjected to a variety of harmful chemicals – chemicals that will seep into the plants and eventually into anyone who eats them.

Neighborhood cats can also be a problem for some gardeners, as they will chew on the plants themselves and potentially use the garden as a litter box. Though you don't have complete control over all these things, they are things you need to take into consideration.

In addition to the sunshine you want your garden exposed to, make sure you keep it safe from unwanted guests, intruders, and chemicals.

The Tools For The Trade

Once you know the plants you wish to use, and you have your yard diagram in place, you can take the next exciting step in gardening – getting your supplies. You can find all the things you will need at your local home improvement store, or you can order them online.

Again, there are a variety of ways you can indulge in your garden plan, whether you wish to use raised beds, or you are going to plant directly into the ground. Regardless of the method you choose, you will need the same basic tools, and follow the same basic outline – but we'll talk more about the outline later.

The first thing you need to decide is whether you are going to plant directly into the ground, or if you are using a raised bed garden.

Typically, square foot gardens are raised beds, and people have gotten creative. You can, of course, use planting pots to keep your plants separate from each other, but people have used watering troughs, wheelbarrows, children's swimming pools, tires, and a variety of other things to plant their gardens.

You can use something you have on hand, or you can start from scratch completely – get creative!

To make a basic raised bed garden, determine the size you want your garden to be, then purchase 4 boards that will correspond with this size. From there, screw each of the boards to the other in a square or rectangle shape.

Following the plan you have already put in place, lay your garden where you have decided you want it to go. Take a tarp and place this inside, pressing it to the ground and up against the sides of your garden.

Next, fill your garden with a healthy soil – preferably one that you have purchased as this soil will be free of any weed seeds.

Pack the soil in firmly, but not too tight. Evenly spread out the top of the soil, and your basic bed is done.

If you are using anything else for the bed, simply fill it with soil. You only need to line the bottom with a tarp if the bottom of the garden is going to be exposed to the bare ground.

Again, this is due to the weeds in the soil, and will help your plants to flourish.

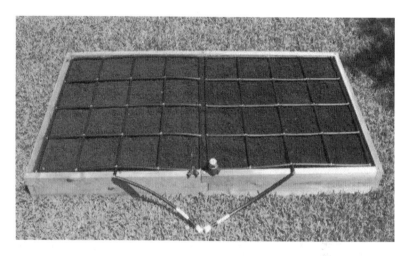

After you have your garden bed, it's time to put in the dividing pieces. Again, you can purchase these at your local home improvement store, or you can order them online. In these two images, you can see the different ways you can do this.

The steel grid method is popular among many square foot gardeners, as it stays in place even when the plants are growing. You can purchase one of these grids to lay over your garden, or you can make one yourself using string, wire, wood, or metal.

165

Measure out equal square spaces, and lay out the material accordingly, securing it in place. You will now have a visual to work with when you put your plants in the ground.

The other popular method is using a cut out grid. This grid is cut out from paper, plastic, or even wood, and each of the squares are then placed in the garden. The plants are placed according to the holes cut into the grid, then the grid is removed.

The seeds grow from where they were planted, and the gardener doesn't need to worry about a grid in the way when they are weeding.

You can choose the method you prefer, and plan accordingly.

In addition to the base of the garden and the planting grid, you will, of course, need other gardening supplies. Don't forget to purchase your own gardening shovel, trowel, watering can (or a watering hose) pots, buckets, and even a wheelbarrow if your garden is large enough.

Don't forget the gloves to protect your hands from the drying effects of the soil, or from the spines on the common weeds. These things can all be purchased at your local home improvement store, or can be ordered online.

Don't be afraid to splurge for quality. When you are dealing with plants, the better quality tools you have, the better your plants will grow – and the more comfortable you will be while working in the garden.

One of the biggest complaints gardeners have is that they aren't comfortable when working in their garden, due to a variety of factors. A tool that doesn't work right, gloves that don't offer proper protection, and hoses that don't offer gentle force will only lead to frustration.

Though you will see you can buy things that are really cheap which are right next to the more expensive version of the product, I recommend you spend the money now to get better items.

You don't have to go crazy with the tools and supplies – just get what you need to grow your garden well, and to feel comfortable while you do it.

Remember to mark what plants you have place where in your garden, as plants can be hard to identify when they are very young.

You can do this through stakes you place at the back of the garden, or you can use the diagram method and draw on the side of your garden what you planted. If you would rather not have either of these, keep a notebook with the layout plan written down, and refer back to it often.

Again, you may feel tempted to skip some of these steps in the beginning, but trust me, once you have your garden in the ground, and the seeds pushing through the surface, you will be glad you took the time to do this.

Now, let's turn our attention to another exciting part of this process – the garden layout.

Garden Plans

It's time to get back to the old drawing board, as now you are going to decide the layout of your particular garden. Again, grab a pen and some paper, then get your ruler and get down to business.

As with the layout of your yard, you are going to mark on the paper specific lengths, as well as how far each length represents. I once again recommend that you use inches, and that you cover your entire garden space.

By now you should know which plants you wish to plant in your garden, so once again you must look at the needs of each of these plants, then plan to put them in the ground accordingly.

Some plants require more space than others, which means that while you can still have them in your garden, you do need to place them carefully to ensure they all fit. Lettuce and radishes, for example, can be planted close together and still do fine.

Tomatoes and peppers, on the other hand, require more space – you won't be able to plant as many of these in your garden as the others.

Again, you can play around with different designs until you find what works for you. Remember to plant them based on their growing preferences, and to place them in the garden for optimal growth.

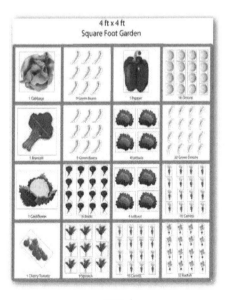

Some gardeners choose to simply plant the plants they like, and place them into the garden where they fit. Other gardeners prefer to be highly systematic with their gardens, and end up planting what looks like puzzles in the ground.

If you choose to plant this way, you do have the opportunity to turn your garden into a work of art as well as a source of food. Take a look at the diagram, and see how this gardener planned to place their herbs and veggies.

Not only will the plants do well if they are placed this way, but the colors will complement each other as they grow, making the garden visually appealing as well as a source of food.

Now, some feel that in order to get a good idea of how your garden is going to look, you will have to take the time to study it over several years with a trial and error method. However, with a simple trick, you can actually get an idea for how your garden will look without having to wait at all.

Gardening trick 101: Planning your garden.

Grab your list of plants, then get online and find images of them. Scale down the images, then print them out. Cut out as many images as you are going to plant in your garden, then piece them together on the table in front of you.

If you don't want to use actual images, simply use the colors each plant will be, and give yourself an idea of what your grown garden will look like.

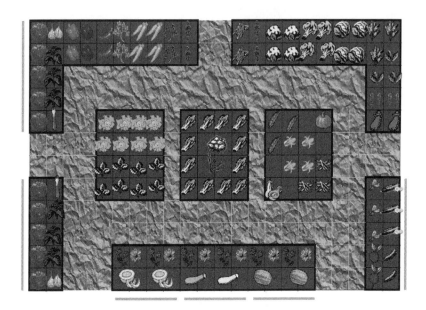

Depending on the size of your garden, you may need to make paths in between in order to reach all the different species. Make sure you factor this into your garden diagram, so you know how the overall look of the garden will be. Again, you can do this using both the garden plan itself, as well as the layout plan you used for your yard. Combine this with the visual of the colors, and you can give yourself an incredibly accurate idea of what your garden is going to look like when it's completed.

Don't be afraid to mix and match the plants you put into your garden, either.

Square foot gardening is a technique which allows you to garden how you want to. Some people use this method with herbs, others use it with vegetables, and still others use it with flowers.

172

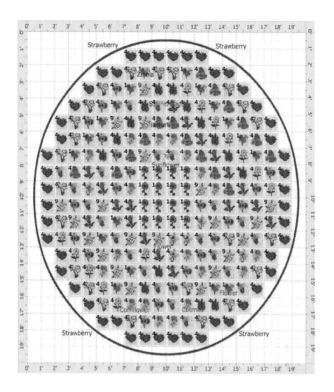

But, if you don't wish to choose, you can do any combination of the three that you like. In this next diagram, you can see how a garden can hold everything from giant sunflowers to the tiny strawberry plants. This form of gardening takes more practice, but with diligence, you can grow one for yourself.

It's all just a matter of planning.

Insider's Tip:

As with the vegetable gardening, you can plan the final look of your garden in advance using images of the flowers or simple using their colors. However, flowers tend to grow vastly different than vegetables, and you will need to compensate for their different needs.

173

The giant sunflower, for example, can reach a height of over 6 feet, and can grow incredibly thick stalks. While this is beautiful to see, the fully grown plants can potentially hide the sun from the smaller plants that didn't grow as tall – which will pose a problem if those other plants need a lot of sunlight.

On the other hand, you can use this to your advantage. Sunflowers, for example, require a lot of sun in the day while strawberries can handle partial shade. If you plan carefully, you can plant the taller plants in such a way that they will give enough shade for the plants that don't require as much sun.

This will require you to do more research in the beginning, but as you can see, all this preparation is going to pay off when you have your plants in the ground. A square foot gardener understands the need to plan, and is willing to put in the time and effort to write it down.

The more experienced you become, the less you will have to do this, but in the beginning, it's crucial you know what you are putting into the ground, and where. Trust me, take the time to do this now, and when your garden is in the ground, you can rest easily, knowing that it's going to grow well and how you wanted.

That's really all you need to get your square foot garden started. After you have your plants in the ground, you cross over into the realm of maintenance. Water the plants according to the recommendation for the variety, and remember to always soften the flow of water into the garden.

Once the plants have become established and start to grow, weed the garden regularly. Remember the time and effort you put into it is going to directly affect the produce and flowers you get out of it.

Inspirational Ideas

If there is one thing you will notice about gardening, it's that it's a highly addictive hobby. All the different things you can grow and enjoy, and all the different ways you can grow them turn gardening into an art as much as it is a hobby.

In this final chapter, let's take the time to look at some inspirational ideas from other gardeners. Look at what others have done, and feel inspired to grow your own. Remember to keep your eyes open. Inspiration can come from anywhere, meaning you may see something on the cover of a magazine, you may see something on your favorite tv series, or you may find something walking down the street that you want to try for yourself.

For the ultimate square foot gardener, creativity is everything. The only limit the gardener has is with their own imagination, as you will see with the gardens here. From gardens that are set in stone to the gardens that are entirely mobile, these square foot gardeners know what it means to make the most of the limited space.

If you are following the guidelines needed for the plants, you can't do it wrong, so get out there and garden!

This gardener has separated each of the plots with paths and fences, giving a charming visual to the garden along with the ease and function.

You can use a variety of fences decorations to give your garden a sweet charm. In addition, planting vine plants next to a fence will encourage them to grow upward, giving you even more space to work with in the garden itself.

Some kinds of fences are also a great way to keep unwanted visitors from disturbing your garden, too!

Herbal gardens are one of the most popular of the square foot gardens. This is largely due to the versatility of the herbs, as well as the similar growing needs.

As you can see in this garden, the gardener has planted a variety of herbs in both the center and the outer ring. Herbs don't require a lot of maintenance, and can be used for a variety of things on a day to day basis, making them a popular choice for beginning gardeners.

Not only can you use them for health, but many of the herbs grow flowers that are pleasant to look at, making herbal gardens a useful hybrid of the flower garden.

As I mentioned earlier, you don't have to use an actual garden when you are square foot gardening. As this gardener has done, you can use pots and planters to grow your plants – and keep them separate from each other.

Growing a garden in a series of pots has a variety of benefits. For starters, you can move your garden whenever you need to. Is something bothering your plants during the night? Move them to the garage until it goes away. Is there sudden construction taking place? Move the plants further from the road.

Do you dislike the layout of the garden? Rearrange the pots until you are happy with how it looks. Each and every one of the plants you would plant in a fixed square foot garden can also be planted in pots and planters. Remember to mark what each of the plants are, and take care of them according to the recommendations.

Square foot gardening also allows you to start a garden even in the most unlikely of places. Take this gardener's idea, for example – it wouldn't appear as though there was enough space in that small corner of the yard, yet they have planted a variety of herbs and flowers.

Square foot gardening is all about inspiration. When you know what a plant needs to grow, you know how to provide that for it in spite of some of the limitations you are facing elsewhere – with space, for example.

All you need is some good, quality soil and the right kind of seeds, and you can turn any space you can find into a miniature garden. Square foot gardening can be elaborate and cover your entire yard, or, as you can see with this little group of plants in the corner, it can take literally a foot to do.

Work with what you have, write down your plans, and stick with them. You can transform any space you have into your own miniature garden, and enjoy the benefits of your hard work within a few weeks.

Now get out there and enjoy gardening – anywhere.

Healing Herbs Garden

Herbs are nature's medicine. This has been true for thousands of years; before humans had discovered how to create antibiotics or the massive range of medicines now in existence. In fact, despite modern medicine not acknowledging the value of herbs; plants are the inspiration for many of the current prescriptions. Herbs are generally referred to as alternate medications and assumed to be a last resort, or for those that have a more 'whacky' approach to life.

Fortunately, this has been changing in recent years and many more medical professionals are accepting the power of an entire range of medications; including herbs. In fact, herbs are a natural way to cleanse and heal your body; the human body consists of a variety of minerals and other naturally occurring chemicals. Doctors strive to keep the various elements in your body balanced to ensure maximum health; herbs have these same nutrients and can contribute to this balance. The real trick is in getting the balance right; healing herbs can work in conjunction with modern prescription drugs to ensure your body is working correctly.

Herbal medicine is a broad title; whilst obviously referring to the product of herbs, there are many different herbs which occur naturally. It is possible to use the seed, roots, flowers, berries and even the entire plant to create the right effect. Learning which one to use can be a long term project! Fortunately this book is designed to introduce you to some of the most popular and commonly needed healing herbs.

You will probably not be surprised to learn that herbs have been used by the ancient Chinese and Egyptians; in fact there is documented proof of the use of these herbs as long as three thousand years ago! Of course, in these days the herbs were used just as they were. It was not until the 19th century that scientists started to examine the herbs and learn to extract the valuable chemicals in order to use them and mix or modify them. This was the start of modern medicines and has evolved into these compounds being made artificially.

There have been questions raised over the decision to create synthetic chemicals instead of using the plant derivative. However, there is certainly no doubt that modern drugs can have a profound effect on many medical conditions. Yet, despite this; as many as 80% of the world's population still rely on healing herbs to deal with any illness. This is an estimation by the World Health Organization and reflects the desire for many people to use a more natural approach to healing.

Living in the modern world provides you access to these contemporary drugs and the benefits of advances in medical science. This does not mean that you cannot use healing herbs as a first or last resort as well. You can even use them in conjunction with prescription drugs.

On a final note it is worth observing that in many cases it is not clear exact what part or substance of the herb is responsible for the healing properties. Herbs can be affected by the environment they grow in and even the plants that grow around them. Even the best prescription drugs may not provide the same benefit as the actual ingredient is not isolated and reproduced.

5 healing Herbs For your Body

Herbs, like any drug can have a dramatic effect on your body and your mental health. Everything thing you do, and the processes which occur naturally in your body, is a result of chemical reactions. Herbs can help to balance your chemical levels and ensure you feel ready to take on any situation. The first five herbs described in this book are ones which are capable of healing physical complaints:

1. Ginger

Healing Properties

Ginger has been used for centuries to help ward off nausea. In fact, it is a common ingredient in travel sickness medicines and will even be recommended by doctors before you take a trip.

Ginger is known to be a powerful antioxidant and prevents the body from reacting to the chemical serotonin. This is what is secreted by your digestive system and even your brain to make your feel sick. It can often be triggered by motion; especially one which is beyond your control.

Ginger has also been linked with reducing blood pressure, risk of cancer and even eliminating the pain of arthritis.

Tools for Growing

Ginger can be grown inside your house or in your garden. You will need a suitable sized container; depending upon the amount of ginger you wish to grow. Shallow and wide is best. You will, of course need some nutrient rich soil and a small trowel. It is best to grow ginger from seeds although it is possible to grow it from existing ginger. However, the results of this can vary as many farmers cover ginger with a growth inhibitor.

How to Grow Ginger

Ginger prefers partial sunlight and will be best to start indoors. Simply plant your seeds and water regularly. The pot must be well draining and you will need to keep the soil moist. It will take several weeks for the shoots to start to show. At this point you can continue growing it inside or replant it into your garden. When you want your ginger you can take the whole root or simply remove part of it; leaving the ginger to continue growing.

2. Chamomile

Healing Properties

Chamomile has been linked with providing better sleep patterns; this is essential for all manner of health issues. Scientists are still realizing just how powerful a tool sleep is in healing your body from a wide range of illnesses. Obtaining an adequate amount of sleep is more than just being in bed for eight hours. It also involves getting quality sleep. Chamomile is a natural herb which will help you achieve this.

It is commonly drunk as a tea and soothes the body, slowing the metabolism and helping to prepare it for sleep.

Tools for Growing

This is another herb which will grow equally well indoors as it does outside. You can plant it in a pot and move it in and out; if you prefer! You will need a good sized planter; it tends to be a fast grower and will produce plenty of beautiful white and yellow flowers. It is these which are used to make the tea. It is also useful to have a mist spraying bottle, a small trowel and some good quality potting soil.

How to grow Chamomile

You can start planting Chamomile in the winter; providing you are growing it inside. It is quite happy with just four hours on sunshine! The seeds should be planted approximately half an inch into the soil. The pot should be at least a foot wide; per plant. The soil must allow for good drainage; you can even add sand or small pebbles to the bottom of your pot.

You will need to keep the soil moist; ideally the growing area should be at least 20 C. Sprouts should appear within two weeks and then you simply need to water them once a week. Within two or three months you will be able to remove the flowers and make tea; or dry them for future use.

3. Licorice

Healing Properties

You will probably associate licorice as a sweet treat and maybe something that you have not had since childhood. However, this is the commercial produced and artificially altered or enhanced product; not the natural herb which can have healing properties. Licorice has been known to soothe a sore throat.

It is also been linked with relieving digestive issues and eliminating stomach ulcers. It can even be effective against heartburn and bacterial infection. It is truly a versatile herb that is often under-rated.

Tools for Growing Licorice

It is possible to start licorice inside from seed in seed trays. You will need some seeds, potting soil and a few pebbles to ensure the soil drains well. It is advisable to have a spray bottle handy as this is the most effective way of watering these herbs.

How to Grow Licorice

Licorice loves the sun; it does after all originate from the Mediterranean! This is why it is best to plant it inside in the early spring or in your garden during late spring. It prefers stony soil to maximize the drainage and needs to be in a sunny spot. Licorice should be watered regularly to keep the soil moist but never soggy. It will take between two and three months for the yellow, or sometimes pale lavender flowers to appear. These can be used to make tea or you can peel the bark of this plant to create a licorice stick.

4. Clove

Healing Power of Clove

Clove is one of nature's most powerful painkillers. It has been used in a variety of applications; from being placed on a sore tooth to being used as a local anesthetic. Clove is also an excellent antiseptic and anti-inflammatory as well as calming the digestive system and releasing excess gas.

Tools for Growing Clove

Just like many of the herbs available it is possible and often preferable to grow this herb from seed. This will assure the quality of the grown plant. You will need a suitable sized container for inside planting, or a planting bed which is at least moist, if not wet. You will need a trowel and a watering system.

Growing the Clove

It is worth noting that although clove grows very well from seed, this herb is actually the produce of a tree and it will take twenty years before it is able to produce any cloves. You may prefer to plant a young tree to reduce this time. Once it does start to produce cloves it will do so in most seasons for several decades!

Once the shoots of this herb have established themselves you can transplant it to the outdoors. It likes to have partial sun and enjoys rainfall; in dryer periods you will need to keep it watered. It is worth noting that this is a tropical plant and is used to a warm climate.

5. Sage

Healing Properties of Sage

Sage is one of the oldest plants to be used as a medicinal aid; it is also commonly used in cooking. It is a natural preservative, antiseptic and is even good at killing a wide range of bacteria. It is often used to relieve the pain of aching muscles; including rheumatism. It is also linked to a reduction in depression, increased mental clarity and can even help to improve your retention of memory.

Tools for Growing

As always the basic tools are sufficient. Sage cuttings, potting soil with good drainage and a planter (if indoors or needed outdoors). You will need a means to water your plants.

Growing Sage

You will find that Sage can be easily grown from cuttings, seeds are actually more difficult. This means you can plant them directly outside if you wish; just before the last frost. Alternatively they can be planted inside six weeks before the last frost. They must be placed in well draining soil and be water every few days to ensure they do not dry out. The herb likes plenty of sunshine and should be planted two feet away from each other as they spread during growing. The average herb will be between one and two and a half feet tall.

5 Herbs which can Improve Mental Health

Healing involves more than just looking after the physical aspects of your body. You need to be mentally fit and healthy to ensure your body is capable of fighting off physical illnesses. The ancient Chinese were very aware of this and devised a variety of herbs to help ensure they were mentally healthy. The following five herbs are all beneficial to your mind and can be easily grown either inside or in your garden.

Although these herbs have been used for many years they are becoming increasingly popular now. One of the biggest reasons for this is because of the amount of stress and anxiety that the average person is placed under on a daily basis. It can simply cause an overload of information. Your nutrients need to be rebalanced and your mind taking off these pressures.

It is worth noting that although many herbs do grow well inside; they will usually grow bigger and provide a higher yield if allowed to grow outside. They will not be constrained by an artificial environment.

1. Bacopa

Health benefits

Bacopa is not a new herb but it is only recently that scientists have realized just how powerful an herb it is. The herb is also known by the name Brahmi and has been shown to help reduce memory loss, slow down the progress of Alzheimer's and even prevent it from occurring. It is also excellent at dealing with people who have attention deficit disorder, epilepsy and can even reduce stress levels! Additionally, Bacopa has been found to reduce high blood pressure and even prevent depression!

Tools for Planting

There is no special equipment needed to plant Bacopa. A suitable container or flower bed, along with a water sprayer or even a hosepipe. You will also need a little time; to ensure it starts its life well. This will undoubtedly lead to a happy and healthy plant.

Growing Bacopa

This herb prefers a partially sunny spot, valuing a little shade every day. Its maximum height when grown is one foot. The plant will re-grow every year and flowers from June to October. It also spreads quickly.

To plant it you will need to use seeds or cuttings. They should be planted directly into a container; this will ensure they can be kept constantly moist. Within a few weeks you will see shoots appearing and you can move the plants to the garden. Re an excellent plant for mixing with other herbs or even flowers. They do tend to attract aphids but these can be removed via a strong water spray or even a soap spray.

2. *Rhodiola Rosea*

Healing Power

This plant is commonly referred to as Goldenroot; it has been hailed by many fitness fanatics as it is known to improve your fat burning potential and improve your energy levels. Even more importantly, Rhodiola Rosea is thought to improve your brain power!

This is one herb that has been used for centuries with positive effects; even the Vikings used it to enhance their strength. More recently, the Russians are said to use it to improve work performance, prevent insomnia, tiredness and even depression!

Tools for Planting

As with any king of planting the tools required are basic; a container if planting indoors, a trowel, good quality soil and a water bottle, watering can or hosepipe.

Growing Rhodiola Rosea

Although this herb originates in the high altitude regions of Asia, it is still possible to grow it at home. The plant generally flowers between May and August and only grows to one foot high and one foot wide. It is tolerant of most soil types; whether sandy clay but prefers to dry soil or slightly moist. Wet soil can damage this plant.

This hardy perennial likes the sun and should be planted in full sunlight. It is advisable to start growing the plant in a greenhouse in the spring. You can then move these to the ground outside in the summer of the following year; when the plant is just over a year old. They should flower this year and every year after that!

3. *Passiflora incarnate*

Healing Properties

This herb is more commonly known as passionflower and has a range of health benefits to assist you. Research has shown that passionflower is especially good at dealing with insomnia and anxiety issues. It can also be effective at assisting with withdrawing from addictive drugs.

This is not the only uses for Passionflower! It has been shown to be effective at dealing with seizures, hysteria and even heart issues such as irregular heartbeat or high blood pressure. It is an impressive herb!

Tools for planting

This is a hardy herb once established that will need very little care each year. Initially you may wish to plant it inside or in a greenhouse. You will need seeding trays and individual pots; depending upon how many you wish to grow. You will also need something for it to climb up and soil which is easy draining. Of course you will need some seeds or cuttings to get started.

Growing the Passionflower

It is best to plant the seeds in the spring after having dried them for at least two weeks in a dark place. You will need to use soil which drains well and keep your seeds watered regularly. There will be very little action for weeks; until you finally see the plant starting to emerge from the ground. It will then establish itself and grow vigorously. The vines on this herb can grow up to thirty feet long; you will need to keep it trimmed! An alternative is to plant it in a pot in the garden; this will limit its roots and growth potential.

In the fall you will be able to remove the leaves; you can dry these and then use them as you wish to gain the above benefits. There should be a sufficient harvest to tide you over to the next fall.

4. *Calamus Root*

Healing Properties

The Calamus root is usually dried and can then be used to make tea or even smoked. It is legal! It is also possible to chew the root; this is generally the most popular option and can be the fastest way of getting the root into your system.

The health benefits of this herb include the ability to calm your mind whilst re-energizing you. Surprisingly it can relieve tiredness despite calming your mind. It is also commonly used as a laxative and can even relieve mild pain

Tools for Growing Calamus Root

The Calamus Root is actually semi aquatic and is often referred to as needing 'wet feet'.

You will need to have a wet environment, such as a pond for it to grow at the edge of. To get it started you will need several paper towels, a plastic bag and then some good quality soil. Although it can grow at the edge of a pond it is happy in rich moist soil.

Growing Calamus Root

The best way to grow this plant is from seed. You will need to start by wetting a paper towel and then squeezing the water out. The seeds can then be sprinkled across the wet paper towel before it is folded in half. The folded towel needs to go inside a plastic bag and be placed into the fridge. The seeds will need to be left in the fridge for four weeks before you can transplant it to its permanent home. Although the seeds will not sprout whilst in the fridge they will be ready to grow.

Calamus Root can grow to six foot tall; if this is higher than you wish then you can plant them in a pot; this will restrict their height to roughly two foot.

Ideally you should plant them in a partially sunny spot with plenty of water. The soil should be rich; this can be achieved by adding plenty of manure. The flowers will appear between May and July although you should wait until the leaves start to turn yellow before you harvest them.

5. *St. John's Wort*

Healing Properties

St. John's Wort is an herb which has been used for many years to treat depression and as an anti-inflammatory. It is also an effective medicine in the fight against changes in behavior due to the menopause or PMS. Surprisingly it can also be very effective at relieving the symptoms of obsessive compulsive disorder. It is worth noting that this powerful herb can react to other medications and you should seek medical advice before you start taking it.

Tools for growing it

You will probably want a pot to grow this herb, some good quality potting soil and a spray bottle for misting it whilst it gets established.

Growing St. John's Wort

This is one herb that loves to live in the sunlight but will cope with partial shade. You can grow your herb from a seed or from a cutting. Seeds will generally flourish; providing you soak them in warm water for several hours.

The plant will spread quickly if it has the opportunity. If you wish to avoid this it is best to put it into a pot and then into the soil. The plant will need to be watered regularly at first to ensure it settles in properly. After this it needs very little care. It is a resilient plant but you may find it preferably to put plenty of mulch around it during the winter to prevent the frost affecting it.

5 of the Best Other Healing Herbs

It is difficult to choose the best herbs to include in a book; there are so many different ones which can have a powerful effect on your body. Healing herbs can do much more than mend the physical issues with your body or the mental ones. They can also provide a good level of protection against issues before they occur. The following five herbs are considered to be some of the best available.

1. Turmeric

Healing Properties

This has been used for many years in some cultures and has been shown to improve the health of your brain and your body. Turmeric is known to speed the healing of cuts and ease aches and pains in the body. It is also a powerful anti-inflammatory. Research has linked the consumption of Turmeric with a decrease in diabetes, the ability to resolve heartburn and indigestion issues and, perhaps most importantly, it has been proved to reduce the rate of heart attacks in patients after they have had by-pass surgery.

Tools for Planting

You will need a container to grow turmeric. You will also need some root cuttings as these are generally better than seeds. The soil needs to be rich in nutrients and you will have to grow turmeric inside unless you live in a warm climate.

Growing it

Once you have got the root cuttings it is as simple as planting them! The whole piece needs to be under roughly two inches of soil and knobs on your root cutting should face upwards. Even in warm climates it is advisable to start them off inside until the shoots are visible. You can then move them outside; late fall is a good time to do this. Initially they will need watering regularly but once they are established you will not need to do much!

The plant takes between eight and ten months to be ready to harvest; this will be indicated by the leaves drying and the plant going yellow. You can dig it up to use the root but make sure you keep a few pieces to grow some more.

2. Cinnamon

Healing Properties

Cinnamon can be added to many different recipes and even to some drinks. It adds a warming feeling and sweet taste which transforms the taste of many items.

Cinnamon has been linked with a reduction in fasting blood sugar levels; making it an excellent tool in the fight to manage diabetes. Research also shows it can help to lower cholesterol and be used as an antifungal and antibacterial aid. It is also impressive that cinnamon has been linked with an improvement in the movement of people suffering with Alzheimer's or Parkinson's.

Tools for growing

Ugh classed as an herb, cinnamon actually comes from a tree; which can grow as high as sixty foot tall! You will need to plant this outside. For this you will need a spade a young tree and some good soil. You will also need a means of watering it regularly.

Growing Cinnamon

Once you have your tree you will need to pick a spot in your garden and dig a hole big enough for all its roots. It prefers a sunny spot although you should not allow it to grow too near your home. The soil needs to have good drainage. You must also be prepared to prune the tree regularly as this will keep its size down to approximately three feet. As soon as the tree is established you can take some of its bark to grind into cinnamon. Younger trees provide a fuller flavor.

3. *Basil*

Healing Properties

Basil is a common ingredient in your food but it also has a range of positive benefits for your health. It has been shown to reduce swelling and inflammation and is particularly effective at relieving stiffness in arthritic sufferers. It is also said to have anti-aging properties by protecting brain cells. It is high in antioxidants and is even good as an antibacterial agent. In short it can have a positive effect on your general health.

Tools for growing

You will need a seeding tray, seeds, quality potting soil and a misting bottle. You may also want a larger pot for when you move it outside; or it can go into the ground.

Growing Basil

You can sow the seeds into your well draining soil roughly six weeks before the last frost occurs; providing you are doing this inside. Once the risk of frost is gone move the seedlings into the garden and plant them with ¼ inch of soil over their roots. They will grow to two feet tall and will need watering regularly if there is no rain. Flowers should be removed straight away and you can start harvesting once the second set of leaves appears; you should always leave the first set on the plant.

4. Aloe Vera

Health Benefits

Aloe Vera is perhaps best known for its cooling effect on the skin; making it effective at soothing sunburn, healing cuts and even lessening wrinkles. However, it is also good for reducing dental plaque; easing constipation and even treating ulcers.

Tools for growing

You will need some quality dry soil and a good location; Aloe Vera loves the sunshine; although too much sunshine can be damaging to the plant. You will need a cutting and a means of keeping it moist; a spray bottle will suffice.

Growing Aloe Vera

You simply need to pick the spot you will be planting in and then make sure that your young cutting or even a young plant is put in the ground upright and all the roots and base are covered with soil. You need to leave some space around it as it will quickly grow outwards. If using a container it should drain quickly. This plant needs to be kept moist but never wet.

As soon as the plant has started to mature you can remove a leaf or two; they should be removed as close to the root as possible and used as you wish.

5. *Oregano*

Healing Properties

This herb has stood the test of time and scientific research. It has a range of benefits including relieving digestive disorders, respiratory issues and even urinary tract infections. It is also known to help reduce the appearance of acne and even dandruff.

Research also shows that this antibacterial and anti-inflammatory herb can help protect you from cancer! Alongside this it is effective at reducing colds, muscle aches, toothache and even heart conditions.

Tools for Growing

The herb can be grown successfully from seeds. You will, therefore, need seeds, seeding trays, a warm spot inside your home and some soil with a high level of nutrients but which drains easily.

Growing Oregano

It is best to put the seeds just below soil level in your seeding tray approximately eight weeks before the last frost of the season. They will need to be watered regularly but not over watered! By the time the last frost has been you should have a good selection of seedlings to plant. It is possible to plants seeds at this point directly into the garden but the seedlings will generally perform better.

Ideally you should plant them one foot apart from each other; they will grow outwards to cover this gap and as high as two feet. They can be planted in their own area or mixed with a variety of vegetables, other herbs, or even flowers!

To encourage dense growth it is advisable to trim them once they reach four inches in height. At this stage you should water once a week and only if the soil feels dry. Other than this the herb will look after itself. It will also self seed; returning by itself the following year!

As soon as the leaves are grown you can start to harvest them although the ones with the best flavor are those removed just before the Oregano flowers. Freeze them or dry them to have some ready all year round.

Self-Watering Garden Systems

Gardening can be great fun; it provides the opportunity to nurture and watch as plants flourish. Not only is it a good way of exercising it is also a very effective method of learning about nature and becoming more at one with the world around you. However, gardening can also be difficult. There are many variables involved in being a successful gardener and many of these are difficult to control. The PH level of your soil can play a part in your plant's health and whether it flourishes or not. Every plant needs sunshine but some can get too much sunshine; shade is necessary! In addition the soil must have enough nutrients to feed your plants or you will need to add food in one form or another. Finally, perhaps the most important ingredient of all is water. Just as humans require water to stay alive, so do plants. You can even find your plants desperate for a drink after days of wet weather; this will depend upon how efficient the soil is at draining the water away. Although many of these variables are not easy to control, watering can be.

Whether you are growing vegetables, fruits or just pretty flowers; it is possible to devise and install a self watering system. There are a variety of different options and you may even come up with your own design! In essence you are looking to ensure your plants receive an adequate amount of water without you needing to do anything. This can be an excellent option for anyone who has limited time or is prone to forgetting to water your favorite plants. Some of these systems can even be used inside the home!

The beauty of a self watering system is that your plants will always have enough water; no matter what the weather does. Even when you are unsure of whether they need watering or not; this can also help if you need to go away for work or simply on vacation. There is no need to rely on others to water your plants and worry about them under or overwatering them. Simply set yourself watering system up and leave it to do its job!

A secondary and very important advantage of self watering systems is that the plant takes the water it needs; when it needs it. Conventional thinking tells you, that in hot weather, you should water your plants in the morning or the evening. This is because if you water them in the day time the water will evaporate before the plant has the opportunity to drink it. However, what if the plant needs it during the day? If you water in the morning you will probably notice your plant has shriveled by half way through the day. With a self watering system the plant can take water as it needs it and be comfortable regardless of whether it is hot or cold.

This book will help you to get started with your own self watering system; copy one of these designs or build on them to make your own; the choice is yours!

5 Low Maintenance Self Watering Techniques

Unfortunately many self-watering systems can be time consuming and even costly to establish. However, once you have created them there is very little maintenance and your plants will always be looked after. You can even add a little liquid fertilizer to some of these methods to help ensure your plants have all the nutrients they need.

1. Irrigation

This has been the method of choice for farmers for many generations as it puts water directly to the base of each plant; which is exactly where it needs to be. This system can take several hours to set up and will cost approximately $40; this cost is dependent on the size of the area you wish to keep watered. Forty dollars will comfortably do a standard back yard.

The process of setting this type of system up can be divided into several steps:

- Using some ¼ inch tubing you will need to run this tubing from your tap around all the plants that you wish to water. If there are large flower beds you can add branches of tubing which will end in a sprayer. It is best to use micro irrigation hose for this; it is ¼ inch tubing with tiny holes in at regular intervals. The tiny holes allow the water to drip into the soil; right by the roots of your plants.

- If you do not purchase pre-punched pipes then you will either need to spend a lot of time punching small holes into your pipe or you can bury emitters into the ground at regular intervals and connect them to your pipe.

- Once you have laid the tubing and connected it to your tap you can turn the tap on a very slow drip. The water will move along the pipe, slowly filling it and dripping out of the holes. This will provide a very small amount of water out of each hole but would ensure that all your plants received water regularly without it costing a fortunate or you contravening any regulations.

It is easy to purchase this tubing as most garden centers will do it. Obviously the amount you need depends upon the size of your garden and the number of plants you need to reach. Emitters and sprayers can be attached but will cost extra. It is worth noting that this system can just as easily be connected to the tap on a water butt; allowing you to use previously collected rainwater.

2. *Shop Bought Automated Drip System*

The first thing to consider when installing a system like this one is whether your faucet will be needed for other uses. If it will then you should purchase a split connector. This will allow your faucet to have a dedicated connection for your drip irrigation system and leave one available for anything else you might need.

The shop bought system works on a similar pretext to the irrigation system described previously. There are many different options which can be purchased and then modified to your needs. However, the main difference with the shop purchased system is not the time taken to install it; this will be approximately the same. It is actually the fact that all the parts you need are included in one package and this will generally include a flow meter. This can be used to monitor the level of water you are using or to control how much you wish to allow round the garden.

Shop bought systems still need to be snaked round your garden; they will provide you with clips to retain the pipe; this allows you to keep it on top of the ground but secure. You can also purchase attachments to cater for specific types of plants or flower /

vegetable beds. Perhaps the greatest asset of this system is the ease in which you can add additional pieces to the system. There are quick fit connectors which will allow you to add extra pipe work in or even remove it; depending upon the changing needs of your garden.

Of course, this type of system will be considerably more expensive than creating one from scratch yourself. This is partly because it comes with several dedicated options and partly because it is neatly packaged into one box! You will need to verify the regulations in force in your area before you can install this type of system. As it runs from a mains faucet and can use sprinklers you may find that its use is restrictive.

An additional bonus of this type of system is the addition of times which can control the water flow. This is not something that is included in the basic kit but is something that can be purchased separately. In effect an electronic timer will open or close a valve to allow the water through the system. This allows you to preset the time or times that the drip irrigation system comes on and off each day!

3. The Water Bottle

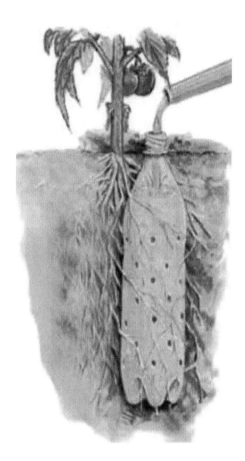

This technique is often used by keen vegetable gardeners as it is efficient but not the best looking option. This may not be something you wish to consider if you have a beautiful flower bed that would be ruined by the presence of water bottles dotted across it!

This system is effectively free to make as it uses recycled parts from your household waste and can be made very quickly. It will water your plants for several days and has no moving parts; which eliminates the chance of breaking the system. In addition you need just a few common household tools to create this system and you can make as many or as few as you like.

You will need to find a two liter soda bottle, or similar. The bottle must be plastic. You can then punch small holes into the side of it at random places. This will allow the water out. You now have two choices; you can dig a hole and bury the bottle so that just the opening is visible; this should be about half an inch above the soil line. Alternatively you can keep the lid on the bottle and bury it neck first in the soil. If you choose this option you will need to cut a hole in the bottom or even slice the bottom off. This is necessary to refill the bottle.

Once the bottle is buried you can fill it with water. The water will find its way out of the small holes but this will take several days; making it the perfect solution if you are unable to look after your plants for a few days; for whatever reason.

The reason this works is because the soil is packed around the bottle and does not allow the water to leave the bottle easily. The wetter the soil becomes the harder it will be for water to escape the bottle as it will not be able to find its way through the soil. This makes the bottle solution idea for many situations as it will adapt to the wetness of the soil.

4. The Gravity System

This is an ingenious system but is only viable for containers within your garden. It could be used within a raised bed, but you would need to create a pond like base to avoid water escaping. This creates the risk of a lack of nutrients for your plants. As such it is better to utilize this method just with containers which you design for this purpose! The cost of this system should be zero although you will need a ballcock as found in standard cisterns.

To start with you will need a big container of water; it is possible to connect this system to the mains supply, however, you would need to reduce the pressure to avoid damaging the valves you are about to use.

214

You will also need a colander or an old plastic bowl that you can punch plenty of holes into. If you are looking to put this into your garden you will need a plastic container to hold the water. You will also need some hose; the length of which will depend upon where your water containers are located and where the plant container is.

To start with the container will need to be placed at the bottom of your container, or a hole will need to be dug in your garden. Above the container you will need to put a lid in place; this will trap the water in the container. You can then create a hole in the lid which will take a piece of solid pipe. This will extend from inside the water container to approximately one inch below the top of the soil. Before you push this pipe into place you should make plenty of small holes in it; this is how the water will get to your soil. Pin prick size holes are best. You may also wish to add some silicon round the spot where the pipe goes into the lid.

You can now lift the lid again and drill a hole through the side of the container and the plastic pot inside. This should be big enough to house the inlet pipe from the ballcock. Secure the ballcock inside the container; as though securing it to the cistern. You must be sure to seal the entry hole with a little more silicon. The lid can now go back in place and be sealed shut. The float arm of the ballcock may need to be adjusted to fit properly. This will need minimal movement as you will simply want it to maintain the level of water inside the pot.

The outside of this ballcock can now be connected to pipe which feeds back to a raised container of water. This will ensure that gravity pushes water into the pot; when the ballcock is in the right place. The water will rise up the rigid pipe and seep into the soil whilst the ballcock goes down slowly; allowing more water into the system. You can even connect a succession of planters to the same water container.

215

5. Plastic Fantastic

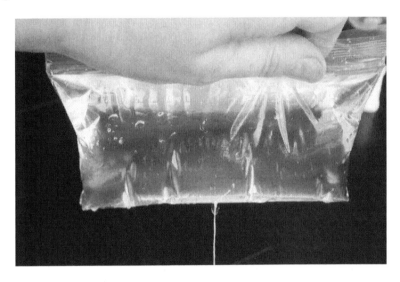

This method of watering your plants can be extremely effective for one pot or several. It will ensure they have enough water to last for several days which can help if you are going away or are merely forgetful.

The basic premise is to use a large plastic bag. You can then tie a little cotton to a needle and push it through the bag once. Pull it through far enough to be able to remove the needle and knot the cotton thread. It should then be pulled back through from the outside; the knot in the thread will stop the cotton coming out.

The cotton can be as long as you want; the idea is that the end of it will touch the soil in the pot you are wanting to self water. It is possible to add several threads of cotton to your bag; each one can go to its own pot; allowing you to water several plants at the same time. The bag will need to be filled with water and hung somewhere. It will have to be close enough to allow the cotton threads to touch the soil in each pot. You can choose whether to seal the bag or not.

An alternative to a bag is a large plastic container. The water carrier should sit higher than the planter or planters you intend to keep watered. Water will saturate the cotton; this can be drawn into the soil as the pot and the plant needs it. The beauty of this system is not just that it is simple; it actual works!

An addition to this technique is to add a mains supply to the plastic water container. You can simply add a valve to allow easy topping up of the container. To become even more autonomous you simply need to fit a float from a toilet cistern into the container and attach it to the main supply. This will automatically keep the level in your container the same; allowing your plants to be watered for an indefinite period of time!

5 More Complex Systems

The systems described so far can be put together in next to no time and can be extremely effective. However, unless you are opting for the irrigation option; there is little to help you keep a larger space watered; which can often be much more challenging and time consuming. Obviously you could pay someone in the area to water your plants every day and this would be a semi-automated system; provided you remember to pay them they should water your plants. Fortunately, there are a range of other options which can be employed to ensure your plants remain watered; no matter what you are doing.

1. The Sprinkler System

This is simple in principle but can take some time to set up properly. It is perfect for watering large spaces, such as your lawn or a specific flower bed. You can even cover your entire garden; if required. However, it is important to check whether there are any regulations in your area concerning the use of sprinklers. You will need to abide by these!

You will need to purchase plastic piping or you can use general hosepipe. You will also need at least one sprinkler and a time controlled valve.

To set the system up you will need to start by locating the pipe work that will connect to your outside watering system. You can then cut the pipe; being sure to shut the water off first, before inserting the electronic valve. This will need to be near a power supply as the valve will be electronically controlled. It is best to locate these items inside if possible. Once you have fitted your new valve you will be able to connect your hosepipe to the outside tap which is connected to this branch of your water works. The pipe will then need to snake across your garden until it locates the sprinkler. To finish you simply connect the pipe and the sprinkler. Before starting the system you will need to set the valve timer. It is best to water your plants morning and evening if your timer can cope with this!

The difficulty with this install is that you will not want hosepipe trailing round your garden. You may wish to bury the hosepipe although this may cause temporary damage to your garden. The alternative is to secure it above ground where people will not walk.

There are two additional considerations with this system. Firstly it is advisable to simply set the system up and assess the most effective location for a sprinkler; depending upon which plants you wish to water. The second concern is whether you live in an area which is prone to frost. An above ground pipe is likely to freeze and the effect can continue into your home; affecting the supply of water in your house. To counteract this you will need to insulate the pipe; remove it in the winter or bury it.

2. The Air Conditioner

The hotter it gets the more likely it is that you will need to use an air conditioning unit. These can be a very effective way of cooling your house. But, at the same time, you will find that they are an effective method of watering your garden!

The air conditioning unit is usually high up; this means you can rely on gravity to send the water round the garden. However, if your garden is too big or angled in the wrong direction then you can opt for an automatic pump. These pumps are hardwired to your electricity supply and will automatically activate when they detect a certain level of water in a container.

To create this system you will need to attach a pipe to the outlet on your air conditioner. The best way of building this system is to create a secondary water container next to the air conditioning unit. As the air conditioning unit works it will produce water; this will gradually fill the container.

You can now attach what is known as a condensate pump to the container. In fact, some of these pumps arrive with built in containers. These pumps work by automatically detecting when the container is nearly full. The pump will then come on and remove all the water from the container before automatically shutting off again.

The water is removed through the exit pipe; it is this which you must run through your wall and into your garden. You can then split this pipe into as many different branches as you want. It is advisable to have a connector on the outside wall; this will avoid the need to replace the pipe right back to the air conditioning unit if something happens in the garden.

In the garden you can use flexible piping or rigid; can also choose whether to feed the water to a specific bed or allow it to drip feed into the entire garden. This is a drip irrigation system but the watering is regulated by the temperature! The hotter it gets the harder the air conditioning will work and the more water the plants will get.

3. *The Recycled Option*

If you are a keen gardener it is likely that you already have a water butt or two in place to capture your rainwater. After all, watering your garden is important but there is no need to spend a fortunate on it! A water butt collects all the rainwater from your roof and this amount of water can happily look after your plants for an extended period of time. Of course, you do not want to water them when the soil is already wet; this would be a waste of your precious water.

Fortunately, there is a way to use this rain water without having to manually fill watering cans and pour them over your garden. The key in this instance is to use the right pump or allow gravity to do the job for you; this will depend upon where the water butt is in relation to the garden which needs watering.

The simplest option is to connect a small hose to the water butt tap and run the pipe into the soil; approximately one inch below the soil line. Around the plants you wish to water make tiny, pin sized holes to allow the water from the water butt to drip into the soil. The soil will only take the moisture it needs.

The main issue with this type of system is that the water will be irregular; parts of the garden will get more than other parts simply because of the way the pipes are laid and how gravity affects them. It is not a high powered system! This is generally acceptable as you will learn to plant according to where the water arrives best.

However, if you need a more consistent flow you will need to look at adding a pump in. The simplest route is to use a submersible pump and have the feed line come over the top of your water butt. You can then put a small hole in the highest point of the pipe. This will create a drip which simply falls back inside the water butt. However, when the pump is off it will allow air in; this prevents back flow from the garden and wastage of water from the water butt! You can then opt for a simple timer mechanism where the pump plugs in and control how often it comes on and off.

4. Soil Sensor System

Once you have built this system you need to do nothing to it except top up your water container regularly. The system, as its name suggests, uses soil sensors to establish whether a plant needs water or not. You will need to purchase some soil sensors!

The system can be connected to a small container situated near a specific plant or container. Alternatively you can connect it to a larger water supply which can be linked to a range of sensors; allowing you to water different parts of the garden. You will need to run pipe work from your water container into the soil near your plants. You then add a soil sensing probe to the soil near where the pipe is but not too close. If you place it too close the sensor will think the soil is very wet as soon as the water starts to feed into it.

The sensors in the soil normally provide a read out to the meter. However, instead you can connect these wires to a relay. The relay will also need power to it. As soon as the sensors detect the soil is dry they will tell the relay which can send power across to a water pump. This pump will send water down the pipe and to the dry area of soil. As soon as the soil is moist enough the sensors will shut the relay off and stop the water flowing!

It is possible to have several sensors in the soil, but you will need a small pump for each area you wish to water. Your own responsibility will be to keep the water container topped up. Alternatively you can connect the water container to the mains supply with a float valve to allow it to keep itself topped up!

5. Automated Rain

An alternative to the drip irrigation methods and others already described in this book is to copy the idea used by many commercial businesses to create a more natural environment. Whilst plants suck water up from their roots, they also enjoy the precipitation from rain water as it sits on their leaves. This can help to prevent burn damage in hot weather and brighten the color of the plant.

The system requires flexible piping to be run from a faucet or a water container. It will also need a pump to ensure the water can effectively get to where it needs to go. If the faucet is close to the plants it may be sufficient to rely on water pressure; but in either situation you will need an electronic valve.

The valve is connected to the mains water, or water container. This will also need to be connected to the electricity. You will then be able to control this valve by setting a timer; allowing the water to come on and off at certain times of the day. Once you have set this up you will need to run your pipe to the area or areas which need to be watered. When you reach the area the pipe will have to move upwards and be held in place by a framework. You can then either fit emitters into the pipes or simply create as many small holes as you like. The pressure of the water running through the pipes will create a mist like spray which will cover the plants; effectively creating an artificial rain on them.

It is advisable to set the timer to come on for half an hour in the morning and evening. This type of system will not soak the soil but it will provide several plants with enough water to keep them alive and flourishing.

PART TWO
Solar Power Energy Self-Sufficiency

In a world where there are a limited quantity of carbon fuels left, many scientists and even individuals are looking to devise new ways of creating energy. Of course, many countries operate nuclear power stations which provide them with all the electricity they need with surprisingly little amounts of environmental effects. However, a nuclear power station is inherently dangerous. If something were to happen at the power plant it is possible to have a disastrous fall out which could affect thousands if not millions of people.

As such, there has been a massive increase in interest in more passive, environmentally friendly approaches to creating energy. Wind and water power are two avenues which have been explored thoroughly within the last few years. Solar power is another potential solution to the energy crisis around the world. In fact, many companies and even individuals have invested in their own solar panels to generate electricity; assist the planet and save funds.

Of course, solar technology is not new. As long ago as the 7th century BC there are records showing a magnifying glass was used to create fire and to burn ants. The third century Before Christ refers to burning mirrors which lit the torches for religious ceremonies. There are even reports of the ancient Greeks using their bronze shields to focus the energy of the sun and set an enemy ship on fire. This has been attempted in more modern times and has been shown to be possible; providing the boat was no more than fifty feet away.

Just two thousand years ago, in the fourth century AD the Roman bathhouses harnessed the power of the sun to warm the rooms via large glass windows. Although the sun has always been used it is in relatively basic ways, until 1767 when a Swiss scientist known as Horace de Saussure devised a box to collect the heat from the sun and cook food. It is recognized as the world's first solar collector.

It was not until 1839 that a French Scientist, known as Edmond Becquerel discovered the photovoltaic effect of the sun. He was experiment with electric generation through an electrolytic cell and realized electricity production increased when exposed to sunlight. The French mathematician August Mouchet continued this work and devised a solar powered engine; they were used for a variety of novel applications.

By the end of the 19th century the first solar cells had been created from selenium wafers and the first solar water heater had been created. Although there were steady developments throughout the first part of the twentieth century, it was not until 1954 that the silicon photovoltaic cell was developed; it was the first cell which could run everyday electrical equipment just from the power of the sun.

The technology has continued to develop with a massive increase in interest at the end of the twentieth century; including the creation of a solar powered aircraft!

Fast forward to the present day and you will find many houses with solar panels on their roofs and the ability to power their own electrical needs. Whilst these have been and will continue to be refined and improved, the basic principle remains the same. It is likely there is a big future for solar electricity and now may be the best time to purchase your own kit and install it to create your own electricity supply.

Parts Involved in a Solar System

Despite the fact that solar power is a massive step forward in terms of energy generation and the potential to save the planet; the number of parts involved in setting up your own system is surprisingly limited. Every install requires at least one solar panel; the more panels you have the greater the amount of electricity you can generate. Of course, the space you have available will restrict your project to some extent.

Initially solar panels were only ever placed onto the roof of buildings, in fact, many contractors would only offer favorable rate for an installation if your roof was south facing. The reason for this was simple; a south facing roof is in direct sunlight all day. However, many companies now accept that south west or even south east facing roofs can harness as much energy as a purely south facing roof.

Photovoltaic Cells

The key part to any solar installation is the solar panel. This is the large sheet of lightly checkered shimmering, almost mirror like substance. The solar panel has no moving parts; this means there is nothing which can go wrong with them. They simply collect the energy from the sun and convert it to electricity. This is done by absorbing some of the photons which are present in the sun's rays. The energy in the photon is captured by an electron inside the semiconductor material. This energy allows the electron to move and occupy a place in the current; generating electricity in the process.

There are two types of photovoltaic cells; those which are made of crystalline silicon and those which are made of thin-film. The thin-film type cell is undergoing extensive research and development and offers exciting potential for the future. On the other hand, the majority of installs at present are using the crystalline silicon type cells.

The solar panel or energy collector is only one part of the system. You will need to connect this to your appliance or to the electrics in your house and potentially to the main grid. There are two different types of system depending upon your intended use of your photovoltaic cell.

The Direct System

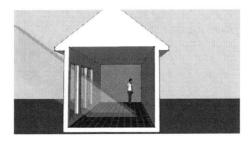

The solar panel can be connected directly to what is referred to as the load. This is the appliance they are supposed to be running. Whenever there is sufficient energy generated by sunlight the appliance in question will work. This may be useful if you need to run and air conditioning pump on a hot day or even ventilation. Of course, when the sun is not shining no electricity is generated and your appliance will not work.

Off the Grid Systems

These are designed to create enough electricity to power an entire house. You will need more than one solar panel. The solar panels are connected to each other and the electricity generated is transferred to a bank of batteries; this is a second vital component. The bank of batteries is then connected to all the electrics in the house and power is available at all times of the day or night; providing there is juice in the batteries.

This type of system not only requires a battery bank, it will need an inverter. This is a device which can convert the DC power generated by the solar cells into AC power which is useable by all your appliances. As well as the inverter you will need to have a charge controller. Every battery can only handle so much energy. If you attempt to store too much electricity in one battery it will overload and can potentially explode. The charge controller prevents the battery from accepting any more electricity once it is fully charged.

Alongside this you will need a decent quantity of cabling to connect everything up and several safety features, such as a surge protector and a range of trip switches. These will help to protect you from any issues. It is also possible to get a monitor which will sound an audible alarm if there is any issue with the system.

Battery Backed-Up Grid

In effect this system is almost identical to the off grid system. You will need an array of solar panels, a battery bank, an inverter and the safety features. However, this type of system is also hooked into the main grid. This is an exceptionally dangerous part of the process and must be completed by a qualified electrician. It is common for the electricity board to send someone to make these connections. The advantage of this type of system is that you will always have power regardless of whether the sun is shining or not. Whilst a battery back-up can support most functions, if there is a specific item which must have power then this system can ensure it does. It is also a comfort to know that you will always have power available!

No Battery Grid

This has become one of the most popular home style systems on the market. The photovoltaic cells generate electricity and send it through cables to all the appliances in the home or business. Every appliance will work as normal; although you will still need the inverter mentioned earlier. Excess or unused electricity is sent to the main grids; which must be connected to your system. The electricity unused by your home is effectively sold to the grid; in return you can purchase electricity from the grid and the two charges should off-set each other.

The system involves the solar panels, an inverter, an array of cables and the usual safety features including trip switches and surge protectors.

This type of system is designed to reduce your energy bills whilst providing you with the same access to electricity as a conventional electrical install. However, the downside of this system, or any which does not have a battery bank, is that there is no power available in your house if the main grid fails.

Installing & Setting Up Your System

Now that you are aware of the different types of system and how few components are required you may be more interested in establishing your own system. Inverters, battery banks and cabling are not incredibly expensive. The main cost of a system is the solar panels. These are not generally cheap, but the more you have the more electricity you can generate which will help to reduce your dependence on the large energy companies, reduce your environmental impact and even ultimately lower your cost of living. Installing a solar system may even be a necessity if you live off grid already; understanding what is involved is the first step towards powering your own home.

To complete a successful install and set-up your home electricity you will need to consider the following issues:

Type of System

The first question you should ask yourself is which system most suits your needs. If you are planning to run your whole house then you will not want to have a direct system. The decision between off-grid, battery grid and no battery grid will be influenced by your location. If you are not near a current electrical system then the cost of connecting to the grid can be prohibitive; the off-grid system may be the right one for you.

If you are able to connect to the grid then this can provide a useful back up and allow you to have power all the time whilst reducing your energy bills and still having power available if the grid fails. The real question when choosing a grid system is whether you wish to have the ability to survive without the grid or not. It is also worth noting that a grid system is generally cheaper to install as there are less parts required and easier to maintain.

Buying the Equipment

There are many government backed schemes which will offer to supply you with your solar panels for free provided you commit to a contract with them. This can help to off-set the cost of purchasing the panels, but will restrict your savings and is only an option if you intend to have a battery less grid system. You will also need to choose a supplier and installer with caution as many of them will charge high rates for the solar panels; this can even off-set any savings you may get by using a government grant.

The alternative is to source the equipment yourself. There are many suppliers of photovoltaic panels on the internet. You should purchase the best ones you can afford; installing them and connecting them up is actually a simple process for any keen DIY'er.

Fortunately choosing the solar cells is relatively straight forward. The majority of solar cells are made in the same way using the same materials; there is no significant difference between those offered by different suppliers. This means you can choose the cells which are cheapest, or the firm which is offering the best deal on purchasing them.

Your solar cell supplier should also be able to supply you with a good quality inverter and batteries, as well as the charge protector. However, these are easy to pick up in a variety of places and may be cheaper elsewhere.

Before you can buy the equipment you will have to decide either the amount of panels you can afford; you can always expand the system later; or the amount you will need.

It is therefore important to consider the following:

Location

Solar panels will attract the most sunlight and therefore create more electricity when they are positioned facing due south. This is because the photo sensitive cells will dramatically reduce in productivity as soon as they are placed in shade. This is not to say it is not possible to generate electricity in a shady spot, but, if this is your only or preferred choice you may need to consider extra panels to gain the power you need.

Traditionally these panels have been mounted on the roof of a building, however, there is an increase in the amount of people and businesses who are choosing to mount them on the ground. You will need to ensure this is permissible with your local planning regulations and your neighbors!

Choosing the best spot to locate your panels will enable you to calculate how many panels you can fit in a spot and how much electricity you are likely to be able to generate. Of course, it is incredibly difficult to predict an exact amount of electricity as the sunshine is not a constant; you cannot tell which days will be cloudy or wet and windy.

Current Situation

Another important factor to consider which should influence your decision; is which type of system is best for your current situation. There are significant financial implications involved in purchasing a system; an average 3KW system will cost approximately $5,000 and you will need to factor in an inverter, battery bank and charge controller. An entire system can be installed for $10,000; whilst this is substantial cheaper than it has been this is still a serious financial commitment. Should you have the funds available then you will be freeing yourself from electricity bills for the foreseeable future. However, you will not recoup the money for several years.

Are finance options available but, depending upon the reason for your impending solar install this may not be the best option. The alternative is to wait or build your system slowly with a long term goal of solar energy and the ability to survive off the grid.

Professional Assistance

If you are keen on undertaking and completing your own projects you will be pleased to know that it is possible to install a personal solar power system yourself. However, it is also worth obtaining some quotes from professionals. You may be surprised at the cost and will certainly find the system is installed without any hassle. Having said that not all professional firms have experience with installing off-grid systems; if this is your chosen option you should confirm they have the knowledge and experience to do the job properly.

Tips to Ensure a Successful Install

There is a distinct advantage to installing your own system which is even better than any financial savings you may make. This is that you will have designed the system and will know how it fits together and what to look at if any part may need to be replaced. This can be invaluable information if there is an issue with the system and it is not possible to contact assistance or to get anyone to help for a period of time. In fact, this concern relates directly to the reason why many people are considering either off-grid systems or battery back-up ones. The increase in natural disasters has increased the number of power outages; having your own system will allow you to navigate these pitfalls with little disruption.

The following tips will help you to complete your install successfully:

Preparation

One of the most important factors in any project is planning before you start. Successful projects always need to be planned and to have a contingency plan. There are several key elements you should consider when devising your plan:

- The average house can survive on a 3KW system which will take approximately twenty one square meters of space; either on your roof or a ground mounted install. Before purchasing any panels you should measure the space you have available. Ideally you should have a larger space than this and have the potential to expand your system in the future.

- Fastenings are vital. Your choice of fastenings will depend upon where you are intending to locate the panels and what your natural weather cycle is like. If you live in an area which is prone to cyclones or tornadoes you will need to ensure your fixing kit is likely to withstand a cyclone or tornado; you do not want your installation ripped apart right before you are most likely to need it.

- There are different types of panels; although many of them now offer similar rates of power production, the panels you choose and even the inverter will affect the power generation and efficiency of the system. Whilst installing on a budget may attract you to the cheaper panels; you may find it more beneficial to choose fewer panels but have the higher quality ones. You can always add panels to your system.

Testing

There is no reason why you cannot test your system before you install it properly. Whilst the panels are relatively heavy you can simply prop them up in your garden on a nice day and connect them up to either your battery bank or directly to your appliance. This can be especially useful if you are new to this type of install and wish to ensure you have understood all the parts of the system properly. This is also a good opportunity to test the equipment and confirm you have everything you need to install the entire system in one go. This can be a particularly useful exercise if you realize you have missed or forgotten one important part.

Information

Solar energy is still a rapidly growing and improving industry. Things which are the best possible today may not be the same tomorrow. It is important to stay abreast of the changes in technology as this will affect the prices of the current available solar panels or may even be worth waiting for if they offer significant advantages. Knowing the latest research and techniques should also make it easier for you to install your system.

Planning

You may notice a nearby house has solar panels; this does not mean that you will automatically have the right to put solar panels on your property. It is essential to check with your local planning department and, if necessary, submit an application. You may also find that erecting them is acceptable but that there are restrictions on the quantity or some other small clause. Knowing what the planning regulations are will ensure you do not fall foul of them and have to remove your install at a later date.

Space

You will almost certainly have considered the amount of space you will need to keep free for the solar panels. However, you may not have considered where the ancillary parts will go. The inverter and batteries, as well as the charge controller all need to be inside and relatively easy to access. You will also need to connect into your wiring. This may be as simple as running cables into the power supply of your fuse box, or may necessitate some new wiring. Whichever path you need to take you will have to consider where the new wires are going; will they be fitted into the walls, out of sight? Knowing the space required and where you locate these items will make your installation process much easier.

Approval

If you are intending to install your system yourself but will be connecting to the grid you will need to gain approval from the utility company. Even if you can achieve solar power without touching the utility meter you may find yourself in trouble as you do not have permission to interact with the utility. To ensure your install is successful it is advisable to contact the utility company first and find out what their requirements are. You can then ensure you comply with them; this will ensure your new system is a success and has the potential to supply you with free power for the foreseeable future.

You are likely to find a dedicated section on their website which will allow you to access the information regarding their requirements and even complete a form to get the paperwork side of the installation finished as early as possible.

Installing your own solar energy system is more than just possible; it is actually fairly easy to do! All you need to do is a little preparation and have some patience whilst you design the system and ensure you have complied with all the relevant legalities.

Electric Usage, reduction and Effective Solar Energy

241

There are several reasons why you might wish to power your home via solar power; the most obvious of which is the long term cost savings. Although solar panels have become cheaper in price it will still take on average three to five years to repay the cost of purchasing and installing the panels. This means that for solar energy at home to be financially worthwhile you need be intending on staying in your current home for at least the next five years. The benefits are then obvious; your energy is free! You will no longer have to concern yourself with electricity bills or power outages; as long as the sun is shining and your system is working properly you will have power!

The second most common reason for installing solar energy stems from a genuine concern for the environment. It is often the case that the general public is informed of an issue but is unable to do much about it; regardless of how they feel or what useful suggestions they may have. Thankfully, solar energy is different. You can install it and make a small difference to the environment; encouraging family and friends to do the same. In fact if you encourage enough people to do this then you can make a significant difference to the environment!

However, a fundamental part of changing your energy system should be looking at your current consumption and assessing how you might be able to reduce it. The less demand you have for electricity the smaller your system will need to be, or, you can make more money by selling the excess electricity to the grid.

Current Usage

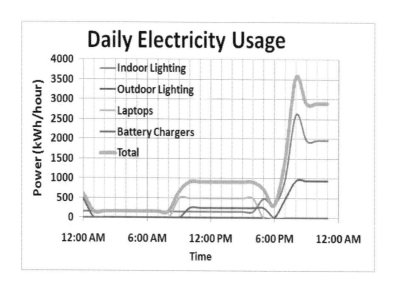

Daily Electricity Usage

This leads to the obvious question of how do you assess your current electricity usage? The most obvious way to do this is to physically monitor what you are turning on and how long it is on for. Combining this with the wattage rating of the appliance will give you an idea of how much electricity has been consumed by every task. This is a very time consuming method but it will provide you with the amount of electricity you are using, your maximum draw during a given period and what things are actually consuming your electricity. You may be surprised!

There is also a technological alternative. You can install a home monitoring system which will establish how much current is going through a specific cable without needing to splice into the cable. This device acts as a data gateway and talks to the sensors which are added to a multitude of appliances. The data is then displayed on screen where you can see how your electricity is being used.

Reduction

The most obvious way to reduce your dependency on the main grid is to reduce the amount you use. There are several easy, logical steps which can be achieved by almost anyone. These include turning lights off when not in a room and not leaving equipment on stand-by. However, there are a myriad of other possibilities which can be extremely effective. These include switching bulbs to LED's which last longer and are better for the environment. Establishing an effective reduction technique can save you hundreds of pounds a year; as well as making you more aware of your electricity usage and which systems are most suited to your needs.

Your Needs

An alternative way of assessing your electricity needs is to look at all the things you current use on a daily basis and how much electricity they use. If you monitor the ways you use electricity then you are likely to notice if everything you currently use is really essential to living comfortably. You will quickly pull aside a variety of items which you do not need to enjoy life; it can be surprising at how positive an effect this kind of approach can be.

Heat

One of the biggest electricity consumers is your heating system. There is no doubt that using electricity to heat your home can be expensive. However, it is possible to reduce this bill even in the coldest winters. There are two different approaches. The first is to simply use the heating system for a little less each day; half an hour less heat can make a difference to your consumption. The alternative is to simply lower your temperature dial. It has been suggested that a one degree reduction can save hundreds of pounds per year of the average electricity bill. However, on approach which is often overlooked is to simply change the way you heat your home. It is possible to add a gas fire or even a wood burner which will dramatically reduce your electricity bill and your reliance on the grid. Combining this will reduce your need for electricity and will keep you warmer than simply using electrical means.

The same principle can be applied to all your appliances; particularly washing machines. By turning the settings down slightly you will consume much less electricity. It may seem ridiculous trying to reduce your electrical consumption if you are looking at going off grid and producing your own. However, the better you understand which items consume the most the easier you will find it to produce enough electricity to cover all your needs.

A solar energy system can be exceptionally efficient; providing you use the latest, most expensive solar panels. However, this may not be an option for you or you may not feel it is the most viable solution. There are other factors to consider including the intended use of the electrical system. The efficiency of any solar panel is calculated by working out how much of the percentage of the solar energy which hits the panel actually converts to electricity. Generally more expensive panels work better; but this may not always be true and may not fit with your plans. The location of your panels will, to some extent, alleviate the need for the most efficient panels. If yours are positioned facing south at the right elevation they will produce more than enough energy for your needs.

DIY Solar Charger For Electric Car

The search for new, environmentally friendly energy is an ongoing process. However, solar power has become one of the most popular options. There are several reasons why this is the case:

- It is clean energy, renewable and, once your panels are installed and set up, free!

- You don't actually need to live somewhere where there is constant sunshine; you may be surprised by how much power can be generated on a cloudy day.

- Solar energy created at home and not required can actually be sold to the main grid. This will either help you to cover the cost of the solar panels or reduce your electricity bill to zero.

- It is comparatively easy to add or even remove solar panels to create the right amount of electricity for your needs.

- Solar power can allow you to go 'off-grid'. You will need batteries and a charging device; you can then store your own electricity for use at night.

Solar energy is not a new form of power, the power of the sun has been harnessed in many different ways for hundreds of years. Even something as simple as starting a fire, with the aid of a magnifying glass and the sun could be described as solar power! What may surprise you is that this technique was used as long ago as the 7th century BC!

In fact, sunlight is reputed to have been used as a weapon in 212 BC when Archimedes used bronze shields to bounce and magnify the sun's rays. The result was impressive; several of the ships belonging to the attacking Romans were set on fire!

It was as early as 1767 that the sun was used to collect heat and power a cooker; examples of solar cookers still exist today and can be easily made at home.

However, it was in 1839 that the photovoltaic cell was discovered. This is the same basic technology which is used today! This discovery was made by the French scientist Edmond Becquerel. He was experimenting with electrodes and an electricity conducting solution; the energy generated was magnified when the cells were exposed to sunlight!

The second half of the 19th century saw a variety of advancements in solar technology; including solar powered engines and the potential of selenium.

Despite a constant stream of discoveries and improvements, it was not until 1954 that Daryl Chaplin, Calvin Fuller and Gerald Pearson created the first cells capable of taking the sun's energy and powering standard electrical equipment.

Now there are solar powered aircraft and electric cars. It was inevitable that the two would and should meet. Using solar power to power your electric car will ensure your environmental impact is virtually zero and allows you to run your car for free!

This book will guide you through the process of choosing the right system for your needs, installing it and setting it up; your electric car will be fully charged and ready to go whenever you need it.

Choosing the Right System For Your car

There are three distinct phases to establishing your solar charging system. The first is to verify the size of the system you require and whether you are charging just your vehicle or your entire home. There are several factors to consider during this stage; this chapter will guide you through them.

The second stage is the installation; this can often seem the most daunting but can actually be very straightforward; simply follow the step by step approach. Finally, you will need to set up, use and monitor your electricity generation and the amount you are using; this will tell you if your original calculations were correct!

Perhaps one of the greatest hurdles to overcome when attempting to power an electric car from a solar charger is how it is possible to recharge the vehicle after a long trip.

Home Based System

The most obvious route to take is to equip your home with solar panels and then use the electricity generated to charge your electric car batteries. This is generally considered to be the best option for anyone with an electric car. The amount of electricity it takes to recharge a car every night will increase the overall cost of your electricity bill significantly. This can even push the rate you pay per unit up.

You should already have an idea of how much the car will cost to charge; this is an important part of your calculations prior to buying a vehicle. If you have not looked into this and already purchased an electric car then you are likely to have noticed the additional electricity cost on your monthly bill.

If you are looking to purchase an electric car then this is a valuable piece of information to help you choose the right one for your needs and power cost.

Understanding the Electricity Required to Power Your Car

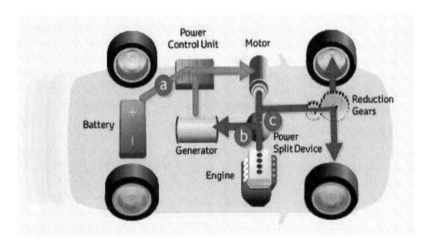

Every type of electric car will have its own electricity rating. You will see it in the dealer or can locate the statistics online. The figure you need to be looking for is its kilowatt hours (kWh) rating. This figure tells you how much electricity is required to allow the vehicle to drive one hundred miles. An average vehicle will require approximately 30kWh; however, this will vary depending upon the performance of the vehicle, its size and its shape.

There are two important calculations you can look at from this; both of them will require you to know your average annual mileage:

1. Cost comparison to gas.

You should be able to work out your average yearly mileage. If you do not know it then simple calculate the number of miles you cover in an average week and multiply it by fifty two.

You will also need to know the cost of your electricity per unit, the cost of a gallon of fuel and the miles per gallon your vehicle will do.

You will then be able to calculate your costs:

Electricity: Annual mileage of 12,000 / 100 * the kWh rating of your vehicle; for the example the average of 30 will do. The resulting figure of 3,600 can then be multiplied by the cost per unit of electricity. For example, if you pay .12 cents per unit it will be $432 to run your car for the year.

Gas: This time your annual mileage will need to be divided by the number of miles per gallon your car does on average. This will give you the amount of gallons of fuel you need. Simply multiple by the cost per gallon, (approximately $2.40) and you will have your comparison cost for the year. 12,000 / 35 * 2.40 equals $805; a substantial difference.

Of course, there are other factors involved in this; such as the cost of charging your vehicle away from home. But the figures will give an idea of the cost savings you can generate.

2. Electricity Usage

The second calculation will simply illustrate how much power you need. This is simply the first part of the cost comparison equation. Your annual mileage divided by 100 and then multiplied by the kWh of your vehicle. In the above example this equates to 3600kW of electricity per year.

You can further divide this by 52 to get your approximate weekly requirements; 69.23 kWh.

It is interested to note that the average American home will use approximately 8,000kWh per year; charging your electric car at home could add half your current bill to the yearly charge.

It is important to understand the amount of electricity your vehicle is likely to use. If you are planning to generate enough power just to charge your electric car then you can fit panels accordingly. If this is in addition to powering your home; this figure must be taken into consideration when calculating the number of solar panels required.

Dedicated Car System

The second option available to you is to install solar panels which are just there to power your car. This can be done simply without connecting to the grid; if you desire. However, this may mean that much of the electricity generated will be wasted. This is not generally considered a viable option unless you are installing the system on a budget and looking to expand it in the future. As the figures above indicate, the cost of a small system could be offset within a few years; particularly if you follow this guide and install most of the components yourself.

On car

There has been some research and testing of systems which can be fitted to your vehicle and allow it to recharge or trickle charge whilst you drive. The intention behind this is to enable you to take longer trips without the need to pay and recharge along the way.

This type of system is only likely to be of interest if you regularly travel large distances. Staying fairly local and the annual vacation will probably not warrant this option which is discussed later in the book.

In fact, once you start monitoring your daily usage of electricity for your electric car you may be surprised by both how little you actually need and how few miles you actually cover!

Deciding the system will allow you to start planning the installation; however, you should also consider the power of the sun in your particular area. The more sunshine you have the better your power generation; if you live in a cloudier area then you may find that there is not enough electricity produced in the winter months to cover your needs. It is best to calculate this before you start your installation as it may affect the number of panels you use.

The average solar panel will produce 250 watts of electricity; in excellent conditions. To calculate how many will be needed simply to power your electric car you will need to look at how much you need on a daily basis. From the above example this will be approximately 10kWh per day.

You will then need to work out how much sunshine you get on the average day; this will depend on your location. If you get five hours of sunlight a day then you can divide your 10kWh by 5 to get 2. This is the amount of kilowatts you need to generate daily to cover your vehicle needs.

A final point to consider before you complete your calculation is to understand that the electricity created by the sun is transformed into Dc energy which then needs to become AC to be used at home. This results in a loss of 20% of your power. You must allow for this is your calculations. 2kw divided by .8 equals 2.5.

If you need to generate 2.5kw of electricity using 250 watt panels; you will need 10 solar panels; this will be enough to power your vehicle. Should you wish to contribute or cover the cost of electricity in your home you will need to factor your home usage into the calculations.

Installing Your System

If you are looking to install a system just for your vehicle and not connect to the grid then it is possible for you to install the system yourself. Obviously you must take appropriate precautions. You may even prefer to have an electrician check the final work before you get the system working.

However, if you are powering your house and connecting to the grid then you will need to have an approved contractor complete the installation to the grid. Without this the electric company will not be able to buy back your excess electricity and they may even disconnect your supply until it can be confirmed to be safe.

The following guide will ensure you have a safe and reliable system for years to come; making it possible to charge your electric car and run your home. It covers all you need to know to be ready to connect to the grid:

Stage 1 – The Equipment

You will need several key pieces of equipment in order to install your solar charger for your electric car and, if required, home.

- Solar Panels – Using the calculations in the previous chapter you should have the number of panels you require to run your house or car. It is worth noting that the production rate of these panels is based on good sunlight. Any day which is not sunny will result in a decrease in the amount of electricity being produced.

If you wish to make sure you have enough electricity even on the darker days then you will need to base your calculations on the amount of light and power produced on these days. This will provide you with enough in the winter months and an excess in the summer; which can be sold back to the grid.

It is important to note that are several factors to consider when choosing which solar panels are right for your installation:

- o Cost; the price of solar panels can vary surprising amount. Whilst your budget may not stretch to the most expensive ones it is worth considering purchasing less panels but having better quality ones. This will help to ensure they last for a long time and produce a consistent amount of power.

    You may also find that there are packages available which reduce the cost per panel.

- o Assess the tier of the manufacturer. Tier one is for top producers whilst tier three is for the majority of the mass marketed solar panels in existence. In general tier one panel are better quality but will cost more to purchase.

- o Tolerance – a panel which has a positive tolerance will achieve the wattage rate it has been advertised at. In fact, it may even produce more than that. If the tolerance is negative then the power rating will only be reached in optimum conditions; in reality you will lose approximately ten percent of the power.

- o Temperature co-efficient – This is a measure of the effect of heat on the panel's capability to produce electricity. The lower the percentage the better the tolerance to heat.

o Conversion – This simply states the amount of power which is converted from solar to DC electricity. The higher the conversion rates the better!

o Solar cells – There are actually different types of solar cells which can be used in a panel. If your panel uses monocrystalline silicon cells it will be highly productive even in temperatures. This is generally considered to be the most efficient cell for creating electricity.

If the panel uses polycrystalline then it will actually offer a similar performance and efficiency to the monocrystalline brands. This is because of recent improvements in technology. These improvements are making this the most popular option for new solar panels.

It is also possible to obtain budget solar panels with amorphous cells; these have very little silicon and are generally considered to be inefficient.

- Inverter – The electricity generated by your solar panels is known as DC; this is not the same as that needed to power your car or home. You will need to convert this to AC electricity. An inverter will do just this for you! However, you will also need the inverter to charge your batteries and allow you to connect to the grid.

Your inverter will need to be able to handle the maximum watts that your solar panels can generate and your household may need. A good inverter will have surge protection to prevent it blowing if there is a sudden surge of power. This is also important when equipment is first turned on; most equipment draws a surge of power before it settles to the typical or continuous range. This figure should also be reviewed to ensure it is high enough to deal with all the electricity you may need simultaneously.

- Batteries – This is an essential part of your system if you plan to be able to access electricity when the sun has set; without needing to draw power from the grid. As your vehicle is most likely to be charged overnight; when there is no sun; it is advisable to have a bank of batteries which can power the charger.

It is worth noting that whilst a standard car or truck battery will work; it will not handle the constant draining and recharging associated with solar systems. You should purchase deep cycle batteries which are designed to handle the ups and downs of solar power.

You will need to calculate the number of batteries you require. To do this you will need to know how much energy your solar panels could produce in one day. This is the rating of the panel (250w), multiplied by the number of hours of sun. In

259

the example above this was five, so one panel could produce 1250 watts per day. If you have ten solar panels then this figure could be 12500 watts per day.

You can then multiple this figure by three or four to cover your electric needs for cloudy days.

To calculate the number of batteries needed you must look at the volt and amp-hour rating of the battery. Multiple the two together, for example 6 volts multiplied by 200 amp-hours equals 1,200 watts.

This is nearly enough to hold one day's supply of electricity from one panel. However, deep cycle batteries are not the most efficient. You should multiple your answer by .6 to establish the real watt rating. This equates to 720 watts. To store the power generated by one panel you would need two batteries.

Unfortunately there are other factors to consider; such as the loss of power transforming the energy and the fact that the panel will probably not be operating at peak proficiency for the entire five hours.

- Charge Controller – Your batteries cannot be continued to be supplied with electricity once they are full; this is likely to cause them to explode! Instead, you will need to have a charge controller. This allows the electricity to be fed to the batteries and then rerouted once the battery or batteries are full. The charge controller can also help to prevent discharge from your batteries.

- Distributor – This part only applies to those homes which are connecting their solar install to the grid. The distributor is situated after the inverter. It accepts the AC power and sends it to a breaker in the main fuse box of your home. From there it can be fed round the circuits of your house. If there is not sufficient power being put in for your needs then the distributor will allow power to be drawn from the main grid as well. If, there is more power being generated by your panels than you need then the distributor will feed it back into the grid. The amount which enters the grid is usually monitored and a credit is supplied on your next electricity bill.

- Cabling – You will, of course, need a fair amount of cabling to run from your panels through the various pieces of equipment and into your home, car charger or even to the main grid. The type and quality of this cable will be controlled by the building regulations in your area.

Stage 2 – The Location

Most solar panels are mounted on the roof of your house and there are special kits to ensure they can be red properly. You should, ideally, have a south facing roof as this will attract the most sunlight and generate the highest levels of electricity.

However, if for any reason this is not possible then it is acceptable to install the panels at ground level; angled towards the sun. Again, the easiest way of doing this is to use specialized kits but it is possible to make up your own securing brackets.

The most important factor is ensuring the panels get the maximum amount of sunlight possible.

Stage 3 – Installation

Once you have organized all your materials you will be ready to install them! As you will probably be working on your roof you will need to ensure you have all the relevant safety equipment and tools to access the roof.

Roof ladders are useful, as is scaffolding. However, you may prefer to hire a cherry picker which can hold you over the roof; allowing you ease of access.

Every panel needs to be taken onto the roof; you will need to exercise care when doing this part of the job. Panels are expensive if broken!

You will usually find that the mounting kit comes with the solar panels. If this is not the case then you will need to purchase enough mounting kits to fit all your panels to your roof.

You should always mount the bottom feet first with angle brackets. Alternatively, rails can be screwed into your roof which the panels will slide into position; each panel will need at least a top and bottom rail to ensure they cannot move; even in extreme weather. The rail approach also allows the panels to stay close to the roof; preventing the wind from getting under them and trying to lift them excessively; there will be a small gap to allow the wind to cool the panels; this will ensure they work more efficiently.

This approach is simple although can be time consuming to mount the rails and ensure the panels are fastened to the rails properly. The bolts holding the rails in place must go into the rafters.

It is important to note that, in order to make the most of the available sun, your panels must tilt at the same number of degrees the latitude lilt of your location; you can easily find this out on the internet.

You should be able to clip the connectors together on the solar panels to ensure they are connected in sequence. This will allow you to connect your cables to the one panel at the beginning of the install.

Electricity

You can now connect your cable to the indicated point on your panels; this will need to go into your house or down the outside; towards where you have decided to keep your batteries.

The other end of your cable will need to go into the DC input end of your inverter. It is worth noting that the black wire is positive, white negative (or neutral) and green is earth.

Once you have connected your inverter you can run a cable from the AC output side of your inverter to the master fuse box. This will be the standard colors that you see in your home as you are now dealing with AC electricity. The solar panels will now direct electricity into your fuse board and round your home. If there is insufficient power the electricity will be drawn from the grid whilst excess will be sent to the grid.

It is important to note that the connection to the main fuse box must be with a distributor to ensure power can flow to and from the grid.

To improve your system you will want to connect the bank of batteries to it; this will help reduce your dependency on the grid. The easiest way of doing this is to simply connect the batteries into your system before the inverter. This approach does require your inverter to be grid activated; it will not detect the batteries but a sensor at the fuse box will ensure they are charged when possible.

Unfortunately, this is unlikely to provide you with power in the event of a power failure.

To deal with a power failure you would need to place the batteries after the inverter with the use of a charge controller. This will return the Ac power to Dc to charge the batteries and then a second inverter after the batteries would convert it back to AC. The batteries would be connected to the grid inverter which could draw power from the grid, solar panels or batteries; depending upon which has electricity available. Of course, you would set it to ensure solar power is replaced by battery and then the grid only if there is no other power available.

This system will work in reverse and provide you with the power in the batteries; topped up by daily sunshine, even if the main grid power is out.

Once you have installed all this and had it checked you will be ready to turn on your system and generate your own power!

Solar Power For The Car

Creating the electricity is not the only thing you need to do to charge your car at home. You can charge your car with a standard plug; but unfortunately this will result in a very slow charge. In general a standard plug will charge at 4 miles per hour; this means if you charge your car for ten hours overnight it will add just forty miles of driving to your batteries!

The alternative is the EVSE – This is dedicated Electric Vehicle Service Equipment. This is a specialist device which actually turns your AC power into DC; your car batteries will run on DC electricity. This means that you could simply run cable from your solar panels to the electric charge point and allow the current to stay in DC. However, you would still need a charge controller to ensure your car batteries do not overcharge and the EVSE to allow your car to plug in. As the EVSE converts AC to DC it may be confused by applying a DC current directly to it.

The EVSE is purchased as a complete kit; it simply needs to be wired into your home electrics. You can then plug your car in and charge it at a much faster rate.

Direct Solar Power on Your Electric Car

In theory it is possible to have a solar panel or two mounted to your car allowing it to charge either whilst driving or when parked. The fact that solar panels produce DC electricity and this is what is needed to charge the batteries means there are very few connections needed.

In reality, this type of car would look a little ridiculous unless the panels are built into the car. Manufacturers are working on this and there is already a prototype which can produce enough power to take the car approximately thirty miles every day; just from the solar panels attached to it! It can also be charged in the conventional way. This is a huge step forward from the original solar panels on electric cars which simply powered one system inside the car. It is, undoubtedly, the way that electric cars will operate in the future; but, at present this is not something which has been achieved. Ultimately a solar paneled car would be able to generate enough electricity to power even on a cloudy day. You would never need to stop or recharge the vehicle!

PART 3
Provide Own Fresh Water

In this era when technology has an important role to play in our daily lives, most of us live in very fast-paced lives. With the many stresses attributed to living in this modern world, the appeal of going back to basics is very strong among people who want to live slower yet more sustainable lifestyles.

One of the repercussions of conventional modern living is that our food supply is running low such that we rely so much on destructive agricultural practices that everything in nature is out of balance. Moreover, we are also running low on the power supply and most of our planet's vast resources of fossil fuels have already been depleted.

To make matters worse, our consumption of fossil fuels has contributed to the release of greenhouse gases that have massive effects on our climate.

This is the reason why many people want to take a step further to live more sustainable lives by going green through homesteading. The basic principle of homesteading is sustainability wherein you by only a few resources and grow your own food. Homesteading also encourages people to use renewable ore recyclable resources.

So what is the difference between farming and homesteading? While farmers grow food for a living, homesteaders grow food to support their family and provide for their own sustenance. They may sell but only the surplus of their produce.

It is important to take note that homesteaders are slowly reviving old survival skills that have disappeared during the advent of the industrial revolution. This means that people are practicing the art of canning their food, baking bread, spinning wool to yarn, making homemade cheese, sewing clothes and other old-fashioned crafts.

So why are many people opting for homesteading? One of the explanations why individuals opt for homesteading is that it is one of the most environmentally healthy ways of living. It is also a simple lifestyle that allows you to appreciate what life has to offer thus you become more responsible to the environment as a whole. Homesteading is more than just gardening, raising livestock and learning old skills. It is all about making things work for your survival. If you are interested in homesteading, it is important that you have the right guide thus this is where books come in.

Homesteading is an earth-based lifestyle of self-sufficiency. It is about reconnecting with nature and getting back in touch with your authentic self. Homesteading is all about learning home survival skills so that you can survive within a limited area of land. In fact, you don't need a big area in your house in order to start homesteading. This chapter will discuss the basic skills that you need to learn in homesteading.

Homesteading is ultimately all about living your life fully and more wisely, all whilst being more respectful to your environment and your body. The aim of this book is to instill inspiration and give you a starting point to kick-start your homesteading journey. And it all starts with one of the most basic necessities: being able to feed yourself and your family.

Gardening

Growing your own food is basically one of the most important skills that you need to learn to grow into a successful homesteader. If you want to adopt this lifestyle, it is important that you start growing your own food. This section will enlighten you on the basics of gardening.

Growing food through gardening is never easy and it can pose a lot of difficulties for anyone who has never grown food at all. It also takes a lot of time and practice to grow your own food and even to start your own garden. Below are the tips on how to start a garden so that you can grow your own food.

- Grow only what you want to eat: When starting a garden, you might be overwhelmed with the different variety of plants you can really grow. If you have a limited space in your house, make sure that you focus on fruits or vegetables that your family will eat. It is no use to grow plants that you don't even consume.

  Once you start growing your own crops, you will realize that they will taste better than store-bought produce.

- Dedicate your time in the garden: If you want to be a successful homesteader, you ought to be ready to spend more time in your garden than usual. Plants grow easily but their productivity largely depends on your caring hands. It may exhaust you easily but there is nothing more rewarding than spending time in the garden and growing your own food.

- Start small and eventually scale up: If you don't have any gardening experience, it is important that you start small and eventually scale up once you get the hang of it. First timers find it easy to become overwhelmed and start a very big garden. In fact, it is very hard to grow a very big and poorly tended garden. To make it easier, you can start with a container or square foot gardening and try two or three crops jut so you will get the hang of it.

- Test your soil first: Make sure that you test your soil first using a basic home soil test kit which you can buy online or from your local garden store. You can also approach your local cooperative extension office where they can provide soil testing for free. If you are planning to test soil, it is important to know that the perfect soil pH for your garden is 7 (neutral pH) but if you have an acidic soil, you can still grow crops like potatoes and other tubers.

- Look for good seed source: Look for good seed source from your local garden stores. Look for seed companies that provide robust seeds. Once you start growing seeds, you can start saving seeds from mature plants. This will allow you to save a lot of money for your future garden.

- Use organic fertilizers and pest control: One of the facets of a homesteader garden is the refusal to use synthetic and conventional fertilizers and pest control. Not only because these synthetic products can have adverse effects on health as well as affect the natural balance of things.

- Invest in reliable garden tools: If you are going to start gardening to raise your own food, you need to invest in reliable garden tools so that they will last for a long time. Moreover, get tools that are sized properly so that you can reduce the risk of injury once you start working in the garden.

- Start composting: One of the main problems that people encounter when gardening is that they encounter plants that have voracious appetites for fertilizer. To supplement the nutrients that they need, you need to make your own compost from dead leaves, kitchen scraps and grass clippings. You can also fortify your compost if you opt for vermicomposting wherein you rely on the power of worms to transform your compost to enriched black gold.

Animal Husbandry

A homestead will never be complete without a small livestock area. Animal husbandry or raising animals for food is very important in homesteading. There are many types of animals that you can raise in your homestead. These can include fish (practicing aquaculture or aquaponics), rabbits, quail, dwarf goats and chickens.

A Borehole

Each and every one of us would not wish to live without this priceless asset, right? In light of this, numerous households are still discovering it difficult to have a consistent supply of this priceless asset. As a result, this makes life intolerable and fairly unpleasant to this group of individuals. Nonetheless, with the help of water well drilling services, this problem could pertain to an abrupt end once and for all.

The majority of individuals particularly those in the remote areas; use this valuable resource to sustain their needs. As a result, it becomes incredibly tough for them in the event that they are without a steady water supply. It is additionally really pricey in case they need to buy this valuable resource. Nonetheless, if you live in a remote location where there is no constant supply of this precious item, you can easily drop a part of your land where professionals can attempt and trace this valuable resource.

The accessibility of a borehole enables you to maintain your farming tasks as this commodity plays an integral role in the growth of yields. Therefore, this guarantees that you are able to initiate irrigation activities in order for your yields to have a constant supply of this asset, particularly during summer time. The availability of a borehole also allows you have a continual supply of geothermal power in your house.

Not only does this help to reduce power related costs, but it also helps to conserve the environment as this method of does not have any effects on the environment. Apart from the benefits of digging a borehole, it is important to know the type of equipment that you need to use for this type of project. It is important to ensure that you have a boring rig that is up to the task as well as a rig that is within your budget.

It is not advisable to ignore the reliability and quality of the rig as this can give you many problems in the middle of the project. Before, choosing a rig to bore your borehole, ensure that you are able to know the manufacturer of that rig as this plays a big part in ensuring the success of your project. Always choose a rig from a manufacturer who has had positive reviews from past users. Texas windmills are also something to look at when considering water well drilling. You should also look into the cost of water well parts because it is highly likely that that will affect your budget.

In addition, ensure that the outfit is easy to use without much trouble. There are different water well drilling companies that can do this job on your part.

Other Sources for Homesteaders

Water is an essential need all homesteaders should address. You need water for drinking, bathing and even for watering your plants and for raising livestock. There are many sources of water that you can use as a homesteader and this section will discuss your many options.

- City water: If you are a city-based homesteader, then you are probably connected to your city's water line. This is the most reliable source of water but the problem is that it may contain fluoride as well as chlorine which are not too environment and health friendly which may not totally appeal to homesteaders.

- Well water: If you are living in a rural area, you can dig a well and install pump and filters to get water from the ground. The best thing about using this source of water is that you can be assured that the water is free from any chemical treatments and they also contain a lot of natural minerals. However, this particular water supply can easily dry out especially if your area is suffering from a dry spell.

- Collecting rainwater: Whether you live in the city or in a rural area, collecting rainwater is a great way to supply and fortify your water supply for your homestead. To collect rainwater, you need gutters and barrels to store the rainwater. With this system, you can save a lot of water every time it rains. However, your rainwater collection system may also collect leaves, insects and other debris that may contaminate your water source. Having said this, you also need to install filters and lids on your collection system. You can use the water collected from rain by just about anything but if you are going to us it for drinking make sure that you boil it first or let it go through a filtering device to ensure that it is safe to drink.

Aside from knowing how to source your water for your homestead, it is also very vital that you understand the steps of purifying your water especially if you are planning on drinking them. To purify water, you will have to boil it for at least four minutes.

Importance of Drilling a Well

There are many uses of water wells. Drilling a well makes the difference in the world for a high percentage of the world's population. Being provided with a fresh supply of water ensures that new crops are adequately irrigated. Water is something that a number of individuals take for granted. We need to understand that in the absence of a fresh supply, we cannot survive and life can suddenly become very desperate and sour.

Wells will be dug for scientific reasons, drinking water, and many other reasons. Knowing how to make such wells is very crucial. The most common method to dig up a well of this sort is water well drilling.

This type of drilling involves using a rig of some sort to reach the aquifer. What type of drill one will use is all dependent on the terrain. A terrain consisting of granite bedrock for a few hundred feet will need a very powerful drill with a few thousand pounds of torque. On the other hand, an aquifer that is not very deep and has a layer of only soil above is requires a fairly lighter drill. The more powerful drill will be more efficient and faster to drill into the ground, where the lighter drill will be more compact and need much less maintenance.

Usually they mount these rigs on the back of some sort of truck, maybe an 18-wheeler for the bigger drills or a flatbed, super-duty pick-up truck for a lighter drill. It is important to note that these drills are not used for everyday drilling. It is more common to find a well that is about twenty meters deep supplying fresh water for a residence or small village. These rigs are for the wells that are hundreds of meters deep. The shallower well is then dug with techniques by hand including sludging, jetting, and hand percussion. One might also need a drill in more extreme situations.

These drills are not only used for water well drilling. They are also used to dig geothermal wells. This is a type of water well but it is specifically designed to supply water to geothermal heating or cooling system for a home or business. Using geothermal wells is a very environmentally friendly process. People have said that using this technique improves water quality. Unfortunately, the use of water well drilling for this type of system is not every common. The issue is that most people just do not know enough about it.

As the green movement grows, it is probable that this type of heating or cooling system will gain popularity. It is a feasible substitute for a traditional system. One of the best features of this type of system is that the most efficient way to have one of these systems in place is to convert an existing traditional system. I have a feeling that geothermal systems will catch on because of this.

Water Well Drilling Equipment

Do not be alarmed when we mention the word drilling. It is perfectly safe once the land you have the land you are about to drill observed. This could be in the backyard of your house and observing the land and knowing what kind of rock of soil is beneath the land will help you decide the right kind of drilling equipment required to get to the water underground.

Drilling of water wells are referred to the structure created or the excavation made underground by boring, drilling or digging to access water from the underground aquifers. The type of the water wells drilled varies and may be classified as dug wells, driven wells or drilled wells. The water well drilling equipment used in the process of excavation depends on the type of the well that would be drilled.

Drilling equipment is mostly heavy with cable rigs that pound into the ground or rotary ones that screw into the ground to make the well. The advancement in technology has made well water drilling easier and faster. This has also enabled the drilling equipment available in more compact sizes. Water supply for a home does not need a large well and if your land is suitable for easy drilling then you should probably go for compact drilling equipment which will be enough to handle the load and manage a neat drilling work. Transporting this equipment to your backyard will also be easy since most of this equipment is usually mounted on large vehicles.

The drilled wells are more commonly dug than the dug or driven wells. It can be terminated in the glacial drift which can be gravel, sand or bedrock. Drilled wells are constructed using the cable tool, hollow rod, rotary, and jetting and auger rigs. The casing material used can be of either plastic or steel. The driven wells need to be excavated only in the glacial drift. They are most common near lake areas and are installed by the homeowners.

The main components used for the drilling of water wells are the boreholes, casing, well seal, grout, screen, and packer and filter pack. Boreholes are the vertical borings used for reaching the underground aquifers. For wells terminated into rocks, the borehole would reach the well casing's bottom. The well seals are mechanical devices that prevent contamination from reaching the well casing. This device is installed after the completion of the water well and it is ensured all well seals and caps are secured, vermin proof and weather tight.

Well casing can be either plastic or steel pipes that are installed inside the water well to prevent the borehole wall from getting collapsed. However, plastic pipes are preferred over steel pipes as they are non-corroding. The grout is the layer of clay or cement placed in between the annular space between the casing and borehole to prevent separation of the aquifers and water well contamination.

Filter pack is referred to the silica sand that is placed outside the screen for stabilization and filtration. This also ensures longer life of the well and improved rehabilitation of the well. The packer is used as water well drilling equipment as it keeps out sand from reaching the well water. The screen acts as a filtering device and prevents sediments from contaminating the well water.

Some of the common water well drilling type includes cable-tool, rotary drilling, hand driving, auger drilling, hollow rod drilling, jetting, downhole hammering, sonic, or directional drilling. The advanced water well drilling equipment helps to obtain a steady water supply for the farmers, household purposes and for fishing purpose. Areas where water supply was not so good before can have water with the help of drilled wells now.

Figure 1: A drill head

Drilling is required in numerous instances, whether it is to excavate something from the ground or to create holes for anchoring. Based on the requirement, there are different types of drilling equipment. Some are listed below.

Drill press

The drill press has a rotary tool that is forced into the ground by turning it at high speed. The primary function of the drill press is to drill holes in the ground. The working mechanism of the drill press gives you precise drilling and a neat deep hole. A drill press can be used for reaming, counterboring, spotfacing, countersinking and tapping, in addition to drilling.

Drill presses are of different types based on their working mechanism. The three main types are an upright sensitive drill press, upright drill press and radial arm drill press. The upright sensitive model is not suitable for heavy drilling. It is best appropriate for light to moderate work. In the upright sensitive range of machines, there are floor style drills as well as bench style drills.

Upright drills are used for heavy applications. The spindle head in these machines is controlled by a geared assembly that produces greater torque and drills the spindle into hard surfaces. In the range of upright drills, there are automatic models as well.

Radial arm drills come with an arm that makes it easy to drill in places where the machine cannot be taken. The arm stretches out to the drilling area and the operator can control it for precision drilling. This is a versatile machine because of the wheel head which moves along the radial arm. The biggest advantage of radial arm drills is that they can be used to drill angular holes in the ground.

Equipment for special purposes

Drill presses might not be suitable for certain special purposes. For example, if you want to drill multiple holes on a plane surface quickly, drill presses are not useful because you need to adjust the machine and drill arrangement for every hole. So, you cannot complete the work in a short time. For such requirements, you need special drill machines called gang drills that can drill multiple holes simultaneously. Gang drills come with multiple heads that can be used for different purposes. Also, drill presses might not be useful to drill holes of very small diameters. If you need holes with a diameter of less than 1 inch, you should choose special kinds of drills.

Some of the drilling equipment used for special requirements are multi-spindle drills, micro drills and turret drills. Each of these machines is meant for a specific purpose. Turret drills are equipped with cutting tools. These are used to extract rock or mineral samples from under the ground.

Auger drills

Figure 2: Auger Drill

Figure 3: Auger drill

Auger drills come with a helical screw assembly used to drill holes in the ground and lift the drilled earth from the borehole. There are two models in auger drills - hollow stem and solid stem augers. Hollow augers are used in soft places such as swamps and solid stems are used in harder grounds.

There are other types of drilling methods and equipment as well. Some of the common ones are percussion rotary air blast drilling, air core drilling, cable tool drilling, reverse circular drilling, diamond core drilling, hydraulic drilling and sonic vibratory drilling.

Steps

Groundwater considered as the most valuable necessity for many needs, ranging from domestic usage to industrial processes. Well is a manmade hole in the land surface into the ground, created to access water and other liquids. All of these vary accordingly their size and usability. Besides the regular groundwater water wells, you can see many wells are dug for accessing oil and natural gas like precious natural elements. All people are advised to find water first before drilling the well. It saves both time and money essentially.

You may think that digging a well feels like a hard labor that will certainly break a sweat. Actually, if you know the right technique to do it, you will find that digging a well is quite easy. At this time, this book is going to give you some easy steps to dig a well. So, just check out the easy steps below.

How to Find Water for Wells and Start Drilling:

As the first step, drilling a well at your backyard requires consideration of the costs as well as benefits against other options. The initial budget of drilling a well is costly compared to the regular water supply charges. And for the households and farm owners, who waited for years to get access to public supply are readily accepting the wells. Along with the setup cost, you also have to plan for installing a pump and maintenance of the well.

Figure 4: A man watering plants

The second step is you need to find the right place for the well. The accuracy of finding well water on the land adds more risk to your project. You cannot dig a well anywhere your land to get access to the groundwater. You have to locate a spot where the well has to be dug with the help of groundwater surveyor professionals. Finding the place with the experts is wiser than other alternatives like asking neighbors or similar. Finding the right position for digging the well is the most primary responsibility for the landowners. When you search for the place to dig a well, you have to make sure that there is a source of water in that region such as running stream and an open body of water. The well is required to be at least 100 feet from a water source so that the water can use the ground as a natural filter. Besides, the well should also be at least 100 feet from any contamination's source like animal area, dump, or toilet.

Figure 5: Water analysis

The experts also help you in choosing the best drilling method accordingly surveying your land and the position of groundwater. They will tell you the required depth of well to get the best access to the groundwater. They may conduct a physical survey using their advanced tools or machinery. The accuracy rate or flawless detection of this method is really superior to anything else.

After getting recommendations from the geological survey experts, you must go further on drilling the well. In fact, you must consider acquiring all necessary permits from the local authorities or certain departments. This is the third step. Here also, you have to pay the charges separately for certain sanctions. While requesting for the approval of your drilling well project, the reports of groundwater surveyor experts may be required.

You need to finish the tasks of finding water first before drilling or applying for approvals. In fact, you may also be asked to clarify regarding your construction method. This process may take more time compared to your previous experience of finding water for wells. The rules differ from one state to another and your land types.

The fourth step is to start digging the well. Digging a well must be about five feet across in the circular shape. Digging a well can be dangerous and it needs at least two people. One digger will work in the bottom of the well with a shovel and pick. Then, he will fill his bucket with dirt and rock to be pulled up by the other person. You have to continue the digging until you get the water in the well about 6 feet deep.

Figure 6: The drilling process

From all available drilling options, you have to choose the ideal one which matches your budget and requirements properly. In fact some people still trying find well water and drill wells using traditional methods. But latest technology driven auger drilling, cable

288

tool drilling, rotary drilling, jetting, and sonic drill among others are more advantageous. All the drilling methods have their own set of features with varied drilling motion, time and tooling requirements, etc.

The fifth step that should be done is to cover the bottom part of your well using four or five inches of the small rocks. This will be functioned as a filter that can keep any wildlife and insects from entering your well from the dirt below.

Figure 7: Reinforcement around the well

The sixth thing is to start reinforcing the edges of the well with brick. You can start it from the bottom. The brick should only be used for the first 5 or 6 layers and then you can use mortar as well. It would be wise if you reinforce the edges using two layers of brick. Moreover, you can continue to the very top with a mortar and the brick. Finally, the top of the well needs to be covered with stone or concrete slab and the hole can be left for the pump. So, after the pump is stalled, the well is ready to be used.

Figure 8: Hand-driven well

If you need to dig large area, it is ideal if you use the backhoe for the digging process.

PART 4
Pantry
Food Preserving

This part will surprise you how simple it is to salt and pickle your foodstuff and end up with uniquely flavored foods. Most of the pickles are not only suitable to consume as they are, they are also great when served with other foods. In addition, they are fitting for all seasons. It is important to note that you can make great pickled edibles from most of the common ingredients, just by salting and pickling.

Read on and enjoy the wide variety of pickle recipes available in the book!

The Real Meaning Of Pickling

Pickling is a culinary art that people of different cultures practice all over the globe. To give you an idea what pickled foods look like, examples include, kosher cucumber pickles, salsas, pickled herring, chutneys, kimchi, miso pickles, and others. These examples are found in different countries, and that goes to underline the fact that pickling is a global practice. The big question, really, is what you do in order to be able to say you have pickled your food.

Basically, to make pickles or to pickle your food, what you do is to dip it in a solution that ensures the food has a long shelf life. Salting food is another complementary way of ensuring your food can last long without getting spoilt. In ancient times, nomadic tribes of Africa and elsewhere would salt their meat to ensure it lasts many days and sometimes weeks. In fact, people of different cultures would preserve their food supplies for use during the winter season or during famine, and for that lengthy preservation they would do salting and pickling.

In Asia particularly, pickling is not a new practice. Word has it that people who built the Great Wall of China used to eat *sauerkraut*, which is a form of fermented cabbage. That takes us to the next point, which is that although pickling is done for food preservation, it is also done to create some interesting flavor in food. Pickling also gets to alter the texture of the food sometimes. So an ordinary type of food may end up tasting exotic and yummy just from the pickling. Incidentally, pickling is what gets you the spicy foods of Southeast Asia and the acidic flavors of Eastern Europe.

Sometimes people use vinegar for pickling, and this is because vinegar is acidic enough to kill bacteria that would otherwise cause food to go bad. Foods like the kosher cucumber pickles that you see in supermarkets secured tightly in bottles, have vinegar as their preservative. Other foods are pickled in salt brine, and that is because it is a liquid that enhances fermentation. The reason fermentation is encouraged here is that good bacteria ends up developing, and that makes the food much less vulnerable to the bad bacteria. And, of course, if the growth of bad bacteria is restricted, it means your food cannot get spoilt quickly.

An Ancient Brine Fermented Recipe

If you are looking for simplicity, this recipe will fit the bill. You will use brine here instead of salt, but guess what? Brine is basically a salt solution. So, is there a difference, really? You can use brine effectively in the pickling of cucumbers, of green tomatoes, of asparagus, of squash, of garlic, of carrots; basically any vegetable you could think of. At the same time, you need to know there is no limit as to the amount of food you can pickle at a go. As for storing your pickled food, mason jars do quite fine.

Ingredients for this ancient recipe include:

(1) Brine

(2) Vegetables of your choice

(3) Spices of your choice

(4) Some leaves to introduce crispiness

Pickling Procedure

- Begin by preparing the brine

- Here you need to measure salt and water in the ratio of 2:1 respectively, where salt is in tablespoons and water is in quarts. Then, of course, you need to stir it properly.

- Chop your vegetables into pieces that one can comfortably bite

- Put your pickling spices together

- You can use any spices of your choice, or simply put together some fresh herbs, some onions and even some garlic.

- Now put your herb mixture or spices in the jar

- Of course, you need to have a jar, or whatever other container, in which to do your pickling, and it is where you need to put your spices or your herbs for starters. These should lie right at its bottom.

- Next, add some black tea so that it lies on those spices

- What the heck? Isn't black tea for making beverage? Well, pickling is a culinary art – yes, art. So you are allowed to be creative. However, you do not have to use black tea as there other food items that are just as effective in keeping your pickled food crisp. You can use horseradish, mesquite leaves, or even oak and any of them will keep your pickled food crisp alright.

- It is now time to include your vegetables

- Take your chopped vegetables and place them on top of the other ingredients in your jar. Even then, you need to ensure that you leave some space above the vegetables within the jar, making a distance of at least 2" (two inches). So from the level of vegetables to the jar brim, it should be a minimum of two inches.

- Add the brine

- Now take the brine you prepared and pour it over the vegetables. As you do so, ensure the amount of brine that covers your vegetables is a minimum of 1" high. We are talking of an inch here as the minimum, but if you can make it higher and your container allows, the better.

- Push down the vegetables

- Before you leave the pickling process to take effect, try and push down your vegetables, so that they remain below the brine. If you find them still rising above the brine, you can use something like small size plate or even some jar lid to suppress them.

- Cap your jar

- You need to cap your jar tightly now that you are through preparing your vegetables for pickling. You need to give them a span of around ten days while seated in an environment of between 65° and 85° Fahrenheit. For every hour the vegetables remain at that room temperature, the more they ferment.

- Keep checking lids for pressure

- You need to keep testing the lid on your jar to see if it is building pressure. If it is, this means the carbon dioxide that the vegetables normally release in the initial days is building up. You need to release this gas, so open the lid quickly but carefully. You will effectively be, kind of, burping your jar, by unscrewing that lid to allow some reasonable amount of gas to go out. You need to screw back the lid after you have allowed that carbon dioxide to escape.

- Finally, store your pickled food in cold

- The final step, after the food pickling duration is up, is to move your food to some cold place, this time well below 65° Fahrenheit. What you will be seeking to accomplish is to store your pickled food in a refrigerator type of environment.

Dill Pickles Recipes

What would you say dill pickles are? Well, they happen to be some popular condiment that people use on sandwiches and hotdogs, and they sometimes use them on burgers and other edible items. To make the condiment, you need to use fresh herbs with great flavors. Examples of such herbs include hot peppers, garlic, and even dill itself, so that you end up creating a tangy taste. Just so you know, dill is a herb in the parsley family.

Recipe Two and Three

Recipe Two

1. Take a dill and wash it, and then put its head in a jar

2. Add ½ teaspoon of peppercorns (whole ones) in the jar

3. Add 1 teaspoon of mustard seed in the jar

4. As an option, you could add 1 teaspoon of onion powder to the mix

5. Instead place of the option of onion powder you could make your addition fresh onions that have been nicely chopped.

6. As another option for you in case you enjoy spicy foods, you can add some hot pepper, probably adding red pepper that has been crushed into flakes

7. Now prepare your brine in this manner:

8. Put 2½ cups white vinegar in a saucepan

9. Add 2½ cups water in the same pan

10. Add ¼ cup pickling salt in the mix

11. Now heat the contents in the saucepan until they begin to boil. Then remove from the fire

12. Next take cucumbers and stuff them in your jar, aiming to fill it up

13. Then take the brine you have just prepared and pour it in your jar as you watch it wash over the pickles.

14. For the space above the pickles, you need to leave only ½" from the jar lid.

15. Finally, put the jar lid on

16. Place your packed can in some kind of bath – often termed the canning bath

17. Let the can rest there for a maximum 5 minutes. Note that leaving the can in the bath for longer would cause the pickles to lose their crunchiness.

18. Now clean your pickle jar using some clean towel and let it cool down further

19. When you deem your pickle jar cool enough, put it in your pantry

20. Note that as for the part of putting your pickle jar in the bath, this is a step you can omit, but substitute that cooling by placing your jar in the refrigerator. So, essentially what you do is place your dill pickles in the refrigerator before you can deem them ready to serve.

21. In case you decide to use this latter method which is refrigeration, ensure that your pickle jar is well closed

22. Then let the jar rest somewhere on your counter so that it can cool down first before you can put it in your refrigerator

23. When you choose to use the water bath for cooling, you will effectively be preventing yeast and even mold from destroying your pickles.

24. For the pickles you have just prepared, it will take a week for them to be ready to serve. During this period, the pickles will be seeping in the flavors to make them enjoyable to consume.

Recipe Three

Ingredients

(1) Sea Salt – 5 tablespoons

(2) Water that is chlorine free – 2 quarts

(3) Horseradish leaves or oak – 4 or up to 6 pieces

(4) Garlic (peeled) – 6 or even up to 9 pieces of cloves

(5) Dill heads (large ones) – 2 pieces

(6) Spices of your choice – e.g. mustard seeds; black peppercorns; or even red pepper flakes

(7) Some fresh strips of horseradish as your secret ingredient that will add to the spicy taste

(8) Cucumbers in plenty

How to Make the Pickles

- Prepare your brine using the chlorine free water

- Into the mix, add the sea salt

- Leave the mix to cool up to room temperature

- Take your jar and add some of your leaves, your garlic cloves, the dill, and a third of the spices you have prepared for use

- On top of those spices, now place half the cucumbers you plan on using, ensuring the long cucumbers come first

- Put another layer of your leaves, garlic cloves as well as some spices

- Continue adding layers of cucumber and following that with spices

- Now pour your brine on top of the pickles and as you do so, ensure you leave an inch or two of free space above the jar content

- Finally cover your content with some of those leaves that have tannin

- Cap your jar properly and store it at room temperature for a period of between 3 and 10 days. You could also do fine if stored in a cellar for up to one month.

How do you tell that your pickles are really ready? Well, the brine you put in will have turned cloudy and will no longer be bubbling. If you are not going to consume your pickles as soon as they are ready, you need to store them in some cold storage.

More Pickling Recipes

Recipe Four to Seven

Recipe Four: A Summer Squash Recipe

1. Chunks of summer squash – one or two pieces (medium size) which need to be diced into ½" width

2. Seasoning, e.g. onions and garlic; or pepper

3. Herbs of your choice, including oregano, parsley, or even dill and cilantro

4. Leaves to keep the pickles crunchy; such as grape leaves, mesquite or oak

5. Filtered water – one quart

6. Sea salt – 2 tablespoons

How to make the pickles:

- Here, you need to dissolve the sea salt in water to make the brine

- Then mix some herbs and the spicing leaves in a jar

- Add the summer squash up to halfway the jar

- Follow that with some more herbs plus seasoning

- Continue adding the summer squash pieces until your jar is almost full, leaving only one or two inches space to the rim

- Now pour the brine you made over the contents in the jar, and press down the squash so that it is submerged in the brine. This will ensure the fermentation is even.

- Finally cover your jar properly and let it sit in some cool place; at room temperature

- Keep checking your jar and burping it every 12hrs to let out the building carbon dioxide

- Leave your content to ferment for a period between 2 and 5 days, your timing depending on the prevailing temperatures.

- After that time, your pickles will be ready

Recipe Five: Pickled Carrot Sticks

Ingredients to use:

(1) Fresh carrot – one or one and a half

(2) Water – one quart

(3) Sea salt – one tablespoon

(4) Garlic – Three peeled cloves

(5) Fresh leaves of cilantro – Two handfuls

(6) Cumin seeds – Half a teaspoon

Follow the procedure used there before and finally store your pickled carrots in a cold place if you are not going to consume it straightaway.

Recipe Six: Pickled Green Tomatoes

This is a recipe that will make your day in the time of season when ripe tomatoes are hard to come by. So, this recipe is not only great for consumption, it is also very convenient. When some people are mourning the absence of sweet red tomatoes, you will be glad you can pickle your green tomatoes to produce a dish with a tangy and flavored taste.

Ingredients to use:

1. Plain water – Around 3 cups

2. Sea salt – 2 tablespoon

3. Dill seed – 1 tablespoon

4. (Substitute for Dill seed) – Coriander seed

5. Garlic – 4 cloves, either peeled or smashed

6. Jalapeno – 1 piece

7. (Substitute for Jalapeno) – Any half piece of hot pepper

8. Green tomatoes that are cherry sized – 2 pounds

As for the methods of making the pickles, you can use any of those illustrated before in the book.

Recipe Seven: Pickled Sweet Potatoes

The Ingredients include:

(1) Sweet potatoes – 5 pounds; washed and thinly sliced

(2) Fresh ginger – 1½ inches; grated

(3) Onion – a single large one and diced

(4) Cayenne powder – 1 teaspoon

(5) Sea salt – 3 to 4 tablespoons

You need to mix the ingredients and treat them in the same manner that happens in the recipes already described, only notice here that you need to crush your sweet potatoes to enable them produce juices better.

An Array of Pickles Recipes

Recipe Eight to Twenty-one

Do you still recall that you can salt your foods by using brine since brine is essentially a water solution? That is why you will notice some salting and pickling recipes listing brine as an ingredient without mentioning salt. And as has been mentioned elsewhere in the book, salting, even without the conventional pickling, helps to preserve foods. Since the presence of natural herbs in pickling also enhances food preservation, the whole process of salting and pickling is not only great for preservation of otherwise perishable foods, it also makes for great flavoring.

Recipe Eight: Salt Pickles

The ingredients include:

1. Plain water – Half a gallon

2. Grain vinegar – One cup

3. Canning salt – Half a cup

4. Sugar – quarter cup

How to make the pickles:

- You need to mix the sugar and the salt and then dissolve them in your water

- Next add your vinegar

- Now let your solution cool down

- Now take your cucumbers, your dill as well as your herbs of hot pepper, grape leaves as well as garlic, and put them all in one jar.

- Next pour your vinegar mixture when it has cooled down in the jar with cucumbers and put on the lid. From this point, you need to wait for around 5 or 6 days and your salt pickles will be done.

Recipe Nine: Peanut Pickles

The ingredients include:

(1) Sugar – 2 cups

(2) Corn syrup that is light – 1 cup

(3) Plain water – ¼ cup

(4) Salted peanuts – 1½ cups

(5) Butter – 3 tablespoon

(6) Vanilla – 1 teaspoon

(7) Baking soda – 2 teaspoon

As for the method of making the pickles, you need to:

- Mix the sugar and corn syrup first in a saucepan

- Add your water to that mixture

- After you have mixed your contents well, heat it and ensure to use medium heat as you stir the contents

- Continue with the process till the heat in your mixture is 285° Fahrenheit.

- Now add in the peanuts plus the butter and begin to stir the contents. When the contents have reached 295° Fahrenheit, get the saucepan off the fire.

- It is at this point that you add your vanilla plus the baking soda and then proceed to stir your contents. You need to mix till you can see foam.

- Take a buttered pan and pour in the mixture, and let it sit for between 8 and 10 minutes

- Pick a knife and mark squares in your content

- When the brittle looks like it is cool, invert your pan and tap it off the pan

- You can even proceed to cut your brittle into pieces according to your guiding squares.

Recipe Ten: Taffy Pickles

The ingredients are:

(1) Sugar – 1 cup

(2) Corn syrup (light) - ¾ cup

(3) Plain water – 2/3 cup

(4) Cornstarch – 1 tablespoon

(5) Butter – 2 tablespoon

(6) Salt – 1 teaspoon

(7) Vanilla – 2 teaspoon or

(8) Peppermint oil – ¼ teaspoon

The way to make the taffy pickles is similar to the method just explained above.

Recipe Eleven: Simple Salted Taffy Pickles

Ingredients to use are:

(1) Sugar – 2 cups

(2) Cornstarch – 1 tablespoon

(3) Salt – ½ teaspoon

(4) Corn syrup (light) – 1 cup

(5) Hot water – ½ cup

(6) Butter – 2 tablespoon

Follow the same method as in the taffy recipe above.

Recipe Twelve: Pickled Nut Bars

Ingredients to use:

1. Butter – ½ cup

2. Flour – 1½ cups

3. Salt – 1 teaspoon

4. Sugar (brown) – ¾ cup

5. White syrup – ½ cup

6. Butter – 2 tablespoons

7. Butterscotch chips – 6 ounces or 1 cup

8. Mixed nuts – 1 can

Use the same basic method of making the pickles, but remember also that it is fine to be a little creative your own way.

Recipe Thirteen: Nut Bar Pickles

The ingredients include:

1. Flour – 3 cups

2. Sugar (brown) – 1½ cups

3. Softened butter – 1 cup

4. Salt – 1 teaspoon

5. Mixed nuts – 1 can

6. Corn syrup (light) – ½ cup

7. Butter – 2 tablespoon

8. Water – 1 tablespoon

9. Butterscotch chips – 6 ounces or 1 cup

Take flour, sugar, butter and salt, and mix them, then heat them at 350° Fahrenheit, baking the mixture for between 10 and 12 minutes. Then mix in a saucepan the syrup, 2 tablespoons of butter, the water, and the butterscotch chips, and then boil the mixture for 2min. Next sprinkle the nuts on the crust, and put the cooked mixture on top of the nuts. Bake your contents for another 10 or so minutes till it turns brown. You can then cut it into bars, ready for consumption.

Recipe Fourteen: Salted Nutty Rolls

The ingredients are:

1. Cake mix (yellow) – 1 packet

2. Soft butter – ⅓ cup

3. Egg – 1

4. Marshmallows (miniature ones) – 3 cups

5. Corn syrup – 2/3 cup

6. Butter – ¼ cup

7. Peanut butter (in chips) – 12 ounces

8. Vanilla – 2 teaspoon

9. Cocktail peanuts – 2 cups

10. Rice Crispy – 2 cups

Use any of the now familiar methods to make this recipe.

Recipe Fifteen: Pickled Peppers

The ingredients are:

(1) Pickling salt – 1 teaspoon

(2) Sugar – 1 tablespoon

(3) Garlic – 2 cloves

(4) Sliced pepper (hot or not hot) – 4 cups

(5) White vinegar – 1 cup

(6) Boiling water – 1 cup

Method

- Put salt, garlic and salt in jar

- Add peppers

- Next pour in the vinegar

- Add in the hot water, leaving about ½" from the top

- Close the jar, put it in a boiling bath for about 5min when the contents should begin to boil

- After that let the jar rest still for 12hrs straight for the pickles to be ready.

Recipe Sixteen: Pickled Green Beans

The ingredients are:

(1) Fresh dill – 2 heads

(2) Hot peppers – 2 pieces

(3) Garlic – 2 cloves

(4) Cayenne pepper - ½ teaspoon

(5) Green beans (fresh) – 1 pound

(6) Water – 1 cup

(7) Cider vinegar – 1 cup

(8) Salt – 2 tablespoons

Follow the method used in the pickled green beans, only this time when you seal the jar, let it stay in the hot bath for 15min.

Recipe Seventeen: Perpetual Pickles

The ingredients are:

(1) Cider vinegar

(2) Dill – 2 heads

(3) Garlic – 2 cloves

(4) Pickling salt – ¼ cup for 1 gallon of liquid

(5) Bay leaves – 2 pieces

(6) Black peppercorn – 1 tablespoon

(7) Mustard seeds – 1 tablespoon

Choose one of the pickling methods above, but you can try out flavored vinegars and even dried herbs if you wish.

Recipe Eighteen: Pickled Crunchy Dill

The ingredients are:

(1) Small cucumbers – Four pounds

(2) Garlic – 2 cloves

(3) Fresh dill – 1 sprig

(4) Black peppercorns – 4 pieces

(5) White vinegar – 2 quarts

(6) Pickling salt – ½ cup

This recipe follows a similar method as the last few. Just ensure any jar with pickles closes properly. If it does not, you need to put it in the refrigerator the soonest.

Recipe Nineteen: Fermented Pickles

The ingredients are:

(1) Salt to make brine

(2) Vegetables – any that is in season

(3) Pickling spices

(4) Herbs to increase crispiness of the pickles

Method

- Mix salt to water in the ratio, 2 tablespoons: 1 quart, then stir

- Chop your vegetables to bite size pieces

- Mix your flavorings, e.g. fresh herbs, garlic, onions

- Throw those spicing herbs into the jar

- Then follow these with the vegetables, but leave some space of about 2" to the top of the jar

- Now pour in the brine you made covering the vegetables properly

Recipe Twenty: Garlic Dill Pickles

The ingredients are:

(1) Garlic bulbs – All the cloves of 3 pieces of garlic

(2) Vinegar – 700ml

(3) Pure salt – 1 teaspoon

(4) Mustard seeds – 1 teaspoon

(5) Spice berries – 3 pieces

(6) Dried chili – 1 piece

(7) Fresh basil – 1 sprig

Method

- Have some water boiling and put in your garlic cloves for one minute blanching

The purpose here is to loosen the garlic skin, allowing it to slip off more easily once it has cooled.

- Put your spices in a jar that has been sterilized

- Now add in your garlic

- Next boil your vinegar and pour it on top of the garlic

- After this, seal your jar containing your pickling ingredients, and let it cool through the night.

- The next stage is to refrigerate your pickles.

Recipe Twenty-one: Wild Garlic Pickles

The ingredients are:

(1) Wild garlic

(2) Vinegar – 1 part

(3) Plain water – 1 part

(4) Alum (sieved) – ½ teaspoon

<u>Method to Follow</u>

- Start off by washing your peeled garlic clean, and cutting off the tip that is green

- Now put the rest of the garlic in your chosen jar

- Next add half a teaspoon of alum

- Add the vinegar too

- Also add 1 part water

- You can now seal your jar and refrigerate it, letting it to remain in that cold environment for a period of between 2 and 3 weeks.

You can use this wild garlic pickle with your meals and everyone will enjoy.

Different Ways of Pickling Eggs

Recipe Twenty-two to Twenty-seven

In this chapter, you are going to read about how to pickle eggs when they are hard cooked and also peeled.

- Prepare your pickling solution

- Boil all the ingredients apart from the eggs

- Next, lower the heat, letting the ingredients simmer for five minutes

- Take a jar and put in the eggs, and ensure they do not exceed 12 in number

- Now take your pickling solution, and when hot, pour it over those eggs in the jar

- Finally, cover your jar and immediately put it in the refrigerator

Recipe Twenty-two : Pickled Red Beet Eggs

Ingredients are:

(1) Red beet juice – 1 cup

(2) Cider vinegar – 1½ cups

(3) Brown sugar – 1 teaspoon

Recipe Twenty-three: Pickled Sweet, Sour Eggs

The ingredients are:

(1) Apple cider (pasteurized) – 1½ cups

(2) Cider vinegar – ½ cup

(3) Red cinnamon candy – 12 ounces

(4) Mixed spice (for pickling) – 1 tablespoon

(5) Salt – 2 tablespoons

(6) Garlic salt – 1 teaspoon

Recipe Twenty-Four: Pickled Spicy and Dark Eggs

The ingredients are:

(1) Cider vinegar – 1½ cups

(2) Water – ½ cup

(3) Dark brown sugar – 1 tablespoon

(4) Granulated sugar – 2 teaspoons

(5) Pickling spices (mixed) – 1 teaspoon

(6) Hickory smoke salt – ¼ teaspoon

(7) Salt – 2 teaspoons

Recipe Twenty-five: Pickled Cider Eggs

The ingredients include:

(1) Apple cider juice – 1½ cups

(2) White vinegar – ½ cup

(3) Onion slices – 6 pieces

(4) Salt – 1½ teaspoon

(5) Pickling spice – 1 teaspoon

(6) Garlic clove (peeled) – 1 piece

Recipe Twenty-six: Pickled Dilled Eggs

The ingredients include:

(1) White vinegar – 1½ cups

(2) Water – 1 cup

(3) Dill weed – ¾ teaspoon

(4) White pepper – ¼ teaspoon

(5) Salt – 3 teaspoons

(6) Mustard seed – ¼ teaspoon

(7) Minced onion – 1 piece

(8) Garlic clove – 1 piece

Recipe Twenty-seven: Pineapple Pickled Eggs

The ingredients are:

(1) Pineapple juice (not sweetened) – 1 can

(2) White vinegar – 1½ cups

(3) Medium size onions (sliced) – 2 pieces

(4) Sugar – ¼ cup

(5) Salt – 1 teaspoon

(6) Pickling spice – 1 teaspoon

It is important to note that many of the salted and pickled recipes in this book go with different types of meals and they fit very well. At the same time, they are great to eat as they are without any other main dish. Something else worth noting is that how you treat your pickles after you have made them depends on the weather. For most of them, you need to refrigerate them as soon as they cool down unless it is winter. However, if you have made your pickles to be consumed in only a couple of days, refrigeration may not be necessary.

Summer Canning

I would like to thank and congratulate you for downloading "Canning and Preserving: 30 Delicious Savory Recipes for Preserving Summer Vegetables". You will enjoy sitting down to feast on this collection of tasty recipes. You will be able to enjoy the tastes of summer vegetables in the middle of the cold winter months. Canning and preserving is a great and safe way to store your food supplies to eat at later times. These methods can help you to prepare foods for the long winter months, when fresh fruit and vegetables are not readily available. Also by making your own preserves, you can save a lot of money, you won't have to purchase as much food from the stores.

Enjoy preparing this collection of healthy summer vegetable and fruit preserves for yourself and loved ones. Think of how nice it will be when you are feasting on a yummy summer preserve, thinking about the warm summer months with each bite! You can enjoy your home canned food again and again if it is preserved properly. Now follow these easy recipes to help you to prepare some healthy foods at very little cost.

The process of pickling has been around for over 4000 years, originally invented to preserve foods. However, today many people love pickled foods because they love the taste of them. The nutritional value of food can also be improved by the pickling process that introduces B vitamins that are introduced by bacteria. Natural preservation and fermentation are the most unique ways of preserving foods. Foods that are naturally pickled and fermented also help to develop healthy gut microbes which help prevent unhealthy ones from developing. Adding these foods to your diet will help with your digestive process and help you to absorb healthy nutrients. You will be pleasantly surprised just how easily you can take some aging vegetables and turn them into a healthy dish that you and your loved ones can enjoy the benefits from!

Enjoy this collection of summer vegetable preserves, and before you know it you will be making them a part of your daily healthy diet. Making changes in your lifestyle such as in your diet that are healthy is going to make you so happy that you decided to add some healthy foods to your diet. This collection of recipes will certainly help to get you started down the road to living a healthier lifestyle!

Jams, marmalades, confitures and other conserves are the products or extracts of fruit, which are preserved by the sugar. All of them vary in ingredients, gel texture and fruit preparation. They can be prepared at home, but there is the difference between each one of them.

Jams can be made by crushed fruit which has thick texture because of the high amount of pectin.

Marmalades are jelly like with pieces of fruit suspended in them. Citrus peels are commonly used in marmalades.

Vegetables are defined as any plant or part of a plant used as food. This includes any plant whose fruit, seeds, roots, tubers, stems bulbs, leaves and flowers are used as food. Examples of vegetables include Tomato, beans, beet, potato onion, asparagus, spinach, cauliflower and so on.

A **vegetarian** is someone who does not eat meat, and occasionally other animal products, especially for moral, religious or health reasons. This means that a vegetarian meal can include things like milk and eggs for those who do not mind.

Reasons for the Topic

There is a reason why I chose to write about the topic. Many health's related killer diseases today bombard the world. Health is one of the most important things for any human being to have, you clearly realize this when you get sick or even see someone close to you who is sick. With good health you will feel better emotionally, physically and mentally and keep the doctor away. You will be able to work well at your given job, your sporting activity or whatever it is that you do. I thought vegetable and fruit recipes are a good idea for anyone trying to live a healthy lifestyle as well as a wake-up call to those who are not. I am interested in recipes from all over the world, this is because using the same recipe day in day out may become boring, I also intend to make your cooking interesting and encourage you to keep cooking.

Health benefits and nutrient of fruits and vegetables

- Reduces risk of heart diseases like heart attack and stroke; vegetables are high in fiber which is important for digestion.

- Protection against cancer; consider using flowering vegetables like cauliflower and broccoli.

- Reduce risk of blood pressure; vegetables rich in potassium like bananas, sweet potatoes, white potatoes, white beans, tomato products, soya beans, lime beans, spinach, kidney beans and lentils.

- Low-calorie level hence reduces your calorie intake naturally.

- Can be a way of losing weight as well as most vegetables have low fats and calories.

- Improved eyesight; carrots are a boost for good eyesight.

- Lovely skin; this is enabled by consumption of vegetables rich in vitamin A.

- Healthy strong teeth by consumption of vegetables rich in vitamin C.

- Formation of red blood cells and iron sufficiency.

Vegetable Preserves

1. Spicy Pickled Green Beans

Ingredients:

- 2 c. white vinegar

- 3 tbsps. kosher salt

- 2 c. water

- 1½ tbsps. sugar

- 1½ pounds trimmed green beans

- 4 small and dried red chilies

- 8 twigs of fresh dill

- 8 thinly sliced garlic cloves

Preparation:

Place all the ingredients except for dill, peppers, and garlic in a large saucepan, bring all ingredients to a boil. Once pan has reached a boil, remove it from heat and add the remaining ingredients and set aside. In a clean mason jar, layer it with green beans. Pour the mixture of vinegar over the beans and cover them. Refrigerate it for one week, before every use stir the jar.

2. Pickled Yellow Squash

Ingredients:

- 1 small red bell pepper

- 1 onion

- 2 lbs. small yellow squash

- 1 tbsp. mustard, ground

- ¾ c. sugar

- 2½ c. cider vinegar

- ¼ c. kosher salt

Preparation:

Take your yellow squash and slice it into thin rounds. Cut onions very thinly lengthwise. Dice your red bell pepper. In a mixing bowl add in pepper, squash, salt and onion. Cover the mixture with some ice and water, and let sit for 30 minutes. In a saucepan add the vinegar, sugar and mustard. Bring to a boil, and once they are dissolved remove from heat. Pour the vinegar mixture over the other mixture that was previously made. Pierce squash with a fork to make sure they have been well-soaked. Cover the mixture and keep in the fridge.

3. Garlic & Coriander Pickled Baby Carrots

Ingredients:

- 1 teaspoon toasted mustard seed

- 1 c. vinegar

- 1 c. water

- 1 pound baby carrots, peeled and chopped

- 1 teaspoon toasted coriander seeds

- 1 smashed garlic clove

- 1 bay leaf

- 2 tablespoons honey

- 1 tbsp. kosher salt

Preparation:

Take the carrots and water and place them in a saucepan. Bring them to a boil. Boil them for 2 minutes, then remove from heat and drain them through cold water. Transfer your carrots to Mason or canning jars. In a cup of water add honey, bay leaf, salt, vinegar, coriander, garlic and mustard seeds. Boil these ingredients in a saucepan. Pour this mixture over your carrots in the jars and allow them to cool at room temperature. After jars have cooled add on the lids and place them in the fridge to store them.

4. Pickled Celery Relish

Ingredients:

- 1 small red Fresno Chile, thinly sliced

- Fresh Ginger, peeled and sliced

- 1 tbsp. kosher salt

- 6 tbsps. sugar

- 1 chopped bunch of celery,

- 1 c. of distilled vinegar

Preparation:

Cut up the celery, removing leaves and ends. Place celery into jars. In a saucepan bring remaining ingredients to a boil, then remove from heat. Pour this mixture over celery in jars, covering it over. Allow jars to sit and cool at room temperature. Secure lids and store in the fridge.

5. Jalapeno Pickle

Ingredients:

- 5 Jalapeno peppers, chopped

- 1 tsp. black peppercorns

- 1 tsp. coriander seeds

- 1 tbsp. kosher salt

- 1 onion, sliced

- 2/3 c. white vinegar

- ½ c. water

Preparation:

Add your coriander, salt, vinegar, peppercorns and water to a pot and bring to a boil. Cook for at least 5 minutes, then remove from heat. Add your jalapenos to mason or canning jars. Pour hot mixture over the jalapenos. Leave jars to cool at room temperature. Once they have cooled secure lids onto them and store in the fridge.

6. Pickled Mixed Vegetables

Ingredients:

- ½ tsp. mustard seeds

- ½ tsp. dill seeds

- ½ tsp. peppercorns

- 2 teaspoon kosher salt

- 1 tbsp. sugar

- ½ c. water

- ½ c. distilled vinegar

- ½ tsp. thyme

- ½ tsp. tarragon

- 1 thinly sliced clove garlic

- ¼ c. carrots, thickly sliced

- 6 oz. green beans

Preparation:

In Mason or canning jars place the herbs, vegetables and garlic into them. In a medium saucepan bring to a boil the vinegar and remaining ingredients. Remove from heat and allow to cool at room temperature. Pour mixture over vegetables in jars, covering them. Secure the lids onto jars and store them in the fridge.

7. *Tomato Salsa*

Ingredients:

- 1 tbsp. oregano leaves

- 2 c. vinegar

- 4 finely chopped cloves garlic

- ¾ c. chopped onions

- ½ c. chopped jalapeno peppers

- 2 c. chopped and seeded green Chilies

- 4 c. chopped tomatoes

- 1 tbsp. fresh cilantro

- 1½ tsps. kosher salt

- 1 tbsp. cumin, ground

Preparation:

Add all your ingredients in a saucepan and bring them to a boil. When bubbles appear, reduce the heat and simmer for 20 minutes. Add the mixture to mason jars and secure lids. Place steel rack inside large pot, fill with water. Place jars into pot on top of rack and boil for 15 minutes. Remove from pot, place on towel on top of counter to cool at room temperature for the day. Once the cooling process is complete store the jars in fridge.

8. *Tomato Taco Sauce*

Ingredients:

- 2 tbsps. oregano leaves

- 1 tsp. cumin, ground

- 1 tsp. sugar

- 1½ tsps. black pepper

- 2 tsps. salt

- 2½ c. distilled vinegar

- 4 chopped and seeded green chilies

- 4 chopped and seeded jalapeno peppers

- 5 c. chopped onions

- 8 quarts tomato paste

- 2 crushed cloves garlic

Preparation:

Add all the above listed ingredients into a large saucepan and bring to a boil over medium heat. Once bubbles begin to appear reduce heat to a simmer. Cook for about 15 minutes on simmer. Add the mix to mason jars, place them into a canner and do the boiling process for 15 minutes.

Place your jars on top of a towel on counter, allowing them to cool at room temperature. Once the jars have cooled place them into the fridge to store them.

9. *Hot Tomato Pepper Sauce*

Ingredients:

- ½ tsp. pepper

- 3 tsps. sea salt

- 1 c. vinegar

- 4 c. chopped onions

- 6 c. chopped and seeded chili peppers

- 10 c. chopped and cored tomatoes

Preparation:

Over medium-heat, place all the above ingredients to a large saucepan. When the bubbles begin to appear reduce to simmer for 15 minutes then remove from heat. Add the mixture into mason or canning jars, leaving an inch-space at top of each jar. Secure the lids and place the jars into canner and put them through the boiling process for 15 minutes.

Place your jars on top of a towel on top of counter. Allow them to cool at room temperature. Once they have cooled place jars in fridge for storage.

10. Canned Sweet Potatoes

Ingredients:

- Sweet potatoes, cubed

- Kosher salt

- Water

- 1½ c. sugar

Preparation:

Wash sweet potatoes, then boil them for 15 minutes or until soft. Remove the skins. Place potatoes in Mason or canning jars. Add a dash of kosher salt to each canning jar. Make syrup by boiling sugar along with 5 cups of water. Cover the sweet potatoes with syrup, leaving 1-inch of space at top of jars. Place them in canner and process the jars in boiling water for 15 minutes. Remove the jars and place on a towel on counter. Allow jars to cool at room temperature. Store jars in fridge.

11. Canning Spinach

Ingredients:

- Fresh Spinach

- Kosher salt

- Water

Preparation:

Wash your spinach until the water runs clear, greens tend to grow close to the ground so they usually have a lot of dirt on them. Remove the stems and any other hard pieces from your spinach. Steam for five minutes or until the spinach is wilted. Place it loosely into canning jars. Add a dash of kosher salt to each jar. Fill jars with boiling water, 1-inch from top of jar. Seal the jars and place them into canner and boil for 15 minutes. Remove the jars and place onto towel on counter. Allow jars to cool at room temperature and then place them in fridge.

12. Avocado Mango Salsa

Ingredients:

- 1 tbsp. chopped cilantro

- Salt

- 1 seeded and chopped habanero pepper

- 1 chopped small red onion

- 1 peeled and sliced mango

- 1 juiced lime

- 1 peeled and sliced avocado

Preparation:

Add your avocado to mixing bowl, and add in all the other ingredients and mix well. Add mixture into canning jars, and secure lids, storing in fridge.

13. *Garlic Dill Pickles*

Ingredients:

- 3 pounds Kirby cucumbers

- 1½ c. apple cider vinegar

- 1 tsp. red chili flakes

- 2 tsps. black peppercorns

- 4 tsps. dill seed

- 8 peeled garlic cloves

- 2 tbsps. pickling salt

- 1½ c. water

Preparation:

Wash and dry cucumbers, cutting them into spears. Remove the blossom end of cucumbers. In a saucepan combine vinegar, water and salt to make brine. Bring to boil over medium-high heat. Equally divide the dill seed, garlic cloves, red chili flakes, black

330

peppercorns between the jars. Pack cucumbers into the canning jars as tightly as you can without crushing them. Pour the brine over the cucumbers, filling jars to ¼ of an inch from top. Tap jars to help remove air bubbles from jars. Wipe rims of jars and secure the lids in place. Add jars to canning pot and boil for 15 minutes. Remove jars and place on towel on counter to cool at room temperature. Once jars have cooled place in fridge. Let the pickles stay for at least one week before eating.

14. Marinated Fava Beans

Ingredients:

- 1½ pounds fava beans

- 2 tbsps. red wine vinegar

- ¼ tsp. black pepper, ground

- ½ tsp. kosher salt

- 2 sprigs fresh rosemary

- 1 tsp. fresh and minced garlic

- 2 tbsps. olive oil

Preparation:

Boil salted water. While water is heating up, remove beans from their pods. Once water is boiling add beans, and cook for about 3 minutes or until tender and green.

Drain the beans and rinse them under cold water. Pop the fava beans out of their casings and set them aside.

Mix the vinegar, garlic, olive oil, rosemary sprigs, salt and pepper in a mason jar. Place lid on jar and shake contents to combine. Add fava beans to jar and secure lid. These marinated beans will keep up to three days in the fridge. Allow the beans to soak for at least 15 minutes in the mix before serving them.

15. Pickled Oyster Mushrooms

Ingredients:

- 1 pound oyster mushrooms

- 2½ c. rice vinegar

- 2 peeled and sliced garlic cloves

- 2 bay leaves

- ¼ tsp. black peppercorns

- 1 tbsp. sugar

- 1 tbsp. pickling salt

- 1 sliced onion

Preparation:

Wash your oyster mushrooms well, and cut them into pieces. Bring a pot of salted water to boil, then reduce heat to a simmer. Add in your mushrooms to the pot and simmer them for 10 minutes or until they become tender. In another medium-sized pot combine onion, vinegar, peppercorns, sugar and salt. Bring the brine to a boil. Drain the mushrooms well, then add them to the brine. Cook the mushrooms in the brine for 5 minutes. Divide the garlic and bay leaves between two prepared pint jars.

Pack jars with mushrooms, onions, covering with brine. Leave ¼ of an inch space at the top of jars. Use wooden spoon and stir contents in jars to help get rid of any bubbles. Wipe jars lids and rims secure on the lids. Place jars into canner and boil for 15 minutes. Place jars on top of towel on counter. Allow jars to cool at room temperature. Store jars in fridge. Allow the jars to rest for at least 48 hours before opening them.

16. Lemon Pickled Cauliflower

Ingredients:

- 2 lbs. cauliflower, florets

- ¼ tsp. peppercorns

- 1 sliced garlic clove,

- 1 sliced lemon

- 2 tsps. sea salt

- 1 c. water

- 1 c. apple cider vinegar

Preparation:

Wash your cauliflower. In a large saucepan combine your sea salt, apple cider vinegar, water, and bring to a boil. In a quart canning jar place two slices of lemon on the bottom of the inside of jar. Top with peppercorns and garlic slices and set aside. When the brine is boiling add your cauliflower to it. Add cauliflower to prepared jar using tongs, and cover with brine. Add two to three slices of lemon on top, then secure lid in place. Allow the jars to cool at room temperature, then place them in the fridge. Will be ready to eat within 12 hours, but the longer they rest the more their flavor will deepen.

17. Pickled Fennel with Orange

Ingredients:

- 1 c. apple cider vinegar

- ¼ tsp. black pepper, fresh and ground

- 1 sliced orange

- 2 tbsps. kosher salt

- 3 fennel bulbs, small

Preparation:

Wash your fennel bulbs and remove the stems, also cut out hard core. On a mandolin slice, paper-thin. Add kosher salt to shaved fennel, toss to combine, and allow to sit for at least one hour. After time is up pour fennel into colander, and press to remove any liquid that developed while it sat in the salt. Return the fennel to the bowl, and toss with black pepper and orange slices. Pack orange and fennel into a quart jar and top with apple cider vinegar. Use a wooden spoon to stir contents, and this will help to get rid of bubbles. Secure lids and keep in the fridge, do not eat for at least 24 hours.

18. Pickled Brussel Sprouts Halves

Ingredients:

- 1 pounds Brussels sprouts

- 2 garlic cloves

- 1 c. water

- 1½ c. apple cider vinegar

- 2 bay leaves

- ¼ tsp. divided yellow mustard seeds

- 20 divided peppercorns

- 1 tbsp. pickling salt

Preparation:

Trim the sprouts and set them aside. In a saucepan add vinegar, water and salt and bring to a boil. Divide the peppercorns, mustards seeds and cloves between pint jars. Pack the sprouts in jars. Pour the brine over your sprouts. Using a wooden spoon to get rid of air bubbles. Wipe the lids and rims and secure them in place. Place the jars into canner and boil, processing them for 15 minutes. Remove and place jars on top of a towel on the counter to cool down at room temperature. Once cooled place jars in the fridge. Allow to rest for at least 48 hours before eating.

19. Marinated Carrots & Mint

Ingredients:

- 1 tsp. pepper, freshly ground

- ½ tsp. sea salt

- 1 minced garlic clove

- 2 tbsps. chopped mint

- 3 tbsps. rice vinegar, seasoned

- ¼ c. olive oil

- 1½ pounds carrots

Preparation:

Peel your carrots and slice them into thick rounds. Simmer your carrots in salted water just until they become tender. While your carrots are cooking, whisk together mint, olive oil, salt, pepper, garlic and vinegar. When your carrots are fork tender, drain them. Toss carrots with vinaigrette and allow them to sit and cool. Add to mason jar and secure the lid and store in the fridge. Allow them to rest for at least 1 hour before eating.

20. Pickled Eggplant with Mint & Garlic

Ingredients:

- 1½ tsps. pickling salt

- ½ c. fresh mint leaves

- 1½ tbsps. chopped garlic

- 1½ pounds peeled and cubed eggplant

- 2½ c. red wine vinegar

Preparation:

Prepare two-pint jars and set aside. Add vinegar to a medium saucepan, bring to a boil. Once it boils add in the eggplant, reduce heat to simmer for 3 minutes. Remove eggplant with slotted spoon and place in a bowl. Add in the garlic, mint and salt, mix to combine. Pack eggplant into jars, top with boiled vinegar. Leave about ¼-inch of space at the top of jars. Place jars into canner and boil for 15 minutes. Remove the jars and place them on top of towel on counter. Allow jars to cool at room temperature. Once they have cooled place jars in the fridge. They will be ready to eat in 1 week.

21. Pickled Red Tomatoes

Ingredients:

- 3 tbsps. pickling spice

- Fresh ginger, sliced

- ¾ c. sugar, granulated

- 2 tbsps. pickling salt

- 1½ c. red wine vinegar

- 2 pounds small meaty tomatoes, Plum

Preparation:

In a pot combine sugar, 1 ½ cups water, ginger, salt and vinegar. Bring to a boil. In the bottom of each jar add 1 tablespoon of pickling spices. Carefully pack prepared tomatoes into jars. Pour the brine over the tomatoes. Leave about 1/4-inch space at the top of jars. Use a wooden spoon to gently stir to help get rid of air bubbles. Add two to three ginger slices to each jar. Secure lids and place jars into canner and bring to a boil and process for 15 minutes. Remove jars and place on top of towel on counter. Give enough time to the jars to cool. Place the jars in the fridge once they have cooled. Allow the contents to sit in the brine for at least 1 week before you eat them.

Fruit Jams And Marmalades

1. Raspberry Jam

Ingredients:

- 4 c. raspberries

- 4 c. sugar

- 1 teaspoon vanilla extract

- ½ teaspoon citric acid

Preparation:

Gently wash and drain the raspberries. Lightly crush them with a potato masher, food mill or a food processor. Do not puree, it is better to have bits of fruit. Sieve half of the raspberry pulp to remove some of the seeds. Combine sugar and raspberries in a wide, thick-bottomed pot and bring mixture to a full rolling boil, stirring constantly. Skim any foam or scum that is seen to rise to the surface. Boil until the jam sets.

Test by putting a small drop on a cold plate – if the jam is set, it will wrinkle when given a small poke with your finger. Add citric acid, vanilla, and stir. Simmer for 2-3 minutes more, then ladle into hot jars. Flip upside down or process 10 minutes in boiling water.

2. Raspberry-Gooseberry Jam

Ingredients:

- 2 c. raspberries

- 2 c. gooseberries

- 4 c. sugar

- Salt

- ½ teaspoon citric acid

Preparation:

Combine fruit and sugar in a wide saucepan. Stir and set aside for an hour. Gently boil fruit and sugar, stirring and removing any foam that rises to the surface. Boil until the jam sets.

Add citric acid, salt and stir. Simmer for 2-3 minutes more, then ladle into hot jars. Flip upside down or process 10 minutes in boiling water.

3. Raspberry-Peach Jam

Ingredients:

- 2 pounds peaches

- 1½ c. raspberries

- 4 c. sugar

- 1 teaspoon citric acid

Preparation:

Wash and slice the peaches. Clean the raspberries and combine them with the peaches is a wide, heavy-bottomed saucepan. Cover with sugar and set aside for a few hours or overnight. Bring the fruit and sugar to a boil over medium heat, stirring occasionally. Remove any foam that rises to the surface.

Boil until the jam sets. Add citric acid and stir. Simmer for 2-3 minutes more, then ladle into hot jars. Flip upside down or process 10 minutes in boiling water.

4. Blueberry Jam

Ingredients:

- 4 c. granulated sugar

- 3 c. fresh blueberries

- ¾ c. honey

- 2 tablespoons lemon juice

- 1 teaspoon lemon zest

Preparation:

Gently wash and drain the blueberries. Lightly crush them with a potato masher, food mill or a food processor. Add the honey, lemon juice, and lemon zest, then bring to a boil over medium-high heat. Boils for 10-15 minutes, stirring from time to time. Boil until the jam sets.

Test by putting a small drop on a cold plate – if the jam is set, it will wrinkle when given a small poke with your finger. Skim off any scum or foam, then ladle the jam into jars. Seal, flip upside down or process for 10 minutes in boiling water.

5. Triple Berry Jam

Ingredients:

- 1 c. strawberries

- 1 c. raspberries

- 2 c. blueberries

- 4 c. sugar

- 1 teaspoon citric acid

Preparation:

Mix berries and add sugar. Set aside for some hours or overnight. Bring the fruit and sugar to the boil over medium heat, stirring frequently. Remove any foam that rises to the surface. Boil until the jam sets. Add citric acid, salt and stir.

Simmer for 2-3 minutes more, then ladle into hot jars. Flip upside down or process 10 minutes in boiling water.

6. Red Currant Jelly

Ingredients:

- 2 pounds red currants, fresh and crushed

- ½ c. water

- 3 c. sugar

- 1 teaspoon citric acid

Preparation:

Add in water, and bring to a boil. Simmer for 10 minutes. Strain the fruit through a jelly or cheese cloth and measure out 4 cups of the juice. Pour the juice into a large saucepan, and stir in the sugar. Bring to full rolling boil, then simmer for 20-30 minutes, removing any foam that may rise to the surface. When the jelly sets, ladle in hot jars, flip upside down or process in boiling water for 10 minutes.

7. White Cherry Jam

Ingredients:

- 2 pounds cherries

- 3 c. sugar

- 2 c. water

- 1 teaspoon citric acid

Preparation:

Wash and stone cherries. Combine the sugar and water and boil the mixture. Boil for 5-6 minutes then remove from heat and add cherries. Bring to a rolling boil and cook until set. Add citric acid, stir and boil 1-2 minutes more.

Ladle in hot jars, flip upside down or process in boiling water for 10 minutes.

8. Cherry Jam

Ingredients:

- 2 pounds fresh and pitted cherries, halved

- 4 c. sugar

- ½ c. lemon juice

Preparation:

Place the cherries in a large saucepan. Add sugar and set aside for an hour. Add the lemon juice and place over low heat. Cook, stirring occasionally, for 10 minutes or until sugar dissolves. Increase heat to high and bring to a rolling boil.

Cook for 5-6 minutes or until jam is set. Remove from heat and ladle hot jam into jars, seal and flip upside down.

9. Quince Jam

Ingredients:

- 4 pounds quinces

- 5 c. sugar

- 2 c. water

- 1 teaspoon lemon zest

- 3 tablespoon lemon juice

Preparation:

Combine water and sugar in a deep, thick-bottomed saucepan and bring it to the boil. Simmer, stirring until the sugar has completely dissolved. Rinse the quinces, cut in half, and discard the cores. Grate the quinces, using a cheese grater or a blender to make it faster. Quince flesh tends to darken very quickly, so it is good to do this as fast as possible. Add the grated quinces to the sugar syrup and cook uncovered, stirring occasionally until the jam turns pink and thickens to desired consistency, about 40 minutes. Drop a small amount of the jam on a plate and wait a minute to see if it has thickened. If it has gelled enough, turn off the heat. If not, keep boiling and test every 2-3 minutes until ready. Two or three minutes before you remove the jam from the heat, add lemon juice and lemon zest and stir well.

Ladle in hot, sterilized jars and flip upside down.

10. Quince and Apple Jam

Ingredients:

- 2 peeled and diced quinces

- 3 diced apples

- 3 c. sugar

- 2 c. water

- ½ c. lemon juice

Preparation:

Place the quinces, lemon juice, sugar, and water in a saucepan and bring to the boil. Simmer for 10 minutes, then add in the apples. Simmer for 10 more minutes, or until the jam is set. Ladle into the warm, sterilized jars and seal. Flip upside down or process in boiling water for 10 minutes.

11. Apple Jam

Ingredients:

- 2 pounds clean apples, sliced

- 4 c. sugar

- ½ teaspoon cinnamon

- 2 teaspoons lemon juice

Preparation:

Place the sliced apples in a large saucepan. Cover with the sugar, add in lemon juice and cinnamon and bring to the boil stirring continuously. Boil for 30 minutes, removing any foam that may rise to the surface. When the jam sets, ladle in hot jars, flip upside down or process in boiling water for 10 minutes.

12. Orange Marmalade

Ingredients:

- 1½ lbs. seedless orange

- 1 grated lemon zest, juiced

- 3 c. water

- 1½ lbs. granulated sugar

Preparation:

Using a mandoline slicer, cut the oranges into 1/8-inch slices. Pile the orange slices and cut them into quarters.

Place the oranges into a heavy bottomed pot or saucepan. Add the lemon juice, zest, and the water to the pot, bring to a boil over high heat. Reduce the heat to medium-low and simmer for 30 minutes, stirring frequently.

Add the sugar and cook for about 20 minutes or until a candy thermometer reads 220 F.

Pour orange marmalade into the newly sterilized jars, leaving 1/4 inch headspace. Cover tightly with lid.

Place jars in a hot water bath. Process for 15 minutes. Cool completely at room temperature.

Store in a cool, dark place. Keep refrigerated once opened.

13. Lemon Marmalade with Cinnamon

Ingredients:

- 1 lb. clean unwaxed lemons

- 2 c. water

- 2 lbs. sugar, granulated

- 1 tsp. ground cinnamon

Preparation:

Using a mandoline slicer, cut the lemons into 1/8-inch slices. Pile the lemon slices and cut them into quarters.

Place the lemons into a heavy bottomed pot or saucepan. Reduce the heat to medium-low and simmer for 30 minutes, stirring frequently.

Add the sugar and cinnamon. Cook further 20 minutes or until a candy thermometer reads 220 F.

Pour lemon marmalade into the newly sterilized jars, leaving 1/4 inch headspace. Cover tightly with lid.

Place jars in a hot water bath. Process for 10 minutes. Cool completely at room temperature.

Store in a cool, dark place. Keep refrigerated once opened.

14. Grapefruit-Lemon Marmalade

Ingredients:

- 3 clean grapefruits

- 2 clean medium lemons

- 4 c. water

- 5 c. sugar, granulated

Preparation:

Cut the grapefruits and lemons into quarters, then slice thinly. Place the fruits and water in a large, heavy bottomed pot or saucepan. Bring to a boil and cook for about 30 minutes, or until rind is tender.

Reduce heat and add the sugar, stirring constantly, until the sugar is dissolved completely. Add ginger and increase heat, cook until it reaches setting point 220 F.

Transfer marmalade to hot sterilized jars, leaving 1/4 inch headspace. Cover tightly with lid.

Place jars in a hot water bath. Process for 10 minutes. Cool completely at room temperature.

Store in a cool, dark place. Keep refrigerated once opened.

15. Orange Marmalade

Ingredients:

- 2 large lemons
- 5 c. sugar
- 4 medium oranges
- 1½ c. water
- 1/8 tsp. baking soda
- 13 oz. pectin
- ½ tsp. butter

Preparation:

Heat the jars in the boiled water to sterilize them. Wash the lids with warm water too.

Peel off the lemons and oranges. Slice them thin and put in baking soda with water in a pan. Cook for 20 minutes and cover the pan. Remove the fruit pulp, get the fruit chopped and save the juice. Include the fruit and juice to mixture and simmer it for 10 minutes. Cover it.

Mix the fruit with lime and sugar in a saucepan. Add butter or margarine for foaming, if required. Heat the mixture over high flame with frequent stirring.

Include pectin, instantly after squeezing the mixture from the pouch. Continue boiling for 1 minute, with continuous stirring. Remove from heat and skim the foam

Ladle the jam in sterilized jars. Cover the lids tightly.

Process them with boiling water method for 10 minutes.

16. Cherry marmalade

Ingredients:

- 4 tbsps. lime

- 4 c. cherries

- 2/3 c. peeled and chopped orange

- 3½ c. sugar

Preparation:

Take a large pan and mix cherries, orange and juice in it. Make them boil at medium heat. Low the flame and add cove with gentle boiling with frequent stirring for 20 minutes. Keep boiling with slow stirring.

Now boil hard with frequent stirring as the mixture gets gel like, for about 30 minutes. Remove the flame.

Pour the hot marmalade into sterilized jars. Remove the air bubble by adding more marmalade. Seal them with lids.

17. Strawberry Lemon Marmalade

Ingredients:

- 6 c. sugar

- 1 tbsp. lime

- ¼ c. peeled and sliced lemons

- 6 tbsps. classic pectin

- 4 c. crushed strawberries

Preparation:

Get the canners prepared. Heat jars with simmering water. Don't boil them. Wash the lids with hot soapy water.

Mix the lemon peels with water in a pan. Cover the pan. Boil the mixture at medium flame and let them boil for about 5 minutes, until the peel gets softened. Drain the liquid.

Now include the lime and strawberries to lemon peel and mix them. Slowly stir the pectin. Heat the mixture at high flame with occasional stirring.

Include sugar and stir until it dissolves. Make the mixture to get boiled for one minutes with constant stirring. Remove the flame and skim off the foam if required.

Pour the jam into sterilized jars with ladle. Cover them with lids and seal them.

Process the jars in boiled water canner for about 10 minutes. Remove the jars and allows them to cool.

18. Gingered Zucchini Marmalade

Ingredients:

- 2 large lemons

- 2 large oranges

- 5 c. shredded zucchini

- 4 c. sugar

- 3 inches chopped and peeled gingerroot

- 1 tart shredded apple

Preparation:

Get the boiled water canner. Heat the jars in simmered water for use. Don't boil. Wash the lids with hot soapy water.

Wash the citrus fruit. Use peeler for removing peel from oranges and slice the peel. Put them in separate pan.

Use sharp knife to cut peel from lemons and oranges. Add the peels in pan.

Make the mixture boil at medium heat with frequent stirring. Boil the mixture until it forms gel like product.

Pour out the jam into sterilized jars. Remove the air bubble and cover them with lids.

Process the jars in boiled water canner for about 10 minutes. Allow them to cool.

19. Meyer Lemon Marmalade

Ingredients:

- 5 c. sugar

- 6 c. water

- 2 medium lemons

- 2 oz. Meyer lemons

- ¼ c. lime

Preparation:

Cut the Meyer lemons lengthwise and put them in stainless steel oven. Add water in it and boil them at reduced heat. Allow them to simmer, uncovered for 90 minutes until lemons get softened and liquid gets syrupy. Press the lemons to generate the juice. Remove heat, cover and allow it to stand at room temperature for whole night.

As the lemons are simmering, take some more Meyer lemons and cut them lengthwise while removing their seeds and cut them into slices. Put them in enameled or stainless steel oven. Add more water in it. Make them boil at reduced heat, allow them to simmer, uncovered for 30 minutes with occasional stirring. Remove the heat and cover them. Let them stand at room temperature.

Pour the lemon mixture via strainer in oven included the lemon slices, press them with wooden spoon to release the juice. Discard the pulp.

Add sugar and lime to the slices. Bring them to boil at high flame, reduce the flame to medium, cook, while keeping them uncovered and stirring for 45 minutes.

Pour out hot marmalade in the sterilized jars. Remove the air bubble and cover them with lids.

Process the jars in boiled water canner for about 10 minutes. Allow them to cool.

20. Three-Citrus Marmalade

Ingredients:

- 3 large lemons

- 6 c. sugar

- 4 medium navel oranges

- 2 pink grapefruit

354

- 4 c. poached zest liquid

Preparation:

Wash the fruit thoroughly and let them dry. Use the peeler to remove the zest of fruit. Cut the zest into strips by using fine confetti. Mix the zest in the pot along with 6 cups of water. Make them boil at reduced flame and allow them to simmer for 30 minutes.

As the zest cooks, cut the white pith off the fruit and separate their membranes.

Drain the zest and save the liquid or cooking.

Take a large stainless steel pot, add zest in it with citrus fruit, 6 cups of sugar, 4 cups of liquid from the zest, and cheesecloth roll. Boil them and cook instantly as the mixture gets heated to 220 degrees.

Stir them before removing the flame for helping the zest to become spread evenly throughout the marmalade.

Pour out hot marmalade into the sterilized jars. Remove the air bubble and cover them with lids.

Process the jars in boiled water canner for about 10 minutes. Allow them to cool.

21. Tangerine Marmalade Recipe:

Ingredients:

- ½ tsp. vanilla extract

- 5½ c. sugar

- 12 oz. tangerines

- 3 lbs. kumquats

- ½ c. vanilla bean

Preparation:

Cut the fruits from the half and remove the flesh and skin. Cut them into thin slices. This will make 2 cups of the kumquat rinds.

Use fine mesh peeler to remove the zest of tangerines, be careful about the thin skin of tangerines.

Cut the peel of tangerines and divide the fruit into two. Put the segments of tangerine in a bowl. Collect the pulp of fruit in a separate bowl.

Mix the slices of kumquat with its juice, zests of tangerine, pulp of tangerines, sugar and water. Boil them, reduce the heat from medium to low and cook the mixture for about 15 minutes. Remove the flame.

Take a large pot containing water and boil it. Put the jars in it along with lids. Pour the hot jam into these sterilized jars. Cover them with lids tightly and allow them to get cooled.

Homemade Dairy Products

This part is a great read for everyone who is keen on maintaining good health. It explains the benefits of consuming organic dairy products and proceeds to teach you how to make those products step by step. One impressive thing about the book is that the methods it explains are not only easy for everyone, but they do not require any specialized apparatus. Whatever you need to make your yoghurt, cheese or butter can be found in any ordinary kitchen.

Another thing you will find impressive is the rich content about the various dairy products. You will learn a host of benefits that come with dairy products, and realize that their usefulness is generally underrated. You will also like the fact that while you can vouch for the fact that your DIY dairy products are organic, you still get to save a substantial amount of money making them at home than when you would buy them from food stores or supermarkets.

Welcome and learn how to make organic nutritious dairy products the most cost-effective and convenient way!

Benefits of Organic Dairy Products

Dairy products are foods made out of milk. Milk and dairy products are very nutritious, and once you are consuming milk, you are very close to completing a balanced diet. Whenever you consume dairy products, you improve your overall health, particularly that of your bones. The main nutrients found in milk and dairy products include minerals such as calcium, potassium, magnesium and also phosphorus. They also have a range of vitamins – B12, B1, B2, B6, A, E and D. They also have niacin, riboflavin and folate. The other very important nutrient in milk is the protein.

Another thing that puts dairy products in a unique position is the fact that a good number of vegetarians get their proteins and essential minerals from dairy products. Yet they are able to avoid high intake of saturated fats by consuming low fat milk or low fat dairy products. In short, you can consume dairy products and still not raise your cholesterol levels. Results of a study conducted in Spain, involving in excess of 5,000 grown-up, indicated that consumers of skimmed milk and low-fat milk were far less likely to suffer from high blood pressure – actually 54% less likely – compared to adults who took no low-fat dairy products or none at all. Those adults were seen to have that advantage over a period of 2yrs.

Consumption of Dairy Products on the Rise

People who like to follow trends may wish to note that Americans have reduced their milk consumption over time, and even of butter. However, this is no indication they are abandoning dairy products. What they are doing is just taking to dairy products that are somewhat different from the traditional ones. For example, consumption of cheese has been on the rise, and the same case applies to premium ice-cream. And it is good the consumers can opt to consume low fat dairy products because they are there and their labels indicate whether their percentage of fat is low.

As an example of how rich dairy products are, take a cup of low-fat yoghurt. If you consume this on a daily basis, it will be providing ⅓ of the required daily calcium intake, and also 17% of the required protein intake. As for Vitamin D, your body may be able to make enough of its own, but that is only if you live in a place that has ample sunshine. Instead of risking deficiency of important vitamins and minerals, it is advisable to consume daily products, because sometimes cereals and other products that are fortified with the nutrients do not provide them in high percentages. For instance, results of a study on a group of adolescents in Finland who consumed products fortified with calcium and Vitamin D were beaten in bone thickness as well as density by another group of adolescents who consumed cheese itself.

Benefits of Nutrients in Dairy Products

1. Calcium

Calcium is great for bone building and strengthening, and also in strengthening the teeth. When the body has sufficient calcium, you develop optimal bone mass, meaning you are not at risk of breaking your bones at the slightest fall. Experts say if you can have three cups of dairy or their equivalent, your optimal bone mass can be well maintained.

A study performed by Spanish researchers concluded that the best source of calcium if you are looking to avoid heart problems is low fat dairy products. They relate it to the proteins involved, which are similar to those found in whey, and which have been known to act like the drugs used to lower blood pressure.

2. Potassium

Potassium is one mineral that helps to keep your blood pressure under control. That is why you need to consume milk, yoghurt or soymilk. Soymilk is a beverage made out of soy, and it is rich in potassium.

3. Vitamin D

Vitamin D helps to regulate the absorption of calcium as well as phosphorus, even as it helps in bone building. Sometimes milk products are fortified with Vitamin D just like soy products, and this makes them an even richer source of the vitamin. Other foods that are commonly fortified with Vitamin D are breakfast cereals, but these are normally not as rich as milk in nutrients.

4. Probiotics

The good bacteria in the yoghurt, referred to as probiotics, can help fight bad bacteria in cases of diarrhea, hence slowing down diarrhea or possibly stopping it entirely. They are also handy in cases of vaginal infections, for the same reason that they effectively fight bad bacteria that would mostly be the cause of such infections. The probiotics are also capable of drastically reducing the symptoms of Irritable Bowel Syndrome or IBS. When suffering this condition, not only do you have uncomfortable bowel movements, you also bloating and abdominal pains.

For people who are concerned about the fat in milk, they can consume low fat dairy products, because those ones have minimum solid fat content. On the overall, organic dairy products are great in improving and maintaining health. And, of course, people usually look younger than their age when they are in good health. They also feel younger, not only because they have strong muscles and the various body systems work well, but also because their bones are strong. This means that for such people, even with advancing age, osteoporosis is pushed away.

When you consume dairy products on a regular basis, you get to lower your risk of heart related ailments as well as diabetes type 2, the type of diabetes that is acquired usually from your lifestyle. A study done by Iranian researchers and targeting men and women, who totaled 827, showed that consuming dairy products, particularly milk, cheese and yoghurt, helped the waistline to remain unexpanded. The metabolic rate of the individuals in the group was also great. Efficient metabolic rate and a trim waistline is a sign of good health, especially a sign of low risk of diabetes and cholesterol related ailments.

Dairy products are also highly recommended for children and adolescents, particularly for that role of bone development.

All Milk is Great for Dairy Products

Sometimes you see whole milk, skimmed milk, milk with a certain butter fat percentage from another, and you may wonder if one is better for making healthy dairy products than another. However, despite the fact already mentioned about whole milk having more saturated fat than skimmed (fatless) milk, the rest of the health benefits remain equal. In short, whether you use whole milk or skimmed milk, you can be assured all the essential nutrients will be present; including calcium, protein and even Vitamin D.

What happens to have the different milk varieties of packed or bottled milk is that all fat is extracted, and the milk is left without any fat, or something is added to suit a certain category of consumers. After removal of fat, at some point some fat is returned to some categories of milk, giving each category its own percentage of fat. Just to give you a good perspective, the butter fat percentage in whole milk is generally 3.5%.

There are times you may wish to make dairy products at home instead of buying ready-made ones from stores, and you may be concerned about the fat level in the milk available. For that reason, this chapter has a list of different categories of milk with their different fat percentages. To help you understand the implication of that percentage in your diet, we shall give you the fat concentration in weight as well.

Fat Level In Dairy Milk Categories

1. Whole dairy milk

It has 3.5% fat, which translates to 8g of fat, 5g of those being saturated fat. An 8oz serving of this whole milk, a cup's estimate, bears 150 calories; 8g protein; 12g carbohydrates, 11g of those being from sugar.

2. 2% Dairy Milk

In an 8oz serving of this category of milk, there is 5g of fat, and calories are 120. The rest of the nutrients are almost the same, although the milk with less fat often exceeds a little bit whole milk in carbohydrates. This is because the amount of fat in whole milk means less lactose.

3. 1% Dairy Milk

This percentage of fat translates to 2.5g of fat. An 8oz serving of this category of milk provides 100 calories.

4. Skim Milk

This is the category of milk that has no percentage of fat whatsoever. Essentially, therefore, it has zero grams of fat. For an 8oz serving of this milk, there are 80 calories.

5. Buttermilk

To get buttermilk, you need to add some active cultures to your original milk. The addition of the cultures leads to production of lactic acid in the milk, and ultimately your milk develops a thick texture, coupled with a tart taste. However, in years gone by, any mention of buttermilk brought to mind the liquid that remained as residue after the milk or its cream had been used to make butter.

For anyone enjoying the taste of buttermilk, you will still benefit from its nutrition, because although all its fat has been extracted, it still has high levels of potassium, phosphorus and calcium, as well as riboflavin and Vitamin B12.

6. Lactose-free Dairy Milk

What is lactose? Well, it is that sugar that is naturally present in milk. Some people are unable to digest it well, and that is mostly because they do not have the enzyme responsible for breaking down that particular sugar.

However, it does not mean you cannot enjoy dairy products owing to your lactose intolerance. There are ways of making organic milk fit for people with the lactose intolerance. Firms that process milk and package it have found a way around the problem, and it entails adding a little bit of lactase into the milk. Lactase is the same enzyme you would find in your small intestines, and which helps to break down the lactose in milk. Once you add the lactase into your milk, it breaks down the natural sugar in the milk, and anyone, including the people with lactose intolerance can consume it and not suffer indigestion or any other lactose related problem.

Dairy Nutrition as per FDA

When you buy consumer products from the supermarket or from stores, you probably see the nutritional value on the packaging. If only you could tell the exact nutritional value of foods that you prepare at home, it can be very helpful in monitoring how healthy you are eating. It also helps to know the amount to serve individual members of your family, especially if there are some with certain intolerances.

You will see here below the level of nutrition you would expect to have in a serving of dairy milk, in the context of the recommended daily nutrient intake. Consider one serving to be around 250mm of milk or an ordinary cup.

The Food and Drug Administration (FDA) has its guidelines made public in the US, and so you can confidently use them to gauge the nutritional value of your foods. The list here below shows the percentage of nutrition you will have covered by consuming a product with the equivalent of one serving of dairy.

(i) Calcium

One dairy serving provides 30% of your daily calcium requirement, and calcium is the main nutrient responsible for making your body and teeth strong.

(ii) Riboflavin

One dairy serving provides 25% of your daily riboflavin requirement, and riboflavin is great at promoting the growth of your body and production of red blood cells. It also helps to enhance your metabolism.

(iii)   Phosphorus

One serving of dairy provides 25% of your daily phosphorus requirement. Phosphorus serves to strengthen your bones.

(iv)   Potassium

One dairy serving provides 11% of your daily potassium requirement. Potassium is a mineral known to regulate the fluid balance in your body. It also helps in regulation of your blood pressure.

(v) Vitamin D

One dairy serving provides 25% of your daily Vitamin D requirement. Vitamin D is credited with promoting your body's absorption of Vitamin D.

(vi)   Vitamin B

One dairy serving provides 22% of your daily Vitamin B requirement. This vitamin is known to help in converting food to energy.

(vii)   Vitamin A

One dairy serving provides 10% of your daily Vitamin A requirement. Vitamin A is great in improving your vision and keeping your skin healthy.

(viii)   Niacin

One dairy serving provides 10% of your daily Niacin requirement. Niacin, also referred to as nicotinic acid, is a compound credited with enhancing blood circulation.

How to Make Organic Yoghurt

There is a big advantage in you making your own organic yoghurt even when there are some available in stores and food stores. Talking of organic dairy products, they are those products made from milk that has been known to have no trace of antibiotics, growth hormones, or any other artificial components injected into the producing animals. At the same time, those organic dairy products have no artificial ingredients added when making them. For example, organic yoghurt is made out of milk alone.

DIY yoghurt making is not only advantageous because you are certain the nature of milk you are using, but it is also great at saving you precious money. All the cost that is loaded on the price of milk because of packaging and overheads do not hurt your pocket when you make your yoghurt at home. And to cap it all, making your yoghurt is fun, and calls for no special equipment. All you need is fresh milk and a yoghurt starter – essentially some culture.

Yoghurt Making Method

(1) Begin by identifying a yoghurt starter

You can buy some ready yoghurt starter culture, or if you had yoghurt before, you might have saved some little amount to use as your starter.

(2) Identify the fresh milk to use

As already explained earlier in the book, you will choose a different type of milk if you want your yoghurt thick from when you want your yoghurt light. At the same time, you will vary your milk type depending on whether you are particular with the fat level.

(3) Take your culture and add it to your milk

Warm your milk up to around 25°C, and then add your starter culture. The assumption here is that you are using mesophilic culture, otherwise when using thermophilic culture you need to heat your milk up to a temperature of between 40°C – 45°C. So, the temperature should be a maximum of 77°F for mesophilic yoghurt starter and 112°F when the starter is thermophilic.

(4) Allow undisturbed milk culturing

As the process takes place, it is important to ensure the temperature does not fall completely. It actually needs to remain constant, and that is why it is recommended you put it in some place with lighting. You could, for instance, put your culturing milk in your oven with the lighting on, but with the heat turned off. Then leave the milk undisturbed for a while. The longer hours you let it stand, the thicker it becomes, and the tarter the taste becomes.

What to Check in the Process

As the culturing process takes place and before the time you have set is up, you are likely to see the yoghurt separating into some whey or liquid of sorts, and some solid part made of curds.

That liquid part is good and nutritious, and it is fine if you would like to stir it back into your yoghurt. Alternatively, you could strain it off and then use it in some cooking or some future culturing. The reason the separation takes place is either that the culturing process has been extra fast, or it has taken extra long. Whatever the reason, you need to keep a keen eye on the process, because once the solids in the milk begin to separate, it cannot be long before the bacteria begin to die. Yet you want your yoghurt rich in active bacteria, because that is good bacteria helpful to your health.

(5) Stop the culturing process

Store your yoghurt in a refrigerator. It is advisable to refrigerate your yoghurt, in fact, for the first 6hrs after you have prepared it, during which time the culturing process stops. Stopping the culturing process in a timely manner ensures the good bacteria remains intact, and hence you have good quality yoghurt.

It is also important to note that after you have exposed the yoghurt to some extreme cold and stopped the fermentation initiated by the starter culture, the yoghurt does not resume fermentation even if you decide later to store the yoghurt at room temperature.

Thickening Your Yoghurt

If you want your yoghurt thick, you can simply drain off the whey – the liquid separated from the curds – and then remain with the solid part. This is commonly referred to as

Greek-style yoghurt. Of course, some people use thickeners that are readily available in the market, but you can avoid them when you are interested in purely organic yoghurt.

Practical Example of Making Yoghurt

The ingredients you need:

(i) Fresh Milk – ½ gallon
(ii) Organic yoghurt – ½ cup

You can add flavoring to your yoghurt if you are using whole milk, otherwise, leave it unflavored. Also expect thick yoghurt that feels quite creamy if the milk you are using is whole. And remember your best option if you are trying to strictly avoid saturated fat is to use skim milk as opposed to whole milk.

To establish how organic your half cup of organic yoghurt is, you need to look at the container label before buying to confirm the yoghurt contains live cultures; that the cultures in that yoghurt are active. The way to do this is by reading the bacteria listed. Yoghurt contains good bacteria and they are the ones that help convert fresh milk to yoghurt. Amid the commonest bacteria in yoghurt, technically referred to as the cultures, are L. Bulgaricus; L. Casei; S. Thermophilus; L. Acidophilus; and Bifidus. They are also termed probiotics and are the ones that make the yoghurt extra healthy for you.

It is important to note that the more variety of bacteria your cultured yoghurt has the better, because the bacteria all work differently. L. Acidophilus, otherwise known as *Lactobacillus acidophilus* or just *acidophilus*, makes your intestines its habitat, and it is known to be the strongest in fighting bad cholesterol in your body. L. Bulgaricus in full is *Lactobacillus Bulgaricus*, and it also helps improve digestion. It is also very helpful in

370

the management of the liver disease, allergic rhinitis, IBS, eczema, tooth decay and other dental problems, colic and other health conditions.

Easy Way to Make Organic Butter

Why would anyone wish to make butter? For one, it is relatively cheap to make your own butter at home, and again you can put the amount of salt you want instead of buying either salted or salt-free butter. Butter is also rich in nutrients, beginning with the eyesight strengthening Vitamin A, which is also great at promoting the health of your skin, your teeth, as well as body tissue and membranes. Butter is also credited with reducing the risk of cancer.

Ingredients to use in Butter Making

1. Organic cream (heavy) – 2 cups

2. Sea salt

Method of Butter Making

- Get a food processor ready

- Pour your milk cream into the food processor

- Process the cream for around 10 minutes

- What you will notice is your cream having turned into some whipped cream that is pretty thick.

- Continue to process the cream in your food processor

As you continue processing the cream, you will notice the conversion from a thick cream into some grainy pieces within some butter milk. Essentially, it will be the liquid part of the cream getting segregated from the solid part.

- Eliminate the liquid

Drain the liquid, which is the buttermilk, from the food processor, to be left with the grainy solid cream.

- Remove the butter pieces from the food processor

A lot of the butter will be attached to the sides of the food processor, and you need to scrape it off.

- Put that butter into a colander

A colander is a bowl with perforations, one that is ideal for straining off liquids from food. Not only will it let go any drops accompanying your butter, it will also be useful as you try to rinse your butter.

- Use cold water to rinse your butter

As you pour cold clean water on the butter, the butter will be clean and the perforations in the colander will continuously release the water after use. You are encouraged to keep turning your butter gently using a spoon as you pour cold clean water over it, until you notice the water remaining clear. This would be a sign that your butter is clean.

- Squeeze out the last drops

To ensure you have butter that is well solid, use a wooden spoon or something just as good, to press out any drops of liquid remaining in the butter. To eliminate the liquid effectively, use the wooden spoon to smash the butter, and that move is meant to ensure that what you are left with is genuine butter that is not inflated by liquid.

- Transfer the butter to a clean bow or a clean jar

- Keep the butter container in the refrigerator or in a freezer

You can use this butter as you wish, and as long as you maintain it clean in your cold storage, it can last for many months without going bad.

Different Ways of Making Organic Cheese

Cheese is one of the popular dairy products that have been in use for many centuries. You can make yours in different shapes and textures as you wish. As a dairy product, it is rich in vitamins, proteins and minerals, and so it is not only consumed for its nice taste but also for its nutritional value.

How To Make Fresh Cream Cheese

One of the easiest ways to make cheese is to use cream. This one will be approximately 7oz.

Ingredients required:

1. Fresh milk (raw) – 4 cups

2. Sea salt – ½ teaspoon

3. Buttermilk – 2 tablespoons

The Procedure:

- Begin by filling four cups with the raw milk

- Place the cups on a saucepan

- Now place the saucepan on a fire source

- Let the milk absorb the heat slowly until it reaches 90°F

- Next, take the sea salt and add it to your hot milk

- Follow that by adding the buttermilk into that milk

Suppose you don't have buttermilk? Well, you can make your own substitute.

How To Make Buttermilk Conveniently

- Measure fresh milk that is raw – 2 tablespoons

- Measure white vinegar – ½ teaspoon

- Mix the two ingredients in a tiny bowl

- Keep stirring for a period between 5min and 10min

That's it – you've just quickly and conveniently prepared your buttermilk.

- Take a clean glass container the size of ½ gallon

- Put the milk mixture in the glass container and place the lid back tightly

- Place the container horizontally on a level surface. The container will essentially be lying on its side.

- Let it remain in that position and at room temperature for a period of 8hrs to 24hrs.

The idea is to wait until the milk has clabbered. Do not be surprised if the milk mixture takes longer to clabber in a cold environment. It is normal if it is the cold season. It has been known to take up to 30hrs.

Observation to Expect

Once your milk is well clabbered, you should expect it to appear like fresh yoghurt; or somewhat like gelatin.

- Take a clean jelly strainer and put your clabbered milk in it

- Alternatively, you can use a thin tea or cheese cloth to do your straining. Just ensure you have layered the piece around four times.

- Leave your clabbered milk to strain for a period of around 8hrs. All along you will be getting rid of the whey, and your residue, which is the cream cheese, will be getting thicker.

Great! That easily, you have yourself some nutritious, nice tasting cream cheese.

Just to make your cheese even more nutritious and all the more delicious, you could add:

- Some raw honey.

- Some raw nuts (probably walnuts)

How to Make Cheese from Sour Milk

Here you are going to learn how to make cheese using raw milk that is sour. In short, if ever your raw milk turns sour inadvertently, probably because you did not put it in the refrigerator, you need not discard it. You can still benefit from its nutrients by making cheese.

The required ingredient here is:

1. Sour milk (raw organic) – 4 cups

Method of preparing the cheese:

- Pour the sour milk in a mason jar made of glass or in such other container, provided it has a lid. The ideal jar size in this case would be ½gallon equivalent.

- Close the container tightly

- Put the milk containing jar in a safe position at room temperature

- Soon the milk will begin to clabber

- Once the sour milk has clabbered, you need to pour it into a strainer or a tea cloth. A cheese cloth would also work.

If you are to use a cloth, it does well when folded nicely around 4 times. The whey, which is the liquid part of clabbered milk, will begin dripping, and you can save it and use it in any way you wish later. In fact, you can use the whey as a starter culture to make yoghurt at a later date. You can also use it when making smoothies any time you want. The only condition is you store it under refrigeration, in which case it can last for a good 6mths.

- Depending on how soft or hard you wish your cheese to be, you need to leave it straining for a period of between 2hrs and 8hrs.

How to Make Butter

This part seeks to educate people about butter and to affirm that it has very many health benefits, and also to explain why butter and related dairy products are within everyone's reach. The book goes further to explain why butter and every other related product is beneficial to your health. You may be interested to know that ghee, which is merely known as a dairy product, is actually a direct product of butter, and that it has special benefits beyond the ones you generally get from butter and other dairy products.

Luckily, this book has clear information on how you can make your own butter, margarine, and even ghee. It also teaches you, in a very simple way, how to flavor your butter while still keeping it all-natural. The book also teaches you how to make low fat butter without losing butter's cherished natural flavor. One of the amazing things this book brings out is that you can enjoy butter and its derivatives without spending too much money.

Read on...

What, Really, Is Butter?

Butter is one of the most popular dairy products. It is one of the products that would be greatly missed if cow milk were to become unavailable, especially among vegetarians. To get butter, you have got to rid the milk of other components, to be left with the fatty portion. This means you can derive butter from milk and still make other products from your milk.

Butter is liked a lot for its rich flavor. In fact, culinary dishes made with butter distinguish themselves from those that are made with ordinary oils and fats. Many people have a preference for butter when it comes to their daily cooking, baking, or even applying directly on bread.

Butter Is High In Nutrition

Butter is one of those foods very convenient to have when unable to venture outdoors freely, for instance, in times of terribly bad weather or times when security is questionable. This is because it is high in calories. In fact, just a single tablespoon of butter has calories equivalent to those in a medium size banana, which are estimated to be 101. Any time you do not have enough food to give you energy, butter comes in handy with its host of fatty acids that are in excess of 400.

Butter also has vitamins, minerals, protein, different categories of fat, including Omega 6 and a little Omega 3. What it has little of are carbohydrates and sugar. The particular

378

vitamins in butter are A and D, E and B12, and also K2. This means you have yourself an antioxidant because of Vitamin E, and you may be able to keep osteoporosis at bay, courtesy of Vitamin K. Butter also has a significant amount of water.

Apart from fueling your body, butter is also credited with reducing inflammation affecting the digestive system, as well as with contributing to the healing of Crohn's disease. And whereas some people may have concerns because of butter's fat content, it is good to know it poses no risk when consumed in moderate quantities. In any case, you can benefit from the presence of mono-saturated fats, which are actually a quarter of the entire fat content in butter, and have your heart protected.

Low Fat Butter

Sometimes people worry about the fat in butter, but as already mentioned, since you are not actually eating butter itself but using a little of it at a time to give your food flavor, and to reap other nutritional benefits, it is singularly unlikely to increase your waistline. However, it is alright to seek out low fat butter, and this mainly the one made out of vegetable extracts. The plant sterols and the stanols found in the low butter catalyze absorption of the LDLs, the fats with high cholesterol, thus reducing the risk of developing high blood pressure.

You can use low fat butter, which many people prefer to view as butter substitute in view of the fact that regular butter is made out of dairy, in recipes that have butter as a requisite ingredient. Owing to the complex process of extracting fats from plants, you may find it a little difficult to make your own low fat butter at home. However, you can always buy some from the supermarket or food stores. As you do your shopping, ensure you only pick the low fat butter that is refrigerated, lest you risk buying some that is stale. One great thing with this plant based butter is that it does not only have low percentages of saturated fats, it is actually free of trans-fats.

How to Prepare Nicely Flavored Butter Recipes

What would you say are some benefits of making your own butter? Well, speak of freshness. You can truly vouch for its date of manufacture – the date you prepare your butter in your own small way – the manner of storage, and, hence, how long it is likely to take before it starts losing its flavor and general freshness. At the same time, you can say for certain there are no artificial or chemical preservatives included in the ingredients, because you did not actually put any; something you cannot vouch for with mass produced butter.

You also have the advantage of choosing your preferred flavor when you prepare your butter at home as opposed to getting some off the shelves. This chapter will show you how you can prepare butter from scratch. It will also show you how you can make butter in different delicious flavors, while still retaining the natural goodness of regular butter.

The Basics of Butter Making

Ingredients:

1.   Heavy dairy cream – 3 cups
2.   Salt – 1 teaspoon
3.   Ice water – 5 tablespoons

Have your food processor ready and pour all your cream in it. Alternative equipment is a hand mixer, whether an electric one or otherwise.

Method:

- Begin to whip your cream and continue till it separates.

After around 2½ minutes of whipping the cream, it will appear like it is thickening, and around the 4th minute the entire cream will be wholly separated. What you will be looking at is a cloudy liquid, but with solids of butter within it.

- It is now time to pour in your ice-cold water.

The reason you add in this water is to help further solidify the butter solids, and to keep the liquid, which is essentially what is known as buttermilk, distinctly separate.

- Next, take a bowl and put a sieve over it, and then pour in it the creamy contents.
- You can refrigerate the buttermilk in your bowl and use it later, probably when doing some baking or marinating.
- Next, focus on eliminating as much liquid as possible from the solid in your sieve, and you can do this by squeezing the contents with your bare hands. Your plan is to remain with dry butter. You can even help the drying process by the use of a clean kitchen towel; or some cheesecloth.

This butter recipe that takes you only 10 minutes to prepare is meant to give you butter of 300g. in weight. You can store it in your refrigerator for 6wks during which time you can add it to your baking, in different dishes, or even apply it on bread.

Now that you have learnt how to make butter from fresh dairy cream, it is time to learn how to give the flavor of your choice to your butter. The advantage you have once you know how to give your butter different flavors is that you can make a large amount of butter at once, slice it into chunks, and keep them frozen. Then any time you want to use some butter with a particular flavor, you just pick one chunk, defrost it, and make your specially flavored butter. With your knowledge and skills, you will not have to buy flavored butter off store shelves.

Recipes for Flavored Butter

(1) Garlic-flavored Butter

Ingredients enough for 8 servings:

(a)   Unsalted butter (softened) – ½ cup

(b)   Salt – ½ cup

(c)   Black pepper (ground) – ¼ teaspoon

(d)   Extra virgin oil – 2 tablespoons

(e)   Garlic cloves (crushed) – 4

(f)   Parsley (freshly chopped) – 2 tablespoons

As for nutrition, one serving of this butter constitutes 0.6g carbohydrates, 14.9g fat, and 134kcal of calories, among other nutrients.

Method of Flavoring Your Butter

You need the ingredients to be at room temperature as you begin to use them.

- Set a bowl before you
- Put in your softened butter, spices of your choice, the herbs and all the other ingredients you have prepared.
- Mix all the ingredients in the bowl thoroughly.
- Set a parchment paper and scoop butter onto it using a spoon
- Next, wrap up the paper and roll it into the shape of a log.

383

- Reach of the paper ends and twist them in order to seal in the contents.
- Store the wrapped butter contents in your refrigerator for around one week.
- If you think you will not need the butter soon, you need to store it in the freezer, where it can safely remain for 6mths.

Note it is always good to slice the butter before freezing, so that you only defrost the piece you need for every use when time comes. Another good storage alternative is spooning your butter into some silicon tray for refrigeration. It actually helps you control your portions.

This method of preparing butter is suitable for all the other recipes in this book. As such, what will follow henceforth are the different sets of ingredients for the different butter recipes.

(2)   *Bacon-cheese flavored butter*

Ingredients enough for 9 servings:

(a)   Softened butter (unsalted) – ½ cup

(b)   Salt – ¼ teaspoon

(c)   Black pepper (ground) – ¼ teaspoon

(d)   Crumbled bacon (crisp slices) – 2 large slices

(e)   Cheddar cheese (grated) – ½ cup

(f)   Spring onion/Chives (freshly chopped) – 1 tablespoon

For general nutrition, this recipe has 0.1g carbohydrates, 11.6g fat, and 110kcal of calories among other nutrients.

(3)   *Jalapeno-Lime flavored butter*

Ingredients for 7 servings:

(a)   Softened butter (unsalted) – ½ cup

(b)   Salt – ½ teaspoon

(c)   Black pepper (ground) – ¼ teaspoon

(d)   Jalapeno pepper (finely chopped) – 1

(e)   Cilantro (freshly chopped) –2 tablespoons

(f)   Lime juice – 1 tablespoon

You will benefit from carbohydrates 0.3g, fat 13.2g, calories 117kcal, and other nutrients from each serving of this butter.

(4)   *Harissa flavored butter*

Ingredients enough for 8 servings:

(a)   Softened butter (unsalted) – ½ cup

(b)   Salt – ¼ teaspoon

(c)   Black pepper (ground) –¼ teaspoon

(d)   Harissa paste (from different spices, including chili) – 3 tablespoons

One serving of this recipe has 0.7g of carbohydrates, 12.2g of fat, 112kcal of calories, and more.

(5)*Butter with the Thai curry flavor*

Ingredients for 7 servings:

(a)   Softened butter (unsalted) – ½ cup

(b)   Salt – ¼ teaspoon

(c)   Black pepper (ground) – ¼ teaspoon

(d)   Thai curry paste – 2 tablespoons

As for nutrition in one serving, this butter contains 0.6g carbohydrates, 13.2g fat, and 119kcal in calories, among other nutrients.

(6)   Lemon-Herb flavored butter

Ingredients for 7 servings:

(a)   Softened butter (unsalted) – ½ cup

(b)   Salt – ½ teaspoon

(c)   Black pepper (ground) – ¼ teaspoon

(d)   Lemon juice (fresh) – 1 tablespoon

(e)   Lemon zest – 2 teaspoons

(f)   Garlic (crushed) – 2 cloves

(g)   Mixed herbs, e.g. basil, thyme and dill (freshly chopped) – 2 tablespoons

As for nutrition, each serving of this butter provides 0.5g carbohydrates, 13.2g fat, 118kcal of calories, and more.

How to Make Margarine at Home

First of all, let us just mention that there is some subtle difference between margarine per se and spreads. For spreads, the fat content is usually lower than margarine. In fact there is the requirement that margarine be made out of 80% fat. On the contrary, spreads could have the fat and oil content as low as 60%, the rest being water and other ingredients with nutrients like protein. However, on a day-to-day use, many people speak of margarine interchangeably.

How Did Margarine Enter The Butter Market?

Well, they say necessity is the mother of invention. It is true in this case because during the industrial revolution of the latter years of 1860s, the urban population was too high that sellers of butter could not meet its demand. And that was when a Frenchman by the name of Hyppolyte Mege Mouries came up with the ingenious idea of making margarine. With his background as a chemist, he came up with a formula that brought out a product so popular it overshadowed butter.

Of course, the reason for the high demand for margarine at the time was its price; butter being too expensive for the working class.

Recommended ingredients

1. Coconut oil – 30g
2. Vegetable oil (e.g. sunflower or olive oil) – 45ml
3. Milk – 10ml
4. Egg yolk – 10ml
5. Lemon juice – 2.5ml
6. Salt – 2.5ml

Method of Preparation

*   Begin by heating your coconut oil using a microwave; just enough to melt it well
*   Take a bowl and put in a good amount of ice
*   Then take a beaker and place it on that bowl
*   Now pour in your vegetable oil

- Add in the coconut oil
- Using a stick blender, mix the two ingredients till you see a milky shade, with the content well emulsified. 60 seconds are sufficient for the blending process.
- Next, add in your egg yolk, the milk, the salt, as well as the lemon juice.
- Mix the contents and blend them until the mixture has all its constituent ingredients evenly distributed.
- Your margarine is about done, and what remains is for you to refrigerate it for setting purposes.

That is how easy you can go through a DIY margarine making process, using oils of your choice and not having to spend money in food stores buying ready-made margarine.

Note that the margarine you have just made does not have the color of the margarine you buy from stores and supermarkets. However, you have done the hard part and giving your margarine color is quite simple. If you wanted to have a yellowish product, all you needed to do was add some drops of yellow food color as you finalized the first stage of blending. Simple!

How to Make Your Margarine Healthier

One advantage you have when you choose to make your own margarine is to include ingredients you prefer, reduce or get rid of ingredients you do not like and, of course, to give your margarine a flavor of your choice.

In this regard, you can opt to include some plant extracts into your margarine recipe in order to introduce plant sterols into your margarine. The plant sterols have the capacity to reduce the bad cholesterol in your body, a positive development as far as keeping away from heart problems is concerned. Also with homemade margarine recipes, you have the option to add spices of your choice, to give your palate a variety of tastes, and in some cases to add unique healing properties from certain spices.

Ghee And Its Benefits

Are you one of those people who imagine ghee to be an oriental ingredient that has nothing to do with other recipes? Well, the fact that ghee is popular in Indian kitchens does not mean you cannot enjoy its flavor and nutritional value too.

The make-up of Ghee

Ghee is even simpler than butter, considering that in butter is comprised of butterfat, water, and milk solids, yet in ghee there is no water and no milk solids. In short, in ghee you have some clarified butter.

Ghee cooks more easily over high temperatures because of the absence of milk solids. Cooking experts prefer to say it has a high smoking point. Ghee actually has a higher smoking point than many cooking oils like coconut oil, canola and the grape seed.

It is funny how ghee came to be, because initially all people knew about was butter. Word has it that butter is as ancient as 2000 BC. It was very popular in

Northern India, then in later years the southerners on the continent sought a way of making their butter last longer. The issue was significant in the south because climatic temperatures there are quite high and hence not allowing a long shelf life for butter and other foods. So the southerners sought to clarify their butter – must have been a trial and error thing at the time. What they produced was clarified butter. So, where is the ghee?

To get ghee, you need to let your clarified butter simmer a little longer. What happens during the process is that the milk solids begin to turn brown. Once you sieve out the caramelized solids, what you remain with is the ghee. As for the flavor, ghee has a nutty flavor that you will not find in ordinary butter.

Simple Method of Making Ghee

- Put butter in a pan
- Put the pan over medium heat

What you should expect to observe in a couple of minutes is your butter splitting three-ways – the topmost layer is some foam while at the bottom should be the solid part (milk solids). Then floating in between the top and the bottom should be what is termed clarified butter.

From here henceforth is the procedure to turn clarified butter into ghee.

- Wait until the butter begins to simmer
- Soon you will notice the water in the butter gradually evaporating
- As the moisture diminishes and the solid part (milky solids) continues to settle at the bottom of your pan, you can hear a sputtering sound.

- Continue heating and you will notice the sputtering sound ending when all the moisture is gone. The part that was the clarified butter will now be golden and more fragrant than the butter initially was. As for the solids at the bottom, they will, by now, be a little brownish.
- Using a spoon, remove the foam that is still showing on the surface
- It is now time to remove your pan from the heat source
- Strain it using a strainer well lined with cheesecloth and into a jar, preferably one made of glass. The intention is to get rid of the milk solids.

After the straining, what you are left with is the ghee.

The Best Way to Store Ghee

Gladly, ghee can last longer than ordinary butter without going stale. It can survive for up to 3mths at room temperature if only you hide it from heat and direct light. However, if you intend to have it for long, it is advisable to store it in your fridge. Once refrigerated, ghee solidifies, and it can last even a year when still fresh. The good thing is it quickly turns into liquid once removed from the refrigerator – just takes between 5 and 10 minutes. In this regards, it behaves like coconut oil.

9 Huge Benefits of Ghee

1. Its smoke point is high

This means it is safer in the kitchen than oils like soybean oil or corn oil, which are mostly genetically modified. Apart from the safety issue, ghee has the capacity to retain most of its essential phytonutrients even when exposed to heat unlike many oils that we consider good for the body. In fact, it is correct to say that ghee is more stable than olive, avocado and other monounsaturated oils, as well as fish oil, flax oil and other polyunsaturated oils. Actually oils like the olive need to be used solely where there is no heating involved; as a salad dressing, for example.

2.   It is rich in Vitamin D, E and A

This richness in soluble vitamins makes ghee good at improving conditions of leaky gut syndrome, Crohn's, Irritable Bowel Syndrome (IBS), and some pancreatic disorders. Ghee also helps a lot with people whose system does not absorb Vitamin A well.

3.   Ghee does not contain lactose or casein

Though essentially derived from dairy milk, ghee does not contain lactose or casein, meaning that people who have related allergies can use ghee without concern.

4.   There is ghee with high levels of conjugated linoleic acid (CLA)

When you are very keen on the health and healing properties of ghee, you can make it from milk from grass-fed cattle. Such ghee has properties that keep bad cholesterol in check, reduce inflammation and tumors, and on the overall, keep reduce body fat.

5.   Helps regulate blood sugar

Ghee is known to support regulation of insulin in the body, and to improve the health of your colon. Other conditions it helps treat include ulcerative colitis and hormonal imbalance.

6. Its taste stands in well for butter

The taste of ghee is so much like butter that people who love butter do not feel shortchanged when they consume ghee instead. Some people have been known to say its taste is even better, still in a butter-like way.

7. It is great in bone strengthening

Ghee is rich in Vitamin K2, which is a fat soluble vitamin that helps in the absorption of important minerals like calcium. Needless to say, calcium is important for bone building. Along the same lines, ghee helps to keep your teeth free from decay. It is also credited with protecting your arteries from atherosclerosis, or more plainly, their calcification.

8. Improves the digestive function

The fatty acids in ghee are known to be of medium chain, just like coconut oil, and so they attract other body fats and help to burn them, and in the process get rid of toxins that are ordinarily difficult to clear. This is to say that ghee can help you lose weight and keep diseases away. Another way ghee helps in weight loss is by improving the function of the gallbladder, which, in turn, catalyzes the working of the digestive system. It also stimulates production of the gastric acid, a factor that also enhances digestion.

9. Ghee helps in detoxification

Once your body is detoxified, you are unlikely to fall ill very easily. Ghee helps in detoxify your body by catalyzing fiber conversion into butyric acid; one known for eliminating toxins.

Simple Clarified Butter and Ghee Recipes

For the recipes in this chapter, you can either use clarified butter or ghee. Either way, your dish will be very palatable.

Flavored steamed potato recipe

This particular clarified butter recipe takes around 40 minutes to prepare, and it makes 4 servings.

Ingredients

(i)   Potatoes – ½ kg

(ii)   Small onion (chopped) – 1

(iii) Garlic (chopped) – 1 teaspoon

(iv) Ginger root (grated) – 1 teaspoon

(v) Lemon juice – 1 tablespoon

(vi) Water – 3 tablespoons

(vii)   Salt – just enough to taste

(viii)   Clarified butter/Ghee – 1 tablespoon

(ix) Cinnamon – a single small stick

(x) Cardamom pods (lightly crushed) – 3

(xi) Cloves – 2

(xii)   Bay leaf (crumbled) – 1

(xiii)   Turmeric (ground) – ½ teaspoon

(xiv)   Cumin seeds – ½ teaspoon

(xv) Yoghurt – ½ cup

(xvi) Garam masala – ½ teaspoon

(xvii) Cilantro (chopped) – 2 tablespoons

Best method of preparation

- Take a saucepan and put in your boiled potatoes
- Pour in water and put the saucepan on fire
- Cover the saucepan and let the potatoes boil
- After 5 minutes of boiling, drain the saucepan

You can prick one of the potatoes lightly with a skewer to gauge if the potatoes are cooked.

- Take your blender and put in the onion and garlic, the ginger, the lemon juice, the water, and appropriate amount of salt, and blend them into puree.
- Next, you need to heat your ghee using a saucepan that you place over medium heat.
- Then put in your cinnamon, the cardamom, the cloves and the bay leaf, and fry them for around 2 minutes.
- After that add your turmeric and ensure you stir the contents as the spicy mixture continues to fry.
- In quick succession, add your blended mixture into the frying pan.

The goal should be to fry the contents until the onion ceases to smell raw. Ideally this should not take more than a minute.

- You now need to rinse your blender with some little water – 2 tablespoons to be precise – and to add that water to the contents in the frying pan.
- Stir that potato mixture and then cover it tightly.
- You need to reduce the heat so that your meal cooks on very low heat.

Let it cook for a period of between 20min and 25min. That is it.

- Take a different pan that is dry and put in your cumin seeds
- Place the pan over medium heat and begin to roast the seeds
- Keep stirring the cumin seeds as they roast until they turn dark brown.
- Next, remove the pan from the heat source and pour your cumin seeds into a bowl
- Embark on pounding the roasted cumin seeds until you have crushed them to a rough state.
- Then add in your yoghurt, the garam masala, and a pinch of salt.

You have now a complete dish to serve. You need to serve your potato dish, which you have made with ghee, and top it with your yoghurt mixture. Then crown it with a sprinkle of cilantro. Enjoy!

For nutritional information, just know each of your servings here constitutes 150 calories, 2.98g fiber, 124mg sodium, 26g carbohydrates, 4g protein, 4g of fat; and only 2g saturated fat and 12mg cholesterol.

The Doro Wat Ethiopian recipe

Though native to Ethiopia, this ghee made chicken stew recipe is appreciated wherever it is prepared across the world.

Ingredients

(i)   Onions (finely chopped) – 3kg
You can use a food processor for the onions to ease the work

(ii)   Large chicken (free-range, preferably) – 1

(iii) White vinegar – 100ml

(iv) Lemon juice – from 1 lemon

(v) Olive oil – 100ml

(vi) Nit'r kibbeh – 3 tablespoons

Nit'r kibbeh is a local name for clarified butter that is commonly used in Ethiopian and Eritrean dishes.

(vii)   Berbere – 6 tablespoons

Berbere is a local name for an Ethiopian chili spice. You can reduce the amount if you do not want your dish too hot.

(viii)   Hard boiled eggs (peeled) – 12

Another recommended mix of spices:

(a) Cardamom – 2 tablespoons

(b) Nigella seeds – 2 tablespoons

(c) Fennel seeds – 2 tablespoons

(d) African basil leaf (optional) – 1 tablespoon

(e) Black peppercorns – 2 teaspoons

(f) Salt – 2 tablespoons

Best method of preparation

- Take a heavy based saucepan and put in your onions
- Use a lid to cover the saucepan and cook the onions over low heat
- Stir the onions occasionally
- Keep your onions cooking without adding a drop of liquid or even oil, until you notice the onions having reduced to around $2/3$.
- As the onions cook, you need to be removing skin from your chicken, and cutting it into pieces. If you want to cut it into 21 pieces the way Ethiopians do, it is well and good.
- Take the vinegar and the lemon juice and mix them in a bowl

- Next, dip in your pieces of chicken, allowing them to remain in there for a period of between 10min and 15min.
- After that drain the chicken.
- It is now time to use a mortar and pestle to grind your mixed spices into a spicy powder.
- Focus on the onions next, adding your oil in the saucepan, the clarified butter and the chili mixture, and stirring the saucepan contents.
- Follow that by adding in the chicken
- Let the chicken cook and boil in its liquid, and then lower the fire to allow your contents to simmer.
- Add in the mixed spices
- Allow the contents to cook and stir occasionally till the chicken is properly cooked. Just ensure the onions do not stick at the bottom of your pan.
- Take a large spoon and skim off whatever oil is floating on the surface of your chicken mixture.
- Now pick each egg at a time and create incisions, so that the food flavor can seep in.
- Once your chicken stew is well cooked, put your eggs in.
- Then remove your meal off the fire.

You now have your Ethiopian chicken stew ready, all cooked with ghee. You can serve it with whatever you want, including rice. Locals serve it with *injera*, a local form of leavened bread.

Honey Making

This chapter, *How to Make Money Beekeeping,* explains how you can invest your meager savings and end up with a million dollar empire within a short time. You will find out how straightforward beekeeping is, and that it is one of the businesses you can embark on with just $1,000 and yet grow your business exponentially.

You will learn the first steps to take once you decide to venture into beekeeping, the different types of bees to choose from, and the best places to target for your market. Moreover, the book teaches you about other bee products that you can earn from beside the honey, without spending an extra cent.

By the time you finish reading the book, you will, very likely, wish to start your own beekeeping project, to supplement the income you earn from your day job.

An Overview of Beekeeping

Are you the material to rear bees and earn income through honey harvesting? Probably yes. Some people have been in formal employment for most of their lifetime, yet they have retired to beekeeping and are doing marvelous. Others are still in their prime and they find beekeeping a serious source of income. However, you need to know how to manage beekeeping the same way you do other business enterprises. You need to seek knowledge of the skills required first, as well as that of marketing your products. Products, yes – and not product – because in beekeeping, it is not just honey you can make money out of. There are other products; and you will not have to incur additional costs to reap from multiple bee products.

Important Points To Note In Bee Management

You want to attend to your bees the way you would other animals, right? Well, when it comes to checking out how your bees are doing in their hives, you do a physical check only when the weather is warm. Otherwise, in the cold season, like in winter, you need to leave the hives alone. And the reasons are simple.

1. In the warm season, you need to ensure you make periodic inspections to see if your bees are doing what you expect them to be doing, like:
   - Is the queen bee laying eggs?
   - Are the workers building honey stores?
   - Is there enough space in your hive for your bee colony to expand?
2. In the cold season, admire your hives from afar. Reason?
   - Your bees do not need you to take food to them just because they are shielding themselves in the hives away from the biting cold. What do they eat then? Well, your colony is comfortable eating the honey already in store. It is as much as the worker bees can do to flutter and keep the queen bee and themselves warm, and they do not need you opening the hive and letting the little warmth they have created escape.
   - The bees let themselves out periodically when the weather is bearable, in order to relieve themselves.

From the points just listed, you are likely to consider the fact that the weather is not uniform everywhere. For that reason, there is no strict program that anyone can prescribe for you as far as management style is concerned. You need to understand your environment and its weather patterns, and then decide the best way to handle your bees. Other factors you need to consider when forming a certain management routine include the types of bees you are keeping, and even the hive style. It is safe to say at the end of the day, you need to tailor your management style according to your personal experience with your bees.

Why Beekeeping Is Not A Dangerous Undertaking

Well, it is not exactly dangerous – not unlike other undertakings like cookery or engineering. One might wonder if a chef doesn't risk getting burnt, or if an engineer doesn't risk getting ground by a machine, but all trades require that you take precautionary measures, so that you keep injuries to a minimum. As they say, as long as you are in the kitchen you can't avoid feeling the heat.

For the beekeeper, there are protective outfits made purposely to ensure the bees do not reach your body and sting you. However, sometimes you may find a bee stuck somewhere within some fold of your outfit, and you may not notice it until it has stung you. Still, there is some good news for you – honeybees are not eager to sting you. They seem to be aware that stinging you is suicidal for them. Yes, when a bee stings you, being a mammal, not only does its barbed stinger remain in your body, but the stinging bee gets disemboweled as it tries to run away, during which time its rear is torn off. Suffice it to say, honeybees sting as a last resort. For most part, they are docile.

Learn About Your Local Bees

Why and how do you learn about your local bees? The reason for learning how the local honeybees behave is that their behavior is greatly influenced by the climate of their area. That is why beekeepers in certain areas may seem more successful than those in other areas. An obvious factor is how warm or cold temperatures in the area are, because the warmer the place is, the more the bees are able to roam around and collect nectar. In warm climates, the foraging season is significantly longer than in relatively cold climates. However, if the area has a very long and cold winter, honeybees will spend most of their time feeding on the honey in store, and probably even require supplementary feeding from the farmer. This simply means that you can expect to harvest more honey in areas with warm climates than you in areas whose climate is mostly cold. Instead of doing trial and error in your learning process, it is advisable to seek advice and guidance from someone in your local area who is already rearing bees.

Understand What Honeybees, Specifically, Are

Honeybees are no different from anything else you may wish to take care of – you need to, first of all, understand what they really are, as opposed to any other bees. It is also important that you know what their needs are, their strengths, as well as their weak points. So, try and learn the lot you can about honeybees, and then narrow down to those in your particular area.

And even once you have begun to rear your own honeybees, it is important that you be observant, so that you can take note of any change of behavior during the visits you make to the hives. You need to be flexible, and that is in order to adjust anything you are doing that affects your bees if the honeybees are reacting negatively. The actions that you take that make your bees healthy and productive are the ones you need to enhance.

Honeybees In Contrast To Other Bees

A honeybee, as you can decipher from its name, is that bee that you can bank on to produce and store honey in one place, where you can find it and use it, and where the bee colony can feed from when the bees cannot venture outside the hive to forage. In fact, honeybees are the only known insects that do not only produce food, but also store it in excess. Besides, honeybees do not only supply people with food, in form of honey, but they also supply them with high value wax. That is precisely the reasons the Europeans who went to America in the 1600s found it attractive to introduce honeybees to that country. Over the years, honeybees have become very valuable in America, and not just for their high value products. They are credited with a significant proportion of crop pollination. That important role the honeybees play in the agricultural system is confined to America alone. Reliable information has it that of the entire world's food crops, 30% are pollinated by honeybees as they seek nectar from one plant to another.

In America, the species of honeybee mostly kept by farmers is the Apis mellifera, and it is the one that the Europeans introduced those many centuries ago. In fact, you'll be hard pressed to find a farmer who keeps any other species of honeybees in America, among the 20,000 species in existent worldwide, even if the country has around 4,400 species of bees (not necessarily honeybees). Some of the bees found in America but not reared by farmers include social bumblebees, solitary tunnel nesting bees, and even solitary ground nesting bees.

Categories and Species of Bees

In order to understand beekeeping and do your beekeeping successfully, it is imperative that you understand what other categories of bees there are besides the honeybees. This will help you to eliminate certain bees when you are taking actions meant to target the honeybees. It is also important for you to know the major specifies of honeybees that exist, and the advantage each of them has, if any, over the others. This helps when you are selecting the honeybees to rear for a business venture.

Honeybees Have Social Castes

How many social castes do honeybees have? Well, the known ones are three, and each one of them has its specific role. Of course there are those that have more than one role, and these roles are important for work to go smoothly within the colony of bees. Once each social caste does its work as expected, the colony survives well and in harmony.

Interesting Characteristics of Bee Social Castes

(1) Queen Bee

Why the queen? Well, lots of reasons. She is well guarded, for one. She does not go out foraging, yet she eats to her fill. Again, she plays a pivotal role in the size of the bee colony, being the one that lays the eggs that ultimately hatch into bees. In fact, in one colony, you will find only one queen bee – so she does not compete with anyone for attention. She is the only bee that reproduces. Sometimes she lays unfertilized eggs, and these eggs hatch into the bees referred to as drones, and at different times she lays fertilized eggs, which later hatch into the bees referred to as workers.

Who Is It That Fertilizes the Queen's Eggs?

Funny enough, it is the queen herself who chooses what bees to fertilize her eggs. She just decides to venture out of the hive one day, and she identifies a location with male bees. She then goes on a mating spree, engaging males to the tune of 80! And then she returns to her hive. It is not for nothing that the queen bee mates with so many partners – she stores all the sperm she returns with from the mating spree, and it is from this sperm bank that she produces young bees for the five or six years that she lives. In short, a virgin queen bee goes out mating, and collects sperms worth a lifetime. Isn't it interesting?

Queen bee does not venture out unnecessarily, and the other time she is known to temporarily move out of the hive is when she spots a swarm of bees and she is drawn to them. That time, being one confident and experienced queen bee, she might decide to join the swarm.

(2) The Worker Bees

These are female bees. And why the heck don't they reproduce like the queen bee? Simple – they are sterile. And since everyone must be useful in the colony, these female bees become the workers. There is good reason why they are termed workers, as they are the ones charged with foraging, with feeding the young bees, cleaning the hive, and even defending the hive from intruders. These workers are the same ones that produce the honey you are looking forward to harvesting, and they are still the same ones that ensure the honey is neatly and securely stored within the hive. In addition, they produce bee wax as well.

The worker bees are one very organized lot. They ensure that each of them plays some role during their lifetime, every one of them working for between 4 and 6 weeks. Unfortunately for them, as they advance in age, their roles within the hive diminish, and they are called upon to venture further away from the hive on duty – which is essentially risky for them.

(3) The Drones

These are the proud males of the bee colony. Theirs is to eat readily available honey that they have no part in producing, and mate with virgin queen bees. They usually venture out of the hive and fly in swarms. No sooner does a drone mate with a queen than he dies. Still, there are those that are not lucky to get a chance to mate with a virgin queen from neighboring bee colonies, and they return to their hive and become content with eating the honey and pollen assembled by the workers.

However, as in the human kingdom, one must work in order to eat. So, when the drones stop going out to mate at the end of the swarm season, and they stick within the hives just eating and doing nothing helpful to the colony, of course the food resources diminish faster than usual, and the workers in charge of foraging get pissed off. So they evict those drones from the hive.

As a beekeeper, you don't want to be too ignorant about bees, their basic species and their characteristics. Knowing the fundamentals of honeybees could help you understand your bee colonies better, and even decide if you want to retain them, to crossbreed them, or to replace them altogether.

The breed of honeybee that was introduced in American from Europe, specifically Italy, was the Apis mellifera, but in its country of origin it is referred to as Apis mellifera lingustica. It is a very calm species of honeybee, and it is not surprising that Americans embraced it when it was first introduced into the country. Apis mellifera is this species' scientific name, and it simply means *honey carrying bee*. Of course bees do not carry honey; what they do carry is nectar – but the name sounds a good enough in identifying the bee. There are other species of honeybees worldwide, and they are eight in number.

The Bee Species to Keep

The different species in existence include the Italian honey bee, the Russian, and even the Carniolian. However, the reality today is that finding a pure species of honeybee is close to impossible. The different species have interbred very much over centuries, and what farmers are more interested in now is having a healthy and strong colony of bees as opposed to specific species of bees. But for the sake of knowledge, here are some well-known honey breeds:

Apis mellifera carnica

The species of honeybees is the same one people refer to as carniolan honey bee.

Apis mellifera caucasca

Some refer to this species as caucasion honey bee.

Apis mellifera scutellata

This species of honeybee was introduced into America from Brazil, after it had been introduced in Brazil during the 1950s. It is commonly referred to as the Africanized bee. Essentially, the species is a result of crossbreeding the original African bee, scientifically known as *A. m. scutellata,* with various species of honeybees whose origin is Europe.

Cordovans

The cordovan bees derive their name from their color, and they are usually crossbreeds of different species or races but what they have in common is the color shade of dark rose or rich burgundy that they bear. In America, the cordovans you find a gentler than other bee races, and they happen to be mainly Italian. At first glance, the color yellow on them stands out, and they do not bear any black color on them. In fact, instead of the usual black legs and head of the Italian species, the cordovans have purplish brown.

The Buckfast

Buckfast honeybees are also a gentle race. They are also resistant to tracheal mites that sometimes invade bees.

The Russian species

This species is relatively recent in the US, their first sale to the public having been the year 2000. First, the United States Department of Agriculture (USDA) imported them from the province of Primorksy in Russia in 1997, and put them on some island in Louisiana to study them. They were wanted primarily for their resistance against mites, and after due studies for around 2yrs or so, they were set out for testing in various US states in 1999. They happen to be very watchful in guarding their hive.

Starline

This species comes from two different Italian breeds as a hybrid and it is very prolific. What you do not want to have are generations of queens from your colonies because they will not be as productive as the originals. So you may need to buy fresh honeybee colonies every year to ensure high yields.

Minnesota Hygienic

This is a honeybee species associated with Dr. Marla Spivak who worked on its production from the University of Minnesota. These bees have such hygienic behavior that they easily keep disease away. For instance, they are able to avoid contracting American Foul Brood disease, which is a problem to other bee species.

Earn from Multiple Bee Products

What is the best way to optimize your beekeeping project? Well, since your interest is in generating as much profit as you can from the project while keeping your costs at a minimum, you will need to think broadly, and see what by-products from your beekeeping you can sell. Of course, you will have mastered how to bring your costs down by having sought advice from your local mentor, and treating your bees in ways that reduce their deaths and enable them to become highly productive.

Why do people mainly rear bees? In reality, there are those who keep bees for fun – call them hobbyists. Those may not worry much about other income generating products from their beekeeping. The other category of beekeepers is the one that has been skyrocketing by the year, after having realized that honey is very high demand worldwide, and that beekeeping gives you room to earn income from incidental products.

Different Income Streams From Beekeeping

(1) Selling honey

The demand for honey has shot tremendously over the years, as ordinary folks and medics realize the health value of the product. At the same time, people want to buy their honey from sources that they trust, hence having beekeepers supplying honey to credit processors and packers.

Rate Of Income From Honey

The statistics provided by the National Honey Board (NHB) has it that it is unlikely a hive will produce less than 20 pounds of honey in a year, but you can have a hive giving you 60 pounds and more in one year. Of course, how well you tend to your bees will matter, although a lot depends on your geographical location and related weather patterns, the temperatures, the variety and richness of local flora, interference from pests particularly mites, and such other pertinent factors.

With the honey output also emerges the issue of prices. Prices of honey are steadily rising as its demand rises, and this can be seen from the 2015 prices that the NHB put at $6.75 for each pound sold at retail and $5.09 for each pound sold at wholesale, as compared to the 2006 prices that were $3.88 and $2.74 respectively. If you have 20 hives, for instance, you will be looking at 400 pounds of honey or even three times that much. That cannot fetch you anything less than $2,700 in a year, and it sure could fetch you in excess of $8,100.

Of course as a beginner it is not recommended that you start big, because you don't want to risk your capital. You can start off with just 2 hives, as you learn what the bees in your location prefer in terms of treatment, and how they behave in relation to the weather condition and patterns.

How Many Manual Hours do Bees Take?

From what beekeepers report in different farmers' forums such as *permies.com*, a 20-hive project could demand a single day of work in a week, or even half a day depending on your management style. Remember you could keep as many hives as you wish, but you need to keep in mind the benefits of having a diversified farm, for example one with orchards and vegetables. Won't you be helping your bees with foraging even as you benefit from their bee pollination? And as with other animals, a well fed bee is bound to generate more honey for you.

411

(2) Selling beeswax

Why would anyone wish to buy beeswax? Well, high demand for the product means there is a way of making more money out of it. As such, you have room to sell the beeswax that your bee colonies produce. Many buyers of your beeswax proceed to make candles out of it, soap, lip balm, and some of them still use it to make edible products such as natural sweeteners and food flavorings. There is definitely a lot more use for beeswax, and so you are unlikely to miss buyers for it. Look at a company like Burt's Bees, for instance, which has markets across the globe including the US and Europe. Their business journey began with the production of candles and lip balms based on beeswax.

(3) Selling pollen

It looks like the world is not about to have enough of bee pollen, so if you venture into beekeeping, this is one product you need to target for an extra income stream. Many companies dealing with natural supplements have hailed bee pollen as being a 'superfood', for its ability to boost people's health naturally. It is said to boost immunity, heal seasonal allergies, reduce the rate and effect of osteoporosis, and generally act as a natural antioxidant.

(4) Selling propolis

Bee propolis is that sticky substances that bees produce and use it to seal any tiny gaps existing on their hive. It is rich in resin and is hailed for its medicinal value, including its capacity to treat sores. It is also a great antioxidant and is valued for boosting immunity. Manufacturers of cosmetics also make good customers for bee propolis, and also those who make car wax. Makers of chewing gum also like it.

(5) Renting out hives on short-term

Why would wish to keep hives for just a couple of weeks? Well, serious big scale farmers do. Bees are great at effective crop pollination, and so they often hire bees for this purpose when they deem the season ripe, for durations ranging from 3 – 5 weeks. Going by 2009 statistics, the rental fee for one hive was around $157 per session. These hive rental services are mostly valued by farmers of almond crops, sunflower, and even canola. The USDA has it that within 2012, the revenue that beekeepers generated from the pollination sector hit a whopping $655 million!

(6) Selling starter hives

Once you are well skilled at beekeeping, why not become the go-to person in your area to supply beekeeping starter kits for beginners? You could supply them with beehives ready with good honey producing bees at a price. You earn yourself some side revenue, and you save them the hassle of researching doing trial and error beekeeping.

In fact, your market is large in this respect because even seasoned beekeepers sometimes want to replace their bee colonies and they can buy new breeds from you. What you might excite you more here, is the fact that if you have excess bees you can always ship them elsewhere – the US postal services comfortably handles this business.

Any Cost Incurred With By-Products?

Generally no – these other bee products that earn you income will be there whether you intend to sell them or not. So why not be business wise and help recoup some of your initial beekeeping costs, by selling the additional products besides honey?

As for beeswax, for instance, worker bees will still produce it from the 8 wax producing glands each has within its abdominal area. What they do is then create cells using the wax, which is normally in form of scales, for use as storage for honey. Of course, these cells also act as protection for young bees at their larval and pupal stages. As far as nutrition goes, beeswax has long chain alcohols, fatty acids, and also some valuable organic compounds.

The bee pollen are those pollen balls that worker bees form wherever they wish, and sometimes it is mixed up with honey and various bee secretions. Many entrepreneurs have learnt to harvest the bee pollen as an individual product, specifically for human consumption. They call it *ambrosia*, which is derived from Greek usage of the word, where referred to a meal for Greek gods that conferred to them longevity and even immortality.

Initial Capital Outlay

Beekeeping is not a business you plan to start when you grow up – financially, that is. When you are starting with, say, 2 beehives, everything you require to get your bees producing honey from A – Z can cost you around $1,000. How many other businesses can you initiate with this amount, fixed costs and recurrent expenditure all factored in? And note that your honeybees can replenish your hives within weeks or just a couple of months depending on how flowery the fields are.

Preparation for the Beekeeping Business

As in all businesses, in beekeeping, you can only anticipate to reap where you have sown. An expert in agricultural extension services, Eric C. Mussen, while based within the University of California, noted that if you keep healthy honeybees and give them enough food and water all the year round, you can reap valuable products from your bees for most of the year.

What Preparation for Beekeeping Entails

1. Get relevant approvals

Consult the homeowners association and even your local authorities, to establish that beekeeping is not prohibited where you want to rear your bees. Then whatever authorizations you may need, get them. Some areas have zoning, and so you either ensure you are within the perimeter where beekeeping is legal, or you get official exemption. In short, before you put any of your precious money into the beekeeping business, ensure you are within the law – both federal and local.

2. Lay out a structured plan

Here, we are referring to the fundamentals, or the preliminaries that you need to have in place, so that you have a good bee farming system in place. They include:

- Consulting with an attorney specializing with matters of agriculture, so that you can become conversant with the laws of beekeeping within your state. If you are in Texas, for example, the attorney will refer you to the Texas Agricultural Code which outlines the dos and don'ts for beekeeping activities in the state, and help you translate them into action.

- Engage a Certified Public Accountant versed in agricultural business, so that you do not incur unnecessary costs or miss opportunity for business out of ignorance or poor accounting systems.

- Seek the services of a insurance agent versed with matters of farming business, so that you can know the extent of your business risk, and how best to shield yourself from possible liabilities.

- Acquire the relevant business license from your local office, and pay for any other required permits

- Seek information from the Department of Revenue in your state, to learn how to go about obtaining the relevant sales tax license. You want all the documentation to be in place by the time you get to sell your honey and other bee products.

3. Identify your mentor(s)

Why seek to reinvent the wheel when others have been there and done it? Get to learn from neighboring beekeepers about the pests and diseases that honeybees in the area are prone to. Learn from them the most marketable honey and bee products in the region.

4. Buy your equipment

You need to acquire good quality protective equipment, and you also need implements to use in the maintenance of your beehives and in the honey harvesting. The specific equipment includes:

- Light colored bee suit to discourage bees from approaching and getting tempted to sting you

- Darkish hat as well as face veil to protect you from the glare of the sun
- A bee smoker which you use to blow smoke into your hive in order to calm your bees when working in the hive
- A bee blower and also brush, which you use to get the bees from where the honey is when you are harvesting it.
- Some other non-essential items which are, nevertheless, helpful; like honeybee feeders and tools to help remove beeswax out of the beehives.

5. Source your bee colony

The most convenient way to do this is through the local beekeepers' association. They can reliably tell you the beekeeper with a good bee colony and prepared to sell, or even the beekeeper with complete starter kits that include hives and their bee colonies. If the local channels prove difficult, you can always order your starter colony online. Go for a supplier who can make an overnight delivery, because you don't your bees taking too long on transit for the sake of their health.

Just ensure that your starter colony of bees has a queen bee and all the other relevant categories of bees need for procreation and honey generation.

6. Do a feasibility study to learn the market

Who wants to serve food without knowing the number of people expected to sit at the dining table? For a successful beekeeping business, you need to do a survey beforehand, to know the outlets that can take up your honey and related bee products once you have supplied your supportive family members and friends.

Establish the food stores that would be willing to put your honey in their display shelves with a view to selling it. Would you be in a position to make beeswax candles for sale in crafts shops as well as gift shops? Or would there be local entrepreneurs prepared to buy your fresh beeswax? What organizations would be willing to buy your other bee products, including the pollen and propolis, and is delivery of those products convenient for you? Do a thorough market study, in advance, and do not forget to check out the open and flea markets.

How To Make Bread

Whether it's for the holidays, a special occasion or a goal for everyday simplicity a lot of people desire to make homemade whole wheat bread. Smelling the freshly baked aroma coming from your kitchen is one of the homiest and soothing fragrances in the culinary world. Making and baking whole wheat bread is healthier for you and can cost much less than traditional 'healthy' store-bought 'whole wheat' bread.

Once the dough bakes in the oven and that beautiful loaf is cooling on your cooling rack, everyone can hardly wait to eat it. A little patience pays off, though. In addition to the satisfaction of making the whole wheat bread yourself, you won't want to go back to the store to buy bread anymore. It just won't satisfy you or your family the same as your home-made, whole wheat bread will.

Making a fluffy loaf of whole wheat bread is easy and once you master the simple skills, you'll want to keep making it. There are different methods by which you can make and bake whole wheat bread. Some people prefer the hand-made, hand-kneaded method. Others prefer using a bread machine. Either option you choose, you can have great success, just choose the method that suits you and your schedule best.

Fluffy, healthy, light and tasty - Freshly Milled Whole Wheat Bread techniques and tricks are outlined here.

How to Grow Wheat

Have you thought about how bread is made? There are many steps. The first step starts on a farm. That is where grain is grown. Bread is made from grain. Grain comes from plants grown in large fields.

Wheat is the grain used to make most bread. There are three main kinds of wheat: hard wheat, durum wheat, and soft wheat. Wheat kernels can be red, brown, purple, blue, or white. Some wheat is planted in the winter. Some are planted in the spring.

Some wheat is hard and contains lots of protein. The protein is very important. It makes bread dough strong and elastic. Flour mills want to know how much protein is in wheat. They pay different prices for more protein.

Some of the steps involved in planting wheat include:

- Study the climate of a region and identify the most appropriate season that allows for planting of the wheat. Does spring or fall have an impact on the planting of the wheat?

- You need to get prepared for the planting time to ensure that your crops will grow and have strong roots.

- Get your land prepared by using quality tools that will make your soil even for instance a rake shovel. You only need to be careful if the land selected has been in use previously for the purpose of farming.

- The next step is to use a shovel to dig big trenches.

- It is now the moment to apply fertilizers on your land or the trenches. Distribute it evenly across your prepared piece of land.

- Everything is set and prepared well for the planting process.

- Place the seeds in the trenches r the prepared area of land and cover with adequate soil so that the seeds do not dry up.

- If the climate around is dry during the time you have planted the seeds, you will need to water them two to three times.

Factors that Lead to Growth of Wheat

When you make the decision to cultivate wheat on your land, you will need to be committed to some arrangements that will ensure that the process is done properly and a successful harvest or yield is achieved. Centuries have changed and it calls for the adoption of new technologies that are more advanced. The new techniques make it easier for the planting process and ensure that people have a significant harvest that can cater for the ever growing population. Farmers need to embrace and adopt the new technologies across the field from the preparation of the land up to the harvesting and even storage.

As we understand, wheat is vital in manufacture or preparation of bread and other commodities like noodles. Most people enjoy wheat as a source of vegetable proteins. Some of the factors and considerations to be given attention in the process of planting wheat include:

- Conducting soil tests. You will need to bring experts on board who will carry out several tests on the soil at your region of selection. They will determine the volume of the soil and outline the soil nutrients to determine if they match with the pertinent requirements for planting wheat. If need be, they will advise on adding external nutrients to improve the fertility or quality of the soil to meet the standards for growing wheat.

- Create diversification and crop rotation plans. A garden is usually a very pretty area but it can also become quite boring to the constant observer. The same plants and flowers appear in the same place each year, making the scenery rather predictable. Not to mention the fact that the soil can become nutrient deficient and creatures such as deer will know exactly where to find their next meal. Use crop rotation to repel deer and pests, replenish up the scenery, and provide other beneficial results to the garden area. This diversification also prevents harmful insects and soil diseases from invading the area. Though the same types of vegetables may be present each year, they will occupy a different area of the garden. A three-year rotation plan is recommended in order to get the best results. You may grow soya beans and rotate them with wheat.

- You need to use clean and processed seeds. When you decide to plant wheat, go to the store and choose that have been cleaned and processed properly. The choices of seeds have on the influence the growth of wheat and the yield. A good choice will lead to a wonderful harvest.

- A nutrient-rich soil. You will need to supplement your soil with extra external nutrients like vitamins, minerals, phosphorous, potassium and nitrogen. Such nutrients will enhance the growth of the plant, its stability and those of roots and contribute to high yields.

- Make use of plant growth regulators. They are used to control the growth vigor & strength of the plant, increase production, improve the weight of the grain, promote early maturity and improve the quality of the wheat. Some of the examples that can be used include Cycocel, Naphthalene acetic acid, Gibberellin, Plant cytokinin and Petroleum fueling agent.

In the olden days, bread was such a very treasured food. Most of the times, it was food for the poor. After the industrialization period, wheat grains would be to flour that was later processed to get rid of germ. What remained was starch that was pure starch.

Making the Bread

Bread Production Flow Chart

Flour and Other Ingredients
⇓
Weighing
⇓
Mixing ⇨ **Resting**

Kneading ⇐

Dividing/Moulding
⇓
Proofing
⇓
Baking ⇨ **Cooling** ⇨ **Slicing**

Packaging ⇐

The process of making bread will require your commitment to be able to achieve the desired results. We have already discussed about the major ingredient for making bread, wheat in regard to the process of preparing the seeds up to time of harvesting.

To be able to make and make whole wheat bread that will come out as the best to test, there are a number of items you will need to have. These are what we will term as the tools of trade in the bread making process.

What are the ingredients?

The following are the vital elements that you will need in order to prepare your bread:

- Whole wheat flour

- Wheat Gluten flour

- Instant dry yeast

- Lukewarm water

- Sugar or honey

- Olive oil or any other healthy oil.

- Salt

The equipment/tools you will need:

- Calibrated Measuring spoons and cups

- A thermometer

- A bread pan

- A Cooling Rack

- A Smooth surface/table

- A Grain Mill

- A large mixing saucepan

- A Mixing spoon

I will explain some of the listed ingredients:

Whole Wheat Flour

The taste of the bread is determined by the quality of the flour used. Your whole wheat bread is affected with the flour used alongside its texture and nutritional value.

There are a number of options involved when making your bread. The first option involves home milling of whole grains of hard wheat. This is the freshest, healthiest and most nutritional flour. It contains most of the nutrients including vitamins, wheat germ, minerals, wheat germ oil, protein and fiber. This has the best nutritional value and texture as compared to any other. It is the best option since it does not need to use white flour.

The second option is the bagged whole wheat flour which can be bought from a grocery near you. This flour is more dense with more fiber as compared to the previous one though it is processed thus germ and essential oils are removed to extend its shelf life. With a longer shelf life, it undergoes oxidation making it to taste bitter. With this option, you will be required to use some portions of white bread flour or increase the amounts of vital wheat gluten to achieve a desired texture.

Vital Wheat Gluten (also known as Gluten Flour)

Gluten refers to the protein section of the bread making flour. It is naturally occurring. At fermentation point of yeast, the starch is consumed and you will see the presence of air bubbles. Gluten plays a big role in stretching the dough and allowing space for holding the yeast. If the air bubbles are allowed to escape, it means the gluten is too little to hold the elastic strands strongly and the bread will be low, crumbly and dense. With gluten flour, your bread will have the desired texture and rises to a height that is considerably good.

Instant Dry Yeast

This is the easiest yeast type that you can use. You may look for the recommended options known as the SAF Instant Yeast and the Fleischmann's Instant Dry Yeast. Check their expiration date to ensure that it is still fresh. Fresh yeast will make your bread to be fresh. You will identify fresh yeast by how it tries to jump off your spoon like those iron shavings that are live.

Yeast is termed as a living microorganism responsible for consuming any starch or sugar and converting them to a gas that will fill the elastic gluten spaces in your dough. Eventually, your bread is made to rise. Excess yeast won't make your bread to rise the more. Instead, it will have adverse effects of making the bread heavy and dense. Ensure that you use the correct measurements.

Water

Water temperature is a crucial consideration that is supposed to be right from the word go. For bread making, the water temperatures should range from 110 to 115 degrees before the addition of the other ingredients. When you add sugar and oil, the temperatures should be within the range of 100 to 110. If the temperature of the water is above 115, it will kill the yeast since it can't survive when exposed to

temperatures above 115 degrees. When the yeast is killed, it won't act the dough correctly making your bread to be dense and flat.

Healthy Oil

Oil is not flavored but it only transmits flavor to other ingredients. It acts as a transmitter. Avoid using whipped butter, low fat spreads or margarine for they are hydrogenated oils and contains water. Such hydrogenated oils will make the recipe to be unhealthy. Apart from the extra virgin olive oil, you may use such other healthy oils like grape seed, organic safflower, organic canola and organic sunflower oil. The oils will keep the bread moist and soft.

Sugar or Honey

Make use of sweet stuff in the recipe with a granulated or liquid option. For the granulated, you may use sugar, brown sugar, sucanat or organic evaporated cane juice while for the liquid option, you may make use 2 Tablespoons of honey, rice syrup, sorghum, molasses or syrup.

When you realize that the bread is too sweet, decrease the sweet element by half. Do not be afraid that you will affect the bread's chemistry, rising or texture. It won't since reducing the measurements of the sweet stuff will not affect anything at all. Avoid using any artificial sweetener because you will end up with something else and not the intended bread.

A Healthy Salt

Salt inhibits yeast from overpopulating the dough. It is just another flavor transmitter like oil. If omitted, your bread will be bland and tasteless. Make sure you use the right measurements so that the result is awesome with each slice of bread having a small amount of salt. Some of the options you may use include mineral salt, sea salt or real salt.

You should note that salt is not supposed to be in direct contact with yeast since it has inhibitive properties that can just kill the yeast. If yeast comes into direct contact with salt water, it will be killed but if flour is added, then everything is fine since the flour will act as a buffer protecting the yeast from salt.

How to measure ingredients

How to measure Whole Wheat Flour & Gluten Flour

The important tip here is making a note of the cup measurement level and ensure that there are no air pockets or interior gaps within the flour. The first technique makes use of the scraper. Once you scoop a cup of gluten or flour, use a straight edge of a knife to level it off by scraping any excess gluten on the top. Level the gluten or flour to be the same with the measuring cup top level.

The second option is using the shaker. As you scoop a cup of gluten or flour, and the cup still in the flour bag, shake it gently to allow the flour to settle and be in level with the cup's top edge.

Avoid scooping and dumping all the flour contents in a large measuring cup. If you do so, you will get air pockets and the measurements will be thrown off. Patiently use the one cup to measure the wheat flour instead of doing it all at once.

How to Measure Instant Dry Yeast

To obtain an accurate measurement, get to know the state of the yeast you are using. If you notice that the yeast is HYPER ACTIVE (by literally jumping off your measuring spoon), you should reduce the amount to ¼ teaspoon. This happens especially when your package of yeast is new.

When the yeast is NORMALLY ACTIVE (only detected by the yeast jumping mildly), take the exact measurements as per stipulated in the recipe.

Do not use any additional yeast with the hopes of better rising dough for it will become wet and the bread will be bumpy.

431

How to Measuring Warm Water

You will use a clear 2 Cup measuring cup and a thermometer to determine the temperature. You should squat for you to take the accurate readings. Use a clear cup that you can easily see through and place it on a level surface. Adjust your eye down to the level of the measuring cup and not bringing the cup to the eye level. Any slant will cause wrong measurements to be taken.

In a situation that it is raining and you are using freshly milled flour, get rid of 2 tablespoons of water. Such kind of flour is so fresh making it susceptible to picking up any moisture found in the air. There is no change if you are using the dead, bagged flour since it is oxidized.

Ensure that the temperature of the water is in between 100-110 degrees F.

How to Measure the Sweet Stuff

This will depend whether the sweet stuff is granulated or in liquid form. For the liquid forms, ensure that the same spoon you use to measure oil is the same used here since it is easier to get the liquid sweet out of the measuring instrument if already coated with oil. When using liquid sweet stuff, ensure that your liquid amounts are decreased.

In the case of granulated or dry sweet stuff, make use of a shaker or a scooper. Use the same procedures you used in the measuring of flour.

Take caution with the amount of the sweet ingredients. If you increase, your dough will be heavy and sticky.

Measuring your Healthy Oil

You will use a tablespoon and measure using your steady hands. Do not shake or freak out. Take an exact measure of one tablespoon. You may measure over a small bowl to take any spillage that my over flour. Add the oil in the mixing bowl that has other ingredients.

Do not add excess oil with the aim of having a more moist loaf because any additional oil will make the bread to be wet in the inside.

Measuring the Healthy Salt

Ensure that your hands are steady and measure a half teaspoon to be used in the dough!

Mixing Techniques

There exist many techniques that can be used to mix your Healthy Whole Wheat Bread Dough. Some methods are great for some other people while others are not. Some take less time like the bread machine while others need more time like Hand-kneaded method. The choice is yours to pick the best that suits you!

The Hand Method of Kneading

This is not a messy method that will leave your counter sticky and flour flying everywhere as many may think. With the instruction provided here, you will be happy to end up with clean floors and counters.

This method requires your input in terms of strength. Your wrist, arm and the upper body should be strong. The method is simple and can be practiced by anyone. Let your counter surface be smooth and have a height that reaches your waist level for easier kneading.

The Bread Machine

If you are a learner in bread making, you should not waste money buying the bread machine since what matters is the flour and not the machine. The bread machines do not contain a pan that is shaped like the real bread. If you buy the bread machine, you will be needed to purchase a Grain Mill for a sumptuous or wonderful whole wheat bread.

The Stand Mixer with Dough Hook

The quality of your bread is healthier and better if you take your time and buy a grain mill instead of the expensive bread machine or the stand mixer. It is good for those who already have the stand mixer but not advisable for those who are yet to buy because it is expensive yet the outcome is influenced more by the flour quality. The other option is considering a second-hand stand mixer if need be.

The Bosch Universal Plus Kitchen Machine

It is a great machine that allows you to prepare up to five 2lbs of bread. It is very wonderful when you need to make multiple pieces of bread at once since it is a nice choice when it comes to have a good time management. This can be so if you already have it since you understand its benefits. My advice for those who are starters is you invest more of your funds in a grain mill then purchase a second-hand bread machine.

It is good to learn all these methods, such that when machine experiences a breakdown and needs repairs, you will be good to go with the other methods to get a fresh bread. It is of great importance to learn more about the methods of hand kneading.

The Hand-Kneading Technique Explained

It is very easy to hand-knead whole wheat bread dough. It is true to the fact that it requires more work as compared to using mixers or bread machine. To hand mix and knead has some therapeutic effects to your body. You should use freshly milled flour and adequately knead to get a good whole wheat bread. You need to knead properly for the rising and texture of the bread.

The Proper Order of Mixing the Ingredients and Bowl Kneading

Mix the water or the liquid the required temperatures, oil, sweet stuff, and instant yeast in a large bowl that will allow the addition of flour.

In another bowl, combine flour, gluten and salt and thoroughly stir using a fork.

Add a cup (of the dry mixed ingredients) at a time to the liquid mixture. Stir every time you add a cup until the mixture is batter-like and smooth. Continue with this procedure until your dough is too stiff to be mixed with a large spoon. You will now have to start hand-kneading it within the bowl.

Apply your hands with olive oil to coat. Press the dough at the center of the bowl into one dusty lump. Press the dough using your oiled palm to make and indention at the center of the lump. Take the dough and fold into halves twice. Continue doing this until there is no dry flour left behind. Once done, you will now move the dough to the counter.

How to Knead the Dough on the Counter.

Select a table or counter area that is smooth and not tiled or porous. Let the counter height match with your waist to avoid straining your back. Let the room space be ample enough to allow for the kneading rhythm and the method of pushing the dough forward.

Coat your hands with oil again and rub any excess on the smooth surface region where the kneading is to be done. Take the dough from your bowl and put it at the center of your oiled surface or counter.

Avoid using flour while kneading because too much of the flour will make the loaf to be dense and heavy and also creates a huge mess.

Use the heels of your hands while kneading the dough. Do not use fingertips which will make you feel tired and can make you not to produce proper gluten strands.

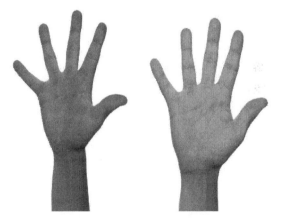

Your palms should be placed in a manner that they are facing down where the dough is, thumbs need to be folded to the sides of your hands, and your thumbnails are supposed to be together, touching and facing each other. This the position your hand should be in to be able to push the dough out. Keep your hands in that same position as you knead, pushing from the center of the dough ball towards the forward position. The dough should be pressing onto the counter and stretching slightly.

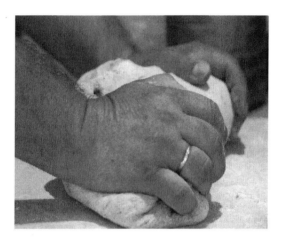

Fold the dough in half and bring the right edge to the left or the vice versa. Quarter Turn the already folded dough. The fold should now be on the top farthest away from you while the two edges are supposed to be closest to you.

REPEAT the above and pause after one push.

Fold dough to the side again, making a Quarter Turn with the seam up and curves down closest to you. Keep repeating until it is a rhythm; kneading forward using your palm heels, stop, folding, quarter turn and repeat.

If the dough becomes sticky, do not flavor the counter and lightly dust the dough before continuing with the kneading. Only use less than a tablespoon at a time and only add when the dusting is fully incorporated and the counter remains clear.

How to Test for Texture and Timing

Kneading times may vary based on a number of factors that include the gluten amount, and strength of the person doing it among others. In general, the kneading process should not exceed 10 minutes.

The **two finger poke** test. Apart from timing, this method can be used to determine the texture. This test will show that the gluten strands have actually formed enough to imply a quick bounce back to signify the dough is ready to make its first rise. This test should be quick.

When you do a quick poke down and the dough is slow to come back to the original smooth state, continue kneading and try the test again after a minute. If it springs back instantly to almost the original smooth state before poking, this will signify that the gluten has been effectively worked on and you may move to the rising procedure. No dents should be noticed when the fingers are removed after poking.

Don't do the two-finger poke test after the rising dough in the loaf pan because your loaf will be deflated. Only do it before the first rise.

Dough Rising Tips

The rising happens twice; the first time is before you shape it and then the second one is after shaping. The first rise happens at around 80 degrees which will be slow and lengthy. For an organized bakery, there is a proofing cabinet to consistently keep warm temperatures for optimum proofing.

Since you are doing this at home, and the bowl is oiled for the first rise, you will see a shiny coating of oil at the top of the dough ball. This keeps the bread from drying out during the rising process.

Turn your oven to low heat for one minute. After the one minute elapses, turn off the oven. Place the dough ball in the warmed oven for about 30 minutes. You should be watchful and keep time at this stage to avoid the dough rising far above doubling its size which will make it to fall or a loaf that is compact, fallen, and wet after the baking process.

Bakeware and Slicing

Bakeware has no effect to the loaf of bread. Loaf pans are in wide use for baking a Whole Wheat Bread. They are for keeping the bread in the shape of a loaf, hence branded the name bake-ware. Different people prefer their own desired loaf pans.

Factors to consider in choosing a quality loaf pan:

- Ensure that you avoid a pan with potential trouble spots like cracks, corroded or other defects.

- The weight of the loaf pan should be heavy and made from a heavy metal material.

Pans are manufactured from different materials. There are glass bake-ware, aluminum bakeware, metal bake-ware and ceramic/stone bakeware. Glass loaf pans are poor conductors of heat and not porous hence not the best option since they will result in a loaf with soggy sides. Metal loaf pans are best heat conductors and affordable. Aluminum loaf pans are poor heat conductors thus bread can take too long to bake and may fall flat. Stoneware loaf pans are both porous and moderately good conductors of heat making them the best option for baking bread.

Slicing your homemade bread

Let the bread cool for approximately 30 minutes.

On cooling, you are now free to slice the bread. The right way of slicing is outlined below:

Use a serrated knife that is long enough to slice the bread. The knife should cut across the width of the bread. You may also consider an electric serrated knife.

Only slice when the bread has cooled to maintain its shape.

Use slightly downward force to slice the bread in a sawing-mood manner.

Start from the top as you slice through to the bottom.

PART 5
Woodworking And Crafts
Wood Pallet Projects

There you are, browsing the shelves of another home and garden store, looking for something that you can put in your back yard. You want something that is unique, fun to look at, and makes you stand out from the crowd, but you don't want to spend an arm and a leg to get it.

You want something that you can put together yourself, and hopefully save a few dollars in that realm. You want something that is as unique as you are, and that doesn't call for you to try a bunch of new things you haven't tried before, or to get a lot of tools you don't have.

Basically, you just want something that you can do yourself, something that makes you happy, and something that doesn't cost you a lot of money to do.

But what?

The more you look at the shelves of the department store, the more it feels as though you are stuck with only a few choices. Perhaps you like one wooden option… but you see that you have to spend a lot more for it, and that you have to have a crew come put it together for you.

Or perhaps you like another, but again, you are stuck with the same old story. It's just like what everyone else has. It's expensive. It's not quite what you were after. So, you sigh and keep up the search.

You know if you want it, you will have to make it yourself. But how? Wood is expensive, the tools you need to make those projects are expensive, and the skills requires are going to take you a long time to learn. You just want your home and garden to reflect how creative you are, but it seems that's just not going to happen.

Until now.

With this book, you are going to learn what you need to do to renovate your home and garden space, with nothing more than pallets. That's right. I am going to show you how to make a variety of fun and creative things, with nothing more than wooden pallets.

No special skills required, just a bit of creativity, some ambition, and a few tools.

In a matter of hours you can have a yard full of things you made yourself, out of pallets you saved from going to waste. Let this book be your guide in the world of pallet creations.

And enjoy your brand new look.

Around the Yard

Simple Pallet Mini Pond

Photo made by: ho8o

What you will need:

Pallets

Hammer

Nails

Paint

Lining

Pump

Saw

Pencil

Measuring tape

Directions:

Start by pulling all the pallets apart. When you have all the wood separated, you are ready to begin.

Measure 20 boards to be 3 feet long. Cut all of the corners of these boards at an angle.

Next, measure 20 more boards to be 18 inches long, and cut all of the boards at an angle as well. Use the photo for reference.

You have 4 posts from the center of the pallets. Cut these so they are 30 inches in length. Now, paint all the wood to be any color you wish.

Measure where you want your pond to be, and dig holes for the posts at equal distances. You are going to hammer the wood to these posts at regularly spaced lengths. Use the photo as reference for how to assemble completely.

Once the entire pond is assembled, place your liner inside, as well as the pump. You are now ready to add water, or even fish!

Pallet Wood Shed

Photo made by: Wapster

What you will need:

Pallets

Hammer

Nails

Stain

447

Tarp

Saw

Pencil

Measuring tape

Directions:

Start by removing the boards on 1 side of 2 pallets. These are going to be the walls for your wood shed. You are going to take the wood from these pallets, and place it against the outside of the pallets so you don't have gaps between the boards any longer.

Hammer these in place, and set aside.

Next, set a pallet on the ground intact. This is the floor of your shed. Hammer the two walls you have made to either side of this board, and set aside.

Completely disassemble another pallet. Use the post board from the center of this pallet for the support beam in the center of the roof. Hammer in place.

You are going to use the wood from the pallet to form the back wall as well as the top of the roof. Hammer these all in place, then apply a stain to the entire building.

Let dry, and hammer a tarp stretched taught over the top. That's it! Your wood shed is ready to keep your woodstove wood safe and dry.

Upcycled Picnic Table

Photo made by: MeganLynnette

What you will need:

Pallets

Hammer

Nails

Stain

Saw

Pencil

Screwdriver

Screws

Measuring tape

Directions:

Start by completely disassembling the pallets, and set all the wood aside in the piles it belongs in.

Next, take your pencil and measuring tape, and measure equal lengths for the legs of the table. I cut mine to be 4 feet long, angled at both ends to stand flat on the ground while supporting the table at the top.

Cut these and set them aside.

Next, you will need to set aside 18 of the boards. These will be cut to be a total of 6 feet, and laid end to end on the frame. You now have all the wood you need for the legs and the top of the table, so all you need is the 2 boards to support either side.

Start by laying out 2 legs side by side, then screwing 2 boards to equal 9 feet across these boards. These are the support arms for the seat, so place them across the legs as you see in the photo. Repeat for the other side.

Stand the legs on end now, and with the assistance of a friend or propping them against a wall, screw the board on lengthwise, to each end of the legs. You are now making the bench and top of the table.

I suggest you add more boards in the center beneath the table for added support after you have screwed the main frame in place. Once this is entirely assembled, sand down all of the rough edges.

Apply a stain first, then paint the color of your choice. That's it! Your new picnic table is ready for a party!

Beautiful Flower Planter

What you will need:

Pallets

Hammer

Nails

Stain

Saw

Photo made by: eren {sea+prairie}

Directions:

Set up the pallet you wish to use on its side, and apply a stain.

Take your saw and cut small lengths of wood, then screw these to the front of your stained pallet. This is going to hold the soil in place.

Drill holes in the bottom of this wood for proper drainage, then fill with soil. That's it! That's all you need for instant flower planters. Pick a sunny spot in your yard, and you are ready to bring in the bees.

Dark Stained Pallet Gate

Photo made by: <u>Wapster</u>

What you will need:

Pallets

Hammer

Nails

453

Stain

Saw

Pencil

Measuring tape

Hinges

Lock

Directions:

I made a long gate for my fence, using 2 pallets placed end to end. You can also follow these directions to make a single width gate... but it's up to you.

Start by removing the boards on 1 side of 2 pallets. These are going to be the walls for your wood shed. You are going to take the wood from these pallets, and place it against the outside of the pallets so you don't have gaps between the boards any longer.

Hammer these in place, and set aside.

Next, take extra wood from another pallet, and place it in the center of these 2 pallets. Screw this in place, so both pallets are together, end to end. Apply a stain all over the pallets, and let dry.

Apply a couple more coats, so the wood gets nice and dark. Measure now on your fence where want your gate to be. Use your pencil to mark on the wood where to place the hinges and lock, and screw these in place before you try to hang them.

Using the help of a friend, make sure you have it properly fit before you screw your gate in place.

That's it! Keep everything where it should be in style.

Innovative Creations

Mini Desk Masterpiece

Photo made by: Mike

What you will need:

Pallets

Hammer

Nails

Stain

Saw

Sandpaper

Pencil

Measuring tape

Directions:

Start by removing all the wood on 1 side of your pallet. Measure your desk where the stand is going to be, and mark on your pallet where you need to cut. Follow these lines with your saw, then use sandpaper to sand down the wood so it's smooth.

Apply a stain to the wood now, bringing out the natural look.

Sand down any other rough spots, and your stand is done!

Rustic Pallet Wagon

What you will need:

Pallets

Hammer

Nails

Stain

Saw

Pencil

Measuring tape

Wheels

Rope

Directions:

Start by sanding down your pallet. You don't want any rough patches or potential slivers from the wood. Apply a stain.

Once the stay has dried, flip the pallet over, and use your pencil to mark where you want the wheels to be placed. Screw them in place securely.

For the handle, I recommend you purchase 2 hooks from your local hardware store and screw them in place right at the front of the wagon. Loop the rope through these hooks and tie securely. That's it! Your wagon is ready for anything.

Quirky Office Desk

Photo made by: pierre vedel

What you will need:

Pallets

Extra poles for the legs

Paint

Hammer

Nails

Stain

Saw

Pencil

Measuring tape

Directions:

Remove all the wood from one pallet and cut the lengths of board in half. Screw these in place on the second pallet, then sand it down so you don't have to worry about splinters.

Make sure there are no cracks or rough spots, then stain. Once the stain has dried, flip the piece over.

Paint all 4 poles the color of your choice, and place them at equal distances at the bottom of your table. Screw securely in place.

Make sure there's no rough spots, and your new table is ready for action!

Practical Pallet Chair

Photo made by: perre vedel

What you will need:

Pallets

Hammer

Nails

Stain

Saw

Pencil

Measuring tape

Directions:

Start by completely disassembling the pallet. You may need 2, so go ahead and take apart 2.

You are going to need 16 boards that are 2 feet long, cut these. You will also need 4 boards that are 4 feet long, 2 boards that are 3 feet long (cut these with their legs at an angle to sit on the floor) and 1 support board.

Sand all of these smooth, and lay them out. Use the photo as a reference, and screw all 16 boards at an angle, these are the seat of chair, use the screw both sets of 4 foot long boards at right angles, then use the photo once more to see where to place the feet of the chair.

Screw the entire piece together, and apply a stain. Let dry, and use a cushion over the top.

Super Slim End Table (Pictured Above)

What you will need:

Pallets

Hammer

Nails

Stain

Saw

Directions:

This end table is incredibly easy to make. Simply cut 1 pallet down the center of each of the support pieces. Sand down and apply a stain, then stack up as you see in the photo.

Apply another stain, and screw in place. Let dry, and you are done!

Little Pallets, Big Projects

Super Simple Chicken Run

Photo made by: <u>Richard Ash</u>

What you will need:

Pallets

Hammer

Nails

Stain

Saw

Pencil

Measuring tape

Chicken wire

464

Directions:

Decide how large of a run you want, and completely disassemble 2 pallets. You are going to lay the boards end to end, and use support boards to screw them all in place. Paint or stain the boards to give a personal touch, then securely attach the chicken wire over the entire project. Make sure all is secure, and you are done!

Planter Bench

Photo made by: Leonora (Ellie) Enking

What you will need:

Pallets

Hammer

Nails

465

Stain

Saw

Pencil

Measuring tape

Directions:

Start with disassembling 1 pallet, and cutting another directly in half. Stack the pallet you cut in half on top of itself, and screw in place.

Take the extra wood from the other pallet now, and place boards up on the sides. You are forming the 'arms' for your bench.

Use more of the extra wood across the back of the bench, screwing this in place. Apply a dark stain or paint over the entire bench, and let dry. That's it! Place all your plants on here for a welcoming, clean garden.

Pallet Compost Holder

Photo made by: Ciarán Mooney

What you will need:

Pallets

Metal posts

Hammer

Nails

Wire

Stain

Saw

Pencil

Measuring tape

467

Directions:

First, decide how big you need your compost enclosure to be, then pound the posts into the ground around this area.

Apply a stain to your pallets, if you like, or paint them. Next, place 1 pallet up against a post, and use the wire to secure it in place. Lift another pallet, and place this next to the first. You can screw this to the first, or simply use wire to hold this in place as well. Repeat for the rest of the pallets around the enclosure.

Garden Grower

Photo made by: Angel Shatz

What you will need:

Pallets

Hammer

Nails

Stain

Saw

Pencil

Tarp

Directions:

Start by completely disassembling your pallet. Decide where you are placing your garden, the dig holes in the corner of this area.

Cut the mid section of your pallets, and use these as corners for your garden. Once they are securely buried, use your saw to cut the boards to the proper length, and screw them in place against these corners.

Finish with a nice stain, then line with a tarp and fill with soil. That's it! Your garden is ready to grow!

Shelf Garden Planter

What you will need:

Pallets

Hammer

Nails

Stain

Saw

Pencil

Directions:

Use the photo as a reference guide for what you are doing, and take apart your pallet. If you like, you can fill in the spaces on the back of your pallet, or you can use a second section of plywood to screw the planter sections to.

Either way, make sure you drill holes in the bottom of the planter, and securely screw these in place against the backing of your choice.

Apply paint or a nice stain, and make sure all is secure. Fill with soil, and you are done!

Have a Seat

Pallet Loveseat

Photo made by: <u>Leonora (Ellie) Enking</u>

What you will need:

Pallets

Hammer

Nails

Stain

Saw

Pencil

Measuring tape

Directions:

Sand down your pallets so there are no rough edges or spots on them. As you can see by the photo, you are going to use 2 pallets as the side of the seat, and 1 pallet as the seating itself.

Use another for the backing of the seat, and 2 extra boards on the front for support. Make sure all is smooth, and screw these together as you see in the photo above. Again, apply a stain or paint if you wish, and let dry.

That's it! Your new seater is ready to go!

Rustic Pallet Patio Tables

What you will need:

Pallets

Hammer

Nails

Stain

Saw

Sandpaper

Photo made by: Michael Coghlan

Directions:

These incredibly easy tables are the perfect addition to any patio or garden. Simply decide how tall you wish for your table to be, and completely sand down your pallets. I use 2 pallets for the height, and a third pallet to take apart and fill in the gaps of the other 2.

Screw everything in place, and make certain there are no rough patches. Apply stain, and you are done!

Rustic Indoor Pallet Table

What you will need:

Pallets

4 extra posts for the legs

Hammer

Nails

Stain

Saw

Pencil

Measuring tape

Directions:

Remove all the wood from one pallet and cut the lengths of board in half. Screw these in place on the second pallet, then sand it down so you don't have to worry about splinters.

Make sure there are no cracks or rough spots, then stain. Once the stain has dried, flip the piece over.

Place the 4 legs of the table at equal distances on the bottom of the pallet. Screw securely in place.

Apply a dark stain to the entire table, and let dry.

Your elegant piece is ready to be placed anywhere in your home.

Pallet Patio Seating

What you will need:

Pallets

Hammer

Nails

Paint

Screws

Screwdriver

Saw

Outdoor cushions and pillows

Sandpaper

Photo made by: SoniaT 360.

Directions:

Much like the patio tables, these require minimal effort. All you have to do is decide on the height you want for your seating, and assemble or disassemble the pallets accordingly.

I like to apply a nice paint to mine, and let dry completely, then screw the taller ones together, plus leave a few of the shorter ones for my more relaxed days.

Let everything dry, and add the cushions, then you're done!

Refurbished Pallet Bookshelf

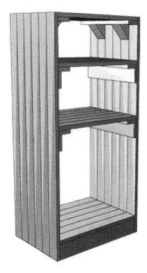

Photo made by: <u>Dr Vedel</u>

What you will need:

Pallets

Hammer

Nails

Stain

Saw

Sandpaper

478

Directions:

Though this might look like a bit of a challenge, this is another easy project. Start by completely taking apart your pallets, I recommend you take apart 2 or three of them.

Decide how big you want your book shelf to be, then reassemble as you see in the photo. Make sure you sand everything down to ensure there are no splinters or rough ends, and add a nice stain or a coat of paint when you are done, and that's it!

Simply Fancy

Easiest Ever Pallet Chair

What you will need:

Pallets

Hammer

Nails

Stain

Saw

Screws

Screwdriver

Sandpaper

Directions:

To make this simple chair, all you need to do is remove the wood from the bottom of 2 pallets. Take 1 of the pallets, and cut ¼ of the end off. Place this pallet at an angle on the other pallet, as you see in the photo above.

Screw securely in place. Take 2 boards from some of the wood you have removed, and screw them to the front of the pallet, lifting the front of the chair, and putting it in a reclining position.

Sand down everything so there are no splinters, and apply a nice stain. That's it! Your chair is done!

Pretty Pallet TV Station

Photo made by: Maria Papadodimitraki

What you will need:

Pallets

Hammer

Nails

Stain

Saw

Sandpaper

Wheels (optional)

Directions:

Start by cutting your pallet in half right down the middle. Set the bottom on top of the top, and screw in place.

Sand down the rough edges, then flip over. If you are going to put wheels on the piece, place these at equal ends of the stand, and screw in place.

Set back upright, and add a nice dark stain to the entire piece. Let dry, and add another. Let dry completely, and your new stand is ready to showcase your entertainment system!

Elegant Glass Table Top

What you will need:

Pallets

Hammer

Nails

Stain

Saw

Sandpaper

Screws

Screwdriver

Glass sheet

Photo made by: <u>Doug Lynne</u>

Directions:

Start by pulling apart several pallets. Apply a nice dark stain to all of them before you begin, so your entire table has a dark stain.

Decide how many different compartments you want to be in your stand, and cut the lengths of wood you need to match these measurements. Sand down the wood so there are no rough edges, and apply another dark stain.

Once all is dry, take your screws and screwdriver, and assemble as you see in the photo. Leave the glass for the very end, and when you are ready, carefully place this on top.

Use hot glue to secure in place, or simply set it inside if you aren't going to move the table often. That's it! Your new table is ready to showcase to your friends and family!

Fun and Fabulous Coat Hangers

Photo made by: Sergio venuto

What you will need:

Pallets

Hammer

Nails

Stain

Saw

Screws

Screwdriver

Paint

Sandpaper

Hooks

Directions:

Decide how big you want your coat hanger to be, and cut the pallet down to this size. Remove the backing, and leave the support boards in place so the wood lies flat against your wall.

Sand down the wood first, then paint it any color you want. The brighter the colors, the better. Let the paint dry, then add the hooks wherever you want them to be.

Add a hanger to the back of the rack, and that's it! Your coat rack is ready to roll!

Fancy Crab Art

Photo made by: sailn1

What you will need:

Pallets

Paint

Nails

Stencil

Saw

Sandpaper

Directions:

Remove the backing from your pallet, and if you want a closer knit section, screw them in place between the boards.

487

If you are good with your art, draw whatever outline you wish across the pallet. I like to use stencils, as they give a more clean looking line. But again, do what makes you happy.

Cut the shape out of the pallet, then sand the wood down so the paint will stay better. Paint the piece any and all colors you like, applying more than one coat if you wish.

Let dry, and hang wherever you wish to show off your work!

The Best of the Rest

Fancy Twin Bed

What you will need:

Pallets

Hammer

Nails

Stain

Saw

Screws

Screwdriver

Sandpaper

Directions:

Start by cutting 1 pallet into thirds, and disassembling another. Leave 2 pallets complete, and sand all the wood down, you don't want there to be any splinters. Assemble as you see in the photo, filling in the gaps of the cut pallet with wood from the disassembled one.

Screw these in place on top of the two intact pallets, and apply a stain or paint to the entire piece. You can also place these on wheels, if you like, but that is up to you.

Once all is secure, you are done!

Leaning Bookshelf

Photo made by: <u>Christine Vazquez</u>

What you will need:

Pallets

Hammer

Nails

Stain

491

Saw

Paint

Screws

Screwdriver

Sandpaper

Directions:

Pull all the wood off the bottom of your pallet, and sand the entire piece. Use some of this wood you have taken, and place it against the pallet frame, only this time, pulling away from the frame so they form shelves.

Screw in place, and sand down the rough edge. Paint the entire piece, let dry, and apply another coat before you place in your home to show off to your friends and family!

Crazy Mandala Paint Piece

What you will need:

Pallets

Paint

Nails

Stencil

Saw

Sandpaper

Photo made by: <u>Amanda Baker</u>

Directions:

Remove the backing from your pallet, and if you want a closer knit section, screw them in place between the boards.

Now, if you are good with freeform art, go to town on this piece, making all the designs you can imagine. If not, you can use stamps, stencils, or anything else you like to make it a rustic, but modern, piece of art.

Have fun and express yourself.

Open Pallet Swing

Photo made by: Joel Washing

What you will need:

Pallets

Chain

Nails

Frame

Saw

Cushion

Sandpaper

Directions:

You can use a frame for this swing bed, or you can use trees or a porch. However you decide to hang the bed is up to you, but I assure you it's a relaxing way to spend the afternoon.

To make the bed, you need to take 2 pallets to 4 pallets and lay them out side by side, the size of the bed is determined by how many pallets you use. Take 4 boards, and add support to each of the pallets.

Screw in place on both the top and the bottom. Sand down all rough edges, and screw hooks in all 4 corners of the pallets. Determine where you are going to hang the bed, then measure how much chain you are going to need to hang it.

Loop the chains through the hooks, and bring together at the top. Make sure all is secure, and your bed is ready to relax.

Charming Pallet Fence

Photo made by: Leonora (Ellie)Enking

What you will need:

Pallets

Paint

Nails

Saw

Sandpaper

Directions:

Remove some of the boards from between the others. This is going to give the pallets a more open feel, making them appear to be more upscale.

Decide how many you are going to need to fence in the area you wish, and do the same to all the pallets. Sand them down, and apply a paint, then set aside to let dry.

In the meantime, determine where the fence is going to stand, and dig holes for the fence posts. You can use wooden posts from a hardware store, or you can use pallets to make the posts. Either way, you are going to paint these as well, and when the pallets are dry, hang them against the posts.

Make sure they are entirely secure, and your new fence is ready to go.

I hope these projects were able to inspire you to use pallets in ways you never thought of before, and that each and every one adds a new bit of charm to your home and garden area.

There are so many things you can accomplish when you use your creativity and some skills, and the more you can use the things around you, the less you have to pick up at the store itself. Use what you have on hand to save money, resources, and time.

Show the world what you can do, and feel proud of each piece you create!

DIY Mini Shed:

The shed is a mainstay of every garden; in fact there are few homes which do not have one. The real question is not whether you need a shed but how big it needs to be. There are many different criteria to consider when deciding on the right shed for your needs. Your budget will feature prominently on this list; a shed is generally an expensive purchase. You will also need to consider what you intend to use the shed for; a small shed is acceptable for simply storing a few garden tools. However, if you wish to spend any amount of time in your shed it is important to consider the design carefully. There are options available which will ensure a spacious shed on the inside with a small footprint on the outside. This will maximize the usefulness of the shed whilst minimizing its impact on your garden.

It is possible to purchase a shed pre-owned and transfer it to your own home. However, this approach will be time consuming and often extremely difficult. You will need access to a good sized van or trailer and will have to take the shed apart. You may find this is difficult as, depending on how long the shed as been in position, the nails, screws and bolts may be rusted in place. Once you have got it apart and conserved the fixings you will be able to start the moving process and then rebuild it. Unfortunately the rebuild process is the slowest part of all as you will need to ensure all the pieces go in the same order and the same place. You will also be limited in your ability to customize your shed as its size and style has already been established.

The most viable option is to build your own shed. At first this may seem daunting, but, this guide will help you calculate the right size and shape shed for the space your have available. There are three main stages of successfully creating a small but roomy shed; the planning stage, collecting the materials and the build. Each of these stages is essential if you wish to create a shed which will serve your needs and cost less than $40.

It is important to note that there are very few places where you will have an issue building a shed. However, it is always a good idea to check with your local planning department to ensure you will not inadvertently fall foul of any regulations. Part of this process is creating a shed which will sit comfortably in your garden; this is one of the reasons wooden sheds have become the preferred option. Although they do require a little maintenance each year, they are generally easy to maintain and will last you for many years.

Planning and Materials

Getting the planning stage right means you will know exactly what materials you need to source and how to put them together. This is an essential part of their plan and the time taken to consider this can easily be as long as the time it takes to build the shed. This guide focuses on a small but roomy shed and not one which is likely to exceed the standard building regulations.

Use of Shed

The first stage of any project is to decide what you will be storing in the shed and what activities you intend to complete inside your new building. If you wish to simply store your garden tools and have a place to sit and rest when working on your garden then your shed can be a small but cozy affair.

However, if you need to pot plants, escape from the rest of the world or simply gain some peace and quiet then you may need to consider making your shed a little larger. The use of your space will be a significant factor in the decision as to what size it should be.

Location

The next item you will need to establish is where you intend to site your shed. Ideally you should find a location which allows easy access but keeps the shed hidden from the main home. You will not wish to have your view ruined by a shed in the middle of your pristine lawn!

It is worth considering which paths are already laid into your garden. It is important to build a path to the door of the shed to ensure that you are not trampling mud back and forth during the wet winter months.

There are also considerations regarding the use; if you wish to use a telescope in your shed you cannot put it under the trees! Likewise, the trees will lose their leaves in autumn; if these fall directly onto your shed they can speed its deterioration; unless they are cleaned regularly. A practical and useful shed should be located where it is most needed. Whilst this may seem like common sense you may be surprised how many people choose a shed's location based on aesthetics; instead of practicality.

Construction

Having established the size and location you now need to consider the material you would like your shed to be created out of. The traditional material is, of course, wood. However, this is not the only option. It is possible to create a shed out of metal sheeting; although you may need to consider painting it to help it blend into your garden. This will be especially relevant if your shed will be visible to your neighbors as they may not like the look of a metal shed!

Plastic is an increasing popular option as it is exceptionally durable and needs very little maintenance. However, plastic is not exceptionally strong and still requires a strong frame work to pin it to. In reality, plastic is only an option for a small shed which is just going to be used for storage.

There are also a variety of environmentally friendly options which you may wish to consider. The most obvious is simply wood that you know has come from a renewable source; the environmental impact is zero. Another substance which is often used to create a waterproof and well insulated shed is rubber. Old tires are plentiful and easy to get hold of. They can be used to create the walls with or without a wooden frame. You can even choose to use hay to create the walls of your shed. Your decision will depend upon the resources near you and the time you have available; as well as how high your concern is for the environment.

Power

In general you will not need power inside your shed if it is simply for storage purposes. However, if you are likely to undertake projects inside the shed or it is a fair distance from your house; there is a good chance that it would be beneficial to have power. It is possible to add a solar panel or two and a battery to create the electricity you need. However, this is a more expensive option and not something that you would be able to do on a $40 budget.

504

It is, however, possible to run a cable from your fuse box to the shed. But, unless you are a very competent Do-It-Yourselfer then you will need to use a qualified electrician to hook your power into place. If this is not an option at this stage it is worth laying a cable in place when constructing the shed and adding the electricity at a later date.

Tools

It is inevitable that you will need a selection of tools in order to build your shed. The assumption of this guide is that you already have these or are capable of borrowing them. If you need to purchase something like a cordless screwdriver your $40 budget will be destroyed.

Alongside a cordless screwdriver you may need a selection of screwdrivers and drill bits. A circular saw is also beneficial although a manual one can be used. You will also need a spirit level, pliers and a tape measure. These should all be items that you already have.

Sourcing the Materials

Building a shed on $40 means you do not have the luxury of visiting your local hardware store and ordering a shed; or even copious amounts of wood. Instead you will need to start thinking about what materials you have at home and what are available within the vicinity which can be used to create your small, but spacious shed.

Obviously if you happen to own a wood then you can chop trees to create walls. However, this is an unlikely scenario! Instead you can start researching which businesses are in your area. One of the cheapest ways to acquire wood for shed building is to locate a local business with an excess of pallets.

Pallets are the perfect material for building a shed; they can be obtained for free and are already strong enough to make solid walls. The only concern when acquiring pallets is that you locate ones which have not been used to carry chemicals or hazardous substances. Even if they have been treated to protect against spills they are likely to have substances which can make you ill. The best pallets are those which have been used by the food industry; they will be clean and untreated.

It is advisable to have at least a dozen pallets although more is better! You will also need plenty of screws and two pieces of thread; approximately five feet long.

Whilst using pallets is fine for the frame and the walls; you will need to consider what roofing material is going to be the best for your shed project. It is possible to purchase roofing felt for as little as $20. This would be a roll of 10m by 1m and should comfortably cover a small shed.

An alternative is to use metal sheeting which can be purchased for as little as $10. It is worth considering how this will make your finished shed look although this is a cheaper option. Plastic sheeting can also be purchased for a similar price and may look aesthetically more pleasing.

It is worth considering the shape of your roof before you commit to any materials. Although a pitched roof can make the shed look nicer and feel roomier inside; it will add to the cost of your roof. An angled roof can be just as effective and use less material; helping to keep your costs down. Opting for a clear plastic corrugated sheet on your roof can provide an additional benefit; you will always have light in your shed; without needing to create windows or add electricity.

Other materials which should be considered before you start your project are those which need to be used to create the foundations. For your shed to be level and long lasting you will need to raise the base above ground level; this will ensure water does not collect round the floor and slowly seep up into the walls. Over time this can rot your shed out from the bottom up; ruining your hard work. The easiest base to create for your shed is made from gravel. In fact you can use small hardcore; with a little patience and luck you will be able to find hardcore being given away for free near you. You may even be able to approach your local authority or local quarry to see if they have any excess which they are getting rid of. It is worth waiting to find the right source as gaining your foundations for free is a very satisfying experience; it also helps your budget to spread further!

It is also possible that you will have the materials you need sat in your garden already. A shed foundation can be made from paving slabs; you may be able to reallocate ones which are already sat in your garden, or, you may prefer to purchase them from your local garden centre. Paving slabs are often as little as a $1 each although you may be able to purchase them second hand cheaper. To create a six foot by four foot shed you may only need between eight and twelve slabs.

It is also possible to use concrete for the base of your shed, however this is generally for bigger sheds and the cost of it will be very likely to put your project over budget.

Used Materials

When considering the materials you need it is worth considering what is on offer on the second hand market. For instance, you will often find paving slabs and gravel being practically given away. In addition there are sometimes cases where a shed is being got rid of. These adverts are usually marked as free to collector but you will need to take the shed apart. This can be time consuming and is probably not a viable opportunity to create your shed. However, there may be valuable bits of material which can be used and make your life easier.

It is, however, important to ensure that you have good quality materials as you will want your shed to last for a significant amount of time. There is little point saving funds on the build and having to do the structure again in a year or two.

As a final point before the building work starts it is also worth considering unusual items which are either very cheap on the second hand market. Even an old boat with a cabin can be utilized to create your perfect small shed.

Getting Started on Your Build

Having gone through all the planning stages you will now know what sort of shed you need, the approximate size and your preferred building material. The following list will provide you with all the materials you need to create a shed approximately two meters by one meter. You can make the shed bigger or smaller simply by adding additional pallets; the average pallet is approximately one meter on each side; hence the chosen shed dimensions:

- Approximately 20 wooden pallets – Free

- Collection of screws; including at least 24 three inch long ones and 24 nuts and washers. You will also need some screws for fastening the roof down. - $10 although you may already have many of these.

- Thread; the best idea is to have four 1 meter pieces and four 2 meter pieces. Cost should be no more than $10

- Gravel or hardcore sourced from any local location for free.

- Pavers or cement blocks to lift the base of the shed off the floor; protecting it from the elements. $10 if you need to purchase them.

- Roofing corrugated sheet; plastic or metal depending upon your preference. Cost should be no more than $10.

Total cost is $40 although it is possible to do this for less if you are able to source more of the materials cheap or free.

You will now be ready to start your foundations!

1. Dig the base

The first step is to dig approximately two inches down into the soil to create the outline size of your shed. You will need to take a pallet apart in order to take the two strongest sides and secure them to each other. This will create a long post; the same size as your finished shed. This should fit into the trench you have dug. You will need to use the spirit level to ensure this piece is in place properly; it must be level. This is vital to ensuring your finished shed is level and strong. You should take as much time as you need to complete this part of the process properly. Once your first piece is in you will need to add a second one on the opposite side; where the shed should sit. Once these are both leveled they can be joined at each end; again this will be using the base section of your pallet. This is often referred to as the block with the bottom deck board and top deck board attached.

BLOCK PALLET

Width

Length

Stringer Board

Block

Bottom Deckboard

HandJack Openings

Opening Height

Chamfer

Lead Board

Deck Spacing

Top Deckboard

You can then continue this process by adding in four cross sections between the original lengthways pieces. The mid sections can be supported by cement blocks or pavers; whichever product you already have or are able to get hold of easily.

This is also the time to consider whether you need to run electricity to your shed. If this is a yes then you will need to purchase some armored cable and dig a trench at least half a foot deep from the foundations of your shed to your home. Armored cable will help to prevent someone digging into the cable by mistake. It is also advisable to note the path the cable takes to help prevent the opportunity to accidentally make contact with it. If this is your desired option then you should make sure that you have more than enough cable and it should not be connected to the mains supply until the shed is finished.

2. Complete the Foundation

Once you have taken the time to create the frame work and leveled it all off you will be ready to fill the interior with your gravel or hardcore. This will help any excess water to drain away and prevent damage to your shed structure.

You will now be ready to start creating the actual shed! You will need to place two pallets onto the ground, upside down. You can now bolt these two pallets together by putting a nut and bolt through the blocks on each pallet. This should prevent them from moving. These two pallets should fit perfectly into the foundation space you have already created.

Ideally the base pallets should be ones which are fully boarded without gaps. If this is not the case then you will need to add extra boards in to fill all the gaps. This will ensure you do not lose items when you are in your shed or leave avenues open for creatures to get into your new creation.

3. Creating the Walls

The walls are simply two pallets stood on top of each other. The long walls will require four pallets; whilst the end wall requires two pallets. You will need to use the thread that you purchased. A hole must be drilled through each of the blocks on one side of both base level pallets. This will need to be in the same spot to enable the pallets to be secured to each other. You can use the washers and nuts to ensure the pallets are tightly secured together. The thread should be cut to allow you to join the pallets in the middle and at the ends to the end pallet. It should also be used to connect the bottom row of pallets to the top; this will ensure the structure is bound securely together.

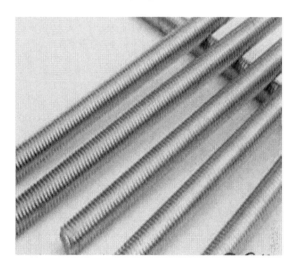

The pallets should be screwed and bolted to the base wood as well as bolted to each other. The three inch screws will come in useful at this stage.

You can work your way round your structure; until the ten pallets are securely fastened to each other and to the base. You will have created a 'U' shape and will be heading towards a completed shed. One important consideration at this point is that the pallets all face the same way. Whether the outer wood is horizontal or vertical it is essential that it all moves in the same direction. This allows for uniformity and provides a good overall appearance.

4. Creating the Roof

The next stage is to create the roof. This adds additional strength to the shed as well as provides a cover against the rain. There are two options for this; depending upon your desired finish and use for the shed.

Both options require you to batten wood round the edges of the walls. Whilst it is idea to use on piece on each side this may not be an option. It is acceptable to batten two pieces of the pallet wood together to create a one long batten. This is the piece that the roof structure will sit on.

It is now time to decide whether you wish to have a sloping roof. This is highly recommended as it will allow the rain water to drain off in whichever direction you choose.

The easiest way to generate a sloping roof is to take the batten you have just created and, before you fasten it to your shed, use it to draw a line across the wood. It should be at least a ten degree angle front to back. You will then need to use your circular saw to cut this angle in situ. You can repeat the process with the other wall and cut a straight line of the back wall to match the new lower height of the sides.

The battens can then be added to the side walls as indicated in the picture. You should also add one or two running parallel to these which will support the middle of the roof line. It is important that a batten is added to the front side of the shed as these roof battens will rest on this and provide the whole structure with strength.

The roof can be screwed or nailed down to the roof battens you have just added. Every screw or nail should be dipped into a silicon sealant before you put it into place; this will help to prevent leakages from the holes created by the screws.

It is also important to note that the roof must overhang the walls on all sides; this will help to prevent the rain from coming through the walls.

5. Adding the Door

At this point you should have three walls battened together and a sloping roof heading away from the door way. As this shed is just one meter wide it is as easy to generate the door out of two pallets. Simply stand them next to each other on the floor and bolt them together in the same way that you have done the side walls and the rear wall. The Pallets should have at least four hinges on them to fasten them to the side wall. This is because they are heavy and will quickly sag if not properly secured.

The two pallets should be the same size as the other end of the shed and the gap you have available. You will simply need to fasten a handle onto the pallets and then a latch and lock onto the frame.

It is possible to cut the pallets in half and make the door half the width of the available space. You can then fasten the other half of the two pallets to your shed. The easiest way of doing this is to screw a batten into the existing shed wall and then screw each of the pieces of pallet wood into this batten. The other side of the pallet will already be the block side; which is strong enough by itself to handle being screwed into the floor and the roof beams.

6. Finishing Touches

You will have noticed that there are some gaps in your shed, this is because, not all pallets are presented as a complete surface. There is usually space to add pallet boars between the existing ones. This is the next job you should undertake as it will seal up all the gaps in your shed. Obviously you will need to follow the lines that the pallets are already set in.

If you do not feel that you want to leave it as a pallet wall you can cover the whole wall with a sheet of chipboard or similar. Whichever end result you choose to adopt it is a good idea to stain the shed or paint it before it gets wet.

You will also need to consider cutting a couple of holes in your shed and fastening some clear plastic to them; these can act as windows as it does not yet have any. You will also spot the gap at the top of your structure; where the roof creates and angle. These gaps can also be filled with clear plastic or even pieces of wood taken from your remaining pallets.

Tips When Building

There are several things you can do to improve the effectiveness of your building.

- The heat and the coldness of the outdoors will affect the wood, it will contract and expand. Painting or staining the outside will greatly help to reduce this affect. However, it is also advisable to line the inside of your shed. The simplest option is black bin liners pinned to the walls. Plastic sheeting or even wood has the same effect and can help to make your shed windproof.

- By only using half the pallet as a door and the other half as a fixed piece you will create the perfect opportunity to run shelves all down one wall. In addition you can put a cupboard at the far end; providing you with plenty of space to store all the important items. Of course, you can make designated spaces for specific items of equipment!

- If you prefer not to have a plastic roof it is possible; with a few extra pallets, to create a pallet style roof. Simply attached your boards to the roof battens you have added to your structure. However, it is unlikely that wood alone will keep the water out. You will, therefore, need to add a plastic membrane on top of the roof before adding more wood above the plastic; this would ensure all rain is kept out of your shed whilst retaining the lodge feel.

- You can also create an apex roof; obviously this takes a few more pallets and will require more felt, plastic sheets or even a number of roof tiles.

- The door furniture can make a big difference regarding how your finished shed looks. It is important to take a moment to ensure you have chosen the right combination.

- If you prefer to minimize the work it is possible to create your shed against an existing wall. This could be a garden wall or even the side of your house. You would need to add a piece of wood to the wall for the roof battens to rest on. However there would be no need to complete the back wall. You would need to seal the roof to the wall to ensure water does not sneak into the back of your shed.

- Perhaps the greatest tip of all is to make sure you take your time with this build. Your preparation and patience will be rewarded with a shed that will last for many years. This is why it is essential to consider all the details before you start work. The right amount of preparation and a good coat of paint at the end will leave people believing you have purchased an expensive shed; not built one yourself!

Fence Building

You see a dog run right through your yard, trampling your flowers and digging holes where you don't want them. Or perhaps you see a group of kids cut through your yard on their way to the park.

Or perhaps you wish to let your own dog outside, but you know you have to stand there and watch him the entire time, or he is going to be the dog that is running loose throughout the neighborhood.

Or even worse, you wish to let your kids go play outside, but with the busy street nearby, you don't want to risk them running out into it without checking for cars. Although it's a beautiful day, everyone is trapped inside until you are able to go out and supervise what is going on.

You feel bad about this, and wish there was a way for you to let your pets and children outdoors, but you just can't risk their safety.

You know a fence would be a good idea, but times have been tight and you know that a fence would be expensive. You've seen the prices at the store, and you know a good fence would cost you several hundred dollars – money that you can't afford to spend right now.

Or perhaps you have finally gotten a little bit ahead in the bank, and you don't want to spend a bunch of money and send yourself back to where you started. The inner turmoil ends up causing you stress – which is the last thing you need in your life.

I would love to put a fence around my yard, but I honestly don't have the money to spend on that right now.

I want to put a fence around my yard, but I don't want my house to look like everyone else's. I want something that is unique.

I want to keep my kids in and the other kids out, but how am I going to do that without draining my bank account?

If you have been trying to find a good fence, odds are you have been thinking this very thing. But, that is where this book comes in. In it, you are going to find everything that you need to construct your own fence, without spending a lot of money to do it.

There's no end to the ways you can create your own fence, and give yourself the peace of mind you have been searching for. Gain inspiration from the fences you see in this book, and secure your home and living space with a fence of your own.

With a little creativity, some work, and a few skills, you will be able to make a fence of your own. And still enjoy having money in the bank when you are done.

The Fences

Simple Striped Fence

Photo made by: koocbor

Give yourself the gift of privacy and enjoy a change in the scenery with this artistic style fence.

You will need:

Wood (begin by measuring your yard and determining how much wood you will need before you begin. This is going to save you both time and money in the long haul)

Fence posts (again, determine how many you will need on the outset of the project)

Screws

Screwdriver

Post hole digging tool

Paint in the colors of your choice

Saw

Directions:

Begin by calling and having the ground surveyed. You don't want to accidentally hit a power or water line. This can be done for free and only takes a few minutes – it's worth doing that before you begin rather than dealing with a burst water line.

Start in one corner of your yard and begin digging holes for the fence posts. You will need to get them at least 2 feet into the ground, so take your time and fit them well. Fill in the holes with soil, tamping it down to ensure that the posts are secure.

Place fence posts at regular intervals, around 10 feet apart depending on the size of your yard.

Take the boards now and screw them in place on these fence posts. Make sure you use several screws per board as these are going to take most of the stress of the fence.

Next, take the remaining wood and your saw, and narrow one end of the board to a fine point.

You can make this a sharp point, or keep it rounded. Screw the boards side by side on the fence, as you see in the photo. You are going to screw these to the boards that are running horizontally between the fence posts, attaching them both at the top and at the bottom.

Once all the boards are secure, apply 2 coats of paint to each board, in the color of your choice.

Allow to dry completely, and you are done!

Naturally Minimalist Fence

Photo made by: Clyde Poole

You will need:

Wood (begin by measuring your yard and determining how much wood you will need before you begin. This is going to save you both time and money in the long haul)

Fence posts (again, determine how many you will need on the outset of the project)

Screws

Screwdriver

Saw

Post hole digging tool

Directions:

Begin by calling and having the ground surveyed. You don't want to accidentally hit a power or water line. This can be done for free and only takes a few minutes – it's worth doing that before you begin rather than dealing with a burst water line.

Following the photo as a reference, you are going to screw the boards in place along the posts. The fence is supposed to have a zig zag shape, so allow for this room when you plan the size of the fence. As you place the posts for the fence, take into account how long the wood is that you are working with. You may need to adjust how far apart the posts are based on the length of wood you are using.

You may need to take a saw and cut the lengths of wood to be close to the same before you begin.

The wood needs to be screwed into place at both ends, offering maximum support for the fence. Make sure all is secure, and you are done!

All Natural Picket Fence

Photo made by: <u>Clyde Poole</u>

You will need:

Wood (begin by measuring your yard and determining how much wood you will need before you begin. This is going to save you both time and money in the long haul)

Fence posts (again, determine how many you will need on the outset of the project)

Screws

Screwdriver

Post hole digging tool

Wooden boards (to screw between the fence posts)

Directions:

Begin by calling and having the ground surveyed. You don't want to accidentally hit a power or water line. This can be done for free and only takes a few minutes – it's worth doing that before you begin rather than dealing with a burst water line.

Start in one corner of your yard and begin digging holes for the fence posts. You will need to get them at least 2 feet into the ground, so take your time and fit them well. Fill in the holes with soil, tamping it down to ensure that the posts are secure.

Place fence posts at regular intervals, around 10 feet apart depending on the size of your yard.

Take the boards now and screw them in place on these fence posts. Make sure you use several screws per board as these are going to take most of the stress of the fence.

Next, take the remaining wood and screw each piece side by side on the fence, as you see in the photo. You are going to screw these to the boards that are running horizontally between the fence posts, attaching them both at the top and at the bottom.

Space them out according to your own size preference, creating a fence that is as secure or as decorative as you prefer. Try to mix and match the sizes for a more natural look throughout.

If necessary, cut the wood to roughly the same length before screwing it in place on the fence.

Make sure all is secure, and you are done!

Artistic Fence

Photo made by: Tony Alter

You will need:

Wooden boards (begin by measuring your yard and determining how much wood you will need before you begin. This is going to save you both time and money in the long haul)

Fence posts (again, determine how many you will need on the outset of the project)

Screws

Screwdriver

Post hole digging tool

Decorations of choice (can be tools as pictured, or you can use anything else you like)

Directions:

Begin by calling and having the ground surveyed. You don't want to accidentally hit a power or water line. This can be done for free and only takes a few minutes – it's worth doing that before you begin rather than dealing with a burst water line.

Start in one corner of your yard and begin digging holes for the fence posts. You will need to get them at least 2 feet into the ground, so take your time and fit them well. Fill in the holes with soil, tamping it down to ensure that the posts are secure.

Place fence posts at regular intervals, around 10 feet apart depending on the size of your yard.

Take the boards now and screw them in place on these fence posts. Make sure you use several screws per board as these are going to take most of the stress of the fence.

Next, take the remaining wood and screw each piece side by side on the fence, as you see in the photo. You are going to screw these to the boards that are running horizontally between the fence posts, attaching them both at the top and at the bottom.

Keep the spacing for the fence close together, setting each board side by side before screwing on the next board on the fence.

Once the main frame of the fence is in place, begin attaching the décor of your choice. Again, this can be something such as tools or pottery, or it can be anything you like. Let your creativity run wild, and show off your style.

That's it, your fence is done!

Barely There Fence

537

You will need:

Smaller, rounded posts

Fence posts (again, determine how many you will need on the outset of the project)

Screws

Screwdriver

Post hole digging tool

Directions:

Begin by calling and having the ground surveyed. You don't want to accidentally hit a power or water line. This can be done for free and only takes a few minutes – it's worth doing that before you begin rather than dealing with a burst water line.

Start in one corner of your yard and begin digging holes for the fence posts. You will need to get them at least 2 feet into the ground, so take your time and fit them well. Fill in the holes with soil, tamping it down to ensure that the posts are secure.

Place fence posts at regular intervals, around 10 feet apart depending on the size of your yard.

Take the smaller posts now and screw them in place on these fence posts. Make sure you use several screws per post as these are going to take most of the stress of the fence.

Attach these posts at the top of the fence, keeping an even line across the entire fence.

Make sure all is secure, and you are done!

Easiest Ever Privacy Fence

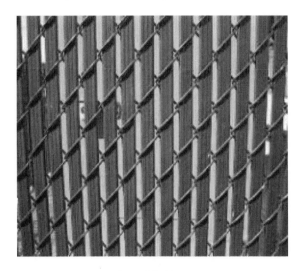

Photo made by: j_regan

If you already have a chain link fence, this is an excellent way to bring in some privacy without having to take it down or change what kind of fence you have. Save money and enjoy more security without breaking the bank!

If you don't have a pre-existing chain link fence, you can easily place one in your yard to start. They are often less expensive than wooden fences, and are easy to put in place.

What you will need:

Chain link fence

Fence posts

Weather proof plastic strips (can be purchased at your local home and garden store)

Directions:

If you need to put up the chain link fence:

Begin by calling and having the ground surveyed. You don't want to accidentally hit a power or water line. This can be done for free and only takes a few minutes – it's worth doing that before you begin rather than dealing with a burst water line.

Start in one corner of your yard and begin digging holes for the fence posts. You will need to get them at least 2 feet into the ground, so take your time and fit them well. Fill in the holes with soil, tamping it down to ensure that the posts are secure.

Secure the section of chain link to the fence posts. These can be screwed into place at the corners, or you can attach them with wire. If you are using wire be use gloves as you attach the fence in place, and snip off the long ends. Make sure anything sharp is folded inward so nothing gets cut or caught on the piece.

Once the fence is in place:

If the strips didn't come precut, take your saw and cut them to the appropriate length. You may need to cut both the length and the width, and if this is the case measure carefully to ensure you get the right size before you begin.

Make each piece as uniform as you can, and keep in mind the thicker you make the strips, the more coverage you will have with your fence.

Once the strips are ready, begin weaving them through the chain links on the fence. It is easier to work from the top to the bottom, and to weave them in completely, one at a time. Make sure you run the full length of the fence as you work from the top to the bottom, and start at the center of the fence and work outward.

Once you have woven the strips throughout the entire fence, take your scissors and cut down any extra length that is on the stripping. Make sure all the strips are uniform, and that there aren't any loose pieces hanging out.

Look over the fence and make sure all is secure, and your new privacy fence is set in place!

Jagged Barrier Fence

You will need:

Wooden boards (begin by measuring your yard and determining how much wood you will need before you begin. This is going to save you both time and money in the long haul)

Fence posts (again, determine how many you will need on the outset of the project)

Screws

Screwdriver

Post hole digging tool

Saw

Paint

Directions:

542

Begin by calling and having the ground surveyed. You don't want to accidentally hit a power or water line. This can be done for free and only takes a few minutes – it's worth doing that before you begin rather than dealing with a burst water line.

Start in one corner of your yard and begin digging holes for the fence posts. You will need to get them at least 2 feet into the ground, so take your time and fit them well. Fill in the holes with soil, tamping it down to ensure that the posts are secure.

Place fence posts at regular intervals, around 10 feet apart depending on the size of your yard.

Take the boards now and screw them in place on these fence posts. Make sure you use several screws per board as these are going to take most of the stress of the fence. Once these boards are in place, apply a bright coat of paint.

Allow this to dry completely before applying another coat of paint. Again, allow this to dry completely before moving onto the next step.

As the paint is drying, take your saw and cut the boards to different lengths. Be consistent with the pattern of boards you are cutting, and try to make 3 different overall lengths for the pieces.

Next, take this remaining wood and screw each piece side by side on the fence, as you see in the photo. You are going to screw these to the boards that are running horizontally between the fence posts, attaching them both at the top and at the bottom.

You can space these as far apart or keep them as close together as you would prefer. As you can see in the photo I have chosen to space them a little further apart than some of the other fences you see, but it is up to you and the level of security you wish to have with your fence.

As you screw these boards in place, set up a pattern that you can follow with the different lengths. Use the same pattern as you work through the length of the fence, creating an artistic look with the lengths of the boards. Make sure they are screwed securely in place.

When you have finished attaching all the boards to the main frame, apply 2 coats of a stain to the wood. Allow the first coat to dry completely before applying the second, and you are done!

Simple Beach Fence

Photo made by: redden-mcallister

You will need:

Wooden boards (begin by measuring your yard and determining how much wood you will need before you begin. This is going to save you both time and money in the long haul)

Fence posts (again, determine how many you will need on the outset of the project)

Screws

Screwdriver

Post hole digging tool

Wire

Directions:

Begin by calling and having the ground surveyed. You don't want to accidentally hit a power or water line. This can be done for free and only takes a few minutes – it's worth doing that before you begin rather than dealing with a burst water line.

Start in one corner of your yard and begin digging holes for the fence posts. You will need to get them at least 2 feet into the ground, so take your time and fit them well. Fill in the holes with soil, tamping it down to ensure that the posts are secure.

Place fence posts at regular intervals, around 10 feet apart depending on the size of your yard.

Next, measure and cut long lengths of wire to run between these fence posts. You will need to wear gloves as you are working to ensure you do not cut yourself with the wire. Cut at least 2 feet longer of each length than you will need, to ensure you do not lose the length as you twist.

Wrap the wire around the fence posts, and begin to twist. Again, I recommend that you use gloves for this part of the project to ensure that you do not scratch or cut yourself on the sharp wire. Continue to twist the wire for a length of 5 inches, then add your first board.

Wrap the wire around both sides of the board, and continue to twist. Use the photo as reference, and add new boards at regular intervals. Continue for the entire length of the fence, using at least 4 lines of wire throughout.

The more wire you use, the more secure your fence is going to be, and the less likely it will be for something to push the boards aside.

When all is secure, cut off the excess length of the wire, and wrap the remaining section around the next post. Bend in the ends of the wire so no one can get cut or snagged on them, and you are done!

Knee High by the Fourth of July Fence

Photo made by: flossyflotsam

You will need:

Wooden boards (begin by measuring your yard and determining how much wood you will need before you begin. This is going to save you both time and money in the long haul)

Fence posts (again, determine how many you will need on the outset of the project)

Screws

Screwdriver

Post hole digging tool

Saw

Paint

Directions:

Begin by calling and having the ground surveyed. You don't want to accidentally hit a power or water line. This can be done for free and only takes a few minutes – it's worth doing that before you begin rather than dealing with a burst water line.

Start in one corner of your yard and begin digging holes for the fence posts. You will need to get them at least 2 feet into the ground, so take your time and fit them well. Fill in the holes with soil, tamping it down to ensure that the posts are secure.

Place fence posts at regular intervals, around 10 feet apart depending on the size of your yard.

Take the boards now and screw them in place on these fence posts. Make sure you use several screws per board as these are going to take most of the stress of the fence.

Measure how tall you wish for your fence to be, then take your saw and cut the remaining boards to this length. Be consistent with your cuts, and make sure they are all the same. You can add a pointed end to the top of the boards, or you can leave them blunt or rounded, whichever you prefer.

Next, take the remaining wood and screw each piece side by side on the fence, as you see in the photo. You are going to screw these to the boards that are running horizontally between the fence posts, attaching them both at the top and at the bottom.

Space the boards according to your own preference, keeping in mind that this is more of a decorative fence rather than a security fence. As you can see in the photo, this fence is spaced slightly wider than some of the other fences you find here.

When you are happy with the spacing and all the boards have been screwed into place, you are ready to paint.

Use the color of your choice and apply a coat to the entire fence. Allow this to dry completely before applying another coat. Again, allow this to dry completely before you allow anything to touch the fence. For a fence such as this you can expect to have to touch up the paint regularly.

That's it! Your knee high fence is done and ready for action!

Recycled Upcycled Ski Fence

Photo made by: zstasiuk

You will need:

Wooden boards (begin by measuring your yard and determining how much wood you will need before you begin. This is going to save you both time and money in the long haul)

Fence posts (again, determine how many you will need on the outset of the project)

Screws

Screwdriver

Post hole digging tool

Skis (source these second hand, you can get excellent deals when you find them through thrift stores rather than paying for them up front)

Directions:

Begin by calling and having the ground surveyed. You don't want to accidentally hit a power or water line. This can be done for free and only takes a few minutes – it's worth doing that before you begin rather than dealing with a burst water line.

Start in one corner of your yard and begin digging holes for the fence posts. You will need to get them at least 2 feet into the ground, so take your time and fit them well. Fill in the holes with soil, tamping it down to ensure that the posts are secure.

Place fence posts at regular intervals, around 10 feet apart depending on the size of your yard.

Take the boards now and screw them in place on these fence posts. Make sure you use several screws per board as these are going to take most of the stress of the fence. Apply a bright coat of paint to these boards, and allow to completely dry before applying another coat of paint.

Allow this to dry, and you are ready to attach the skis.

Next, take the skis and screw each piece side by side on the fence, as you see in the photo. You are going to screw these to the boards that are running horizontally between the fence posts, attaching them both at the top and at the bottom.

Be careful as you are attaching the skis so you don't crack or break them. Use thin screws and be careful not to screw the skis on too tight. Hold the screwdriver straight ahead, and do not use an angle as this is going to make the skis more likely to break when you screw them in.

You can space them as far apart or keep them as close together as you like, keeping in mind that the further you have them apart, the more likely it is for something to get through. If you are using this for decoration, you have a lot more freedom with how far you can space the skis.

When you are happy with the spacing and have screwed all the skis in place, look back over each piece and make sure all are secure and none of them have broken.

That's it! your new ski fence is done and ready for action!

DIY Wood Fired Hot Tub

You may have heard about hot water tub or even saw it on the lawn of your friends, but you are not aware of what hot water tub is. Well no need to worry, hot water tub is something which will make your lifestyle healthy by adding up such things to it which will not only relieve your body stress but also make you feel fresh and peaceful. Today every person has a tough and hectic routine. It is not possible to take out time from the hectic routine of any spa or yoga treatment, but a body is always in need of peace and calm environment. How will you feel when you can provide such environment to your body at home? Well, hot water tub is one option which is available to you at home.

You must be thinking that having one hot tub at your home may cost you a huge amount of money, but the reality is quite different from it. The hot tub is one of those elements that you can build at your home by using few simple elements. These elements are easily available in the market. Upcoming chapters will give you detailed information about how you can make one hot water tub at your home. It will also tell you about the health benefits of this water tub. Therefore, do not waste your time and get to know about how you can also enjoy a hot bath at your home.

What is Fired Hot Water Tub?

A hot tub is a simple thing. The main objective of the hot tub is to hold people in hot water. As all of us know that water does not heat up by itself, therefore there is something needed along with the tub which is heat up the water present inside the tub. Many people who use hot tub mix oils with the water and also leave dirt in it. The dirt present inside the hot tub results in a growth of bacteria. The bacteria inside the water can cause diseases in the bathers and can affect the health of bathers negatively. Therefore, it is better to replace the water present inside the hot tub from time to time, in order to keep the water clean and safe for bathers. The main issue in changing water is that when you change the water present inside the tub, then you will have to heat it up. This heating process of new and clean water present inside the tub will cost you more. As heating of the water is an expensive mechanism and increases the cost.

For a hot water tub, you will also need a number of other elements. One of these elements is filtration system. You will have to filter the water for removing all the harmful materials from it. This filtration can be done with the help of proper system. When you fill the tub with water, then filtration process will remove all the impurities from the water. These impurities can be in any form but can be harmful to the health of bather in either way. Therefore, along with having other things, a proper and active filtration system is also needed.

Anti-bacterial chemicals are also a part of your hot tub, and you will have to put certain chemicals in the water that will keep bacteria away. These chemicals also keep your body away from the disease. No matter for how many hours your body remains in the water, it will remain clean and without getting affected by the bacteria. By putting these chemicals, you can easily place the hot tub outside your house and in your lawn. The water will not be affected by the bacteria that are present inside your backyard.

As the whole tub is loaded with water as you will have to soak your body inside it. For soaking the whole body, the limit of water must be enough inside the tub. Therefore, it is filled with an adequate amount of water. To heat up the whole water present inside the tub, it will take time. You will have to keep the water at bathing temperature for few hours for making it hot enough. For hours, it will need a constant supply of heat so that water will be hot enough so that you can soak your body. Therefore, place the water under heat for hours until it is perfect.

You will require a thermostat as you will have to check the temperature of water from time to time. This thermostat will let you know that what is the current temperature of the water. As you will have to take a bath in water at a certain temperature as lower than that will not be as fun for you as you planned. Whereas higher temperature of the water than you expected may also result in burning your body. Therefore, a thermostat is necessary to keep water at certain temperature range for an enjoyable hot tub bath.

Another important thing that you need along with the hot water tub is insulating cover and top. This insulating top or cover will keep the heat inside the water while the tub is not in use. If you do not have any such thing than heat may be lost from the water while the tub is not in use. Losing heat will make it difficult for you to retake a bath. You will have to repeat the whole process of reheating water for making the temperature equal to how much you planned about. Therefore, keep an insulating cover and place it on top of the hot water tub while not using it.

All these elements will make your simple hot water tub into something complicated. However, some of the people still make it simple by keeping the things under convenient level. They only add up those things in the hot water tub which are easily available and are only considered as necessary. While they eliminate all the other elements by calling those as not necessary. They add up all those things that can make their hot water tub bath convenient and fun time. Few people look forward to a wood fired hot tub. While on the other hand, few people make their hot tub by keeping in view their need and requirements. If you are one of the individuals that is planning to make their hot water tub, then there are many elements that you will have to consider. Along with which you will also need to make several important decisions.

You will have to consider the material of hot tub that you want to use for making one for your home. Along with deciding on the material, you will also look forward to a variety of heating system that you can use for your hot tub. You will also have to decide that for how many persons you are designing the hot tub. According to the number of persons, you will have to keep the size of the hot tub. The hot tub must be large enough so that few people can take a bath and soak their body at the same time. You will also keep in mind that it must not be a leak from any side for preventing water loss. Along with all these decisions, you will have to keep in mind what your budget is so that you spend money according to it.

Choosing Your Tub Material

When people are planning to build a hot tub by themselves, most of them go for wood. As wood is easily available and usually an easy material to deal with. Along with these benefits, there are many other advantages that one can enjoy while he is using wood for this purpose. You can get wood easily from anywhere. You can get any shape and quality of wood as it is available everywhere. Along with availability, you can get wood at a cheaper price as compared to other materials which will, in turn, decreases the overall cost of your hot tub.

Other than wood, many people also look for other materials for making their hot tub at home. The most important thing is that how you want your hot tub to look like along with how skillful you are in using the tools. If you want to give a unique and beautiful look to your hot tub, then you can go for such materials which will give a professional look to it. while if you are not aware of how to use the tools, then it is better to go for simple materials. Otherwise, you will have to take help from some skillful person while using tools.

Many people choose large scale tanks for making hot tub at their home. They use tanks which are used for providing water to the cattle. You can find these tanks made up of galvanized steel or rubberized plastic. The size of the tank is depended on your choice that for how many people you are building one. Along with it a shape of the tank which you will use for your hot tub also depends upon your choice. If you are about to build a hot tub for your use, then go for a narrow tank. Such a tank is perfect for solo soaking. You will need less water for such a narrow bath. When the amount of water is less, then it will take less time to heat up. If you are preparing to build a water tub for more than two people, then round tank is perfect. Round tank can easily hold multiple people at one time.

If you are good with using tools and want such a hot tub which will look good, then wood is the right choice for you. When it comes to wood, cedar is one of the best choices. Cedar is perfect and does not get effected by the weather conditions to a large extent. The smell of cedar is another aspect which makes it one of the best choice. Another advantage of using cedar is that when it absorbs water, it swells up. When the boundary of the hot tub swells up, then its joints will be sealed which prevent leakage of water from it. Cedar also looks good and will give a high-end look to your hot tub. Another advantage is that you can easily find one according to your decking.

Choosing Your Heating Method

After choosing the right material, here comes a turn for choosing which method you will use for heating the water inside the hot tub. There are two heating methods that are largely used for heating hot tub water. One of those methods is an internal burner while the other method is an external burner.

- **Internal burner:**

The internal burner is also known as snorkel stove. It is a most efficient method used for heating water inside your hot tub. Galvanized aluminum is used for making such kind of burner. All the sides of such burner are sealed completely except its top. The top is left open so that you can put wood from it and smoke can also come out of it. The whole unit of an internal burner is placed inside the water. The main reason of keeping it inside water is that the heat can easily transfer from the sides of the burner into the water of the hot tub. This method is quick as compared to other methods the main reason behind it is that heat is not lost even from the sides of the burner. Water is getting proper heat from all sides, therefore, getting heat up easily.

- **External burner:**

As the name depicts, an external burner is the one which is placed outside the hot tub. Water is piped out from the tub with the help of pipes. These pipes transfer heat from the fire to the water. Then water is again supplied to the hot tub. If the external burner is built and placed in the right place, then convection method is used for supplying the heat to the water properly and constantly. You will not need a pump for this purpose. However, this method is a slow method of heating water as heat reaches water slowly. When heat reaches slowly, it takes time to heat up full tub filled with water. Due to slow speed, this method is not considered as effective as compared to other methods.

However, as compared to other heating methods, these methods are mostly used and efficient. You will not need to use electricity in both of these methods for heating up water. When you use any such method that requires electricity, then your overall cost will increase. Heating water inside the hot tub is not a process that takes a couple of minutes, but you will need hours for completely heating the water. When you use electricity for hours for heating the water, then it will cost you so much.

It is recommended to purchase an already designed heater from the market rather than building one from the available materials. As if you are not able to do welding properly then your whole burner will be a big fail. When your burner is not efficient, then you may not be able to take a hot tub bath. Therefore, it is better to purchase one or else get professional help for designing it.

Way to soak

You must be thinking that why there is no information about chemicals and filters till now as mentioned earlier that you will need both for your hot tub. One of the reasons behind it is that wooden hot tub is very much different from the electric hot tub. The Wooden hot tub is usually small. Therefore, for a small tub, it is better to change water rather than filter it from time to time. Changing water in a small tub is not a difficult task. Whereas it gets dirty easily in a small tub, therefore, filters may not be effective in this regard. When you have used the water for a day, it is better to change the water in a week at least. Treating this water, again and again, is not the right option. Simply remove the used water from the water and refill it with clean and fresh water. As you have not combined any chemicals to this water inside the hot tub, therefore, you can use this water for your plants. Simply throw the water on the lawn and fill the tub with fresh water. If there are chemicals, then avoid throwing it in the lawn.

Most of the people who are using wood burner are quite happy with it. They are of the view that changing water in a wooden hot tub is very easy and do not need much effort. You can make your water ready to soak in a small-time period by using a wooden hot tub and wooden burner. It will also make your body close to natural settings, and you can have positive effects on your health rather than negative one. Many people add few drops of hydrogen peroxide in the water inside the wooden hot tub. These few drops increase the life span of water present inside the tub.

Hot tub and cover

The Hot tub is considered as a life time investment which will eliminate the need of spa. You can get the facilities of a spa right at your home place by taking a bath in this hot tub. However, along with a hot tub, a durable and proper fitting cover is also must with it. One of the main reason of keeping this cover is to for safety purpose. This cover will prevent a great number of accidents. If there are small kids or pets at your home, then there are chances of slip-off of both which can be harmful to their health. Therefore, a cover will prevent their slip-off inside the water. Your property will also keep safe due to the usage of hot tub cover. Otherwise, hot water can damage it. This cover will also keep the surface of hot tub safe during bad weather conditions. When there is extreme sunlight, then there are chances that the surface of the tub may get affected which can remain safe due to this hot cover. Even during a storm, a tarp can be easily blown off while cover will keep it safe.

Along with all these, you can also save your money and time if you own a hot tub cover. The reason behind it is when the water will be covered then the heat will remain inside the water. So, you will not have to use electricity for heating it again which is reduces the overall cost and time. Water will also remain inside the hot tub, and it will not be lost due to evaporation. Therefore, you can almost cut your electricity bill in half if you own a hot tub cover and can save the heat as well as water.

Along with all these benefits, one of the most obvious benefits of having a hot tub cover is cleanliness. When you cover the water, you will keep it safe from pollutants and dust. Your water will be clean even after days due to this durable covering. Your water will also remain free from debris. No need to change water after every day as the cover will keep it clean and safe from dust. Another advantage is that cover will also keep the unwanted people away from your hot tub. You can open it up only to family and friends.

Hot Tub Bath and Health

If people get to know about the thing that you are taking hot tub bath on a daily basis, then may take it as a part of your leisure routine. While the reality is that it is much more than just a simple leisure routine part. There are only a few people who are well aware of the benefits of a hot tub bath on your overall health. Researchers have done some researches and found out that there are significant benefits of taking a hot bath in a tub. They also look at the effects of such kind of bath on your health.

Most of the people who are suffering from pain and aches in any part of their body look forward to expensive message for the sake of relief. No matter that hot tub bath will relieve the body pains that you are having from past few years. It will also open up your blood vessels for proper and better blood flow inside your body. When the blood passes through the vessels easily, then blood pressure will also decrease. Along with decreasing blood pressure, blood flow and blood circulation will increase. When blood circulation is improved then body pains and aches are removed. Your body will be able to digest the food particles in a better way and will also strengthen your immune system. When immunity is enhanced, you can fight against the diseases in a better way. You can take hot tub bath as an important part of your diet. As it will solve all your digestion problems and will enhance your metabolism. When your friends come to know about the benefits of the hot tub bath, they will also add it up in their routine.

Massages are considered as a booster of the healing process of your body. massage results in promotion of relaxation reduce stress and smoothly stretch your connective tissue. With special features of the massage, you can save a great amount of money with the help of hot tub bath every year. No matter hot tub may not be as physically intense as that of massage, but the access you have to get a massage results in decreasing the necessity of having one. Your stressed muscles and tensed nerves get a chance once in a month to get better. While with the help of routine hot tub bath you can easily relieve this stress on a daily basis.

Daily stress greatly affects your body joints. You may feel pain in your joints which can be reduced with the help of daily relaxation exercise. The weight or burden over your body is almost reduced to 90 percent with the help of hot tub bath. The burden is not only released from your body, but the stress on your mind is also reduced. When there is no burden on your body and mind, then you will feel lighter and fresh as compared to stressful life.

When you enjoy all this benefits due to hot tub bath, then you will feel sleepy. Sleepiness is another sign of healthy life. When you get better and perfect sleep, then you can improve your performance as well as your memory. The Hot tub will reduce the stress and will improve your sleeping habits. When you sit in the hot water tub, then your body temperature is increased. This increased body temperature is perfect for cold nights and even work during sunny days. When your temperature drops after taking a hot water tub, then it is signed by your body that sleep time is near. When you sleep more, your health is likely to improve along with it. Studies showed that if you take hot tub bath for 15-20 minutes an hour before going to bed will result in deep and calm sleep. You will relieve the stress from your body and mind which will make your body ready to take some sleep.

Stress not only affects your mind, but it also has adverse effects on your body especially your heart. Your digestion will also slow down, and your breathing will not be normal anymore. Due to tension and stress, your whole body suffers. Have you tried yoga or meditation? How these activities affect your stressed-out body similar is the case with hot water tub bath. Your body will feel peaceful in the same manner as that of after yoga or any other such exercise. A hot tub bath will make your body feel light and peaceful. A Hot tub bath is considered as a perfect solution for relieving stress after a tough working day. After a hectic day, hot tub bath is a treat for your body. It will create a therapeutic environment for your body.

Along with these benefits, hot water tubs are also considered as one of the best methods of reducing body weight and manage level of sugar in your blood. It is considered as best option for those people who want to lose weight but do not have time for exercise. Type II Diabetes condition can be improved with the help of hot tub bath.

One of the other group which gets great benefit from hot tub bath is athletes. In order to prevent themselves from having a body injury along with reducing fatigue due to overusing their muscles. People suffering from medical conditions like chronic fatigue syndrome and fibromyalgia can also take advantage of hot tub bath for making their medical conditions better. When you include hot water bath in your life, then you may not need to use anti-inflammatory and analgesics drugs. Therefore, athletes and all such people who have aggressive level exertion in their life can take help of hot tub bath for making their body healthy and fresh.

Many people refuse and ignore the power of hot tubs bath in their life, but the history is evident that how hot tub bath is helpful in your life. Previous generations used it for medical purpose in order to treat your health conditions. Hot tub bath makes your body peaceful and relieves sore joints. It is also helpful for weight loss and improved blood circulation.

How to build Hot Tub?

After getting all the required information about what hot tub is and how you can build one, it is time to get information about step by step process of building one hot water tub for your home.

1. The process starts with finding an affordable source of clear cedar lumber. Make sure that the cedar that you found may not have knots in it. These knots can make your tub to leak. Make sure that you found some better place where you can find clean cedar. Make sure that you have some extra cedar pieces along with you for making a number of accessories like cup holder etc.

2. Draw the rough model of how your hot tub will look like. Measure the length and depth of the hot tub for making it easy for you to make one. Mention everything related to your tub like its shape and look on the paper along with the sketch of the hot tub.

3. When you are done with the sketch, it is time to cut the wood in staves for making a hot tub. Make sure you calculate the dimensions of the stave and mark it on lumber for accurately cutting the pieces. Also, keep your mind that you will also need staves for the floor of the tub. Therefore, cut the staves in such manner that you can make the corner of the tub as well as its floor in a proper manner.

4. After cutting the staves, it is time to join the staves for making your hot tub. Make sure that you complete this step carefully. If you do not pay enough attention to this step, then there can be leftover areas in your hot water tub.

5. Use cove joint for joining the stave. Make sure you give it enough time so that it can settle down. For completing a full joint, you will have to run

each of the board almost four times. If you join the pieces of the cedar properly, then cedar will swell perfectly.

6. After joining the walls of the hot tub, it is time to design its floor. Make sure that you set specific depth on the floor of the hot tub. For floor use dado joints. Use a ratchet strap for keeping all the part of the floor in its place.

7. Now it is time to compile your hot tub parts together. First of all, combine the staves together by using a hammer. Blow the hammer gently on the staves for keeping all the parts together. For holding the tub together, use vinyl-coated cable. Make sure that you use this cable in such a manner that it will not damage the wood. Use stainless steel buckle for keeping the cable intact in its place.

8. Use leftover pieces of cedar for making benches inside your hot tub bath. No need to worry if there are knots in the bench as benches are only for seating purpose. You can make benches in any shape, and the hexagon is an ideal way for it.

9. Attach a garden hose to one side of the hot tub. This hose will help you out in releasing water from the tub.

10. After your hot tub is ready, it is time to fill the tub with water. You can use any source of water depending upon its availability. This water will also let you know about whether there is any leakage in the hot tub or not.

11. You can make your internal burner, but it is better to purchase one. Go for a wood stove and place it inside the hot tub. Make sure there is a pipe along with the stove so that the pipe will smoke out.

12. Your hot tub is ready to use, simply turn on the stove, let the water heat up to the required amount. Check the temperature of water from time to time. When it is close to desired range, soak your body in the hot tub. Enjoy the hot bath and relieve all the body stress leaving it relaxed and fresh.

Cool Down Without Air Conditioner

It is a little known fact that air conditioning can be as expensive to run as a heating system. It simply depends upon where you live as to which product you use.

Estimates suggest that heating is responsible for two thirds of your energy bills; with the average CO2 emissions in a mild state being 4,700 pounds. Air conditioning can produce an impressive 6,600 pounds which is significantly more.

It is therefore easy to see why an air conditioning unit should not be your first priority when looking to live off-grid. Even if you have a huge array of solar panels you may struggle to keep up with the demands of your air conditioner.

Living off-grid does not mean that you do not use electricity. However you should evaluate your current uses of electricity it see if they can really be justified in an off-grid scenario.

The first air conditioning unit was invented in 1902 by an American; Willis Carrier. It was, of course, a large piece of equipment; designed for commercial use. However, by the 1920's it had shrunk considerably and was a common feature on residential buildings. In fact, it is said that the advent of air conditioning made the great migration in America possible!

If you live in the warmer areas of the globe then air conditioning is often seen as a vital part of life. Although it is possible to survive in the extreme heat, it is better to be comfortable; particularly when you are working.

What you may find more interesting is that electronic air conditioning may only have been in existence for 115 years, but there have been a variety of methods used to keep houses cool in the past. It is these methods that you can implement to stay cool and comfortable regardless of what time of day it is.

Some of these methods are those that were adopted by the ancient Egyptians whilst others are more modern and use materials which are only available in modern society.

Many methods will work better and be more cost effective if you build them into your off-grid home when you design it. Of course, this is only applicable if you are intending to build your own home and not simply convert an on-grid one to off-grid.

Choosing to live without air conditioning does reduce the amount of electricity you need to generate. But it also reduces your negative impact on the environment. Both of these are powerful reasons to discover the secrets of air conditioning without the air conditioner.

It may also help to know that your use of an air conditioner actually produces more CO_2; increasing the damage to the atmosphere and trapping more heat than would otherwise be an issue. The result is increased air temperatures and a greater need for air conditioners. A vicious circle is formed from which the best escape route is to stop using air conditioners.

By deciding not to use an air conditioner you are saving yourself funds and saving the planet at the same time! There can be very few incentives greater than that one.

10 Ancient Methods of Cooling Without the Air Conditioner

Although some of these methods do require you to incorporate them into a new build; it is possible to retrofit many of them to your current home. The important part is to understand how these systems work and decide if it is for you or not.

The average air conditioner works by sucking in the warm air round it. This air is then passed over the piping inside the air con unit. The pipes are full of cooling fluid; which is often branded. This attracts the heat from the air and removes it; allowing the cooler air to continue its journey; exiting the air con unit as cool or even cold air.

In the process of absorbing the heat, the cooling liquid will gradually warm up. It is then passed through a condenser which removes the heat; allowing it to continue to cool the air in your home. The warm refrigerant in the condenser is moved to the outside unit where it is blasted with a fan; ensuring the refrigerant cools and is ready to start its journey all over again.

A good air conditioner does not cool your home; it removes the excess heat.

1) Reed Windows

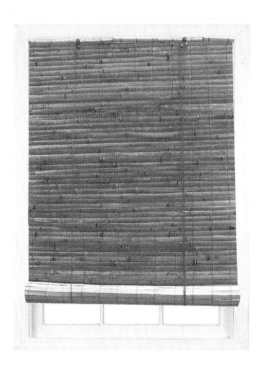

The ancient Egyptians had an innovative and reliable way to cool their homes without the need for any electricity. The method is still viable today.

Simply collect reeds and soak them in water. Once they are wet you can hang them across your windows. Ideally you should hang them on the outside to avoid them dripping into your home.

As the wind blows through your window space it will connect with the wet reeds and cool. The air entering your home will be cool and moist; making your home comfortable.

If you don't have reeds within your local area then a wet cloth can be just as effective. All you need to do is to keep an eye on the cloth or reeds and make sure they stay wet.

2) Salting the Water

Another technique that has been used successfully in the past is to add salt to water, before freezing it. By adding salt to the water you will lower its freezing point.

Although it will defrost at the same rate as standard ice, it will be colder than regular ice.

To get the maximum effect from this ice you need to place the ice in a bowl directly in front of a fan. Then simply turn the fan on. It will blow through the ice block, dramatically cooling the air as the ice melts.

You can reuse the bottle and even have multiple bottles stored in your freezer; allowing you to bring out a new one each time a bottle has melted.

This method does use electricity to run the fan but this is significantly less than the amount you would use to power an air conditioning unit.

3) Ice

An older option and alternative to salting water and freezing is simply to have huge blocks of ice. In the past ice was stored in cool houses between the winter and the summer. It was then brought out.

You could and still can lie against the ice to feel the coolness on your skin; or you can simply break pieces of to rub on your body. Alternatively you can simply suck the ice until it melts; which will help to cool your internal body temperature.

This is a viable method although not especially practical as you will need to store the ice somewhere and it will need to be kept outside; unless you want wet floors.

4) High Ceilings

In the past people considered the design of their houses very carefully. This is something you can do if you are building your own off-grid home. High ceilings which can be artificially lowered will allow you to maximize the air space and minimize temperatures in the summer.

In the winter you can lower the ceiling and keep the house warm. Both of these tactics work on the fact that hot air rises; it is hard to heat a house with a large ceiling taking all the heat. This will help to reduce the heat inside your home during the hot summer months.

5) Verandas

One of the most effective ways to reduce the effects of the sun in your home is to build a veranda. It should at least cover the east to west side of your home; although you can have it going all the way round. The veranda will prevent the heat of the sun from being beamed directly into your home.

It will also provide a shady part outside the home where you can relax and feel relatively cool.

If you build it all round your home then it will provide a shady spot at all times of the day. Even if you are in an existing home it is relatively easy to add this type of feature to your home.

6) Damp Blankets

Another method which worked very well before the air conditioner became available was using damp blankets.

The premise was simple; you soak the blanket in cold water and then wring them out. This leaves them damp; not wet. You can then lay the blanket over your body when you go to sleep. The dampness will feel cool and the heat of you and the room will cause the moisture to evaporate; without getting you wet.

You may need to get up in the night to rewet your blanket; but this is preferable to tossing and turning all night long.

7) Aligned Windows

Many houses used the principle of aligned windows to help keep them cool. This generally only works if you have a window on each side of the room; the house is only one room thick.

579

The windows on each side of the room must be lined up with each other. This can create a cross breeze which blows straight through your home. The result is the movements of air which can make the room feel considerably cooler.

You can extend this principle by having bigger windows upstairs and smaller ones downstairs. This will encourage the heat to leave at the top of the house and effectively suck cooler air in at the bottom.

8) Tree Planting

A more extreme form of cooling your home is to plant a tree. It will need to be a quick growing tree for you to appreciate its effects! If you plant the tree to block the midday and afternoon sun from your home then you will notice that your house is much cooler than it used to be.

However it is worth noting that whilst this technique is effective, it is best used on houses which have a lot of sun all year round. If you only have a couple of weeks of excess heat then you may wish you had not planted the tree the rest of the time!

Trees do create shade but they can also prevent your home from drying properly; making it damp and more likely to have mold issues. It is, therefore, essential to consider carefully before planting a tree.

9) Painting your Roof

If you look at the flat roofed houses of many Mediterranean countries you will note that the houses and the roofs are painted white. This is because white reflects the sun; helping to keep the house cooler on the inside.

If you can get to your roof easily or are still considering the best way to create your off-grid home; then you may need to factor a white or very pale roof into the equation. It makes a significant difference to the temperature inside your home.

10)   **Outside Cooking**

Every appliance you have plugged in will generate heat. Of course, some items must remain plugged in; such as your refrigerator and freezer. To minimize the heat that your house is creating you should unplug everything else. If it is not being used then unplug it!

The one appliance which puts out a huge amount of heat is your oven. You will probably need to cook at some point during the hot weather. However, this will simply increase the temperature in your home.

It is therefore advisable to undertake all cooking either in an outside kitchen or on the barbeque. This will help to keep the temperature of your house comfortable.

10 Modern Ways to Stay Cool Without Air Conditioning

The air conditioning units used today are remarkably efficient but still cost a lot of energy and funds to run. This is why people of the modern age have continued to come up with new ways of cooling their homes and themselves. After all, the real point of cooling your home is to keep your own body temperature balanced. If you can achieve this without cooling your home then this is certain t save you funds.

The following methods may seem unorthodox but they will all help you to stay cool; even without a conventional air conditioning unit:

1. **Drinking Water**

Your body has its own ways to control its temperature. Sometimes this simply needs a little boost and you will find the results make the heat much more bearable.

Although there have been studies for many years regarding the effect of hot drinks on the body; it would still appear that an ice cold drink s more effective at mooring body temperature.

By increasing your water intake and drinking more cold water your body will work to warm the water before processing it. In this process you will boost your metabolic rate and cool your body as your body needs to use the heat you are generating to warm the water you have just drunk.

In effect you will be losing less heat to the room and reducing your own body temperature. All you need to do is consume a glass of water regularly. Of course, you might also need the toilet more often!

2. Electric fans

An electric fan will not cool the room. Even on its cold setting it only moves the air round the room. However, this air movement can affect the feel of the temperature inside your off-grid home. As air moves past your skin it is likely to collect the moisture sat on the skin's surface. This will make you feel more comfortable and cooler; even though it may not actually affect your body temperature.

You can also face an electric fan at the open window. It will push the warm air in the house out the window; effectively allowing cooler air to come in and replace it.

3. Reverse Room Fans

Another option is if you have ceiling fans installed. Even if you do not currently have them they are actually very easy to add to your current home. Of course, the cost of running these fans will need to be considered when creating your off-grid electricity supply.

If you set these ceiling fans to run in reverse they will actually pull the hot air upwards; instead of pushing it down. Providing you have a window open at the top you should be able to expel the hot air and pull in cooler air.

This can make a dramatic difference to the temperature in your home and be exceptionally beneficial when you need to sleep. Opening a top vent does not present a risk whilst the ceiling fans are generally quiet enough to allow you to sleep!

4. Curtains, Shutters and Blinds

This is a very effective way of cooling your home and one that has been used for many years. You will need to have thick curtains or reflective blinds.

First thing in the morning, when the air is coolest, you should open all your windows. This will allow the hot air to escape and your house to cool significantly. As soon as it has cooled and the outside temperature starts to rise, or you have to go to work, you close all your windows and curtains / shutters or blinds. This will trap the cooler air in your home.

You may be surprised at how effective this is at keeping the house cool during the day. In the evening you can repeat the process of cooling the home.

The downside of this approach is that your doors and windows are constantly closed; it may keep the house cooler but it will also keep the sun out; making your home feel darker and cooler than it should.

5. The Whole House Fan

If you are planning a new, off-grid home then you may wish to consider including a whole house fan. This is something that can be retrofitted to your home but will set you back approximately $1,500.

The whole house fan has a large fan fitted above all the rooms. It sucks the hot air out and into your loft space. This air is then removed from the building through the vents fitted into your loft.

The air in the house is replaced by cooler air from ground level.

This system is not as efficient as an air conditioning system but it is very effective, particularly if you only suffer from excess heat for a few weeks of the year.

6. Cooling pillows

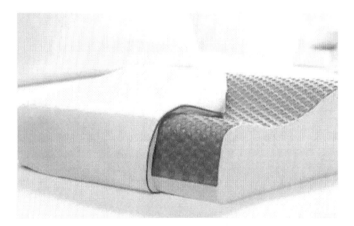

This idea will not help to cool your home but it will help you sleep at night, regardless of the temperature of your house.

It is worth noting that the cooling pillow is not a new idea. In the past pillows were filled with buckwheat as this draws heat from the body as opposed to reflecting it back.

The modern cooling pillow works in the same way. It is filled with a cooling gel which effectively takes the heat from your face. As 80% of your body heat is emitted through your head this can be a very effective way of reducing your body temperature and helping you to stay cool.

Unfortunately, it is necessary to purchase a pillow with a thick layer of gel or the more modern PCM filling to get the best effects overnight.

7. Orientate your Home

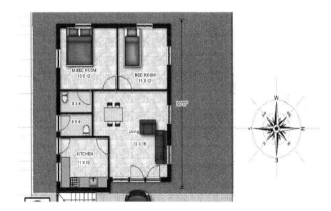

This is definitely only an option if you are looking for a new home or about to build an off-grid property. Where most people like to locate a house which faces in a southerly direction you can be looking to face yours to the east.

This will provide you with the warmth of the morning sun to heat your home for the day; but it will keep the worst of the heat out during the day time. You can easily move into the sun if you are feeling cool and your house will still feel the heat during the day; but it will not get as warm as one which faces directly to the sun, all day long.

8. Tinting Windows

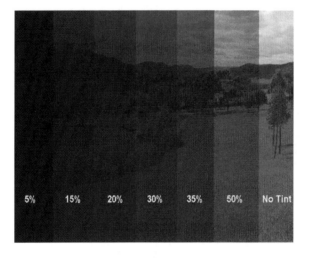

Another good technique to help prevent your house from getting too warm is to tint the windows with a UV tint. This will prevent the UV rays from entering your home and dramatically reduce the amount of heat inside your house.

As an added advantage a UV tint will stop the light hitting your furniture and causing premature aging.

590

The best way to do this is to use a secondary frame. This will allow you to block the heat in the summer but remove the tint and allow the heat in during the cooler months. After all, you do not want to save on your air conditioning costs if you then have to start heating your home

!

9. The Dehumidifier

Hot air can make you feel exhausted and sleepy; however, hot moist air is ten times worse than dry air. Whilst too much dry air may be bad for your skin, eliminating some of the moisture, or humidity, will make your house feel much cooler and far more comfortable.

It is also very easy to do! Simply purchase a dehumidifier and plug it in. These devices use a fraction of the electricity that an air conditioner unit does and will remove an impressive amount of water; making you instantly feel better.

You do not need to leave them running all the time; simply switch them on for approximately an hour in the hottest part of the day. You will need to check the water collector as you do not want it to overflow!

Water collecting can be emptied onto your plats to help them get a little moisture back. Even your cooling can assist the environment!

10. **Midday Snooze**

One way to beat the heat of the sun without resorting to air conditioning is to submit to the midday siesta. This is still a tradition in many countries and can be very effective.

As well as feeling rested during the day you will have an energy boost which keeps you going much later into the night; allowing you to be more productive.

Again, this approach will not cool your home, but it will make the temperature more bearable when you are in your home.

Building Your Own Air Conditioning Unit

If you have created an off-grid home and the ideas in this book have proved to be ineffective or impractical, it is still possible to build your own air conditioning unit.

You do not need to be an advanced engineer or spend a fortune on expensive parts; you simply need to follow the steps in this chapter and ensure you are generating enough electricity through your solar panels to power your new air conditioner.

It is fortunate that air conditioning is a necessity when the sun is hottest; you should be able to generate a significant amount of power. Of course, this will be dependent upon the number of solar panels you have and the electricity they generate.

Here's how to create your own air conditioning system:

You will need:

- A bucket with lid

- PVC pipe

- A table fan

- Spray paint

- Bucket liner - preferably Styrofoam

- Drill

- Hole saw

To make your air conditioner:

1. The first step is to put two one gallon lots of water in your freezer. They need to be frozen before you can use your air conditioner.

2. Next add your Styrofoam liner to your bucket; this means purchasing one that is approximately the same size as the inside of the bucket.

3. Drill a ½ inch hole, with your hole cutter, through the bucket and the liner. Be sure to hold them together to get a neat hole.

4. Repeat this process twice. You will end up with three holes in your bucket; all in the same horizontal line.

5. Take the base and the cover off your table fan

6. Draw round the front of the fan on the bucket lid. Your fan will sit inside the bucket with just the cover outside so cut this hole to make sure this is possible!

7. Cut the fan opening out of the bucket lid, you can use a craft knife or a saw to achieve the desired result.

8. Spray your bucket, lid and even the fan. You can choose the color or colors!

9. Take your ½ pipe and cut it into three sections. Each piece should be approximately three inches long.

10. Insert these pipes into the holes in your bucket. They should be a snug fit, if not use silicone or hot glue to hold them in position.

11. Place one of the gallons of frozen water into your bucket. It is advisable to be freezing one whilst you are using the other bag; this will keep a constant supply of ice available.

12. Add the cover to the fan and mount it into your lid; the fan side should be facing into the bucket.

13. Snap the lid in place and position your air conditioner in your desired location. Make sure it is close enough to a socket.

14. Now turn the fan on.

The fan will blow air out of the three holes you created in the bucket. As the air is being blown over the melting ice it will be cooled and come out as cold air, as effective as a commercial air conditioning unit!

Once the ice has meted you will be able to refill the freezer bag with the water and freeze a new block of ice.

In the meantime your spare ice block can be placed into the bucket and the fan turned on again.

This air conditioner will effectively run for as long as you want it too; providing you have ice available. It will also only cost the price of running a fan; which is much less than commercial unit costs to run.

This makes it an exceptionally attractive option for any home which is off-grid; the amount of electricity you will need to generate is minimal! In fact, it is possible to install one small solar panel just for your fan; this will ensure you can run the DIY air conditioner for as long as you need to; at virtually no cost.

There are actually many different version of a homemade air conditioning unit but all of them work along the same principle; using a fan to blow air across ice.

However, there is one alternative which may be even better suited to an off-grid home; it does not even require electricity!

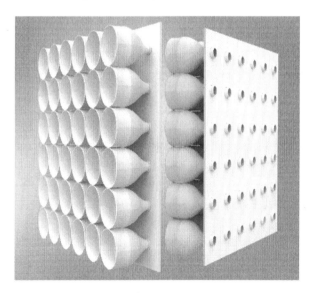

You will need:

- A window sized board

- A hole cutter

- Plastic bottles

- A drill

This is exceptionally easy to make:

1. Start by drilling holes into your board. The need to be the size of the neck of your plastic bottles. You will want to put five or six across and a similar number down. You must remember to leave enough room for the bottles to sit next to each other.

2. Next cut enough plastic bottles to fit the number of holes you have. The bottles must be cut where they are at their widest. This will minimize how far they stick out but maximize air collection.

3. Remove the bottle lids and push them through the holes you have drilled.

Then mount it in a window or door opening. The large end of the bottle should be outside your home with the small end inside. Air will be pulled into the outer edge of the bottle and then forced through the small opening. The reduction in pressure reduces the temperature of the air; pushing cool air into your home.

Whilst this method may not provide you with air as cold as that passed over ice; it is an excellent way of cooling a house which is off-grid and has limited available electricity.

It is worth noting that this technique will not dramatically affect the temperature of your home. But, it will encourage air movement which can make your house seem cooler than it actually is.

Buying an Air Conditioning Unit

Of course, being off-grid does not mean that you cannot have electricity or purchase a standard air conditioning unit. In fact, at approximately $100, a standalone air conditioner is an excellent way to keep cool during the summer months.

But, it is generally at odds with the environmental impact of air conditioners which is one reason that drives many people to go off-grid.

There are a variety of other ways to help cool your home and yourself which can be tried:

- **Unplug off all unnecessary electrical devices**. Anything plugged in will emit heat; even if they are in standby mode. Unplug everything you don't need and save your electricity.

- **Wear the Right Clothes.** Stick to cotton and linen clothing. These are breathable items and will allow the air to move round your body. The same approach should e adopted for your bed sheets

- **Freeze your sheets.** Fold your bed sheets, place them in a bag and freeze them for just a few minutes. Then make you bed and jump in; it will feel deliciously cool!

- **Ice Packs** – Your hot water bottle can be a cold ice pack. Simply two thirds fill it with water and freeze it. Then take it to bed and allow the coolness to distribute during the night.

600

- **Cold Target.** The fastest way to cool down is to apply ice to your wrists, neck, elbow or ankles. Try it; you will be surprised at how effective this simple trick is.

- **Hammocks** – These can be an effective and comfortable alternative to your usual bed. As they are suspended there is air flow on all sides; which will help to keep you cool.

- **Ground Floor sleeping.** Hot air will naturally rise; making your upstairs much hotter than downstairs. To help you stay cool during the day and the evening, you should stay downstairs. This includes sleeping on your mattress or a hammock close to the lowest floor in your house.

Set Up An Internet Connection

The internet has become the most powerful and most used tool on the planet. For many people it is a simple a means to express their feelings, vent frustrations or even just pass the time. However, the internet also represents one of humankind's greatest achievements!

Every piece of information you could wish to know is on the internet. Whether you want to know about the various different animal species or how to survive a doomsday scenario; the information is on the web. Sometimes it will take a little more looking to find the right information; especially if your search reveals hundreds of different results.

But the internet is more than just an information highway. There are now thousands of people who make their living through the internet. It can be used to allow remote working from your existing firm, or you can choose to go it alone. The internet can hook you up with new clients and customers across the globe.

Eve social media sites play their part. They can be used for expressing your own thoughts and building interest in your online or even offline businesses. However, social media can also be used to share information. This can range from the quality of a product to ways to help starving children across the world.

It is certainly true that the internet has changed everyone's lives for the better; many people would struggle to survive without a good level of connectivity.

Of course, needing to have access to the internet can become a bind! There are two main issues with needing to be connected to the internet:

1. Privacy

The first issue is that it is becoming increasingly difficult to survive on the internet without giving away many of your personal details. As well as hundreds of genuine sites which use these details for marketing purposes; there are hundreds of internet sites which are trying to steal your funds, passwords or your identity!

The result is that all your personal details will become available; this can make it very difficult to remain anonymous online.

2. Off-grid

There is increasing interest in the idea of separating yourself from the conventional lifestyle. Most people are to get a job, spend the money they earn on items that they don't really need and then, eventually, retire.

However, it is possible to break the mold and live a different kind of life; one where you are more in charge of the everyday processes. This is often referred to as an 'off-grid' experience. These people focus on growing their own foods and living a life which is more in balance with the Earth.

Whilst this intention is admirable, it does often mean that you will have no internet connection at home. You are unlikely to be near an internet connection point and may not want to subscribe if you are. Yet, the internet holds huge amounts of data that can make your life easier. It is the ideal companion for anyone trying to live off grid.

Fortunately there is an answer! It is possible to live off grid and still access the web; it simply takes a little more planning and some work on your part to establish your own internet connection. This book will show you how this is possible!

Creating Your Own Internet Connection

If you have decided that an off-grid existence is the right lifestyle for your needs then you are likely to have moved away from the more populated places and be busy setting up your own vegetable garden and learning to live off the land. Electricity and the internet may not feature highly on your initial list of requirements. But both can easily become essentials in your new way of life. Electricity makes many things easier to accomplish whilst the internet enables you to locate information and create things that you might not know how to do.

Once you decide that you need the internet you will need to decide the best way of creating your own internet connection. This will depend on your internet access requirements:

Use Your Cell Phone

It is possible to connect to the internet via your cell phone. Even if you have decided to live off-grid it is likely you will have retained a phone for emergency use.

Your phone will already be configured to connect with the internet although you will need to have your data on. You will also need to consider the charges your phone provider will make if you exceed the monthly data allowance.

Simply turn your data on and then enter your wireless settings on your phone. Select the option to use your cell phone as a hot spot. This will allow you to connect to your phone from your computer and access the internet.

It is likely that this will provide a slow internet connection; you should avoid downloading movies or other large items. It is a mobile solution which can be used anywhere; you simply need to be within range of one of the satellite towers.

The Wireless Provider

It is possible to register with a wireless provider to establish a decent internet connection. To be able to achieve this you will need to be able to see a mobile broadband repeater. You can confirm with a local wireless provider where these are.

If you have this line of site then you will need to purchase a special device; these are known as hotspot devices; there is a good selection of affordable options available online or in your local phone store.

A hotspot device will need to connect to a Wi-Fi antenna; again you can buy these easily or you can make your own. This can be done from something as simple as a Pringle's tube!

All you need is a metal can, such as the Pringle's tube, a female N connector, a small piece of copper wire, a female RP-SMA to male N connector and a USB Wi-Fi adaptor from which you can remove the aerial.

It is also necessary to have a soldering iron, wire cutters, a file and even a drill.

The idea is to create a piece of wire which emerges from the middle of the can. To do this it is best to solder the copper wire to the centre of the female N connector. You then need to mount this inside the Pringle's tube or metal can. The easiest way is to drill a hole in the side of the can; you will need to know exactly where this should be which will depend upon the size of your can. You can then mount your N connector through the hole and tighten it in place with a nut.

Now simply use your other connector to link the N connector on your aerial to the USB Wi-Fi adapter; after unscrewing the aerial that came with the adaptor. Plug it into your computer and test it out!

The further you are from the broadband repeater the more powerful your antenna will need to be. You may even need to raise the antenna significantly off the ground to ensure you get a decent signal.

This method of connecting to the internet is very easy as no configuration is required; other than installing the USB Wi-Fi software.

So far, you have been reliant on local wireless internet nodes to generate a signal which you can tap into. However, there are more advanced options which will allow you to create your own means of connecting to the internet:

Satellite Internet

This is generally seen as a more costly and complex approach to having internet access off-grid. Although this is true, it is often worth the additional hassle, especially if you are looking at connecting to the internet in an off-grid scenario. Quite simply it will provide high speed internet regardless of where you are located.

It is worth noting that the option to access the internet via a satellite will involve a monthly subscription. This is due to the fact that you will need to decode the satellite signal and cannot do this without a valid decoding key; which is part of the card you will get for your satellite receiver.

You have two choices regarding the satellite dish;

1. Manufactured

When you subscribe to a satellite internet service most suppliers will provide you with a dish that you will need to erect in the garden. It is very similar in appearance and construction to those which you get for satellite TV.

2. Make it yourself

The second option is to make your own dish. This can be done out of something like a stainless steel strainer. It will need to be approximately fourteen inches in diameter.

You will then need to drill a hole in the bottom of this dish. You will need to put a USB connector head comfortably in this hole.

Next, you should put a USB cable through your hole and then plug it into your USB connector. This can then be glued securely into position.

You should now be able to plug the other end of your USB into your laptop and establish a link between the two with a wireless network adaptor.

The dish is then ready to use; you will need a compass or satellite finder to know which direction to point it in.

You can either secure the dish to a tripod to allow you to move it to the right location, or you can secure it to the wall of your house, or even the roof of an RV.

It is worth noting that a homemade satellite will only be able to track one satellite. Many of the commercially available models can track three or four different satellites simultaneously. This will provide you with a much stronger signal.

To actually access the internet you will need a satellite receiver and a subscription to a satellite service. There is no way, at present of connecting to satellite internet for free. You should also be aware that satellite internet is generally very fast but that speed will reduce during peak times and you need a clear line of sight to the satellite. Inclement weather can reduce the signal you receive or even prevent you from getting online!

The advantage of a satellite system in a crisis situation is that you will be able to receive satellite signals even when the usual internet access methods were crippled. As long as there are satellites in orbit you will still be able to pick up some data!

Create Your Own ISP

Another interesting option is to build your own ISP: Internet Service provider. This is not a free option and might be a little more than you need for your off-grid home. However, if you have other homes in the vicinity you may be able to create one ISP for all of you and possibly reduce your internet costs.

You will need battery back-up units and a power supply. Even if you are on-grid this is important for when the power goes down. Power can come from a generator, solar panels or even a wind generator.

You will also need HVC units; these are basically large fans to keep the equipment cool; if it overheats it will shut down.

The next step is to choose an internet provider and create a peering arrangement. There will be a charge for this part of the service but it is essential! The best approach is to use two different peering providers as this will ensure a good connection at all times.

You will then need at least one good quality computer to act as your internet host. If you are creating this network for your own use then all you need to do is connect this main computer to your wireless router and you will be able to access internet anywhere on your site. If you are doing it for a small community it will be necessary to add cables and additional routers to ensure everyone can get a signal and connect to your ISP.

This process can be technically challenging and you may wish to get additional support. It may also be more than you need for an off-grid set-up.

611

Ham Radio

You may be surprised to find out that it is possible to access the internet via a Ham radio. In fact, this is something which is commonly done by sailors when they are at sea.

Of course, you would be best advised to keep your internet use simple if you adopt this approach.

You simply need your ham radio and a radio messaging system. This will allow you to send data packages and even emails to the next station along. In this way it is possible to both send and receive data. As the internet is merely data, it is possible to link with it and pull down the information you need; simply by using a messaging service.

The service uses repeater nodes; these pass DX signals on to the next station; the same signals as the internet uses. By hooking a computer up to your Ham radio you will be able to receive and transmit data on one channel and connect to the internet!

Dial Up

This is not a viable option for anyone hoping to live in the middle of nowhere! However, if your need to communicate and access the internet is due to a massive catastrophe then you may find it possible to access dial up internet. You will need to know a number for one of the dial up services; you can even subscribe via your own phone line; if you have one.

Even when the power is out, your phone line will have its own power; this means that dial up will still be available. Although it is a slower way of accessing the web, it is a viable option if the is a problem with the energy supply and no means of accessing the internet through your usual router and cables.

Of course, if the disaster has destroyed the phone lines as well this will not be an option! It may, however, be an option for those living remotely as it may be easier to drop a phone line to your remote location than it is to add fiber optic cables or even power lines.

Future Options

The main aim for the future at present is to create a true wireless network which can be accessed by anyone on the planet; through a standard wireless connection. There have been several attempts to achieve this but no success as yet. However, SpaceX is now launching a bid to add a number of low orbit satellites which would allow such wireless access all across the planet.

If this is successful then you will be able to connect via Wi-Fi; regardless of where you are! This will represent a huge step forward for the internet and your ability to use the internet after a disaster on when off-grid. Instead of needing to power computers, routers and wireless networks, you will only need enough power to access your cell phone!

5 Ways to Stay Connected Without Electricity

The ability to connect to the internet allows you to gain access to all the information you need and to find out what is happening in a disaster scenario.

Even if you are simply after an off-grid lifestyle you will want and often need to access the internet. However, there are issues with accessing the internet in these situations. The actual connection to the internet is not always easy to resolve, but, as the last chapter indicates, there are ways of getting connected. Your preferred method will depend upon your technical knowledge and the situation you find yourself in.

Unless a disaster has befallen the entire world, there will still be some internet functioning; accessing it could make the difference between life and death!

This chapter deals with ways to connect to the internet without electricity when in an off-grid scenario. It may not always be easy, but it is possible!

1. Generate Your Own Electricity

The most obvious way to stay connected when off-grid and without power is to generate your own power! This will allow you to power your computer, router and even a variety of other pieces of equipment.

In reality, this is the most effective way to live off-grid. After all, choosing to step away from mainstream connectivity and reliance on corporations controlling energy; does not mean you do not want the modern luxuries. It does mean that you are looking for a life more in touch with nature and one that is controlled more by your choices than those forced upon you.

There are several ways to generate electricity when off-grid. The starting point should be to purchase a couple of small solar panel chargers; these will allow you to keep your cell phone charged. Even off-grid this is a vital piece of equipment in an emergency.

You can then consider installing large solar panels on your roof; or even free standing on your land. The better the quality of your panels the more light they will attract and the greater the electricity produced. Solar panels need to be connected to a transformer and fuse to ensure the power can be safely delivered to your devices. In addition, it is advisable to have a bank of batteries and a charging switch; electricity generated by your solar panels can be stored and used when it is dark.

It is also possible to create your own wind generator. This is a simple fan on the end of a tall pole. As it turns a motor a current is generated which can then be used to power your equipment. Wind power is generally considered to be irregular and not as good an option as solar panels. However, if you have a plentiful supply of wind it can be an option; or it can work alongside your solar panels.

Generating your own electricity means that you should always have power; allowing you to connect to any internet which is still in existence! It is also worth considering the amount of electricity you will need before you start to set up a system. Being off-grid means you will not be able to simply switch back onto a mains supply or even to sell any excess electricity you have back to the grid. Will, therefore, need to balance the amount of power you are likely to need with the cost of purchasing all the equipment.

Generation of your own electricity can also be achieved via the use of flowing water; although this is a much rarer way to generate electricity for a single home. It is worth being aware of this method as you may end up with a river going through or next to your land.

2. High Powered USB Wi-Fi Modem

Your own power source can be used to power a high powered USB Wi-Fi modem. This will look for wireless network within a set vicinity. High powered USB Wi-Fi modems can cover large distances looking for networks.

The idea scenario would be to locate a free service in your vicinity. This will provide you with free internet access whenever you need it. If you cannot find a free network you will need to locate one that is close enough and has not been locked. You will then be able to access it and surf the web as much as you like.

However, it is worth noting that using a free Wi-Fi network or someone else's open network does present a security risk. You should never disclose your personal or financial details on an open network. If there are hackers they will quickly be able to steal your information.

The effectiveness of this solution will depend upon your location. The more rural you are the less likely it is that you will be within range of another network. It is also possible that the network will be turned off from time to time; you will have no control over this!

3. Hot Spots

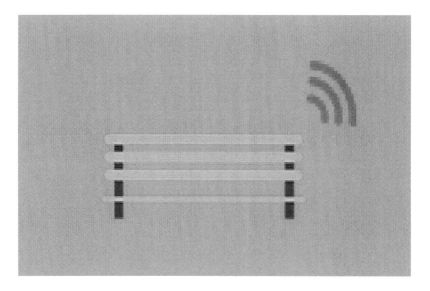

Another way to stay connected when you have no electricity is to rely on others having power. This is likely if you are in an off-grid scenario and not so likely if you are recovering from a disaster!

There are several options regarding what others may be able to offer. The first option simply requires you to locate a hotspot in your area and connect to the internet when you need to by visiting the right spot. You may even find that your house is a hotspot!

Having to visit a specific spot to get internet access may not be the most desirable option but it is a viable way to stay connected without electricity; even if it only a short term solution whilst you generate your own power.

Hotspots do require you to access them via your cell phone; this can then be your portal to the internet or you can turn your cell phone into a hub and access the internet on your computer or tablet. For this you will need a valid data connection; it will not be able to handle large downloads easily but can be useful for general surfing.

It is also possible to use a hot spot by paying for the service as you need it. Although this may not be the most cost effective solution it will, again, enable you to stay online without needing to have power at your home.

One benefit of using the internet this way is that you will only use it for what you really need; anything you can manage without you will do so. This avoidance of reliance on technology is part of what going off-grid is all about!

4. Generators

It is, of course, possible to purchase a generator and have this for your use when you are off-grid. Depending upon your location you may need to purchase a quiet generator or even build an enclosure for it.

It is best to keep a generator outside as it will emit fumes which are dangerous in a confined space. You can build an enclosure from scrap pieces of wood and even line it with sound insulation. This will help to keep the noise of the generator to a minimum. However, you should ensure there are vents on both sides of the enclosure as this will ensure the generator does not get too hot.

Most generators will only power a few pieces of equipment; they are not seen as an ideal solution for the long term unless you are planning to have a very large generator. They can, of course, be exceptionally beneficial for short term use. This includes when you are setting up your off-grid home or after a disaster.

Another thing to consider when deciding whether to get a generator or not, is which type is best suited to your needs and environment. You can get generators powered by:

- Gasoline – or petrol, as it is also known. This is easy to get hold off although may be more difficult during a power outage; simply because the gasoline needs to be pumped out of the tanks electronically. Gasoline generators are generally small and portable as well as being relatively cheap.

- Diesel – A diesel powered generator will be more expensive to purchase but will last for longer on a tank of fuel than a gasoline one. In general this type of generator will last for a long time providing it is properly maintained. It is also much easier than gasoline to start when the weather is cold.

- Biofuel – This is usually a mixture of animal fat or vegetable fat and diesel. It works in the same way as diesel but is generally better for the environment. However, this is generally the type of generator which makes the most noise.

- Emulsified Diesel – This is a mixture of diesel and water. It is blended with a mixing agent and is designed to be cheaper to produce and slightly better for the environment than the traditional diesel fuel. It can be difficult to maintain the water to diesel ratio although this is vital for the sake of the engine.

- Propane – It is possible to run a generator from propane gas. This is often considered to be one of the best options. Propane can be stored for much longer than gasoline or diesel; it is also relatively easy to get hold of; even after a power cut.

Propane offers very few emissions and is actually quite clean for the environment. However, it is a more expensive option. The generator is generally more to buy and you should have a licensed professional to fit it. Unfortunately, the clean emissions come at a price. They will generally burn fuel much quicker than a diesel generator and will not last as long as they operate under higher pressures. It is the quietest type of generator you can buy.

- Hydrogen – This surprising contender is not as well known, considerably more expensive to buy but offers a clean supply of electricity at no cost. Hydrogen is everywhere but this generator uses water. Water has a large amount of hydrogen which is extracted and used to create electricity. This type of generator will require extra safety precautions but is a viable and attractive option for long term electricity.

5. Cell Phones and Mesh Networks

The final way to stay connected without electricity, or even generating your own, is via your cell phone and a mesh network. This is something that is becoming increasingly common and offers internet access to almost anyone; regardless of location and budget.

You will need to charge your cell phone but this can be done via a small USB solar panel or by visiting local shopping malls and plugging your phone in whilst you have a coffee.

The mesh network works via many people using cell phones. By purchasing a simple piece of equipment; known as a mesh radio, you can combine the power of your phone with any others in the area. The signals are meshed together to enable them to travel for several miles. At this point they can be boosted on by another group of meshed phones or be distributed to the relevant parties.

This method of communicating is still being built on and improved. It will provide very limited access to the internet but is a very effective way at transmitting messages between people over fairly sizeable distances.

It is worth considering this new technology as it is likely to improve in the next few years. It will become a viable network option for anyone who is currently living off-grid and a fantastic way of staying in touch in an emergency situation.

As the data is transmitted via radio waves, it will work even after the electricity is off; you just need to have several phones connected to give it the required boost. The networks will grow in size and all data is encrypted to ensure it is passed on safely and in one piece. There is even a feature which allows you to literally shout out to see who is in the vicinity.

624

As the network grows it will be possible to send additional packets of data; making it possible to send and receive pictures and videos; the whole internet could be visible via this method in just a few years! This is definitely one of the most exciting options to watch at present.

PART 6
Well-Being And Beauty
Home Doctor

This book, *How Not to Get Sick during Winter Season: 29 Homemade Remedies That are Approved by Doctors* is a great book to read if you want to lay off chemical based medicines and get through winter without chest congestion, joint pains and other winter related ailments. It shows you the ailments that are prevalent in the winter season, and also the remedies that you can prepare on your own at minimal cost. Gladly, most of the remedies mentioned in the book have been given a clean bill of health by qualified doctors, and that will give anyone preparing for the winter season much needed confidence as far as maintaining health is concerned.

It is a good idea to try and prepare the recipes even when you are not suffering from any winter ailment, because the recipes are not just medicinal but also nutritional. Read on...

Ten Major Winter Ailments

Can you visualize the weather in winter? It is cold, in some areas it is not just cold but dry, while in other areas it is both cold and wet. One common factor in these scenarios is extremity – the cold is extreme, likewise the dryness, and sometimes even the wetness. You can find a place drizzling all through winter while the cold cuts through people's spines and numbs the limbs. All that harshness is acceptable especially because it is foreseeable, but it does not mean that people have gotten comfortable with the running nose and the cold rushes for those who suffer in this manner, or any of those uncomfortable effects of cold weather.

What happens is that they try to make do, swallowing a pill every now and then, as they pray for the season of discomforts to end quickly. Unfortunately, while such pills are good in relieving congestion in the chest and warding off pneumonia, a good many of them have side effects. For that reason, some people have learnt to avoid taking the medication unless their issue becomes a serious medical case. Luckily, you do not have to live with the discomforts that come with the extreme winter weather. There are some natural remedies that you can use to sooth any irritations that you may suffer in your respiratory system and even on your skin. If you are equipped with the right information as you are about to be after reading this book, you can even keep many of the winter ailments at bay, and you will not have to talk about cures. After all, prevention, in all cases, is far better than the effort to cure.

Ailments That Threaten People in winter

When contemplating prevention of ailments, it is important to know first the ailments that are likely to attack people over winter. According to the National Health Service of the UK, there are around 10 different ailments that are likely to be triggered by the cold winter weather, or to be made worse. These ailments include:

(1)   Common cold

Sometimes the cold might not have originated with you but rather passed to you through contact, where you touch infected surfaces like door knobs and such. Other times you could just keep re-infecting yourself when you use a handkerchief and while you may think this is inevitable, you can actually protect yourself by using disposable tissue in place of a handkerchief.

(2)   Sore throat

Mostly, when you get a sore throat in winter it is because you have a viral infection. In such times, you may need something more than just gaggling some salty water.

(3)   Asthma

Asthma is underlined by wheezing and also being short of breath, and it is a condition often triggered by cold such as that of winter. Sometimes victims even use inhalers to open up the respiratory system, but helpful as they are, these rescue inhalers have their shortcomings.

(4)   Norovirus

Beware of this winter bug that gets people vomiting. Although you can easily rehydrate yourself to counter the negative effects of vomiting and diarrhea, you would be better off preventing yourself from catching the norovirus in the first place.

(5)   Suffering joint pains

If you ask people who suffer from arthritis, whose major manifestation is joint pain, they will confirm the pain is aggravated in the cold season. In winter, such people sometimes experience stiffness of the joints in addition to the intense pain. It is such symptoms that natural remedies target, so that you remain healthy in winter and stay out of pain.

(6)   Cold sores

Why get so stressed that cold sores come in to underline the fact that your body is under extreme stress? You can learn about natural remedies and proceed to use them as preventative measure against cold sores.

(7)   Heart attack

For people who suffer from high blood pressure, the condition is likely to become more serious in winter. This happens as the heart strives to pump blood more effectively to keep your body warm.

(8)   Suffering the condition of cold hands

If you have witnessed someone's fingers and toes turn blue, or even red or white in winter, they are, very likely, suffering from a painful condition that persists in winter. Some people reckon you have no choice but to live with the symptoms, but this is not exactly the case. You can preempt this condition and probably even alleviate it by making use of natural remedies. In the meantime, you need to maintain warmth by wearing socks as well as gloves in winter.

(9)   The condition of dry skin

When you have the cold season being accompanied by reduced humidity, you are likely to have skin problems. If you are to use moisturizers to keep your skin moist in such times, you had better use the natural ones, as they do not have any significant side effects.

(10)   The flu

A very dangerous winter ailment is the flu. It is actually a known killer. Although anyone can suffer the flu, people are more vulnerable when they are advanced in age, say, being over 65yrs of age; and when they have other health conditions such as diabetes. Although these days there is a flu jab that people have for protection, there are also natural remedies that serve to boost your immune system, so that you become less susceptible to the flu.

Natural Homemade Remedies for Winter

The Elderberry And 3 Other Homemade Remedies

The elderberry syrup

The elderberry syrup is made from the red berry or even the bluish black berry, a fruit that is often used to make jelly and also wine. You can consume the syrup to ward off colds and related winter ailments, and gladly, it is a remedy that you can make at home. For this recipe, you can bank on it to protect you from the winter flu and intense cold.

According to Dr. Madeleine Mumcuoglu who has done a lot of research while at the Israel University called Hadassah-Hebrew, elderberries have the capacity to weaken the enzyme that viruses engage in penetrating the body's healthy cells of the nose and throat. That is how these natural berries protect you from cold and flu in winter.

Ingredients to make the elderberry syrup:

(i)   Black elderberries (dried) – 2/3 cup or 3 ounces

(ii)   Plain water – 3½ cups

(iii)   Ginger root (dried) – 2 tablespoons

(iv)   As alternative: Ginger root (fresh) – 2 tablespoons

(v)   Cinnamon powder – 1 teaspoon

(vi)   Clove powder – ½ teaspoon

(vii)   Raw honey – 1 cup

The method to use:

• You begin by putting water into your medium size saucepan

• After that you add your elderberries and your ginger, plus the cinnamon as well as the cloves

• What you need to do now is add the honey

• Boil that mixture and after boiling it you cover it

• Then reduce the heat and let the mixture simmer for around 45min or so

• Boil that mixture well until the liquid has evaporated, reducing to half the original amount

- At that juncture, you need to remove your boiled liquid from the fire so that it can cool well enough for you to handle it.

- Now mash the softened berries by use of something flat such as a big spoon

- Finally, you need to strain that content, pouring it into some glass jar or some bowl.

- Allow the liquid to cool down and when it is lukewarm, you proceed to add a cupful of honey

- Stir the honey well to get distributed well in the liquid

Your remedy is now ready for use, so put it into a mason jar, or in a big glass bottle of around 16 ounces.

Do you want to know the best dosage?

(a)   ½ teaspoon for children is a good dose

(b)   ½ tablespoon or even a whole tablespoon is good enough for grown ups

Incidentally, you need to take this dose once a day for prevention of flu and colds, but for curing such ailments, you need you need to take it every 2 or 3 hours till the cold symptoms have disappeared.

The Vapor Rub

This is another remedy that you can use on your feet and also on your back plus your chest to protect you from the winter colds. It calms your coughing, if you have a cough, and it also clears chest congestion.

The ingredients you need are:

(i)   Olive oil – ½ cup

(ii)   Coconut or almond oil (Alternative for olive oil) – same measurement

(iii)   Beeswax pastilles – 2 tablespoons (level)

(iv)   Eucalyptus oil – 20 drops

(For a children recipe, 4 drops of eucalyptus oil are sufficient)

(v)   Peppermint oil – 20 drops

(Even here, 4 drops of peppermint oil are sufficient for children)

(vi)   Rosemary oil – 10 drops

(Avoid using Rosemary oil on recipes for young children)

(Optional) Cinnamon – 10 drops

For the cinnamon option, you can substitute with clove oil

(Avoid taking the cinnamon or clove oil option on recipes for young children.

Here is the method of making the vapor rub:

• First of all melt your beeswax using whatever oil you want, using a double boiler

• After melting the beeswax, proceed to add your essential oils into it

(For baby recipes, you need to add only half your essential oils)

• It is now time to do your mixing, ensuring that every ingredient is evenly distributed in the mix

• Then pour your mixture in a container with a lid for storage. In fact, you can use some small jars or just some tin containers.

This is a recipe you can comfortably use as per need, without worrying about discomforts or overdose. Just ensure that the recipe for young children, including babies, is not very concentrated.

Cod Liver Oil that is fermented

Cod liver oil happens to have soluble vitamins as well as Omega 3 fats. It is, therefore, great as a supplier of these nutrients, and particularly Vitamin D in winter when the sunshine is scarce or non-existent. Of course, here we are talking of nutrients that keep common colds and related ailments away in the cold winter season.

Luckily, you do not need to do much to get the fermented cod liver oil. You could buy some fish liver and ferment it before extracting your oil. According to Dr. Weston A. Price, you could effectively use fermented cod liver oil or even butter oils to maintain your health during winter.

Herbal DIY Cough Syrup

This homemade syrup hastens healing even after you have caught some winter ailment, including those that do not involve coughing. The herbs you use in this recipe are soothing to the throat and the ease any coughing you may be suffering while promoting comfortable sleep. Owing to the fact that honey is highly concentrated, you may wish to use the remedy on children over a year old.

The ingredients to use:

(i)   Filtered water – 1 quart

(ii)   Ginger root – ¼ cup

You can use this root either grated or even dried

(iii)   Chamomile flowers – ¼ cup

(iv)   Marshmallow root – ¼ cup

(v)   Cinnamon – 1 tablespoon

(vi)   Lemon juice – ¼ cup

634

(vii)   Honey – 1 cup

The method to make the cough syrup:

• You begin by pouring your filtered water into a saucepan

• Then you add your dried herbs

• The next step is placing your saucepan onto fire to boil the contents

• Once they boil, you need to reduce the heat and let the contents simmer

• Take your time until the amount in the pan halves

You are actually looking to have one cupful of liquid once you have strained the content. For effective straining, you can use some cheesecloth or even a mesh strainer with fine wire.

• It is now time to add your lemon juice plus the honey

• At the time of doing this, your liquid needs to be still warm; and then you stir the mixture properly.

• You finally have your winter home syrup remedy ready, and you need to store it in some airtight container

• Store it in your fridge and you will have a winter remedy that can last a whole 2mths.

For dosage, 1 tablespoon suits adults while 1 teaspoon suits children.

More DIY Winter Remedies

Three Of Winter's Best Remedies

Winter Broth

Broth here simply means stock, which is essentially some rich infusion you make by boiling bones from well reared animals, and then mixing that soup with vegetables as well as herbs and also spices. So, today, the good news is that broth is not only useful for culinary purposes and exceptional flavor, but it is also handy in warding off winter ailments.

The ingredients you need for to serve 16 people:

(i)　　Bones – 2 pounds

(ii)　　Chicken feet (optional, to get more gelatin) – 2

(iii)　　Onion – 1 bulb

(iv)　　Carrots – 2

(v)　　Celery – 2 stalks

(vi)　　Apple cider vinegar – 2 tablespoons

As an option, you can also add:

(vii)　　Parsley – 1 bunch

(viii)   Sea salt – 1 tablespoon

(ix)   Peppercorns – 1 teaspoon

(x)   Herbs or even spices of your choice – just enough to taste

(xi)   Garlic – 2 cloves (to add in the last half hour of your cooking)

How to prepare the winter broth:

• If you have the time, you can roast the raw bones first in an oven, particularly if they are from beef, just to improve the flavor of your broth. A period of 30min at 350°F is good enough.

• After that you can put the bones in a big stock pot, around 5 gallons.

• Then pour over the bones your filtered water

• Follow that with vinegar

• Allow your mixture to settle for between 20min to half an hour. The presence of the acid from the vinegar enables the bone nutrients to be more readily available.

• Now take your vegetables and chop them, and then add them into the pot. At this point, leave out the parsley as well as the garlic, in case you are using them.

• It is time to add some salt and pepper, and also any spices or even herbs you may be using.

• Put your pot on fire and let it boil.

• Once the pot contents have boiled vigorously, you need to lower your fire, and allow the contents to simmer.

• As it simmers, make a point of scraping off the floating impurities. You will see some foamy layer and you can scooped it out with ease using a large spoon

• Check for this frothy layer every 20 or so minutes and clear it. This exercise needs to go on for around 2hrs. If the bones are from an animal that has been grass fed, you are likely to see less foam.

• You need to leave your broth to simmer for around 8hrs

• In the last half hour of cooking the broth, you can add your garlic as well as your parsley, if they are part of your ingredients.

• Finally, get the cooking pot off the fire and allow the contents to cool

• You can now proceed to strain the contents so that you can get rid of any pieces of bone as well as vegetables.

Once your broth has properly cooled, you need to pour it into a glass jar, like the size of a gallon, and then store it in your fridge. You can use this broth safely for a period of 5 days. However, if you intend to keep it for a longer period, you can always freeze it.

The Garlic

This is one of the easiest natural winter remedies. All you need is raw garlic, and there are different ways of preparing it for consumption.

• You can simply mince the piece of garlic, put it in water and then drink that water.

638

• You can also put the garlic in your soup when boiling it

• Alternatively, you can fry the garlic in food.

The garlic in all those states is potent enough to speed up your recovery when you have any of the winter ailments listed in chapter one. Keep consuming the garlic in intervals of a few hours, and before long, you will be feeling much better.

Natural Probiotics

Probiotics have been in use from time immemorial, and the father of modern science, Hippocrates, advocated for them for their effectiveness in healing gut related ailments. According to Hippocrates, the gut becomes even more sensitive in winter, and so the need for probiotics is even higher. Coconut water and goji berries are just some of the probiotic examples.

Some of Winter's Greatest Natural Remedies

Eight of Winter's Greatest Remedies

Echinacea

This is one herb that protects against colds by boosting your immune system. The parts of this herb that are useful in relation to medication include its roots, its leaves, and even its flowers.

All you need to do is get some of the herb's extract and then take between half a teaspoon to one full teaspoon of the tincture after each 2hrs. You need to continue taking it in this dosage until the symptoms of cold disappear.

Goldenseal

This extract that is bitter in taste can help you to kill bacteria during infections, and it can help to cure any cold that may attack you in the winter season.

The way to use the goldenseal is by taking tiny doses of it as it is quite potent, and you do this in form of capsules or even tinctures. For a warning, you need to be conscious not to give goldenseal to expectant women and also to people suffering hypertension.

The ginger cure

You can make some tea-like beverage from ginger and drink it, and this is bound to ease any congestion in your chest as it warms up your body. At the same time, this recipe acts as an anti-inflammatory, soothing and healing your sore throat. It is also great at fighting anti-bacterial infection.

One of the easiest ways to prepare this recipe is by letting your fresh ginger simmer for around 20min, and then straining it, before adding a little honey. You can also use dried ginger and prepare it the same way. Finally, squeeze out some fresh lemon juice and add into your ginger mixture if you are comfortable with lemon. This is a cure you can take side by side with soups or meals like French fries.

The Slippery Elm

You need to get some lozenges of slippery elm, and these you can find in food stores, particularly those dealing with healthy foods.

You will require:

Bark of slippery elm (dried) – 1 tablespoon

Clean drinking water – 1 cup

All you need to do is put the dried elm into your cup of water, and then you strain it before drinking it.

This remedy is great at soothing the sore throat. It contains mucilage, something that has the capacity to coat your throat, helping it to relieve coughs.

The thyme remedy

Thyme is a herb with anti-bacterial properties, whether used as fresh or in dried form. It, thus, wards off cold related infections in winter, and keeps you protected as you consume it.

It is effective when you use it in soups or any of your stews, and it still has a great flavor. To make this winter remedy:

You can begin by pouring water that is near boiling point into your pot

Then you add to it a pinch of dried thyme, or even fresh thyme.

You then follow that up by switching off the heat.

641

To use the remedy effectively, you need to create some tent using something like a towel, nicely draped over your head and also your pot concurrently. After that you can breathe in the steam from this natural remedy for a period of 5 min.

The astragalus

Using the natural herb, astragalus, strengthens your body so that as time goes by it is able to withstand ailments. It is very handy in the winter season when the body is threatened by cold related ailments.

You can take this remedy in form of a capsule or even a tincture, to keep off colds and the flu. It also works when you consume it in soups or even in rice. Ensure you remove the actual herb before drinking your remedy or the food with the remedy.

(1)   The eucalyptus remedy

Your ingredients are:

(i)   Eucalyptus essential oil – a few drops

(ii)   Boiling water

(iii)   The easiest way of making the eucalyptus winter remedy is by:

(iv)   Putting a couple of drops into the boiling water

(v)   Then switch off the fire soon after that

Your winter remedy is ready, and you can use it immediately by first draping some towel over your head and over the basin with hot water. You can then proceed to breathe the vapor for some five good minutes. The remedy's anti-bacterial properties will begin working, and also its expectorant properties. In essence, if your chest was heavy and the breathing difficult, the chest will feel lighter and you begin to breathe with more ease and comfort. Remember essential oils are not meant to be ingested but for external use.

The Siberian Ginseng

This potent winter remedy is also referred to as *Eleuthero*, which is short for *Eleutherococcus senticosus*. It is one of those cherished herbs that strengthen your immune system, making you ward off many of winter's ailments.

The ingredients you need:

(i)   Siberian ginseng

(ii)   Cardamom

(iii)   Ginger

(iv)   Cinnamon

(v)   Plain water

To prepare this remedy, you need to:

• Boil your water first

• Then put in your ingredients for them to boil with the water

• Once the natural ingredients are well blended, you need to reduce the heat of the fire, leaving the contents to simmer for around 20min.

• Finally, you can strain the contents.

The way to make use of this winter remedy is to drink 2 or 3 cups of it every day.

Mullein tea

This beverage that is made from the flowering plant, Mullein, is great in making a natural expectorant, which can keep your respiratory system open and clear all through winter. Moreover, it has a soothing effect which is very important particularly when you have a cough.

The ingredients for this recipe are:

(i)   Boiling water – 1 cup

(ii)   Mullein leaves – 1 tablespoon

(iii)   Honey – some

(iv)   Lemon

What you need to do is:

• To pour the boiling water on top of the Mullein leaves

• Then leave the contents to steep for around 20min

• After that you need to strain the contents

• Finally, squeeze lemon juice into the contents and add the honey.

The honey and the lemon do not only contribute to the healing, but they also serve to reduce the bitter taste of Mullein. What you have just made is Mullein tea, and it is a great winter remedy.

DIY Remedies To Ward Off Winter Ailments

14 Great DIY Remedies

The Tulsi remedy

This is a winter remedy made from basil leaves. It protects you from bacterial infection when you take the tea made from the leaves.

You can make your own tulsi remedy by brewing the leaves into a form of beverage. For strong protection against illness, experts recommend that you take 2 or 3 cups of the tulsi tea on a daily basis.

Yin Chiao

The ingredients are:

(i)   The honeysuckle leaves

(ii)   The forsythia leaves

What you can do at home is make a decoction out of the ingredients shown, and then you drink it just like tea. It should ease congestion and any symptoms of a cold like sneezing.

Sage

The same sage herb that is known for its culinary properties is also great at curing sore throats. It is also useful when it comes to drying up sinuses.

All you need to do to prepare the recipe is make a concentrated tea-like beverage from the sage leaves, in the ratio of 4 ounces: 2 teaspoons when measuring water to sage respectively.

Ensure its warmth is at room temperature before gargling it. Once you gargle the same amount of sage mixture three times in a day, your sore throat will be gone before you know what is happening. However, when it comes to drippy sinuses, you need to actually drink the sage beverage or tea for them to heal.

The Ginger Licorice remedy

This root remedy is great at boosting your immune system in winter. It soothes the throat and treats the winter coughs and colds. It has been hailed for its healing properties by herbalist, 'Dr' John Raymond Christopher.

The ingredients you need are:

(i)   Water – 2 quarts

(ii)   Ground Licorice root- ¼ cup

(iii)   Fresh ginger (unpeeled) – 1 finger

Method of preparing the recipe:

• You need to put the water in a pot

• Then add your licorice root

• Add the ginger next

• Put your pot on the fire and let the contents boil for around 10min

- Finally strain the contents

- Your ginger licorice remedy is finally ready for consumption

The Oregano remedy

Ingredients:

(i)   Oregano oil – 3 or 4 drops

(ii)   Water – 1 glass

You just need to dilute the Oregano with the water and then drink. This remedy is known for reducing nasal congestion. As long as you do not mind its not-not-so-nice taste that gives it the name Satan's urine, your respiratory system will be fine all through winter.

The Echinacea remedy

This is a tea-like beverage made from Echinacea, a flowering herb with great healing properties. You can take it in winter to boost and also stimulate your immune system, so that you can keep winter ailments and pains at bay.

Ginger tea

The ingredients are:

(i)   The ginger root (fresh)

(ii)   Lemon juice (fresh)

(iii)   Honey

You need to make a drink like tea from these ingredients and then drink it to fight the winter colds.

DIY natural cough syrup

Ingredients:

(i)   Honey – ¼ cup

(ii)   Apple cider vinegar (ACP) – ¼ cup

Once you mix the two ingredients properly, your cough syrup is ready. To keep the winter ailments at bay, you need to take 1 tablespoon in interludes of 4hrs.

The honey remedy

Dr. Oz recommends that you consume raw honey as it is, neither filtering nor heating it. It has the power to boost your immunity and keep winter colds at bay. Even the American Academy of Pediatrics says it is advisable to give honey to 1yr olds and those younger.

The honeyed lemon remedy

You just need to put some honey in water that is warm, and then squeeze in some fresh lemon juice. According to Dr. Benjamin Asher, this remedy will cure your sore throat.

ACV remedy

Apple Cider Vinegar is a great cure for sore throats and it works through gargling.

Natural salt remedy

Dr. Asher reckons that you can cure an irritating throat and other discomforts caused by dry air by gargling natural salt. Some winters are not just cold but also dry, and so salt is a handy natural winter remedy. You can also make nasal drops from it in order to loosen the mucus making breathing difficult.

Chicken broth remedy

Chicken broth is a great natural remedy, and Dr. Amy Myers recommends it together with bone broth in general. Chicken soup is great for winter particularly if you consider it has cysteines, substances that thin mucus. It is even better for killing germs when you add hot peppers as well as garlic in it.

The Olbas oil recipe

You need to put a couple of Olbas oil drops in some hot water in a bowl. The way to cure your cold with this remedy is by leaning over the bowl and covering yourself and the bowl using a towel. You will feel your congested vessels relax, and the aching vessels and muscles soothed.

Medicine Handbook

During the immense hour of crisis, there are many factors which play very important role in fighting for your survival. There have been a lot of research being done regarding this aspect. Medical stuff is very much related to the human life savage and surviving the critical circumstances. So, here is the complete guide for all those who are interesting in making the profound first aid medical kit for surviving the drastic conditions.

In this book, a brief list of few of the basic items is made up which are very important to carry with you all the time in your kit box. There are some other items which must not be overlooked while preparing the survival kit like bandages, antiseptics, injections and so on. The first chapter of the book includes the brief list of such basic items.

The detailed list of medicines along with their usage is given in chapter 2. Other than the prescribed medicines, don't forget to get consultations from your doctor or pharmacist to use any other medication.

At the end, few natural remedies are mentioned in the third chapter of the book. It is better to go for the natural remedies as they don't cause much side effects.

Five items to put in your medical kit today

If you have a well-maintained first aid medical kit, you can effectively take care of the emergency wounds and injuries. You should have at least medical kit at home and also carry it while traveling. You can store the kit anywhere easily where it is saved from the reach of children. Be sure that kids have the proper understanding of the purpose of each item of the medical kit.

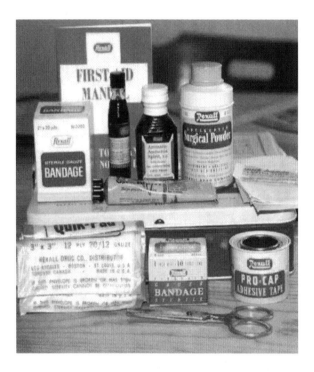

It gets difficult to handle things in case of medical emergency especially during the disasters. Being fully equipped with the useful resources, proper training, skills and the complete aid items can prove to be lifesaving.

You can purchase the medical kit from any medical store, or you can make the one for you. You can use it for specialized tasks and circumstances. The basic items which every kit should include are:

Basic items

- Thermometer

- Manual guide

- Adhesive tape

- Duct tape

- Eyewash solution

- Antibiotic solution

- Cold packs

- Elastic bandages wrap

- Triangular patch bandages

- Aluminum finger splint

- Eyeshield or pad

- Antiseptic solution

- Bandage strips or "butterfly" bandages

- Soap solution or hand sanitizer

- Plastic bags

- Safety pins

- Nonstick sterile bandages or roller gauze

- Breathing barrier

- Syringe, medicine cup or spoon

- Cotton balls

- Disposable non-latex gloves

- Petroleum jell

- Turkey baster or other bulb suction device for flushing wounds

Medications

- Calamine lotion

- Laxative

- Anti-diarrhea solution

- Aloe Vera gel

- Antacids

- Antihistamine, like diphenhydramine

- A cough and cold medicine

- Hydrocortisone cream

- Auto-injector of epinephrine

- Personal meds which don't need the refrigeration

- Painkillers, such as acetaminophen (Tylenol, others), aspirin (never give aspirin to children), and ibuprofen (Advil, Motrin IB, others)

Emergency items

- Sunscreen shield

- Insect killer

- Emergency space blanket

- Cell phone workable with solar charger

- Emergency contact numbers, like phone numbers of the family doctor or pediatrician, emergency road service providers, local emergency services, and the poison help line.

- Waterproof matches

- Whistle

- Medical forms for each person

- Small notepad and waterproof writing instrument

- Medical history forms for each person

- Small, waterproof flashlight or headlamp with extra batteries

Checkup your first aid kit

Kit your first aid medical kit a recheck o regular basis and make sure that the flash lamps and their batteries are in good condition and replace the items which are expired or is used up.

Consider about having a course of first aid medication by any of the organization in your state or from Red Cross. You can get the complete info regarding these courses from online sites or through the phone numbers.

Make your kids prepared for any medical emergencies for every age. In this regard, Red Cross offers different first aid courses like the classes planned for aiding kids in understanding and using the items of first aid kit.

As the SHTF and any other medical situation occur instantly, there are several things which should be done quickly for absolute turmoil. In the majority of the medical emergencies, if the quick response is not taken then it may lead to life-threatening situations, but can be avoided if quick actions are taken. For example, a small cut which if gets in contact with the tainted water can cause the quick infection.

For such cases, the preppers are trained for carrying out quick medical treatments in emergencies. They are learned not just about the basic first aid treatments, but also taught completely about using the natural ways of curing the injuries.

Here are five most important which you need to include in your kit and offer the best natural alternatives for curing the various medical problems.

1. Books

You can't be completely proficient at any of the medical expertise without complete study and its implication. If you consider getting the different medical courses in the community colleges, the fire departments, county extension organizations, and veteran community, then this give you a better edge in acquiring the complete knowledge about the medical emergencies and solving them in time.

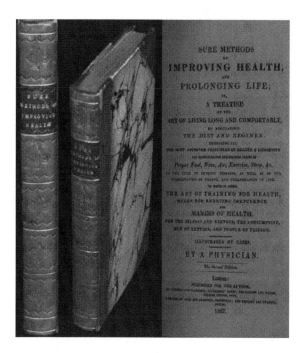

It is very necessary to have a guide about your stock up along with the medical items in the aid box. Following are few essential handbooks and literature which can help you a lot in solving medical issues:

• Wilderness Medicine, Beyond First Aid

• Wilderness Medicine Book

• Field Guide Book of Wilderness and Rescue Medicine

• The Survival Medical Handbook

• A Barefoot Doctor's Manual

• Herbal Antibiotics: Natural Ways of Treating Drug Resistant Bacteria

• Medicine for the Outdoors

• Prepper's Natural Medicine Handbook

2. Kitchen Staples

As many of people have the restricted space in shelves, it is important to put there only the stable food items and the products which can help you in multiple ways. There are some of the kitchen staples which can help you in this – such as providing the medical aid. For example, you can make the antiseptic solution with the help of the dilute solution of the baking soda and bleach. This is known as the Dakin's Solution and kills the dangerous viruses and bacteria.

3. Honey

Honey has been used as a poster child for alternating the antibiotic. In fact, many researches have revealed that there are some types of honey which can kill few species of fungi, superbugs, bacteria, rendering it viable to be used as the antibiotic.

According to the Jeremiah Johnson, a nutrition expert, Honey is very good for healing the wounds, cuts, and abrasions inside the mouth as it is a demulcent which helps for the abraded tissues and also acts as a medium which kills the microbes.

4. Medicinal Herbs

Using the health enhancing herbs is another way of curing the wounds. The herbs like garlic, lavender, thyme and oregano can aid in protecting the wound from any injection and healing it. As Jeremiah Johnson recommended in her book about the presence of 3Gs in the medical kit: Garlic, Ginger, and Ginseng. Moreover, it is essential to know that which herb is used for which purpose. Few herbs are used as the painkiller and reduce pain effectively. Some of the herbs which you need to include in your aid box are given below:

- Aloe (Aloe vera)

- Lavender (Lavandula angustifolia)

- Comfrey (Symphytum officinale)

- Calendula (Calendula officinalis)

- Tea (Camellia sinensis)

- Gotu Kola (Centella asiatica)

There are few kitchen herb items that can be used for stopping the bleeding. It has been found that cayenne pepper is the best alternative of the QuickClot. This herb contains the natural ingredient known as capsaicin, which helps in reducing pain and can be used for different other medical purposes.

5. Essential Oils

For prolonged disasters, there are chances of extended bacterial and viral infections which can lead to many deaths. In history, essential oils were considered as the best natural remedy for soothing the medical issues which modern meds are now being made for. One of the most enchanting aspects of these oils is that they are capable of killing the dangerous bacteria without affecting the good bacteria.

Instead of targeting only one symptom, like modern medicines, essential oils are effective for multiple problems. There are two kinds of oils which you must include in your medical stock up:

- **Antibacterial Oils**

Because of the increasing amount of the antibacterial diseases, most of the essential oils like cassia, cinnamon, basil, cypress, clove, eucalyptus, lemon, tea, lavender, myrrh, orange, geranium, peppermint, thyme, oregano, rosemary, marjoram, and melaleuca are in use for antibacterial purposes.

- **Antiviral Oils**

The oils which are studied for controlling the viral infections are cinnamon, basil, eucalyptus, lemon, tea, myrrh, orange, cassia, lemongrass, peppermint, frankincense, thyme, oregano, rosemary, marjoram, and melaleuca are in use for antibacterial purposes.

Top two medicines to be included in the medical kit

Have you wondered about the situation when you are in any medical emergency, and there is no doctor around or no, medicine, what would happen then?

The survival medicine kit is going to help you in this case. Be sure that you include every important thing in it so that you could survive when disaster comes.

If you are passionate about keeping yourself prepared for such situations, consider regarding the making of the stock up of the necessary medications and antibiotics so that you don't need to depend on the fish antibiotics or have to black market the meds.

Top survival medicines to stock in medical kit

If you are looking for the items for long term survival and dealing with any kind of medical emergency, here is the brief list of the meds which you must add in your first aid kit.

1. Activated Charcoal Tablets

Activated Charcoal is known as the black magic med of the survival medical kit. This is the highly recommended medicine which should be there in your first aid box. The activated charcoal has many advantages (from whitening of teeth to lowering of the cholesterol level) and is an ideal medicine for the emergency removal of toxins. This drug, via absorption, captures the toxins from the body and flush them out of it.

Another major benefit of Activated Charcoal is that it aids in alleviating the bloats and gas. With the help of Activated Charcoal capsules, the digestion can be regulated. It protects your body from getting overdosed with the dangerous toxins. Because of its large surface area, it has high rate of absorption which keeps many substances from being entered in the digestive tract of body.

In acute uses for food poisoning, digestive illness, diarrhea, intake of toxins, vomiting, etc. And keep in the poison control figure in the record for the cases of toxin ingestion in your body.

2. Ammonia Inhalant Drug

The Ammonia Inhalant is the latest day edition of the smelling salts. It is made for arousing the patients who get fainted. This is usually an overlooked survival med, but imagine how it feels to bring someone back to life with the small swift of the ammonia inhalant.

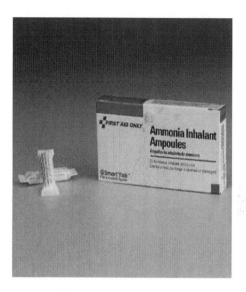

3. Antibiotics (amoxicillin)

Usually, fish antibiotics are not considered safe for the usage of humans, but the role of these antibiotics in treating the medical issues during the modern era is inevitable. Amoxicillin or Fish Mox is the fundamental product of the prepper's stock up which is used in the extensive catastrophic circumstances where a physician or medicines which are needed for the treatment are not available.

Amoxicillin helps in treating the bacterial infections, however also offers the severe allergy in few patients causing the sudden and intense death.

It is better to consult your doctor about this drug to check if this is a right medicine for you and your family members in case of survival circumstances when the prescribed antibiotic is difficult to find. Keep in mind that this antibiotic is originally made for fish, not for humans, but can be, used in cases when no urgent treatment is available.

The Fish Mox can be put in the stock, but should not be used in the ordinary way or without the consult of doctor.

4. Anti-diarrheal

One of the important survival kit medicine is the anti-diarrheal. Some of them are:

- Imodium® A-D or any other anti-diarrheal for controlling the symptoms of diarrhea.

- Kirkland includes the active ingredient

(Loperamide HCI 2mg.), which is available at low price.

5. Antihistamine anti-allergy medicine

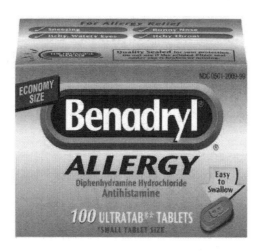

Benadryl is the diphenhydramine, which is the product of antihistamine, an anti-allergy medicine. This drug is being used since 1946 in relieving the perennial and seasonal allergy illnesses. It heals the bee sting readily.

6. Aspirin (painkiller)

Aspirin can't be used by everyone; however, it is important to put in the stock of first aid medical kit as it helps in saving the life during heart attacks. It also helps in relieving pain and being a pain killer; you can use it for different reasons. Keep the small packets of aspirin in your medical kit box.

7. Boiron Oscillococcinum

Boiron Oscillococcinum is a homeopathic medicine for treating the flu and cold symptoms. This medicine relieves the symptoms like body pains, headache, fever, fatigue, and chills. Boiron Oscillococcinum doesn't result in the drowsiness or react with any other medicine.

These are found in the form of the sweet taste pills which get dissolved readily if placed under the tongue and doesn't need to be swallowed by water or chewed. This drug works best for the flu and fever in particular.

8. Colloidal Silver (natural antibiotic)

This is the strong and a natural antibiotic, antifungal, antibacterial, and antiviral, Colloidal Silver helps in soothing various skin diseases like the sun burns, reducing scarring, soothing the herpes sores, and treating boils, ringworms, and warts.

Colloidal Silver is the product which faced a huge amount of medical claims, however, survival stocks should include this as a necessary item. By the manufacturer of the Colloidal Silver Antibiotic, there is no germ of disease which can survive in the presence of even a small trace of Colloidal Silver.

Colloidal Silver can be used for treating the wide variety of the infections and diseases, both for the external and internal use. Many big pharmaceutical firms don't acknowledge the claims regarding this drug because of the extensive advantages of this medicine.

As it is not advisable to self-medicate in any way, but there may come few moments when it gets hard to overcome the disease. Most of the medical kits include Colloidal Silver in their pharmacy packs as it is considered the natural antibiotic which can be used without any prescription. It works as an alternative to the prescribed antibiotic medicines and deals with different kinds of infections.

9. Digestive enzymes (Enzyme supplements)

Your stomach may not behave same after you change your diet. Most of the backpackers get overdosed frozen food items and this lead to various imbalance of digestive enzymes. The problem can be settled by restoring the enzyme balance in the body. Probiotics are considered good, which are the good bacteria used for reducing the digestive gas, bloating and improving the immune system.

10. Frankincense (natural immune system's booster)

Frankincense oil is being used since the biblical era and is considered as the Gift of the Kings. As it is used for healing the myriad of skin, small cuts, incisions while reducing the inflammations, scars of the body. This is an essential oil which helps against the various infections and boosts the immune system of the body.

11. Fresh Green Black Walnut Wormwood Complex (parasitic medicine)

Fresh Green Black Walnut Wormwood Complex is a bit weird item in the list of the survival medical kit. This is the strong extract which is taken from the hulls of the green, black colored walnut trees and has been in use for decades as an herbal tonic for promoting the healthful microbial action. It is added in the medical kit for the killing of parasites.

While any disaster or a survival situation, you may be in the area where there is not the stable supply of the clean drinking water so be prepared for clearing out of parasites from water by using the Fresh Green Black Walnut Wormwood Complex solution. This conventional herbal treatment is used to promote the growth of healthy bacteria and highly recommended for adding to the list of medical aid kit.

12. Goldenseal (immune system support)

Goldenseal is a famous antifungal and antibacterial medicine which promotes the formation of the healthy immune system. Goldenseal is also known as the Indian Turmeric or the Ginseng's little brother, which contains strong, potent medical attributes.

It kills the germs which come to its contact especially the mucus layer and doesn't absorb into the blood of the body, which leads to many benefits but can build up fluctuation if the blood pressure. That's why it should be taken with the consultation of a doctor. It also helps in curing cancer and digestive abnormalities.

13. Hurricaine (tooth pain reliever)

Nothing is more painful than a toothache. Hurricaine is a gel which helps in anesthetizing of the muscles thus provides the temporary relief of the pain and discomfort in teeth and the gums. In the past, the pain in the teeth remained one of the main reasons for suicide as there was no cure for this problem. This drug is a good solution particularly when the dentist is not around.

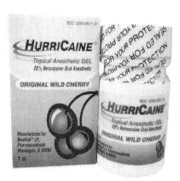

14. IOSAT (Potassium Iodide pills)

Including the IOSAT Potassium Iodide tablets in the medical stockpile, is being practiced since 1982 and its usage is certified by FDA for a long time. It is recommended by the health official Department of worldwide for preventing the thyroid cancer especially in those people who remain in expose to the radioactive species of iodine in the nuclear reactors of the detonators of any nuclear weaponry.

The radioactive species of iodine can emit rays which travel thousands of miles through the wind, as it happened during the disaster of Chernobyl and Fukushima. The thyroid is the part of the body which absorbs the iodine and stores it in it.

After the approval of FDA, Potassium Iodide is allowed for exposure as the thyroid doesn't get harm if it gets saturated safe amounts of the stable iodine. This prevents the absorption of the extra amount of iodine in the thyroid for a long period, and the radioactive iodine of in taken can be disposed of the body via kidneys.

Potassium iodide is the survival peppered medicine which is usually ignored, and even then it is necessary to be included. The issue is that when you require it, it is not readily available because of the health departments which forbid its sale.

Potassium Iodide if found in the form of the capsules, which can aid in maintaining the level of beneficial iodides high within the body especially in the thyroid gland. It supports the normal detoxification processes of the body such as removal of the heavy metals and also cures the sickness caused by the radiation.

15. Melatonin (sleeping aid)

Many survival medical kits include coffee and tea for various purposes. They must also have something in their stock which could induce sleep to them. Melatonin is a sleep-inducing item. Coffee and tea large amount of the caffeine which can stay you awake but help in boosting the energy level of your body while strengthening your endurance and protecting you and your family from an attack of dangerous diseases.

During the hour of crises, your mind is hyperactive with thousands of kinds of thought and worries which keep you up all night, but sufficient sleep is very necessary for gaining the proper level of energy and working on the effective strategy to fight against the crisis.

That's where Melatonin gets very important to use. It is great for those who face occasional insomnia, those who are with jet leg or if they want to enhance their quality of sleep.

16. MiroLAX stool softener (constipation relief medicine)

You may be consuming the food stuff which you don't eat in the normal routine so that it may lead to the bowel motions fluctuations more frequent. MiroLAX is a stool softening medicine which helps in digestion of every food item from fried, oily stuff to frozen, dried food. The prescribed amounts of the medicine can relief the temporary constipation problems while softening the stool. It can be used in the form of the solution by mixing it with any beverage.

17. Oregano Oil (an anti-inflammatory)

Oregano oil is very effective for the vaginal infections, flu and cold, and is a host of many other homeopathic usages. It comes in the packing along with the protection from the bed bugs, lice, fleas, mosquitoes and also tapeworms.

18. SaltStick Caps Plus (dehydration remedy)

Did you ever notice that it is inevitable to prevent the cramping pains during or after the long distance walk or high mountain hikes? By the experience of the marathon runner, SaltStick is considered as an electrolyte salt which includes caffeine and sodium solution which is a beneficiary item to be included in the medical kit.

Along with the reduction of the pain in the muscles, this medicine is entirely based on the veggie ingredients and helps in lowering the heat stress, while maintaining the level of electrolyte and energy. It is a great option for the people who go for hunting expeditions.

19. Tea Tree oil (only for external use)

The tea tree essential oil is the best immune system booster and known as the powerful immune system stimulant. It is strong antifungal and is very effective against various types of infections especially for topical use. It can aid in fighting against the three classes of disease causing organisms including viruses, fungi, and bacteria and the studies show that Tea Tree essential oil when used for massages before surgery can help in fortifying the body and lowering the post-surgery shocks.

Tea Tree Oil can aid the problem of measles, cold, sinusitis, and viral infections. It is a quite penetrating oil which helps in curing the infections and boils or even seeps via toenails. It is a good remedy for the athlete foot.

Avoid in taking the teas tree oil as it may end up destroying the internal digestive duct. Few people apply it for treating the sores of mouth and lips, but this is dangerous concoction for some and is not worth to risk for few people. Never ingest the oil.

20. Thieves Oil (pandemics)

Catch this notion: use the thieves oil to aid the prevention of the different infection.

Natural medicines in the medical aid

If you are interested in making a list of the natural survival preppers medicines and the homeopathic remedies, here is a brief list provided which includes the essential oils, home remedies, and in conservative medicines.

- **Aloe Vera:** Aloe Vera provides the relieving remedy for sunburns.

- **Camphor:** Camphor is used for the acne, aromatherapy baths, facial steams, massages, diffusers, and cuts.

- **Coconut Oil**: is used for cooking purposes.

- **Doctor Christopher's Anti-Infection Formula:** this formula provides the extreme peace of mind for flu infection.

- **Echinacea**: is the famous antiviral and anti-bacterial medicine which is used for the treatment of flu and cold.

- **Elderberry:** has been proven effective against the swine and avian flu. Its extract is made as Sambucol which is safe to use for kids without causing any side effects.

- **Epsom Salts:** Epsom salts are used for flushing out the toxins from the body while improving the absorption of the nutrients and soothing the pains in muscles.

- **Honey:** Honey is perfect to be used as a topical antibiotic and helps in killing dangerous bacteria.

- **Hydrogen Peroxide:** being an important first aid medicine, hydrogen peroxide helps in avoiding the infections even due to small cuts, burns, and scrapes. It can be used as the debriding agent too while removing the mucus, phlegm and other fluids linked with the sore mouth. The small bottles of hydrogen peroxide are added in stock as an essential component of survival medical kit.

- **Peppermint oil:** is ideal to use for the health and helps in keeping the small critters away. Spiders can be killed by peppermint oil and rodents. 100% peppermint can be used to burn the small nostrils.

- **Salt:** Salt is an active ingredient for cooking, preservation and medical uses.

- **Ginger Capsules:** Ginger is effective for treating the reflux, stomach problems, nausea, and morning sickness. It is beneficial for overcoming the motion sickness during the travel. It aids the soothing of the stomach after any digestive disorder or food poisoning.

- **Arnica:** This is the topical crème which is used for healing the muscular pain or any wound, or any kind of trauma. It is only for external sue for bruises and cuts. It has been found that it reduces the healing time of the sore muscles and injuries if used topically after the cut.

- **Cayenne Powder:** is an excellent addition to different food items, it is even better to be included in the medical box. Topically, this helps a lot in stopping the bleeding readily. It can also good for heart patients and clears the blocks in the vessels.

- **Chamomile:** this derived from the bulk of the Mountain rose herbs and is used to make the soothing tincture which aids in calming the children who are ill or have got trouble while sleeping. This tincture also helps in relieving the pain of tooth gums. The dried flowers of chamomile are used to make the poultice along with some gauze.

The brewed chamomile is used as a tea which is a relaxing drink taken at night and if cooled, it is rubbed against the stomach of infants to relieve the belly pain. Sometimes it is added in the bath water of kids as it relaxes the skin and induces the relaxation. Keep the tincture with you all the time.

- **Comfrey:** Comfrey is an external herb which induces the healing treatment for injuries and cures the broken bones. The poultice made by the plantain and comfrey is used for treatment of wounds which immensely reduces the healing time and aids in avoiding the infections. The homemade "Neosporin" along with this and other herbs can be used for treating the bug bites, bruises, cuts and severe injuries.

Other than this few homemade remedies compose of other herbs which can cure various types of cuts and injuries. It is possible to use the dried herb for making poultices and salves at home.

- **Eucalyptus Herb and Essential Oil:** You can keep this oil all the time with you. In this oil, eucalyptus herb is used as a face seam for solving the problem of congestion or the sinus issues. You can make it mild by adding the petroleum free vapo rub for treating the coughing and respiration disorders. The essential oil can also be used in diluted form if mixed with coconut oil or olive oil and implied externally on the chest and feet.

Thinking about the stress and poor nutrition with the low rate of hygiene and the total inadequacy of the medical care is an actual threat for human life and is being catastrophic day by day. It is better to remain prepared for the worst conditions, but for any kind of health related and diet issues, get advice from your doctor in advance so that you can add any extra medicine in your medical box.

Happy endings... it is better to own a medical box even if you don't use it much specially for long journeys and survival expeditions. Save the life of your family members and loved ones. Be cautious about any of the social activities occurring

678

around you and remain updated about everything specially regarding the medical techniques and outbreaks.

Nail Fungus Treatment

There you are, working another day and earning another dollar. Your feet get hot, your socks get sweaty, and you are just ready to get home and take off your shoes and socks.

Put your feet up and get them dry. Maybe put on your slippers. All you can think about is how nice it is going to be to cool down and dry off. Until you get home, that is.

Once you do, you realize how wet your feet are. They may smell, they may not. They may hurt. They may not. They may feel wet and soggy. They may not. Really, you never know what your feet are going to look like, until you take your socks off.

Then, you see the issue. You have oddly colored toe nails. Or perhaps you see that there are some cracks in the edges. Or perhaps you see that there is even growth. The short story is you have a fungus infection, and you need to get it taken care of.

You need to go to the store. You need to get something that is going to fix your problem, but you feel embarrassed. You don't want to hand the checker the box with the solution in it, and you don't want to have to stand in line hanging onto the medicine.

But there is a better way. There is an entirely all natural way you can handle this problem without ever telling anyone that you have toenail fungus. Sure, you know that it's a common problem. You know that you need to get it taken care of, or it can only get worse. You know that the only way for it to get better is to treat it, but no matter how common it is, you don't want the rest of the world to know that you have it.

That's where the all-natural solution comes in. You can take care of the problem at hand, you can do it easily, and you can do it on the sly. You don't have to tell anyone that you have toenail fungus, and you don't have to ever deal with this problem again.

This book is going to take away all of the guesswork in this problem. You are going to find the solution you need for the issues you have, and you are going to have the results that you want, guaranteed.

So are you ready to rid yourself of this for good? Good. Let's get started.

Toe Fungus: An Overview

The thought of toenail fungus is enough to make some people cringe. You may not realize it now, but there are millions of new cases of toenail fungus in the United States alone every single year.

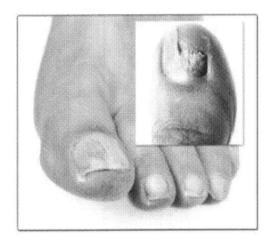

Over three million new cases emerge in the United States, making this condition one of the most common conditions that plagues the population.

The result is an unsightly nail, or set of nails. The infected person can experience abnormal growth of their nails, chipped or cracked toenails, or discolored toenails.

In fact, the general symptoms are very common, and while you are able to go to the doctor to test if you have it, you can very easily diagnose this condition in yourself at home.

The conditions are obvious:

- **Brittle toenails**

- **Dry or cracked toenails**

- **Unsightly toenails**

- **Odd growth on the nails, or abnormal growth of the nails**

- **Discolored toenails**

- **Several toenails infected at a time**

- **Only one toenail infected at a time**

- **Smelly feet**

- **Possibly pain on the nail or in the toe itself**

As you can see by this list, it's really easy to test and see if you have the condition. If you aren't sure and you really want the opinion of a professional, then by all means go into the doctor, but know that this isn't necessarily a dangerous condition, it's just one that needs to be treated when you realize you have it.

Many people out in the world today do not know they actually have toenail fungus. They may feel pain, but more often than not toenail fungus is an entirely painless condition that only results in poor toenail health. It can be spread among nails, and even from person to person with the right kind of contact.

What this means is that you can catch it not only from your own conditions, but you can also catch it from such things as gyms, the public swimming pool, and even through trying on shoes at a department store.

Of course, there are a lot of precautions you can take that will help you not catch this in the first place, and we are going to take a look at those first, but then we are going to look at other causes as well as how you can treat those.

1. First of all, the best thing you can do to keep yourself protected when you are out and about is to wear shoes and socks

2. If you do happen to be in a place with your feet exposed, make sure you clean them thoroughly with hot, soapy water, and that you dry them completely after you have finished

3. Refrain from trying on other people's shoes or socks

4. Refrain from trying on shoes without socks on, no matter where you are

5. Always change your socks after you have tried on shoes, and clean them immediately

6. Always wash your feet after you have tried on shoes, no matter where you are or what you have been wearing while you tried them on

7. Always take the cautious route, no matter where you are or who you are with

As I have mentioned, there are millions of new cases of toenail fungus every year, and the more you expose yourself to the outside world, the more you are going to be exposed to this fungus.

On the other hand, there are countless people out there that may not know they are infected, and as a result they are accidentally spreading the fungus to the world around them without a clue they are doing so.

This is why you need to take every precaution to protect yourself and your feet while you are out and about in the world. The more you do this, the better your chances are of not developing the fungus again.

Of course, this is only a rough overview. You will want to know for a fact what you can do to treat the nails, and how you can prevent this from happening to you again.

Not to worry. In the chapters to come, we are going to look at how you can treat this condition entirely at home, and what you can do to keep it from coming back in the future.

A complete win all around, there's nothing better than treating the condition at home!

Easy Treatment 101: Caring For Your Nails

Now, let's dive into the fun part of this problem... the solution.

These are tried and proven methods that are all highly effective. You need to stay consistent with them, but if you do, you are going to get the results you are hoping for in a matter of days.

Remember that consistency and persistency are the best policy.

Apple Cider Vinegar

What you will need:

Baking soda

Large bowl

Sponge or light scrubber for your foot

¼ cup apple cider vinegar

Directions:

In a large bowl or dish, fill halfway with warm water. This dish needs to be large enough for you to fit the infected foot into it.

Pour in the other ingredients, and soak the foot, making sure all nails are completely submerged by several inches of water.

Soak for half an hour.

Pour out the water in the tub, and take your sponge or scrub and gently scrub the infected toes.

Rinse well with water as hot as you can stand, but be careful to not burn yourself. Once completely rinsed, sprinkle with a bit of baking powder and dry completely.

Leave your foot to air out for at least another half an hour. You want to ensure that your foot is entirely dry before you cover it again.

Sleep with your feet bare.

Repeat these steps every day for a couple of weeks, and the condition will clear up.

White Vinegar

What you will need:

¼ cup white vinegar

Baking soda

Large bowl

Sponge or light scrubber for your foot

Directions:

In a large bowl or dish, fill halfway with warm water. This dish needs to be large enough for you to fit the infected foot into it.

Pour in the other ingredients, and soak the foot, making sure all nails are completely submerged by several inches of water.

Soak for half an hour.

Pour out the water in the tub, and take your sponge or scrub and gently scrub the infected toes.

Rinse well with water as hot as you can stand, but be careful to not burn yourself. Once completely rinsed, sprinkle with a bit of baking powder and dry completely.

Leave your foot to air out for at least another half an hour. You want to ensure that your foot is entirely dry before you cover it again.

Sleep with your feet bare.

Repeat these steps every day for a couple of weeks, and the condition will clear up.

Tea tree oil

12 drops tea tree oil

Baking soda

Large bowl

Sponge or light scrubber for your foot

Directions:

In a large bowl or dish, fill halfway with warm water. This dish needs to be large enough for you to fit the infected foot into it.

Pour in the other ingredients, and soak the foot, making sure all nails are completely submerged by several inches of water.

Soak for half an hour.

Pour out the water in the tub, and take your sponge or scrub and gently scrub the infected toes.

Rinse well with water as hot as you can stand, but be careful to not burn yourself. Once completely rinsed, sprinkle with a bit of baking powder and dry completely.

Leave your foot to air out for at least another half an hour. You want to ensure that your foot is entirely dry before you cover it again.

Sleep with your feet bare.

Repeat these steps every day for a couple of weeks, and the condition will clear up.

Coconut oil

Baking soda

Large bowl

Sponge or light scrubber for your foot

½ cup fractionated coconut oil

Directions:

In a large bowl or dish, fill halfway with warm water. This dish needs to be large enough for you to fit the infected foot into it.

Pour in the other ingredients, and soak the foot, making sure all nails are completely submerged by several inches of water.

Soak for half an hour.

Pour out the water in the tub, and take your sponge or scrub and gently scrub the infected toes.

Rinse well with water as hot as you can stand, but be careful to not burn yourself. Once completely rinsed, sprinkle with a bit of baking powder and dry completely.

Leave your foot to air out for at least another half an hour. You want to ensure that your foot is entirely dry before you cover it again.

Sleep with your feet bare.

Repeat these steps every day for a couple of weeks, and the condition will clear up.

Orange lavender oil

Baking soda

10 drops orange oil

10 drops lavender oil

Large bowl

Sponge or light scrubber for your foot

Directions:

In a large bowl or dish, fill halfway with warm water. This dish needs to be large enough for you to fit the infected foot into it.

Pour in the other ingredients, and soak the foot, making sure all nails are completely submerged by several inches of water.

Soak for half an hour.

Pour out the water in the tub, and take your sponge or scrub and gently scrub the infected toes.

Rinse well with water as hot as you can stand, but be careful to not burn yourself. Once completely rinsed, sprinkle with a bit of baking powder and dry completely.

Leave your foot to air out for at least another half an hour. You want to ensure that your foot is entirely dry before you cover it again.

Sleep with your feet bare.

Repeat these steps every day for a couple of weeks, and the condition will clear up.

Baking soda

1 cup Baking soda per day

Large bowl

Sponge or light scrubber for your foot

Directions:

In a large bowl or dish, fill halfway with warm water. This dish needs to be large enough for you to fit the infected foot into it.

Pour in the other ingredients, and soak the foot, making sure all nails are completely submerged by several inches of water.

Soak for half an hour.

Pour out the water in the tub, and take your sponge or scrub and gently scrub the infected toes.

Rinse well with water as hot as you can stand, but be careful to not burn yourself. Once completely rinsed, sprinkle with a bit more of the baking powder and dry completely.

Leave your foot to air out for at least another half an hour. You want to ensure that your foot is entirely dry before you cover it again.

Sleep with your feet bare.

Repeat these steps every day for a couple of weeks, and the condition will clear up.

Oregano oil

Baking soda

15 drops oregano oil

Large bowl

Sponge or light scrubber for your foot

Directions:

In a large bowl or dish, fill halfway with warm water. This dish needs to be large enough for you to fit the infected foot into it.

Pour in the other ingredients, and soak the foot, making sure all nails are completely submerged by several inches of water.

Soak for half an hour.

Pour out the water in the tub, and take your sponge or scrub and gently scrub the infected toes.

Rinse well with water as hot as you can stand, but be careful to not burn yourself. Once completely rinsed, sprinkle with a bit of baking powder and dry completely.

Leave your foot to air out for at least another half an hour. You want to ensure that your foot is entirely dry before you cover it again.

Sleep with your feet bare.

Repeat these steps every day for a couple of weeks, and the condition will clear up.

Listerine mouthwash

Baking soda

1 measuring cup full of mouthwash

Large bowl

Sponge or light scrubber for your foot

Directions:

In a large bowl or dish, fill halfway with warm water. This dish needs to be large enough for you to fit the infected foot into it.

Pour in the other ingredients, and soak the foot, making sure all nails are completely submerged by several inches of water.

Soak for half an hour.

Pour out the water in the tub, and take your sponge or scrub and gently scrub the infected toes.

Rinse well with water as hot as you can stand, but be careful to not burn yourself. Once completely rinsed, sprinkle with a bit of baking powder and dry completely.

Leave your foot to air out for at least another half an hour. You want to ensure that your foot is entirely dry before you cover it again.

Sleep with your feet bare.

Repeat these steps every day for a couple of weeks, and the condition will clear up.

Olive oil

Baking soda

1/3 cup olive oil

Large bowl

Sponge or light scrubber for your foot

Directions:

In a large bowl or dish, fill halfway with warm water. This dish needs to be large enough for you to fit the infected foot into it.

Pour in the other ingredients, and soak the foot, making sure all nails are completely submerged by several inches of water.

Soak for half an hour.

Pour out the water in the tub, and take your sponge or scrub and gently scrub the infected toes.

Rinse well with water as hot as you can stand, but be careful to not burn yourself. Once completely rinsed, sprinkle with a bit of baking powder and dry completely.

Leave your foot to air out for at least another half an hour. You want to ensure that your foot is entirely dry before you cover it again.

Sleep with your feet bare.

Repeat these steps every day for a couple of weeks, and the condition will clear up.

The Best Blend

Baking soda

10 drops tea tree oil

12 drops orange oil

½ cup apple cider vinegar

Large bowl

Sponge or light scrubber for your foot

Directions:

In a large bowl or dish, fill halfway with warm water. This dish needs to be large enough for you to fit the infected foot into it.

Pour in the other ingredients, and soak the foot, making sure all nails are completely submerged by several inches of water.

Soak for half an hour.

Pour out the water in the tub, and take your sponge or scrub and gently scrub the infected toes.

Rinse well with water as hot as you can stand, but be careful to not burn yourself. Once completely rinsed, sprinkle with a bit of baking powder and dry completely.

Leave your foot to air out for at least another half an hour. You want to ensure that your foot is entirely dry before you cover it again.

Sleep with your feet bare.

Repeat these steps every day for a couple of weeks, and the condition will clear up.

Aiding The Process: Proper Treatment

I know when you are infected with something such as this, you want it gone, and you want it gone now.

That is more than reasonable, but the truth of the matter is it does take time. In order for the fungus to die and your toenail to heal itself, you are going to have to spend the time working on the nail and making sure it really does heal.

This means you are going to spend time soaking the nail in the bowls, and you have to take the time to do this every single day. Each day you let go by without soaking your foot, you are giving the fungus the opportunity to grow and take root in your nails all over again.

The main thing you have to realize about toenail fungus is that it is a living thing, and it is going to take root as much as it can.

If you want to eliminate it from your foot, you have to kill it, which means you have to take the time to win the battle.

This fungus is designed to live in incredible conditions, which means in order to kill it, you have to prove yourself to be better prepared and more resilient than the fungus is. This fungus is alive, and it wants to live on the nail, which means it is going to put up with a lot of treatment before it dies.

On the other hand, when you are consistent with the treatment, you may find that it's a relatively short amount of time you have to spend on the nail in order to heal it. It really comes down to perspectives, and the more time you are willing to invest in your nails, the better off it is going to be.

But, it is very important to remember that you have to also use other precautions when you are treating this condition.

The fungus is looking for a place to live, and the more you expose your nails to the spores, the more likely it is to take root right back where it started.

In other words, you may well be re-infecting yourself right after you go through one of the treatments.

So, I want to ensure you are taking all of the precautions necessary to make sure you are not giving yourself undue exposure to the fungus all over again. Here is a list of things you need to do when you are doing the treatments that will ensure you get rid of the fungus for good, and you do not bring it back when you are finished.

1. **Wash and dry. This is a rule of thumb for you, on everything. Wash and dry the bowl when you are done, wash and dry the tub if you pour the water out in the tub.**

   Wash and dry the towel that you use to dry your foot.

2. **Use gloves. All nails can be infected with this fungus, and you don't want to expose your finger nails to the fungus while you are trying to remove it from your toes!**

3. **Make sure that cleanliness is on top of the list.**

I know I said something to the effect of washing twice, but let me assure you... this fungus doesn't like water. It likes moisture, but not water. This means that the more you keep soap and water on the area when you are cleaning, the more you are going to drive it away.

On the other hand, the more you keep the area dry when you are not doing a direct treatment on your nails, the more likely the fungus is to die out and not come back

Your goal is to keep your nails as hostile as possible toward the fungus. When you make an environment that they can't live in, they aren't going to try. You just have to keep the upper hand in the battle, and in no time at all you are going to have your nails back.

Winning the Battle: Keeping Your Nails Your Own

It's true... the thought of toenail fungus is one that is gross, no matter who you are and how many times you have encountered it. To make matters worse... the thought of catching the fungus from someone else makes the condition that much worse.

This means if you have ever caught it, you know what it is like, and you certainly don't want to bring it back in. If you aren't sure how you got it in the first place, this can be a bit of a challenge, but one that is well worth rising up to if you don't want to deal with the treatment again.

No matter how many times you have treated this before, if you get it again, you have to deal with the same treatment over.

And if you have ever dealt with this treatment before, you know that it can take a fair amount of time to deal with it. This is something that you are going to want to avoid, no matter who you are.

And, one of the biggest ways you can avoid a treatment is to avoid the issue that requires the treatment, which is what we are going to talk about next.

You know that toenail fungus is common, which means you can be exposed to it all over the place. It doesn't matter how clean you are, if the person in the pool across from you has it, then you are going to be exposed. And, it doesn't matter how badly you don't want it to take root on your toes, if you are exposed, you are running the risk.

This means we need to look at the things that you can do that will keep this condition at bay. Things that you can do in the world you live in on a day to day basis that will erase this problem right out of the picture for you. Thankfully. These things are not only easy to do, but they can be as effective in preventing the condition as the treatment is in clearing it up.

1. Wash and dry

A good rule to keep in mind is that if you are outside, you are exposed. Always wash your feet at least once a day, and make sure they are dry!

2. Avoid contact with other people or conditions

You can't always control the circumstances you are in, but if you know you are in a situation that may have gotten you exposed, go back to the first rule, and wash and dry.

You may be exposed and not realize it, or you may see your exposure right when it happens. Either way, wash and dry.

3. Maintain good hygiene

Don't just wash your feet, wash your socks, your clothes, your shower... anywhere your feet are exposed.

You want to keep your environment perfect for your feet, not for the fungus.

4. Maintain a good diet

The healthier your nails are, the harder it is for the fungus to take root. Consume lots of vitamins and minerals, and you will see a wealth of benefits... including on your feet!

5. Keep your feet clean!

As upsetting as it is... the best way to deal with any kind of infection is to be as clean as clean can be. If you keep your feet washed and dry, if you wear socks in your shoes, and you change to dry socks when you are finished with a sweaty activity, and you keep the environment foot friendly, you are going to have healthy nails as a result!

The one most important thing I want you to remember is that everyone can get toenail fungus, and if you do have it, it's no indicator that you are unsanitary. What is important is that you get it under control, and that you do what you can to keep it that way.

You can catch it anywhere, but the fact is you can treat it just as easily, as long as you are willing to keep things clean, and you fight it like a fungus.

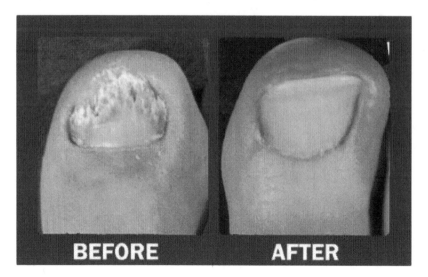

Handcrafted Soap And Skin Care

The use of essential oils dates back thousands of years; they have been used in religious ceremonies, to aid in healing and even as an important part of aromatherapy. An essential oil is simply nature bottled! Every distinct smell in nature can be captured. The smell may originate from the seeds of a plant; their flowers or even the bark of a tree; in all of these items it is possible to find oil. The oil can be removed from the plant; most typically by crushing the relevant part. The resulting liquid is the essential oil and is a volatile compound.

The term volatile is given as these oils tend to be capable of quickly changing from a solid or even liquid state to a gas. The change happens at room temperature and is the reason why the smell of essential oils can be so powerful. This rapid change to a gas form allows the oil to spread quickly across the room.

There are thousands of different oils available on the market; everyone is unique as even oil from the same species of plant can vary in quality and smell depending upon the condition of the plant and the soil; as well as other environmental factors. These oils have been and are still widely used as a form of alternative therapy; although many people disclaim them as there is no scientific proof of their effectiveness. However, despite this Eucalyptus oil has become popular in many products ranging from use as a cleaning product to a health aid in the form of nose drops, throat sweets or even to aid keep insects away from houses and food stocks. There are many other essential oils which are regularly used in a variety of ways and are accepted by society.

There are several ways of extracting the oil from a plant:

- Distillation – This is the process of removing oil by placing part of a plant into water. For instance the leaf of the Eucalyptus. The heat of the water causes the volatile oils to vaporize. These vapors are then condensed backed into a liquid form and ready to use.

- Expression – This is generally used when extracting citrus oil and simply refers to crushing, or cold-pressing the peel of a citrus fruit to access the essential oil which is normally available in a high quantity.

- Solvent – When you are dealing with oil which is too sensitive to be extracted through the above methods you may find that a solvent is added to the plant material. This draws the oil out of the plant and it can then be removed from the solvent by the distillation process.

As volatile compounds it is important to follow some basic safety guidelines when dealing with these oils; this will ensure you can craft a beautifully aromatic soap or skin care product:

- These oils must be recognized as a natural product which are generally strong and have not got additives in; some oils can burn.

- All oils should be stored in their original bottles and the lids kept closed tight. This not only reduces the risk of a leak and damage to the surrounding items it will prolong the life of the oil. Lids left loose will allow the small to diminish. Essential oils should also be stored in a cool, dark place; sunlight will cause them to quickly degrade; plastic bottles should be avoided.

- You should never touch the undiluted essential oil with your bare skin. The bottles have pipettes to use and you should never mix these up as you will damage the smell. If you are at risk of splashing it on your hands then it is advisable to wear latex gloves.

- Essential oil which is to used on the skin should never be more than 3% oil.

- Oils should always be kept away from children; drinking them or even playing with them can be harmful.

- You should always check with your doctor before using an essential oil if you have a serious medical condition.

- Alcohol should never be drunk whilst using essential oils

- Always perform a small skin test before using oil for the first time.

- Finally, you should always was your hands thoroughly before and after you use the oil; whether diluted or concentrated.

Following these guidelines will ensure you gain the benefits from these powerful natural substances; without the risks.

10 Simple Hand Soap Recipes

One of the most common uses of essential oils is to use them when making soap. This will allow you to enjoy the aroma every time you wash your hands or face and the oil can be beneficial to your skin; depending upon which one you have used. The following recipes all make excellent soaps with a slightly different use for each one:

1) Citrus Soap

This soap has a beautiful, fresh fragrance and can be very effective at exfoliating your skin. You will need some glycerin soap which comes in blocks. Melt several of them in the microwave; preferably in a glass bowl to ensure the flavor is not tainted. Whilst they are melting you can either have your citrus oil ready or you can make it yourself by crushing the peel of your favorite citrus fruit; ideally use several different ones such as oranges and lemons. It is acceptable to have very small pieces of peel in the mix as this will aid the exfoliating effect.

As soon as the glycerin has melted you will need to let it cool slightly before you add your essential oil. It is essential to stir your mixture thoroughly to ensure the flavor spreads evenly as the glycerin sets.

You can then pour the mixture into the container; this can be any size or shape. It will need to cool for one hour at room temperature and then one more hour in the freezer. You will then be able to remove it from the container and use it or slice it into smaller chunks with a sharp knife.

2) Chai Latte Soap

This soap is designed to warm your hands whilst leaving them clean and soft. It is excellent for during the winter months when the weather is harsher.

You will need to slowly blend together 90g of palm oil, coconut oil and olive oil with some cocoa butter and castor oil; 30g of each. You will also need 100g of water and 46g of Lye. Once it is fully prepared you can pour it into plastic cups and allow the mixture to cool slowly.

You will then need to make a second dose of this; approximately half the size and add a small amount of titanium dioxide; this must be dissolved in water first. This addition will make a white mixture which can be added to the top of your cups to create a latte effect. The most effective way to get it white is to whisk it for approximately ten minutes. They will take 24 hours to set properly and then ten minutes in a freezer before they just slide out of their molds.

3) Scented bar soap

This is your base soap; you will need to use Lye to create it and you must wear gloves as Lye will burn through clothing and skin. Fortunately it is completely removed during the creation process. You can add any essential oil you like to this mixture.

You will need to measure three quarters of a cup of water; preferably distilled. Then slowly add a quarter cup of Lye whilst stirring continuously. There will be fumes; it is best to stand back whilst stirring to avoid breathing these in. After a few minutes the water should become clear.

In a separate container mix one cup of olive oil, almond or sunflower oil and coconut oil. This mixture should be warmed in the microwave for approximately one minute. You will now need a thermometer to confirm the temperature. The Lye and water mix must be approximately 120 degrees and the oils approximately 100 degrees. Once they hit the right temperatures mix them slowly together;

ideally pour the lye into the oil. It should be stirred for at least five minutes; you will see it start to clear. Ultimately it should look like a vanilla pudding!

This is the point you can add essential oils. You will then need to pour your mixture into an appropriate container and leave it to set for at least twenty four hours. It should then be firm to touch; if it is not then leave it for another twenty four hours. At this point you will be able to remove it from its container and cut it to the size you require. It is then best to leave it on a wire rack for four weeks to cure properly; turning it regularly. It is then ready to use and should be wrapped or placed in an airtight container.

4) Lavender Soap

You will need to select your preferred choice of oil; there are many different manufacturers although the smell should always be the same! Simply add the essential oil to the soap recipe above; it can be used on its own or paired with almost any other oil to make a delightful smell which will help to keep your skin soft. It is reputed to be good for the relief of headaches and a variety of skin conditions such as eczema and sunburn.

5) Cedarwood Soap

Cedarwood essential oil has been shown to act as an effective antiseptic and an anti-inflammatory. It generally has a woody scent and is an effective exfoliate. In fact it is known to help remove oils and other dirt which have become embedded into your skin. It is best used by people with normal to oily skin and can be exceptionally beneficial if you work with your hands a lot; such as a mechanic. A few drops of this essential oil in your soap mixture can be supplemented by almost any other flavor to make the soap of your choice.

6) Patchouli Soap

If you use too much of this essential oil you will know about it! It is a powerful oil but has excellent anti-inflammatory properties as well as being good for dry skin. It is best to use a few drops of this oil mixed with another fragrance of your choice.

7) **Rosemary Soap**

You will probably have already come across this scent. When mixed with the soap mixture above it creates a delicate yet uplifting fragrance. It is also considered a stimulant; helping you feel better and ready to face the day. Because it is a stimulant it should be avoided by anyone who is pregnant or has epilepsy.

8) **Peppermint Soap**

As you would expect, this soap offers a fresh, minty smell which is invigorating and will help to clear your sinuses in the morning. It has even been associated with reducing the effects of a cold. It is also known to be an effective antiseptic although it is not recommended to be used if you have dry or flaky skin as it can dry your skin out further. IT is for this reason it is best to only add a few drops to your soap; ensuring the flavor and benefits are there without excessive skin drying.

9) **Bergamot Soap**

It has been suggested that bergamot oil can improve your mood and even inspire confidence. The oil comes from a citrus fruit which is a cross between an orange and a lemon. It has also been associated with reducing the appearance of scars on the skin as well as effectively killing many types of bacteria.

The oil is known to reduce headaches and can be effective as relaxing muscles. Adding fifteen drops of this essential oil to your soap mixture will help you soothe those aches and pains away!

10)   Tea Tree Soap

Tea tree is a well known essential oil which is used in multiple applications; particularly as a health benefit to heal skin and improve the appearance of damaged skin. There are actually over three hundred species of teat trees; this means you will need to experiment with which specific tea tree oil is right for your soap. You can even use this soap to wash your hair as tea tree is known to help reduce or eliminate dandruff.

10 Essential Oil Hand Lotions Recipes

Because of the natural healing and antiseptic properties of many essential oils they can be exceptionally effective ingredients when making your own hand creams. In fact, although these are described as hand lotions they are generally very effective when used across your body to look after your skin. Essential oil hand creams should become part of your daily skin care routine as they will help to keep your skin looking and feeling younger.

1) Calamine Lotion

Calamine has been known throughout history as a soothing essential oil. Mixed with the following ingredients it can be an effective deterrent to many insects and soothe after a bite.

Simply mix four teaspoons of clay and four of baking soda with one tablespoon of sea salt. Then slowly mix in a quarter cup of water. This can be adjusted to suit your mixture; you do not want it too liquid! Once this has been mixed add a teaspoon of glycerin to keep the mixture smooth. You can then place it in a container and use as needed.

2) Vanilla Lotion

Mix a quarter cup of carrier oil with two tablespoons of coconut oil, one ounce of beeswax and two teaspoons of shea butter. This should be done in a bowl inside a sauce pan of water; to ensure the mixture melts slowly. Once they have all melted you can take it off the stove and add one teaspoon of vanilla extract. You should then pour it straight into a container and leave until it reaches room temperature before using. You can whisk this to make a creamier mixture; if you prefer.

3) Coconut Oil Body Butter

This mixture is thick and creamy and will make your skin feel fantastic as well as moisturizing it.

Simply add one cup of coconut oil to a teaspoon of vitamin E oil and five or six drops of your preferred essential oil. Almost any flavor will do; you can even mix them.

Next use an electric whisk to mix the ingredients thoroughly. It will take at least five minutes before they reach a light, almost airy consistency; this is now ready to use! Simply add the mixture to a suitable container and use regularly to enjoy the maximum benefits.

4) Whipped Peppermint

You should already be aware of the benefits of peppermint. This mixture will provide you with a lotion that can be used on your hands or any part of your body. You will need to place half a cup of each of the following ingredients into a bowl; coconut oil, shea butter and cocoa butter. This should then be placed into a saucepan of warm water over a hot stove. The mixture will melt slowly and you can add in half a cup of sweet almond oil, one teaspoon of vitamin E and four drops of peppermint.

Once you have mixed these ingredients thoroughly you will need to leave the mixture into the fridge for approximately one hour. It should then be firm but not solid. Then, using an electric whisk mix the firm ingredients until you have a creamy mix; this can then be placed into a container and is ready to use. Just be careful not to keep it anywhere too warm!

5) Lavender Hand Cream

Mix quarter of a cup of sweet almond oil with three tablespoons of coconut oil and three tablespoons of olive oil. You will then need to heat this slowly on your stove until it has melted. This will need to be stirred constantly. Then add four tablespoons of grated beeswax and approximately forty drops of lavender oil.

Next, allow the mixture to cool in a fridge for ten minutes before pouring it into your choice of container. It can then be left to cool. Then enjoy!

6) Lemon Hand Lotion

This mixture is designed to give you a lift when feeling a little down or simply to help you get started in the morning.

All you need to do is mix six tablespoons of lemon juice with an equivalent amount of glycerin. You can mix by hand although it is recommended to use an electric whisk. This will reduce the amount of time taken to create your lotion; it will also create a creamy, lighter mix.

Once it has been mixed thoroughly you can place it in a container and use straight way. Easy!

7) Summer Lotion

This lotion will make you think about the warm summer days; it is a great pick you up for a cold winter day! It is also exceptionally easy to make and can be ready to use within a few minutes!

717

Place half a tablespoon of raw honey with the same quantity of aloe vera in a small bottle. Then add three tablespoons of calendula oil and ten drops of chamomile oil. You can also add ten drops of lavender if you wish. Close the lid of the bottle and shake vigorously for several minutes. It can be used immediately although it is even better cooled; keep it in the fridge.

It can be an effective treatment of sunburn as well as a moisturizing hand and body lotion. It is worth noting that as it has raw honey in it you should not use it on a baby under one year of age.

8) Lavender Moisturizer

This is a fantastic lotion to moisturize your skin and leave you with an amazing glow! Simply mix one cup of Shea butter with one cup of coconut oil, a third of a cup of arrowroot powder and eighty drops of lavender oil. These need to be mixed with an electric whisk until you have a consistency like whipped cream. You can then place it in suitable containers and use immediately.

It is worth noting that the mixture makes a lot of lotion; you can halve the ingredients if you choose to. It is also possible to leave the arrowroot out; its purpose is to dry the mixture slightly to ensure your skin is not left looking oily.

9) Essential Exfoliating Body Scrub

Every day you skin will shed dead cells. This happens all over your body and is a natural process. To ensure your skin glows and is healthy it is essential to remove these dead cells. The best way to do this is to use an exfoliating scrub:

You will need to put one cup of sea salt in a large bowl; preferably glass so the flavor is not tainted. The add half a cup of olive oil and five drops of each of the following essential oils; ylang ylang, lavender and frankincense. Slowly stir all the ingredients together until the mixture is thick and creamy. Then put it into a pot and use as necessary – covering your body once a week should be sufficient.

10)   Mixed Oil Salve

This salve uses lavender to sooth and nurture your skin as well as tea tree to heal and lemon to invigorate. Simply place two ounces of coconut in a bowl and add five drops of each of the three essential oils mentioned above. Mix it all thoroughly and when satisfied with the texture put it in a pot to store until needed. You can use this whenever your skin needs a lift!

12 Alternative Hand Crafted Essential Oil Care Products

Essential oils have been part of the alternate medical scene for thousands of years; the medicinal and therapeutic properties of plants are an important part of traditional medicine in many cultures. In recent years it has become more recognized in the west; the following recipes will help you to make the most of what nature has provided.

1) Hair Serum

As well as looking after your skin you should take care of your hair with this simple but effective mix:

Start by putting two ounces of castor oil into a dropper bottle. Then add five drops of ylang ylang, rosemary and lavender. Shake the bottle vigorously for several minutes to ensure the ingredients are thoroughly mixed. Simply apply half a dozen drops to your hair and wait twenty minutes before you wash your hair normally. You can do this morning and night if you wish.

2) Essential Bath Salts

This essential oil concoction is excellent for using tin the bath; it will relax your muscles and invigorate your body whilst encouraging a quick recovery from any sports related injury.

Add one cup of Epsom salts to a big bowl and then mix in ten drops of both the essential oils; Panaway and Aroma Siez. You can even add a few drops of lavender if you wish. Once you have mixed it all thoroughly pour it into a suitable container and put between one quarter and half a cup in each of your baths. You will be impressed!

3) Essential Cellulite

No one wants cellulite; especially anywhere it may be visible. This mixture will help to reduce and even eliminate the issue.

Add one cup of organic coffee to a glass bowl and mix in half a cup of olive oil. Continue mixing this as you add ten drops of grapefruit essential oil and five drops of cypress. Once it is mixed thoroughly add it to a container and either use across all your body in just on the cellulite prone areas.

4) The Essential Perfume Choice

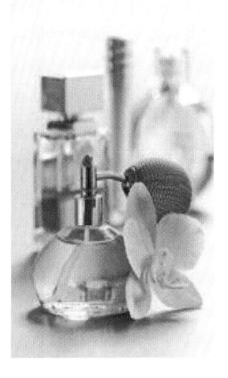

This is a light and fresh fragrance but it is possible to adjust the aroma by adding more or less essential oils; or even using different ones!

You will need a roll on bottle. Add three drops of grapefruit oil, two of frankincense and one of both bergamot and copaiba. Then fill your bottle with coconut oil. This should be about a tablespoon of coconut; if you need two then double then essential oils!

Put the lid on your bottle and shake vigorously; you can then use it as needed; ideally on your wrists and sides of neck.

5) Peppermint Shaving Cream

Peppermint is known for its ability to sooth and to reduce inflammation. This makes it the perfect ingredient into a shaving cream.

To create this place one third of a cup of shea butter and one third of a cup of coconut oil into a bowl; this should be sat in a pan of hot water on the stove. Keep the heat low and this will slowly melt. Once melted pour it into a glass bowl and immediately add three tablespoons of olive oil. It should then cool for fifteen minutes before you add one teaspoon of castile soap and eight drops of peppermint oil. Mix thoroughly before placing into the fridge for one hour. Once it starts to harden remove it and whisk until creamy. It can then be put into a suitable, preferably glass container ready to use when shaving.

6) After Shave

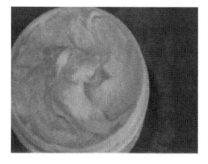

Using this mixture will soothe your skin after a shave and make it small fantastic!

Add half a cup of aloe vera gel to a glass pump bottle and then put half a cup of witch hazel in. Next add two tablespoons of jojoba oil and one teaspoon of vitamin E oil. Mix before adding ten drops of orange essential oil and ten of sandalwood. Shake the mixture well to ensure it is mixed completely and then the pump action lid can be used to squirt it onto your skin as required.

7) Anti-Stretch Essential Cream

This lotion was originally envisioned for women who are pregnant and suffering from enlarged breasts and stomachs. However, it is excellent for any sort of stretch marks:

Place half a cup of shea butter in with half a cup of cocoa butter in a bowl set in a pan of hot water. Once melted add one tablespoon of vitamin E and a quarter cup of olive oil as well as five drops of both geranium essential oil and lavender.

Again the mixture will need to cool for approximately one hour. You will then be able to whisk it until creamy. You can use this daily to achieve the best results on stretched skin.

8) Essential Relaxation

There are times when you may be struggling to relax or even get to sleep. This spray is designed to soothe and calm your nerves allowing you to rest your mind and body.

Place two ounces of magnesium oil in a spray bottle and add twenty drops of any of the following oils; lavender, tangerine, peace and calming, cedarwood or roman. You can even mix the oils.

Shake the mixture well and then apply a little to your feet and rub into them twenty minutes before you go to bed.

9) Essential Eczema Cream

Eczema is a serious skin condition and the irritation can be greatly reduced by the regular use of this cream:

Place a quarter cup of shea butter and a quarter cup of coconut oil in a bowl set in a pan of hot water. Allow the mixture to melt slowly. Once this has been completed allow it to cool for ten minutes before adding fifteen drops of lavender and five drops of tea tree oil. Next, place the mixture in the fridge to cool until it

725

starts to solidify. Although it can be used like this it is generally easier to whisk it until creamy and then store in a container. You can apply it as much as you like to any affected area of your skin.

10)　Essential Toothpaste

Looking after your teeth is an essential part of your healthcare regime. Unfortunately it is often the case that you do not know exactly what is placed into commercial toothpaste. This alternative natural version is a much better solution:

Mix quarter cup of baking soda with a quarter of a cup of coconut oil. You can then add a teaspoon of sea salt and six drops of your preferred essential oil; peppermint or orange are excellent choices.

Once mixed thoroughly store in a suitable container and use a small amount each time you brush your teeth. You should avoid dipping your brush into the mixture to avoid contamination.

11) Essential Lipstick

Your lips can easily suffer dry and chapped skin during the colder months and even in the warmer months from the heat of the sun! A good lipstick such as this will help to protect and revitalize your lips:

Melt two tablespoons of almond oil in a pan with one teaspoon of beeswax and one teaspoon of cocoa oil. You can then add a variety of natural ingredients to obtain your desired color; choose from beetroot powder, turmeric, cinnamon or alkanet root. You may need to experiment to get this right! Then simply add a few drops of your favorite essential oil and store ready to apply when needed.

12)   Essential deodorant

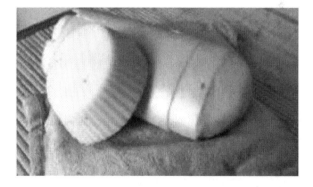

This is truly an essential product to the majority of people! It is also very easy to make at home!

Mix a quarter of a cup of baking soda with a quarter cup of arrowroot powder and four teaspoons of cornstarch. You can then mix in one third of a cup of coconut oil and ten drops of your preferred essential oil. Sweet orange, lavender or

727

frankincense are all excellent choices but any will do! You should then be able to put the mixture into a roll on jar and apply as normal!

Homemade Hydrating Face Mask:

You catch a glimpse of yourself in the mirror, and you feel shocked. You know you are beautiful, but you wonder why your skin is riddled with blemishes, or why you constantly battle that oily feeling.

You want your skin to be dry, but not too dry. You want your skin to be exfoliated, but you don't want to expose yourself to the harmful chemicals that are found in most facial masks on the market today.

You want results, but you don't want to end up spending an arm and a leg to get them. So what are you going to do?

Obviously, the best way to get what you want is to make it yourself. But the world of face masks is huge, and you may not know what you can put into yours to get the results that you want.

Thankfully, you have come to the right place. In this book I am going to show you everything you need for dozens of different facial masks, and provide you with simple and easy directions that will deliver the results you want in no time at all.

With these recipes, you can achieve that youthful, perfect glow you have been dreaming of without wasting your money or your time on the chemical laden facial masks for sale at the store.

This book is going to change the way you take care of your skin, and leave you feeling soft, strong, and ready to face your day. What makes this deal even sweeter is that these masks not only clean and tone your skin, but it will also protect your face from the sun's harmful UV rays.

There is no end to the ways you can indulge in your own facial masks, and whether you use these recipes to the letter, or you mix and match to create your own recipes, you are going to fall in love with the masks, the results, and the skin you're in.

Are you ready to indulge in facial masks that will give you luxurious and spa like results? Excellent.

Let's get started.

The Recipes

Hello Hydration

What you will need:

1 tablespoon coconut oil

1 banana

1 tablespoon coconut milk

Directions:

Combine all ingredients in a bowl, making it as smooth as you can. If there are any soft lumps, make sure to smooth them entirely before application.

Spread the mask evenly over your face, then sit back and let it set for 20 to 30 minutes.

Wash mask off with warm water – making sure you completely rinse off the mask.

If desired, you can wash off the mask with the normal face wash you use daily, but water works just fine.

Repeat twice a week.

Smooth and Shine

What you will need:

1 tablespoon steel cut oats

1 banana

1 teaspoon apple cider vinegar

1 tablespoon goat milk

Directions:

Combine all ingredients in a bowl, making it as smooth as you can. If there are any soft lumps, make sure to smooth them entirely before application.

Spread the mask evenly over your face, then sit back and let it set for 20 to 30 minutes.

Wash mask off with warm water – making sure you completely rinse off the mask.

If desired, you can wash off the mask with the normal face wash you use daily, but water works just fine.

Repeat twice a week.

Pore Perfector

What you will need:

1 banana

1 teaspoon steel cut oats

1 egg

Directions:

Combine all ingredients in a bowl, making it as smooth as you can. If there are any soft lumps, make sure to smooth them entirely before application.

Spread the mask evenly over your face, then sit back and let it set for 20 to 30 minutes.

Wash mask off with warm water – making sure you completely rinse off the mask.

Repeat twice a week.

Perfectionista

What you will need:

2 eggs

1 teaspoon apple cider vinegar

1 teaspoon goat milk

Directions:

Combine all ingredients in a bowl, making it as smooth as you can. If there are any soft lumps, make sure to smooth them entirely before application.

Spread the mask evenly over your face, then sit back and let it set for 20 to 30 minutes.

Wash mask off with warm water – making sure you completely rinse off the mask.

If desired, you can wash off the mask with the normal face wash you use daily, but water works just fine.

Repeat twice a week.

Magic Glow

What you will need:

½ cup powdered milk

1 egg

Splash of vanilla

Directions:

Combine all ingredients in a bowl, making it as smooth as you can. If there are any soft lumps, make sure to smooth them entirely before application.

Spread the mask evenly over your face, then sit back and let it set for 20 to 30 minutes.

Wash mask off with warm water – making sure you completely rinse off the mask.

If desired, you can wash off the mask with the normal face wash you use daily, but water works just fine.

Repeat twice a week.

Happy Face
What you will need:

½ cup prepared oatmeal

2 tablespoons plain Greek yogurt

1 egg white

Directions:

Combine all ingredients in a bowl, making it as smooth as you can. If there are any soft lumps, make sure to smooth them entirely before application.

Spread the mask evenly over your face, then sit back and let it set for 20 to 30 minutes.

Wash mask off with warm water – making sure you completely rinse off the mask.

If desired, you can wash off the mask with the normal face wash you use daily, but water works just fine.

Repeat twice a week.

Grease Fighter

What you will need:

The whites from 2 eggs

1 tablespoon honey

1 teaspoon apple cider vinegar

Directions:

Combine all ingredients in a bowl, making it as smooth as you can. If there are any soft lumps, make sure to smooth them entirely before application.

Spread the mask evenly over your face, then sit back and let it set for 20 to 30 minutes.

Wash mask off with warm water – making sure you completely rinse off the mask.

If desired, you can wash off the mask with the normal face wash you use daily, but water works just fine.

Repeat twice a week.

Princess Skin

What you will need:

2 tablespoons honey

2 tablespoons oatmeal

½ cup plain Greek yogurt

Directions:

Combine all ingredients in a bowl, making it as smooth as you can. If there are any soft lumps, make sure to smooth them entirely before application.

Spread the mask evenly over your face, then sit back and let it set for 20 to 30 minutes.

Wash mask off with warm water – making sure you completely rinse off the mask.

If desired, you can wash off the mask with the normal face wash you use daily, but water works just fine.

Repeat twice a week.

Luck of the Draw

What you will need:

1 egg

2 tablespoons goat milk

1 tablespoon coconut oil

Directions:

Combine all ingredients in a bowl, making it as smooth as you can. If there are any soft lumps, make sure to smooth them entirely before application.

Spread the mask evenly over your face, then sit back and let it set for 20 to 30 minutes.

Wash mask off with warm water – making sure you completely rinse off the mask.

If desired, you can wash off the mask with the normal face wash you use daily, but water works just fine.

Repeat twice a week.

Clear Days

What you will need:

8 drops myrrh essential oil

2 egg yolks

1 tablespoon dry milk

Directions:

Combine all ingredients in a bowl, making it as smooth as you can. If there are any soft lumps, make sure to smooth them entirely before application.

Spread the mask evenly over your face, then sit back and let it set for 20 to 30 minutes.

Wash mask off with warm water – making sure you completely rinse off the mask.

If desired, you can wash off the mask with the normal face wash you use daily, but water works just fine.

Repeat twice a week.

Blemish Banisher

What you will need:

12 drops myrrh

1 tablespoon goat milk

1 teaspoon apple cider vinegar

1 teaspoon unsweetened coconut shavings

Directions:

Combine all ingredients in a bowl, making it as smooth as you can. If there are any soft lumps, make sure to smooth them entirely before application.

Spread the mask evenly over your face, then sit back and let it set for 20 to 30 minutes.

Wash mask off with warm water – making sure you completely rinse off the mask.

If desired, you can wash off the mask with the normal face wash you use daily, but water works just fine.

Repeat twice a week.

Tropical Storm

What you will need:

2 tablespoons grapefruit juice

1 teaspoon apple cider vinegar

3 tablespoons dry milk

1 egg white

738

Directions:

Combine all ingredients in a bowl, making it as smooth as you can. If there are any soft lumps, make sure to smooth them entirely before application.

Spread the mask evenly over your face, then sit back and let it set for 20 to 30 minutes.

Wash mask off with warm water – making sure you completely rinse off the mask.

If desired, you can wash off the mask with the normal face wash you use daily, but water works just fine.

Repeat twice a week.

Berry Blossom

What you will need:

2 tablespoons honey

2 tablespoons milk

2 tablespoons plain Greek yogurt

Directions:

Combine all ingredients in a bowl, making it as smooth as you can. If there are any soft lumps, make sure to smooth them entirely before application.

Spread the mask evenly over your face, then sit back and let it set for 20 to 30 minutes.

Wash mask off with warm water – making sure you completely rinse off the mask.

If desired, you can wash off the mask with the normal face wash you use daily, but water works just fine.

Repeat twice a week.

Rise and Shine

What you will need:

2 tablespoons mayo

1 tablespoon goat milk

1 teaspoon oatmeal

1 egg white

Directions:

Combine all ingredients in a bowl, making it as smooth as you can. If there are any soft lumps, make sure to smooth them entirely before application.

Spread the mask evenly over your face, then sit back and let it set for 20 to 30 minutes.

Wash mask off with warm water – making sure you completely rinse off the mask.

If desired, you can wash off the mask with the normal face wash you use daily, but water works just fine.

Repeat twice a week.

Blooming Beauty

What you will need:

1/3 cup mustard

1 egg yolk

1 banana

Directions:

Combine all ingredients in a bowl, making it as smooth as you can. If there are any soft lumps, make sure to smooth them entirely before application.

Spread the mask evenly over your face, then sit back and let it set for 20 to 30 minutes.

Wash mask off with warm water – making sure you completely rinse off the mask.

If desired, you can wash off the mask with the normal face wash you use daily, but water works just fine.

Repeat twice a week.

Delicate Flower

What you will need:

1 tablespoon lemon juice

1 tablespoon apple cider vinegar

1 banana

2 tablespoons powdered milk

Directions:

Combine all ingredients in a bowl, making it as smooth as you can. If there are any soft lumps, make sure to smooth them entirely before application.

Spread the mask evenly over your face, then sit back and let it set for 20 to 30 minutes.

Wash mask off with warm water – making sure you completely rinse off the mask.

If desired, you can wash off the mask with the normal face wash you use daily, but water works just fine.

Repeat twice a week.

Sea and Sun

What you will need:

1 avocado

1 teaspoons salt

1 teaspoon lemon

Directions:

Combine all ingredients in a bowl, making it as smooth as you can. If there are any soft lumps, make sure to smooth them entirely before application.

Spread the mask evenly over your face, then sit back and let it set for 20 to 30 minutes.

Wash mask off with warm water – making sure you completely rinse off the mask.

If desired, you can wash off the mask with the normal face wash you use daily, but water works just fine.

Repeat twice a week.

Funshine

What you will need:

2 tablespoons black tea leaves

1 tablespoon honey

1 banana

Directions:

Combine all ingredients in a bowl, making it as smooth as you can. If there are any soft lumps, make sure to smooth them entirely before application.

Spread the mask evenly over your face, then sit back and let it set for 20 to 30 minutes.

Wash mask off with warm water – making sure you completely rinse off the mask.

If desired, you can wash off the mask with the normal face wash you use daily, but water works just fine.

Repeat twice a week.

Happiness Fusion

What you will need:

1 tablespoon grapefruit juice

1 teaspoon lemon juice

1 teaspoon cinnamon

1 egg yolk

Directions:

Combine all ingredients in a bowl, making it as smooth as you can. If there are any soft lumps, make sure to smooth them entirely before application.

Spread the mask evenly over your face, then sit back and let it set for 20 to 30 minutes.

Wash mask off with warm water – making sure you completely rinse off the mask.

If desired, you can wash off the mask with the normal face wash you use daily, but water works just fine.

Repeat twice a week.

Your Go-To Mask

What you will need:

1 avocado

1 egg white

1 banana

2 tablespoons goat milk

Directions:

Combine all ingredients in a bowl, making it as smooth as you can. If there are any soft lumps, make sure to smooth them entirely before application.

Spread the mask evenly over your face, then sit back and let it set for 20 to 30 minutes.

Wash mask off with warm water – making sure you completely rinse off the mask.

If desired, you can wash off the mask with the normal face wash you use daily, but water works just fine.

Repeat twice a week.

Under the Sea

What you will need:

2 tablespoons coarsely ground salt

1 teaspoon warm water

12 drops lemon essential oil

10 drops myrrh essential oil

Directions:

Combine all ingredients in a bowl, making it as smooth as you can. If there are any soft lumps, make sure to smooth them entirely before application.

Spread the mask evenly over your face, then sit back and let it set for 20 to 30 minutes.

Wash mask off with warm water – making sure you completely rinse off the mask.

Repeat twice a week.

Behind the Mask

What you will need:

1 banana

1 tablespoon honey

1 egg whites

Directions:

Combine all ingredients in a bowl, making it as smooth as you can. If there are any soft lumps, make sure to smooth them entirely before application.

Spread the mask evenly over your face, then sit back and let it set for 20 to 30 minutes.

Wash mask off with warm water – making sure you completely rinse off the mask.

If desired, you can wash off the mask with the normal face wash you use daily, but water works just fine.

Repeat twice a week.

The Real Deal

What you will need:

2 tablespoons brown sugar

1 teaspoon lemon juice

1 teaspoon coconut oil

Directions:

Combine all ingredients in a bowl, making it as smooth as you can. If there are any soft lumps, make sure to smooth them entirely before application.

Spread the mask evenly over your face, then sit back and let it set for 20 to 30 minutes.

Wash mask off with warm water – making sure you completely rinse off the mask.

Repeat twice a week.

The Sunshine Coast

What you will need:

2 kiwis, skin removed

1 avocado

1 lemon wedge, peel removed

Directions:

Combine all ingredients in a bowl, making it as smooth as you can. If there are any soft lumps, make sure to smooth them entirely before application.

Spread the mask evenly over your face, then sit back and let it set for 20 to 30 minutes.

Wash mask off with warm water – making sure you completely rinse off the mask.

If desired, you can wash off the mask with the normal face wash you use daily, but water works just fine.

Repeat twice a week.

Southern Bell

What you will need:

1 overripe peach

1 tablespoon honey

1 tablespoon oatmeal

Splash of goat milk

Directions:

Combine all ingredients in a bowl, making it as smooth as you can. If there are any soft lumps, make sure to smooth them entirely before application.

Spread the mask evenly over your face, then sit back and let it set for 20 to 30 minutes.

Wash mask off with warm water – making sure you completely rinse off the mask.

If desired, you can wash off the mask with the normal face wash you use daily, but water works just fine.

Repeat twice a week.

Amelia Sunrise

What you will need:

2 tablespoons nutmeg

1 teaspoon cinnamon

1 teaspoon goat milk

Directions:

Combine all ingredients in a bowl, making it as smooth as you can. If there are any soft lumps, make sure to smooth them entirely before application.

Spread the mask evenly over your face, then sit back and let it set for 20 to 30 minutes.

Wash mask off with warm water – making sure you completely rinse off the mask.

If desired, you can wash off the mask with the normal face wash you use daily, but water works just fine.

Repeat twice a week.

Starry Eyes

What you will need:

½ cup coco powder

1 banana

1 teaspoon heavy cream

Directions:

Combine all ingredients in a bowl, making it as smooth as you can. If there are any soft lumps, make sure to smooth them entirely before application.

Spread the mask evenly over your face, then sit back and let it set for 20 to 30 minutes.

Wash mask off with warm water – making sure you completely rinse off the mask.

If desired, you can wash off the mask with the normal face wash you use daily, but water works just fine.

Repeat twice a week.

Calypso

What you will need:

2 tablespoons coco powder

½ avocado

1 egg yolk

Directions:

Combine all ingredients in a bowl, making it as smooth as you can. If there are any soft lumps, make sure to smooth them entirely before application.

Spread the mask evenly over your face, then sit back and let it set for 20 to 30 minutes.

Wash mask off with warm water – making sure you completely rinse off the mask.

If desired, you can wash off the mask with the normal face wash you use daily, but water works just fine.

Repeat twice a week.

Cash on the Barrel

What you will need:

2 limes, peeled

1 kiwi, peeled

1 teaspoon lemon juice

Directions:

Combine all ingredients in a bowl, making it as smooth as you can. If there are any soft lumps, make sure to smooth them entirely before application.

Spread the mask evenly over your face, then sit back and let it set for 20 to 30 minutes.

If desired, you can wash off the mask with the normal face wash you use daily, but water works just fine.

Wash mask off with warm water – making sure you completely rinse off the mask.

Repeat twice a week.

Muddy Mask

What you will need:

¼ coco powder

1 tablespoon powdered milk

1 egg white

Directions:

Combine all ingredients in a bowl, making it as smooth as you can. If there are any soft lumps, make sure to smooth them entirely before application.

Spread the mask evenly over your face, then sit back and let it set for 20 to 30 minutes.

Wash mask off with warm water – making sure you completely rinse off the mask.

If desired, you can wash off the mask with the normal face wash you use daily, but water works just fine.

Repeat twice a week.

Fair Skinned Maiden

What you will need:

2 egg whites

1 teaspoon plain Greek yogurt

1 teaspoon baking soda

1 teaspoon vanilla

Directions:

Combine all ingredients in a bowl, making it as smooth as you can. If there are any soft lumps, make sure to smooth them entirely before application.

Spread the mask evenly over your face, then sit back and let it set for 20 to 30 minutes.

Wash mask off with warm water – making sure you completely rinse off the mask.

If desired, you can wash off the mask with the normal face wash you use daily, but water works just fine.

Repeat twice a week.

Winter Wonder Spell

What you will need:

2 tablespoons coffee grounds

10 drops peppermint oil

1 banana

Directions:

Combine all ingredients in a bowl, making it as smooth as you can. If there are any soft lumps, make sure to smooth them entirely before application.

Spread the mask evenly over your face, then sit back and let it set for 20 to 30 minutes.

Wash mask off with warm water – making sure you completely rinse off the mask.

If desired, you can wash off the mask with the normal face wash you use daily, but water works just fine.

Repeat twice a week.

Summertime Gladness

What you will need:

6 strawberries

1 tablespoon plain Greek yogurt

1 tablespoon honey

Directions:

Combine all ingredients in a bowl, making it as smooth as you can. If there are any soft lumps, make sure to smooth them entirely before application.

Spread the mask evenly over your face, then sit back and let it set for 20 to 30 minutes.

Wash mask off with warm water – making sure you completely rinse off the mask.

If desired, you can wash off the mask with the normal face wash you use daily, but water works just fine.

Repeat twice a week.

Go with the Flow

What you will need:

1 tablespoon orange juice

½ cup brown sugar

½ avocado

Directions:

Combine all ingredients in a bowl, making it as smooth as you can. If there are any soft lumps, make sure to smooth them entirely before application.

Spread the mask evenly over your face, then sit back and let it set for 20 to 30 minutes.

Wash mask off with warm water – making sure you completely rinse off the mask.

If desired, you can wash off the mask with the normal face wash you use daily, but water works just fine.

Repeat twice a week.

Spring Showers

What you will need:

½ cup rose water

1 tablespoon green tea

1 egg

Directions:

Combine all ingredients in a bowl, making it as smooth as you can. If there are any soft lumps, make sure to smooth them entirely before application.

Spread the mask evenly over your face, then sit back and let it set for 20 to 30 minutes.

Wash mask off with warm water – making sure you completely rinse off the mask.

If desired, you can wash off the mask with the normal face wash you use daily, but water works just fine.

Repeat twice a week.

Fresh and Free

What you will need:

1 tablespoon lemon juice

1 tablespoon apple cider vinegar

3 tablespoons cinnamon

Directions:

Combine all ingredients in a bowl, making it as smooth as you can. If there are any soft lumps, make sure to smooth them entirely before application.

Spread the mask evenly over your face, then sit back and let it set for 20 to 30 minutes.

Wash mask off with warm water – making sure you completely rinse off the mask.

If desired, you can wash off the mask with the normal face wash you use daily, but water works just fine.

Repeat twice a week.

Exfoliation Station

What you will need:

½ avocado

½ cup steel cut oats

1 egg yolk

Directions:

Combine all ingredients in a bowl, making it as smooth as you can. If there are any soft lumps, make sure to smooth them entirely before application.

Spread the mask evenly over your face, then sit back and let it set for 20 to 30 minutes.

Wash mask off with warm water – making sure you completely rinse off the mask.

If desired, you can wash off the mask with the normal face wash you use daily, but water works just fine.

Repeat twice a week.

It's a Trip

What you will need:

½ cup coco powder

3 teaspoons nutmeg

2 teaspoons cinnamon

¼ cup goat milk

Directions:

Combine all ingredients in a bowl, making it as smooth as you can. If there are any soft lumps, make sure to smooth them entirely before application.

Spread the mask evenly over your face, then sit back and let it set for 20 to 30 minutes.

Wash mask off with warm water – making sure you completely rinse off the mask.

If desired, you can wash off the mask with the normal face wash you use daily, but water works just fine.

Repeat twice a week.

Summer Vacation

What you will need:

½ cup blueberries

2 tablespoons lemon juice

1 egg white

Directions:

Combine all ingredients in a bowl, making it as smooth as you can. If there are any soft lumps, make sure to smooth them entirely before application.

Spread the mask evenly over your face, then sit back and let it set for 20 to 30 minutes.

Wash mask off with warm water – making sure you completely rinse off the mask.

If desired, you can wash off the mask with the normal face wash you use daily, but water works just fine.

Repeat twice a week.

Destination Sunshine

What you will need:

1/3 cup yogurt

2 tablespoons green Macha tea

1 teaspoon apple cider vinegar

Directions:

Combine all ingredients in a bowl, making it as smooth as you can. If there are any soft lumps, make sure to smooth them entirely before application.

Spread the mask evenly over your face, then sit back and let it set for 20 to 30 minutes.

Wash mask off with warm water – making sure you completely rinse off the mask.

If desired, you can wash off the mask with the normal face wash you use daily, but water works just fine.

Repeat twice a week.

DIY Chapsticks and Lip Balms

This book, *DIY Chap sticks And Lip Balms: 18 Recipes of Flavored Lip Balms to Protect Your Lips from Cold, Wind and UV Rays*, is about lip balm recipes. In it you will find the most popular recipes, which also happen to be easy and convenient to make. You will also learn how your lips will influence the status of your oral health.

As you read through, you need to look out for recipes that have ingredients with properties matching your taste and needs. For instance, if the weather is dry, you may wish to go for the recipe that has plenty of moisturizing oils. In case your lips are chapping after a bout of flu, you may wish to find the recipe containing soothing oils. All in all, you will learn from this book how to keep your lips healthy, and how to make them look youthful and sensual. Welcome!

How to Maintain Beautiful Succulent Lips

Guess what makes lips a significant part of your body. Is it because it keeps dust and debris out of your mouth? Well, you have a great function right there, and, in fact, you can say in summary that lips play a vital role in maintaining oral health. In short, to avoid oral infection and related ailments, you need to practice hygiene on your lips on a continuous basis.

Still, there is the cosmetic part where your lips draw people's attention to you, and whereas you may not necessarily be vain, you will actually feel good when your lips look good. And doesn't looking good give you a boost of confidence? Plus there is the uniqueness of your lips. It is not only the shape and thickness of your lips that emphasize who you are; it is also the shade of your lip color. That is why you want to use lip balms that are appropriate in maintaining your lips' succulence as well as color.

Tips To Keep Your Lips Healthy and Attractive

(1) Exfoliating

Why is exfoliation important? For one, you exfoliate your lips using a good lip scrub, and the purpose is to get rid of any dead skin cells, so that the skin can generate fresh skin cells. And what do you use for proper exfoliation? You have a number of options, and one of them is the use of a lip scrub that is abrasive, say, like a sugar scrub. Once you have removed the flakey skin, you can then rinse off your lips, which are, by now, smoother.

Another nice way of exfoliating your lips is applying some petroleum jelly, and then you massage your lips using a clean cloth that is damp. You just need to move that cloth in circular motions and you will have the flakey skin peeling off.

(2) Apply some oil or lip balm

At this stage, you want to ensure your lips can retain the moisture they have within them. For that reason, you need to apply almond oil, olive oil, or even almond oil or some lip balm. Any of these products will not only help to maintain the natural moisture within the lips, it will also provide extra hydration to the lips.

(3) Make your environment a bit humid

Did you know that staying in a dry environment can make your lips chip? That is the reason it is a good idea to do something about the atmosphere around you, specifically making it a little humid. The best way to go about introducing some humidity into the atmosphere is the use of a humidifier. This one infuses moisture into the air around you, and so you can rest in such a place for hours without your lips getting dry or chipped. You can use this method particularly during the dry winters.

(4) Adhere to a regular and healthy beauty regimen

Do you know how you do this? You only need to make up your mind what beauty products you want to incorporate in your routine. That way, it will be relatively easy to tell the culprit if your lips begin to manifest signs of eczema. Experts reckon the main cause of lip eczema is allergy, and such an allergy would normally emanate from any of the products you are using. It could be the lipstick, the toothpaste, the face wash, and the like. For that reason, the best way to know what is causing your eczema is to eliminate one product at a time from your beauty routine. Then you will be able to note when signs of eczema disappear. Is it, for instance, when you omit to apply your lipstick or when you leave out the face wash?

Simple Homemade Lip Balm Recipes

Are you aware there are myriad types of lip balms you can buy from stores, supermarkets and beauty shops, to use in your beauty care routine? The question is – do they all contain skin friendly ingredients? Are all the ingredients healthy for you and also friendly to the environment? Since you may not be certain that the company has made full disclosure on the product label, you may feel better making your own lip balm. For starters, you would be able to ensure that all the ingredients included in your lip balm are natural, and they are ingredients you are not allergic to.

4 Natural Lip Balm Recipes

The luscious lavender recipe

The ingredients are:

- Olive oil – 4 tablespoonfuls

- Beeswax (grated) – 1 tablespoonful

- Honey – 1 teaspoonful

- Vitamin E oil – ¼ teaspoonful

- The lavender essential oil – 7 drops

- Cocoa powder (optional) = 1 teaspoonful

- Some natural lipstick (optional) – 1 teaspoonful

As for directions to make the lip balm, you need to mix your selected oils, the beeswax, as well as the honey, all in some small bowl of stainless material, or better still in a stainless pot. You then put that container in a double boiler for the purpose of warming the contents. The idea is to warm the content on low heat, until you ensure your beeswax has properly melted. Once that is done, you can proceed to whisk in the Vitamin E and the essential oil, as well as the cocoa powder. Also add your lipstick, if you have chosen to use some.

After this, place the bowl with your mixture in some shallow pan containing ice cold water, then go on whisking the mixture fast. It is at this point that you put in the honey. Whisk the content till your honey has been properly incorporated. The mixture you need is now done, and it is time to pour the balm into your chosen container or tube. Once you have put your balm into one of those, you need to allow it to cool and settle for the next 3hrs.

Any idea how this lip balm ends up looking like? It has some dark aubergine shade, and then once you apply it on your lips, it comes out as some light mauve.

The Coco -Rose recipe

This recipe, as the name hints, contains some content from the Rose plant, and in case you did not know, the Rose is soothing. For the same soothing effect, you could also choose to substitute the Rose with chamomile or even hibiscus.

There is another advantage of making this recipe. Any excess balm you may have comes in handy as a hand balm. In fact, it will do well on any other part of your body.

The ingredients are:

- Coconut oil – 2 tablespoonfuls
- Cocoa butter (grated) – 1 tablespoonfuls

- Rosebuds (dried) – 1 tablespoonful

- Vitamin E oil – ¼ teaspoonful

- Rose essential oil (optional) – 3 drops

To make your recipe with the listed ingredients, you need to put the coconut oil in some stainless steel container like a bowl, and then you melt it on low heat. Once your oil has turned proper liquid, it is time to add the rosebuds. You then need to stir the mixture well. Leave the mixture for an hour as it steeps on low heat, and then strain it, letting the oil flow into a clean bowl. Of course, this goes well when you are using a cheese cloth for sieving the rose bud remnants, or some sieve made of fine mesh.

The next step is to wipe the bowl you had been using originally, and pouring back the oil you just sieved. You then need to return that oil to continue heating. It is at this point that you now add in your cocoa butter, where you stir it till it melts. Then you get that container off the heat and add your Vitamin E oil, plus the essential oil. You then stir the contents thoroughly before transferring them into some suitable small container. After this, let the balm settle for a good 3hrs, when it is meant to be properly set for use.

One thing you need to note is that lip balm with coconut oil as an ingredient easily melts, and so you need to ensure you keep it away from heat. That includes body heat, and so you cannot go putting it in your pocket. In fact, ideally, you need to avoid packing this lip balm in a tube because you would be risking a leak.

The Minty Chocolate Recipe

The ingredients are:

- Beeswax (grated) – 1 tablespoonful

- Coconut oil – $1/8$ cup

- Shea butter – ½ tablespoonful

- Cocoa butter – ½ tablespoonful

- Honey – ½ teaspoonful

- Cocoa powder – 1 teaspoonful

- Vitamin E oil – $1/8$ teaspoonful (equivalent to the amount you squeeze out of 2 Vitamin E capsules)

- Peppermint essential oil – 3 drops

When it is time to make your lip balm with the listed ingredients, you begin by placing your Shea butter and the cocoa butter in some small heating container like a pot, or even a double boiler. Then you add your coconut oil in the butters. The next step is to heat that mixture over low heat for some 20 minutes, all this time stirring the contents. Since you would not wish your butter to begin turning, kind of, gritty, ensure the heat you are using does not exceed 175°F. Finally, while the contents are still on the fire, add your beeswax and stir it in. Only when this too has properly melted do you proceed to take the container away from the heat.

It is now time to add your Vitamin E oil, your essential oil, and also the cocoa powder. You need to whisk your mixture properly after adding these ingredients, so that all your ingredients are well incorporated and your mixture has become smooth. That is all you need to do and you will have your lip balm ready to put into your chosen tube, or even in some tin. Before you can call it a day, it is important that you let your lip balm container rest for 3hrs, so that the lip balm inside cools down properly and also sets.

Of all the three recipes you have already read about in this chapter, this minty chocolate one is the one that does best in a lip balm tube. The reason is that it easily solidifies, and you do not run the risk of the lip balm leaking out. In fact, it is one you can comfortably carry in your pocket. Something else you need to know is that the cocoa ingredient you include in the recipe does not influence the color the way you might expect. So, instead of having your lip balm in a shade close to brown, you end up having it in some light tan. What you will admit once you have begun using the lip balm, is that you have a wonderful scent in the mint. The balm also has a delicious flavor, but surely why lick your lips and then end up with dry lips?

Tinted lip balm

Has tinted got something to do with shade? Yes, it has something to do with the color of your lip balm, meaning it does not come with a shouting color, but rather treats your lips and makes them tender in a, kind of, conservative way.

The ingredients are:

- Beeswax – 2 tablespoonfuls

- Coconut oil – 2 tablespoonfuls

- Grape seed oil – 1 tablespoonful

- Some lipstick of your choice

- Essential oil of your choice – 4 drops

In this recipe too, you can use a double boiler for the heating process, or you can just use a saucepan and some small glass bowl.

The method of making this lip balm recipe is simple. You need to begin by heating water in the saucepan, ensuring it does not get to a boiling point. You then put in your glass bowl the beeswax, the grape seed oil, plus the coconut oil. Once you have done this, you need to place the bowl right inside the saucepan with the hot water. You then proceed to grate some lipstick off your lipstick stick, adding the contents into the glass bowl. You can simply use a butter knife for this purpose. Mind you the lipstick is just meant to give some color to your lip balm.

The next step is to ensure you mix those ingredients as the hard ones melt, and once that is done well, you put the saucepan off the heat source. It is now time to add your essential oil into the balm mixture. Of course you could use more than one essential oil, if you so wish, as long as they make up a total of 4 drops. You need to choose your essential oils, mainly based on the scent you want your lip balm to have. At this juncture, all you need to do is let your mixture cool, and you have your lip balm ready – just within 5 minutes! After this, you can proceed to pack your lip balm as you wish. Guess how many pods of lip balm you can get out of this recipe? A whole 12 pods!

How to Keep Your Lips Looking Young

3 Lip Balm Recipes That Keep Lips Youthful

The Coconut Rose with Vanilla recipe

The ingredients are:

- Coconut oil – $^1/_8$ cup

- Beeswax – ¼ cup

- Shea butter – ¹/₈ cup

- Vanilla extract – 1 teaspoon

- Rose petals (either dried or fresh) – ¼ cup

- Sweet almond oil – 1 teaspoon

If these ingredients look a lot, it is only because they are meant to produce six tubes of this nicely scented lip balm.

How to prepare the lip balm:

You begin by putting your ingredients in some small saucepan, and then mixing them up as well as you can. You then proceed to heat the contents on low fire. The preparation for this recipe can be made easy by the use of a microwave to melt the solid ingredients like the beeswax. In the case of a microwave, you need to put in the saucepan for 30 seconds and then remove it to see how far the melting has gone, and of course you do some mixing as you check this. If not everything is well melted, you need to return the saucepan into the microwave, and keep doing it on a 30sec interval till all ingredients are thoroughly mixed up.

You can then strain off the Rose petals. However, you could still leave them in and your lip balm will still be usable. In fact, they may even make your lip balm look even more appealing to the eye. The final step in this preparation is putting the lip balm into its clean containers, and then giving it a couple of hours to cool. You may wish to note that the melting point for beeswax happens to be 145°F, and that when the time comes, it has no problem solidifying well enough to occupy a lip balm tube.

The Peppermint Balm recipe

The ingredients are:

- Peppermint oil – 8 drops

- Almond oil (or another carrier oil to dilute the peppermint oil)

- Beeswax pellets – 1 tablespoonful

- Some lipstick shavings

In making the lip balm, you need to begin by mixing the beeswax and the almond oil in some glass jar. After that you are required to shut the jar with some lid. You then need to put that jar with its contents in a pot, which you can then place on some source of heat. The idea is to get the beeswax melted, so that you can proceed to mix it with the carrier oil. This, you do on medium heat. The next step is to add your peppermint oil into the glass jar, and you use a dropper. The reason this recipe has 8 drops and not more is because if you exceed that amount, your lip balm might burn your lips, which is not a pleasant experience at all.

What follows now is addition of the lipstick shavings, which you basically do to give some color to your lip balm. This recipe is that simple, and you can now proceed to put your prepared mixture into your preferred tubes or other suitable containers. Of course, you do not hasten to pack your lip balm, but you allow it to rest for around 2hrs, during which it cools and hardens appropriately.

The Hemp-Honey recipe

As you can see, this lip balm recipe contains honey, and this is an ingredient with proven healing properties. So, whereas this book is not about healing agents, being able to heal some lip sores or probably some cold symptoms of sorts can be the icing on the cake.

The ingredients are:

- Beeswax – 15g

- Carnauba wax – 1g

- Cocoa butter – 10g

- Shea butter – 5g

- Almond oil – 20ml

- Hemp oil – 2ml

- Manuka honey – 10ml

- Citrus essential oil – 8 drops

The way to prepare this recipe is easy, just like the others contained in this book. You begin by preparing a double boiler, and then melting a mix of your beeswax, the carnauba wax, the cocoa butter plus the Shea butter, and even the almond oil.

Only after that mix is nicely melted do you proceed to add your hemp oil, as well as the honey. By the time you are finished stirring all those ingredients, your stuff should be in form of liquid. Of course, you should anticipate some hitch getting all your honey properly mixed as it is not soluble in oil, but although heating fails to help out with this, a milk frother can be of help. You use it to make the honey mix well with the other ingredients, mainly so that it can be evenly distributed.

The next step is to get your mixture of ingredients off the heating source, so you can proceed to add in your essential oils. Before you leave your balm mixture to cool, you need to blend the essential oils you added well, preferably using the frother.

You are now through with your hemp-honey recipe, and after it has cooled, you can pack it in the tubes you have chosen for future use. As usual, the lip balm you have just prepared will require some 2hrs or so to set, and then you can term it ready for use.

Classy Lip Balm Recipes with Healing Properties

Do you know that essential oils that have not been adulterated with artificial substances have great healing properties? As a consequence, products that incorporate such essential oils in their makeup also become bearers of similar healing powers. It is for this reason that many people are going for natural products that use natural essential oils as main ingredients. You, too, can benefit from the healing powers of essential oils by way of lip balms. You can opt to make your own lip balms that are based on some of the most potent essential oils, and you will end up enjoying, not just the healing of damaged lips, but also the beauty that comes with nicely moisturized lips. This chapter lists some of the best lip balm recipes you could ever find, and you can prepare them in the comfort and convenience of your home.

3 Classy Lip Balm Recipes

Fruity Lip Balm recipe

The ingredients are:

- Coconut oil – 4 tablespoonfuls

- Petroleum jelly – 3 tablespoonfuls

- Beeswax shavings – 1 tablespoonful

- Some squirt of deeply colored fresh juice

In preparing this recipe, you begin by mixing the coconut oil, the petroleum jelly, as well as the beeswax shavings, all in a bowl. You need to use a bowl that is appropriate for the microwave. Once those ingredients are well blended, it is time to heat them for one minute, and you can use your microwave for that.

The next step is to add your squirt of fresh juice into your mixture, so that it acquires the color you prefer. Note that such fresh juice does a good job of making your lip balm look appealing, and you will have avoided the use of artificial food color. Imagine how easy it is to prepare this classy looking lip balm! You can now fill your chosen containers with the balm, and then allow the containers and their ingredients to cool. If you so wish, you can put them in the refrigerator for a good hour or so, just to hasten the cooling and hardening process.

The Wedding Balm recipe

If you know how nice the resultant lip balm is, just know it is fitting for a bridal party. Can it get any better?

The ingredients are:

- Some lip balm base
- Lime essential oil – a couple of tablespoons, probably 4
- Some edible mica powder (optional)

772

Note that it is alright to omit the mica if you are not interested in coloring your lip balm. As for the essential oil, you do not have to stick with lime. You can substitute that with any other nicely flavored essential oil you wish.

You prepare this recipe by mixing your lip balm base once melted, and your chosen essential oil, and then you add some amount of mica powder. That is all you need to do, and you will have a nicely flavored, easy-to-handle lip balm. Of course proper melting of your balm base means you heat it over low fire. . About the measurements, if you choose to utilize 4oz of balm base, you can make around lip balm tubes to the tune of 20. As for the mixing, it is preferable that you use plastic chopsticks to do the task, as there is no risk of chipping the way wooden items might do, getting tiny splinters into your lip balm.

The Pink Tinted Lip Balm recipe

Here, the ingredients are:

- Beeswax (grated) – 2 tablespoonfuls

- Coconut oil – 2 tablespoonfuls

- Sweet almond oil – 2 teaspoonfuls

- Red lipstick – a chunk of it

- Eye shadow powder (shimmery) – ½ teaspoonful

- Peppermint essential oil – 10 drops

The way to make this recipe is simple. You need to put all your ingredients in one container, say, a glass bowl, and you proceed to melt them, possibly using a double boiler. Ensure no beeswax flakes remain.

The next step is to add your essential oil in the mixture, where you mix everything properly again. Note that you add the essential oil only after removing the mixture from the fire. After a proper mix, you are done. You can now use a medicine dropper to fill up your chosen balm containers. You then need to let the containers having the lip balm rest at room temperature, or if you choose, in a refrigerator.

Easy-to-make Lip Balm and Chapstick Recipes

8 Recipes To Keep Your Lips Healthy And Appealing

Lemon & Sunflower recipe

The ingredients are:

- The Lemon essential oil – 10 drops

- Sunflower oil – 2 tablespoonfuls

- Coconut oil – 1 tablespoonful

- Beeswax – 1 tablespoonful

You need to grate the beeswax and then mix it with your lemon and sunflower oils, plus the coconut oil too. Then you need to process those ingredients over low heat until the wax is well melted and mixing well with the rest of the ingredients. It is fine to add a drop or two of the essential oil whose scent you want prominent, even after you have taken your balm mixture off the heat source. At the same time, if you find your balm mixture firming up before you are satisfied with the mixing you can always return it to the mild heat to melt a little once again.

You can now use a dropper to fill your preferred containers with lip balm. As for cooling, 10hrs are long enough to have your balm cool and set appropriately.

Butter based lip balm recipe

The ingredients are:

- Shea butter

- Cocoa butter

- The lavender essential oil

- Beeswax

This is one of the simplest lip balm recipes to prepare. All you need to do is to measure one part oil and one part butters, and also one part beeswax, and then you mix them up thoroughly. Once you have gotten the mixture melted nicely and well mixed, your lip balm recipe is complete. All you need to do is pack your balm into tubes and let it cool for around 2hrs.

Mango-vanilla recipe

This recipe that is meant to make around ten to fifteen lip balm tubes uses the following ingredients:

- Mango butter – 1 tablespoon

- Cocoa butter – 1 tablespoonful

- The virgin coconut oil – 2 tablespoonfuls

- Beeswax (shredded) – 2 tablespoonfuls

775

- Vanilla extract (pure) – 1 teaspoonful

As for preparation, you need to follow the method you used with recipes in chapter 2.

Beeswax-coconut recipe

The ingredients are:

- Pure beeswax pastilles – 2 teaspoonfuls
- Shea butter (organic and raw) – 1 teaspoonful
- Coconut oil (organic) – 3 teaspoonfuls
- Peppermint essential oil – 10 drops
- Tangerine essential oil – 10 drops

Use a similar method as the previous recipe.

Shea butter coconut chap stick recipe

The ingredients are:

- Coconut oil (organic) – 2 tablespoonfuls
- Shea butter (organic) – 2 tablespoonfuls
- Beeswax – 2 tablespoonfuls
- The chamomile essential oil – 4 drops

To prepare the recipe, you need to follow the method used in the previous recipe.

The coconut-lavender recipe

The ingredients are:

- Coconut oil – 2 tablespoonfuls

- Sweet almond oil – 2 tablespoonfuls

- Beeswax pellets – 1 tablespoonful

- Vitamin E oil – ¼ teaspoon

- Lavender essential oil – 8 drops

Once you mix your coconut oil, the sweet almond oil, the Vitamin E oil, and then you add the beeswax and melt the content, you will have made a mixture fit to create a chap stick. However, for some irresistible scent and nice flavor, you may wish to add the lavender essential oil.

The Cocoa butter-coconut chap stick recipe

The ingredients are:

- Wintergreen Essential oils – ¾ teaspoonful

- Coconut oil – 3 tablespoonfuls

- Cocoa butter – 2 tablespoonfuls

- Beeswax – 2 tablespoonfuls

- Vitamin E oil – 3 drops

For this one, the method of preparation is the same as the previous one.

Papaya whip chap stick recipe

The ingredients are:

- Beeswax – 1 tablespoonful

- Coconut oil – 1 teaspoon

- Cocoa butter – 1 teaspoon

- Orange lipstick shavings

- The mandarin essential oil – 2 drops

As for the procedure of making this recipe, you need to follow the one used at the beginning of this chapter.

Conclusion

Homestead tax exemption is an important benefit because your home is exempt from property taxes. For instance, if the value of property is $80,000, it is eligible for $15,000 homestead exemption. The property will be taxed at $65,000 and you can save a good amount of money. The amount of homestead tax exemption may vary according to the tax laws of your state.

If the owner of a property dies, these protections may extend to the surviving family of the homeowner. This type of homestead is known as a probate homestead and it will be set aside for the convenient life of spouse and children. It can reduce property taxes and protect their family from creditors. According to the laws of some states, a homestead property can be automatically transferred to the surviving spouse of the homeowner.

Homesteading laws of a state require you to sign a homestead declaration and it can protect your house from creditors. Creditors can't seize a homestead property or proceeds from the sale of a homestead house. For instance, if a state protects $300,000 of the value of a homestead from creditors, a value of $150,000 will be completely protected. Though, the creditors can take $50,000 from the value of $350,000.

Made in United States
Troutdale, OR
08/19/2023

12192427R00434